World Yearbook
of Education 1988

Education for the
New Technologies

Edited by Duncan Harris (Series Editor)

Kogan Page, London/Nichols Publishing
Company, New York

Previous titles in this series

World Yearbook of Education 1982/83
Computers and Education
Edited by Jacquetta Megarry, David R F Walker,
Stanley Nisbet and Eric Hoyle

World Yearbook of Education 1984
Women and Education
Edited by Sandra Acker, Jacquetta Megarry,
Stanley Nisbet and Eric Hoyle

World Yearbook of Education 1985
Research, Policy and Practice
Edited by John Nisbet, Jacquetta Megarry and Stanley Nisbet

World Yearbook of Education 1986
The Management of Schools
Edited by Eric Hoyle and Agnes McMahon

World Yearbook of Education 1987
Vocational Education
Edited by John Twining, Stanley Nisbet and Jacquetta Megarry

First published in Great Britain in 1988 by Kogan Page Limited
120 Pentonville Road, London N1 9JN

British Library Cataloguing in Publication Data

World yearbook of education – 1988
  1. Education – Periodicals
  370'.5   L16

  ISSN 0084-2508
  ISBN 1-85091-525 3

First published in the USA in 1988
by Nichols Publishing
an imprint of GP Publishing Inc.
PO Box 96, New York, NY 10024

Library of Congress Cataloging in Publication Data

Main entry under title:
World Yearbook of Education: 1988
1. Education – Periodicals

ISBN 0-89397-299-1
LC Catalog No. 32-18413

Printed and bound in Great Britain
by Billing & Sons Ltd, Worcester

Contents

List of contributors

Introduction

Duncan Harris

Summary: The chapter reflects on different types of education for new technologies, starting from the introduction of cars into two fictitious countries. What are the needs of a society in the throes of the impact of the ubiquitous microtechnology? The authors were not briefed on 'new technologies' but most chose information technology or informatics. The focus on things and information can lead us away from the essentially human aspects of education: caring for one's 'neighbour'. 'Education for' was also left to authors, who interpreted in a variety of ways. The authors must have their say. The book is divided into four sections: the basis and needs for education for the new technologies; national perspectives, case studies of particular initiatives, and questions about education for the new technologies. Guidance is also provided on chapters relating to particular areas and aspects of education.

Introduction: a fictitious example of adapting to a new technology

Two countries in the world were unfamiliar with the motor car. Both countries decided to start importing motor cars to enhance their transport systems and approached the education of the population in different manners. Courses were mounted in the schools and in the adult literacy classes.

The first country focused on the car itself. Wherever possible a motor car was provided for the learning. The focus was on how it worked, the premise being that there were limited repair resources in the country, so that the more people who were aware of the workings of a car and the basic repairs needed, the more likely it was that the cars would be kept running. The first part of the course focused on the theory of the car: the internal combustion engine, ignition, carburation, hydraulics for the brakes and the clutch, servo mechanisms, electrics, electric motors and alternators, gears, clutch operation, corrosion, tyres and so on. The next step was to focus on the repairs: dirt in the fuel system, punctures, bleeding the brake system, simple bodywork repairs. Finally, in order to enable the learners to have a clearer understanding of the car, the design process was outlined and the learners were required to carry out a simple design producing a cardboard model with at least one working part.

The second country focused on a quite different set of aspects. Initially the focus was on how to drive the car and special controlled areas were provided for practising. The next phase was a short course on applied psychology (although not given that frightening label) where the learners were introduced to the ideas of aggression, the design of cars in relation to competition, feeling of power, lack of physical outlets for aggression, focusing on the other people who drove cars, on the pedestrians and on the animals that were common on the roads of the country. Finally there was an introduction to the ideas of pollution and the use of the country's limited resources: the less that the car was used at high speeds and with heavy braking, the longer the time that the car would last without spare parts, which required expenditure of the limited resources.

The two countries carried out their respective programmes of education. The first country had a large number of accidents. There was considerable damage to property and to the cars. The carnage was so great the country eventually banned the motor car as an evil user of the limited resources and a killer of the citizens. After another 15 years the country had become poorer and poorer, with ever-dwindling development in the provision of reliable and rapid transport for its agricultural and mineral resources.

Meanwhile the second country had some problems with the repair and maintenance of its cars but initiated a short training programme to produce a small number of expert mechanics. It had least accidents of any country in the world. The benefits had been seen as the development of the roads, bridges, communication systems along the motor routes, all of which would provide much-needed employment. In 15 years' time it had built up a network of roads, telephone and electricity systems that followed the road routes. The country had become prosperous with rapid transit of its products to its borders and ports, with goods being exported to the places where they received better payments.

While it is clear that neither of the education programmes was perfect, there were more long-term benefits possible in the second education programme, which took into account the social, economic and personal development of the population. The technological aspects were seen as the servants of the needs of the community, rather than the possible follow-up from a well-trained technological population. Both programmes could be perceived as having a heavy vocational bias; however they represented part of the education not all of it.

New technologies and education

Recent talks given at the Royal Society for the Development of the Arts and Manufactures in the UK have painted the scenario for the possible needs of a future society related to new informative technologies. The development of such a society in the throes of a new technological phase raises some interesting issues. It is clear from the economic aspects, social effects and actual practice of these developments that interpersonal relationships, planning for long-term effects and the need to think divergently are key issues for the successful development. The population will clearly require to be educated for the new technologies. It is noticeable that the focus is not on the technology itself (Gershuny, 1987; Shirley, 1987; Handy, 1987).

When briefing the authors, I did not define 'new technologies'. It has been interesting to see how different authors have interpreted the systems that are dependent on microelectronic developments of recent years. The developments can be viewed from a variety of perspectives. If technologies are perceived as extensions of people, then the extensions associated with the microelectronic technologies are: memory, access to data, processing data, control of a range of mechanisms. The extensions are focused around the brain and the nervous system rather than extensions of manual attributes associated with the industrial revolution. These are the technologies known as information technology or informatics.

It is already clear that predictions made over the last ten years about the impact of the new technologies vary from the expected to the unexpected. The impact on employment, production processes, world trade and communication was predicted by authors such as Barron and Curnow (1971), Gosling (1981), Stonier (1983) in the UK and Toffler (1980) in the USA. The social implications and the educational implications were less clearly identified at that time. Some authors made little attempt to address the educational scene.

Education and society

There are fundamental difficulties in addressing the ideas of education for the new technologies. Should education lead or follow society? Most education systems are either controlled by the state or by local representatives of the people. If education is seen to be leading society it could be accused of social engineering. If it follows society it can be accused of educating for the past rather than the future. From the chapters in this book the state of the art seems to be ambivalent. There are chapters which address the wider social and societal aspects of the new technologies and address the problem in general terms from that perspective. The more pragmatic contributions seem to show either a tendency towards putting more and more into the curriculum or to the means by which learners interact with the curriculum content. The main focus is on teaching and the teachers rather than learning and the learners. The lack of clear directions in which to progress raises many questions about the educational systems that are reflected. Most authors address institutionalized educational systems rather than education as a lifelong process.

Critics will no doubt identify many examples of good practice that are omitted. The purpose of the *Yearbook* is to reflect current thinking and current practice, covering education from the early years to adult education. Inevitably such sampling will be thin and the editor's selection will be idiosyncratic In addition an attempt has been made to sample countries, although the sample is exclusively from the North, or developed, countries. There are clear implications of the widening of the North-South divide, particularly in the communication of information for trading. The divide has extended since the warnings of some years ago (Cherry, 1971). I am very conscious that the majority of the world's countries are not represented in this book. Is this a reflection of uncaring attitudes to those less fortunate than ourselves?

It would appear that a further problem is the divide between learners from homes of professional and educated people and learners from homes of manual workers and less educated people. In some countries there are also gender differences of access and cultural differences too.

Associated with the development of the new technologies there has also been a redirection of education towards vocationalism. The approach is supported or queried in every chapter of the *Yearbook*. The use of the technologies can be seen as a means of meeting the needs of educating for the new technologies. Many of the national developments have this approach. Alternative learning strategies are also identified.

The ideas of information, knowledge, communication and control are a recurring theme but the distinction between private knowledge and public information is raised.

The range of electronic media cannot all be featured in a book of this length. An editor has to make some decisions about where to draw the line. There are already many publications covering the use of television, radio, computers and interactive videos. Only where national or international decisions are focused on one particular piece of hardware, the computer, has the general area been addressed. However it does seem to me that the perception of the computer is in some ways a misnomer for the variety of devices now in use. In addition the focus is not on the computer but the needs for education to address the impact of current devices and systems on the individual and society.

The essentially human aspects of education are sometimes forgotten in the following of technologies. If the implications of the new technologies include more people working from home or more people locked into communication via electronic media, I would suggest that crucial aspects of human existence will become essential aspects of education. The socialization associated with meeting at the workplace will be missing (Shirley, 1987), with the reduced effect of the family already prevalent in many societies. Where do children develop values, interactions with other human beings, respect for other human beings? The role of formal education may focus much more on the affective elements of learning rather than the current heavy emphasis on cognitive ones (and those mainly in the printed or written form). The use of spoken language could become increasingly important as an aspect of compulsory education. All the aspects identified here are related to a caring human being, a person focused on the coexistence with other people in that locality, in that country, in the world. We all have common resources founded on air, earth and water, the crucial resources of human existence. The new technologies may enable us to see and hear what else is happening in the global village, but cannot involve us in caring for and supporting those in need (Handy, 1987). We all have a desire to be needed. Several of the authors have raised issues such as these when questioning the idea that there is something special about education for the new technologies. Perhaps what is special is that these aspects of human existence need to become the very essence of education rather than the periphery of education. Morals, values, actions are the elements of a civilized society. There is a need to argue these values out with other human beings, which requires meetings where visual as well as aural cues are essential. The proximity of another human being and the limits of their personal space boundaries help in enabling and limiting the relationship. There is no way that any electronic medium can substitute that aura. The days of the large educational establishment with hundreds or thousands of learners may be numbered but not the environment where people meet together to learn about one another, and to help one another in learning.

Interpretations of education for the new technology

The title of the *Yearbook* this year is *Education for the New Technologies*. Again, the authors were not given an elaborate interpretation. There seems to have been a variety of interpretations in addition to the more obvious one. The idea of education *about* the new technologies is at least in part incorporated in some of the papers. Another more subtle approach is the idea of education *through* (or using) the new technologies. By the very utilization of the new technologies and familiarization with their strengths and weaknesses in an educational context there is implied education for the new technologies. Access to databases provides a good example. However access alone does not incorporate a reflective and thinking educational approach. It may provide a basis for the existence of education for the new technologies, but it is not in itself education for the new technologies. Some educational processes through the new technologies incorporate the reflective approach and such an approach is more realistic. Education *in spite* of the new technologies is the approach in which opposition to technological determinism is taken to the extreme of ignoring the existence of the new technologies and trying to carry on as before. The role of a vocationally based education is aimed at meeting the impact of the new technologies head on. Most chapters incorporate the vocational approach to education, whilst the remainder query the same approach. The book does not set out to provide answers but to encourage discussion and reflection around the issues. The emphasis on a more relevant and vocationally based education seems to cross national and political barriers. (Will the motor car be such a central part of the educational system of those two fictitious countries?) Will there be such an emphasis as the new technologies become a more hidden part of our daily lives?

Education for whom? It would have been possible to put together this book for any sector of the educational system: compulsory, post-compulsory; primary, secondary, college, university; continuing education at work, adult education. I felt that the problems had many similarities. Should technological developments play such an important part in their educational system that educational programmes nationally, in sectors of the system or even locally, were based around this ubiquitous piece of micro-technology? In ten years' time will the whole educational system have become geared to the latest technology, say biotechnology?

Education obviously has a key part to play in the familiarization of humans with the world around them and in drawing out the features of the natural, the man-made, the relationships between people and the society in which they live. The focus on the man-made may lead us to lose sight of our limited resources; the need to survive at the expense of all others seems to be an underlying aspect of education worldwide. Will focusing on new technologies bring about further destruction of the environment, the development of new and terrible means of power (be they weapons of war, weapons of trade or weapons of manipulation)? Could the focus on the new technologies enable us to ask questions about their effects, their costs, their implications in our daily lives and those of others? That would be nearer to my perception of education.

However, let the authors declare their own positions. In asking authors to write for the *Yearbook* I originally envisaged three major sections, but a fourth part has evolved. The outsides of the sandwich are the ideas and questions about education for the new technologies. The inside parts are two layers of present practice.

Structure

Part 1 sets up the basis and needs for education for the new technologies. The four contributors identify information as the crucial area. In Chapter 1 Mary Tasker and Ian Jamieson (UK) set the scene in a historical context, raising the issues of the role of education and its relationship to the disadvantaged. They perceive information as something to access, manipulate and understand. Martin Tessmer and David Jonassen (USA), in Chapter 2, see learning as information processing, the key being learning strategies. Jonathan Anderson (Australia) in Chapter 3 develops a rationale for new technologies in education, with information access being the key. In Chapter 4 John Whiting switches our attention to adult learners with needs to learn and five levels of needs. He focuses in particular on learner-learner communication from a personal learner work station. These four contributors have raised issues, ideas and questions from which the next two sections can be critically reviewed.

Part 2 outlines four national perspectives. Rhys Gwyn reviews recent and current developments in schools in the UK in Chapter 5. Mikhail Draganov and Raina Pavlova outline current and proposed developments in schools in Bulgaria in Chapter 6. Horia Pitariu covers the range of developments including the Informatics High Schools and adult learners at work in Romania in Chapter 7. Finally Lise Fogh outlines current proposals for developments in Denmark in Chapter 8. The national initiatives which are regionally based (as in Denmark and the UK) have co-ordination and dissemination problems, which are not apparent in the centrally controlled initiatives (as in Bulgaria and Romania).

In Part 3, specific initiatives, the bulk of the case studies are from the UK. The purpose of this section was to reflect more on grass-root initiatives. From conferences and conference reports in different countries I feel that these are a fair reflection of what is happening. Peggy Nightingale from Australia sets the scene in Chapter 9 by identifying the needs of university lecturers for staff development activities. More staff development, but for lecturers, in further education (non-degree, post-compulsory) is outlined in Chapter 10 by Chris Bell, with proposals to enable innovation dissemination. David McConnell (Chapter 11) describes an investigation into the use of computer conferencing for the in-service education of teachers focusing on student learning styles. Dick Ewen outlines the Technical and Vocational Education Initiative in Chapter 12 — a local development of a national initiative. The adult learner at work is the focus of Chapter 13 by Clive Hewitt.

The final section, some questions, relects on practice. In Chapter 14 Roland Lauterbach (W Germany) raises issues about the role of primary education and its interaction with new information technologies. George Chryssides (UK) raises questions about vocationally-oriented education systems in Chapter 15. Finally Steen Larsen (Denmark) discriminates between information and knowledge and reflects on the new technologies in education from both psychological and sociological perspectives, leaving us with the social functions of education — back where we started in Chapter 1.

Should you wish to follow only certain aspects of education, a rough guide is:

Vocational Education	All chapters
Primary Education	Chapters 4, 6, 9, 15
Secondary Education	Chapters 2, 4, 6, 7, 8, 9, 13
Post-compulsory (Non-degree)	Chapters 8, 11, 13

Post-compulsory (Degree)	Chapters 8, 10, 16
Adult/learning at work	Chapters 5, 8, 14
Teacher training/staff development	Chapters 6, 7, 11, 12
Learning strategies	Chapters 3, 4, 6, 7, 11, 12, 17
Practice with new informative technology	Chapters 6, 7, 11, 12
Social aspects of education	Chapters 2, 4, 6, 7, 8, 9, 15, 16, 17

References

Barron, I and Curnow, R (1971) *The Future with Microelectronics* Open University Press: Milton Keynes

Cherry, C (1971) *World Communication: Threat or Promise* London: Wiley Interscience

Gershuny, J J (1987) Lifestyles, innovation and the future of work *Journal of the Royal Society of Arts* CXXXV: 492-502

Gosling, W (1981) *The Kingdom of Sand: Essays to Salute a World in Process of Being Born* Council for Educational Technology: London

Handy, C (1987) The future of work — the new agenda *Journal of the Royal Society of Arts* CXXXV: 515-525

Shirley, S (1987) The distributed office *Journal of the Royal Society of Arts* CXXXV: 503-514

Stonier, T (1983) *The Wealth of Information* Thames Methuen: London

Toffler, A (1980) *The Third Wave* Morrow: New York

Part 1: Basis and needs for education for the new technologies

1. Schooling and new technology: rhetoric and reality

Ian Jamieson and Mary Tasker

Summary: Four basic questions in relation to new technology and schooling are posed. The first asks what changes new technology is bringing about in the spheres of work, the home, family life and in leisure activities. The second asks whether these changes are truly widespread and revolutionary. The assessment of the evidence of change brought about by new technology concludes, firstly, that to date the changes are neither widespread nor revolutionary, and secondly that technological change is always filtered through the mesh of sociopolitical and economic factors and that ultimately these and not technological factors are crucial. The final two questions concern new technology and schooling. The third asks provocatively why schools need to change because of technological developments. The attempts to introduce new technology into schools, particularly in Britain, are charted as examples of 'technological panic' on the part of government, and the arguments for change are critically examined. The final question asks what sorts of changes to the organization of schools and the school curriculum ought to be encouraged in the light of developments in new technology. The article concludes by asserting the central place of the humanities and the social sciences in the curriculum.

Introduction

Why should schools teach literacy and numeracy to the nation's children? Such a question appears fatuous to all but anarchists and radical deschoolers. Not only does society require a literate and numerate citizenry for its effective functioning, but individual citizens need to be literate and numerate if they are to realize their own wishes and self potential in a society which is dominated by numbers and words. The same beguilingly simple analogy is used to justify the introduction of information technology in schools. Our economy and society, it is argued, are being transformed by new technology. It is thought to follow that schools must invest increasing amounts of time and money in equipping students to deal with this phenomenon.

It is necessary to unpack these arguments and to question them at every point for they will be shown to have embedded in them a range of unexamined assumptions and unwarranted assertions. There are four basic questions that need answering. In the first place we need to enquire what is the nature of the changes that the new technology is bringing about in society. Our second question is whether these changes are so truly revolutionary and widespread that they will transform people's very existence. Thirdly, we will examine certain features of modern education and ask, in view of the answers to the first two questions, why do schools need to change? Finally, we will turn to the most important question of all for schools — in view of the developments in new technology, what sort of changes, if any, should there be?

New technology and societal change: the present

New technology is widely regarded as one of the great transforming features of modern society. At the heart of the transformation is the rapid technological change in the field of information handling, unprecedented since the invention of printing in the 14th century. We have witnessed an increase in computer power of about an order of magnitude every six years or so for the last 30 years. When this is combined with significant decreases in the price of computer power, and matching developments in communications facilities due to the advent of satellites and fibre optics, then it is easy to understand why many people regard new technology as one of the most significant agents of change in modern life.

The potential of the new technology for transforming society is denoted by the use of such phrases as 'the second industrial revolution', implying that just as the first industrial revolution, which was based on certain technological discoveries, transformed society, so too will the second, But of course the first imdustrial revolution was not a revolution driven solely by technological change. As historians of the period have clearly shown it was the coming together at a particular moment of a complex set of technological, economic, social and political forces. In whatever way we describe the changes that are currently taking place in the advanced industrial nations, whatever the phrases we use to describe them, from the 'second industrial revolution' to 'post-industrialism', such changes are *not* solely the result of changes in new technology. The 'technological imperatives' will be strained through the same social, political and economic sieve of society that they have always been. William Schockley is no more the only father of the second industrial revolution than James Watt was of the first.

The first industrial revolution was at heart a transformation of the workplace and of people's work habits; is new technology bringing about a similar transformation of work today? It is easy to find examples where new technology has made significant changes in the workplace. The printing industry and the trading of financial services are good examples of total transformations, but such examples are notable for their rarity. For example, there are very few current examples in the UK of completely computer-integrated manufacturing (CIM) plants or of flexible manufacturing systems (FMS) (Jones and Scott, 1987). Such systems, where the whole business is computerized — manufacturing, warehousing, re-ordering of parts, as well as the financial and administrative systems — are 'state of the art' systems rare even in the USA and Japan. It would not be true to say, even at a less sophisticated level, that new technology was transforming the workplace. By 1985 there were only 3,200 industrial robots in Britain used by 740 firms (*The Times*, 17.2.87). The degree of penetration is considerably higher for countries like the USA, Japan or West Germany but even there they are not commonplace in manufacturing industry. Certain aspects of manufacturing technology have been more affected by new technology than others. Computer numerically controlled machines (CNC machines) are commonplace, as is computer-aided design (CAD). The quality control of machined parts has been transformed by microprocessor controlled equipment.

It is easier to see the effects of new technology in the world of the office than on the factory floor. It would certainly be true to say that more basic operations have been altered here than in the factory. This is because the nature of office tasks, centered on information flows, lends them to transformation by information technology, and because new technology in the office is relatively cheap compared to that required in the factory. Although word processing, electronic databases and systems of financial and stock control are commonplace, it is still relatively rare to find fully electronic or paperless offices.

In other parts of the working world not adequately covered by our distinction between the office and the factory the same general picture emerges. While it is possible to see specif-ic applications of new technology which transform particular tasks, for example electronic point of sale systems (EPOS) in shops, or electronic funds transfer (EFT) in banks, or even the use of expert systems by a widening range of professionals in areas like law, medicine and health, it is not yet possible to talk of a general transformation of the working world. It is our contention that the blue-collar and white-bloused workers of 1958 would find the working world of 1988 for the most part instantly recognizable.

It is customary to contrast work with leisure. Is our leisure world being transformed by new technology? The short answer to this question must be no. Although it is possible to identify certain ways in which new technology has influenced the leisure patterns of certain segments of the population the change is not significant. A small amount of the increase in leisure time can be attributed to new technology-influenced labour saving devices in the home, but the main instruments of this change, washing and drying machines for clothes and the ubiquitous vacuum cleaner, are essentially old technology. Only the microwave oven is purely the product of the new age. Video cassette recorders (VCR machines) have made a considerable penetration into British homes with over 9 million in use by 1984 (*Euromonitor*, March 1985), and Britain also has a very high density of microcomputers (3.5 million by 1984). And yet there is no evidence to suggest that these examples of new tech-

nology have significantly altered the leisure experience of the mass of
the British people. Going out for a meal or a drink is still the most
popular leisure activity outside the home, while watching TV, garden-
ing and listening to records and tapes are the most popular within the
home. In terms of leisure-related expenditure, the purchase of meals
outside the home and books and newspapers take the proportionately
largest slice of the family leisure income. Walking, a distinctly 'low tech'
activity remains the most popular sport (*Social Trends,* 1986).

At the heart of societal structure in the Western world stands the
family and the home. Is there any evidence that new technology is
making radical changes in home and family life? This is an area where
research is rather sparse. In one of the few summary articles, Ferguson
(1985) argues that 'what debate there has been about their [new technologies'] intended or unintended, desirable or undesirable, social,
economic or cultural consequences, has centred on the symbolic
metaphor of the household as an "electronic cottage" within a "wired
nation" of similarly equipped households.' She goes on to point out,
however, that this futurologists' vision is 'rather rare in the 1980s and
unlikely ever to become the family norm even in the 1990s' (Ferguson,
1985).

New technology and societal change: the future

The introduction of new technology and how it affects social and
employment trends has been an important issue not only in the post-
war period but throughout the history of industrial development. We
can learn at least two important lessons for the future by looking back
on the first industrial revolution. The first is that changes happen gradually; at certain moments it is possible to see the two systems, the old
and the new, existing side by side. This is clearly the case at the present
time: the executive working at home on her networked computer exists
alongside her more junior compatriots still pounding typewriters; the
CNC machine exists alongside the mechanical lathe. The second lesson
is that technological determinism does not provide a satisfactory explanation of the relationship between technology and society. Changes in
technology do not automatically bring about radical changes in the
world of work, let alone other parts of society. What changes new technology brings about are always mediated by the political process,
whether this is at the level of the individual firm or of society.

It is because technological determinism is so obviously mistaken that
it becomes difficult to foresee future trends. The only prediction that
one can make with certainty is that the future is not clear. Let us examine
some of the more common predictions about the effects of new technology and assess the available evidence.

One of the first and most enduring predictions about the effects of
new technology was the apocalyptic vision of a workless society made

redundant by the microchip. Sherman and Jenkins (1979) in Britain and Nora and Minc (1978) in France were the first amongst countless researchers who predicted the 'collapse of work'. These predictions are deterministic: as Rajan (1987) argues, they are based on the dictum 'science discovers, technology executes and man conforms'. Employment is influenced by a complex set of factors, not just technology. Some of these factors might be capable of moderating any adverse impact on employment, others may only accelerate it. For the economy as a whole, it is very difficult to provide an indication of the technological impact on jobs. Most commentators seem to agree that the high levels of unemployment in many European countries are largely the result of economic recession rather than new technology. For example, a recent study of manufacturing industries by Northcott and Rogers (1985) has shown that over a two-year period, information technology is directly implicated in some 34,000 job losses in Britain, 30,000 in West Germany and 12,000 in France. Many official estimates of job losses put the figures lower and point to corresponding job gains in industries supplying new technology (Williams, 1984), while estimates from the influential Institute of Manpower Studies at the University of Sussex come to a higher figure by including not only intra-firm displacement but also intra-industry displacement (Rajan, 1985; Rajan and Pearson, 1986). It is impossible to say what the future employment prospects are for those students who are still at school. Although the 'doom scenarios' considerably outnumber the scenarios in the camp of the optimists, it is certainly possible to envisage considerable employment being created by the demand for new service products related to information technology (Gershuny, 1986). As Gershuny (1987) argues, 'If we adopt appropriate policies, the new technologies of the eighties need not be job displacing, any more than those of the thirties were.' In the end it is a question of policy, not technology.

If the prediction of job loss is one of the firmest predictions associated with new technology, then fear of 'proletarianization', occurring through the de-skilling of craft and clerical work, is also firmly entrenched in the futurologists' folklore, largely through the influential work of Braverman (1974). The majority of empirical studies of the effect of new technology on work skills fail to confirm the Braverman thesis. What they all show is the *complexity* of the world of work. As Sorge *et al* (1983) show in their study, foremen, for example, can be downgraded to serve primarily as facilitators ensuring that jigs, tools and materials are available; or they may be upgraded to use terminals to compile programs and to initiate changes in them. Jones (1982) has shown how the respective roles of workers, supervisors and programmers vary even between plants all undertaking small-batch engineering and using similar numerical control technology. The conclusion of the Institute of Manpower Studies enquiries in different industries on the effect of new technology on work skills was that in 50 per cent of the sampled firms the overall effect was neutral, in 30 per cent the net effect was one of re-skilling, while in the remaining 20 per cent the net effect was one of de-skilling (Rajan, 1987).

An issue which spreads beyond the world of work, although it embraces it, is the effect that information technology has on our personal power as decision-makers. Once more the frenzied predictions of the futurologists lurch between an Orwellian vision of an all-seeing and all-knowing state, which dominates decision-making via its access to knowledge gathered by the invasive capabilities of new technology (state access to our financial, employment and criminal records etc), in contrast to much greater involvement by the individual in organizational and public life because information technology has the potential to give us all access to the relevant information. There are few useful empirical studies in this area. Campbell and Connor (1986) show that in Britain there are 13 big state computer systems containing 1,258 million records and indicate that it is both difficult for the public to get information about them and out of them. Studies of the workplace reveal a complex picture. Innew a summary article on the effect of new technology on decision-making in work organizations, Warner (1984) shows that the locus of decision-making can either move up or down in an organization with the advent of new technology. He concludes his review on an optimistic note.

> In the *long run*, the new communication technology could possibly be intrinsically 'democratic' in its influence on the workplace, as it could potentially enhance the greatest access of the greatest numbers, to paraphrase Bentham. In a way, this could parallel an earlier technological development, namely the printing press, which by reducing communication costs increased the potential for democratic involvement (p.209).

One of the most important predictions about the 'second industrial revolution' does not focus on what might happen in specific sectors or institutions in society like the world of work or education, but predicts instead that the most important effect of new technology will be on making these traditional distinctions redundant. New technology certainly raises important *locational* questions for society.

The technology exists for many jobs to be done at home. Rank Xerox has already initiated 'networking' arrangements with some of its specialists, whereby they now work from their homes. A *Financial Times* survey of 255 large UK companies reported that two-thirds believed that by 1988 they would be employing executives working from home (Cane, 1983). Rumelt (1981) has drawn attention to a far-reaching degree of dispersion in work locations which is made possible by new technology. He suggests that when information technology is combined with CAD/CAM, whole segments of the production process can be spatially and organizationally separated. Once computers begin to specify the requirements for parts fabrication in a standardized language, and once the automated facilities exist to turn these specifications into a part, the need to have all the stages of engineering within the same location, or even the same enterprise, diminishes.

The potential for a dramatic locational shift of employment to the home raises important questions about the validity of the sexual division of labour and the family wage. Ferguson (1985) asks whether the traditional division between 'instrumental' income-earning males and 'affective' child-and-elderly-caring females will be re-encountered in a 'hi-tech' guise. She argues that

> gender and occupational differences are already emerging in the information creation and processing activities (however defined) done at home, and in their differential status and rewards. For professionals of either sex the union of telecommunications and computers confers freedoms from time and place. For part-time working mothers, the advantages of home-based, flexi-time word processing, for example, provides a solution to the problem of combining paid work with child (or elderly parent) care; but at a cost. These costs include lower earnings, little job security or opportunity of occupational advancement.

Nevertheless the possibility of working from home that the electronic future opens up may have an important effect on women's job aspirations and achievements. The success of F International, an all-women company of computer programmers working from home, indicates that such a future can be realized. It is developments like these, particularly if they are accompanied by high financial rewards, that may lead to a restructuring of roles within the family. As Rose (1985) points out, the renegotiation of gender roles and relations would be the single most important process leading to the re-evaluation of the nature and meaning of work.

It is not just in the potential for locational shifts of employment that the home begins to take on more significance. Its locus as a centre for consumption can also be enhanced by developments in information technology. Tele-shopping has been on trial in Britain since 1980, and its development is held back not by technical factors but by commercial ones (Davies and Howard, 1985). Media satellite communication means that Europeans can tune into each other's broadcasts, and commercially run video stations like Rupert Murdoch's Sky Channel can be received in ten European countries. This could have important implications for the 'cultural integrity' of the home and of individual nation states. Of greatest significance for education is that the potential role of interactive communications services in the household challenges the monopoly of the teaching and other professions, when their hold on specialist knowledge is broken by the existence of software designed to fit individual learning, medical, legal, financial, psychological and social needs. Insofar as it is the case that the major job of the professions is in the management and interpretation of information, then there is a real possibility that this job can be accomplished by fifth and sixth generation computer software delivered to the self-educating, self-servicing household of the future.

Technological change and schooling

One of the great problems of modern schooling is the nature of the relationship between the curriculum and the needs of a modern industrial society. One of the distinctive features of industrial market societies is that change is endemic, a permanent feature of the society. There seems little doubt that the advent of new technology will intensify the pace of change. The most important question to be answered is whether the changes we have described warrant a wholesale change in schooling.

The difficulties in answering this question should be clear from our preceding analysis. It is our contention, first, that new technology has not, as yet, made any radical changes in society; secondly, that it is extremely difficult to make predictions about future changes. We would also add that even if we could be sure that developments in new technology would transform society, it would not *necessarily* follow that the nature of schooling should change. A great deal depends not only on the nature of societal change but on one's view of the nature and purpose of schooling.

In England the debate about the nature of schooling has since the 19th cese 'modentury been influenced by the needs of society and in particular the needs of the economy. With the emergence of a more science-based society in the 18th century new schools were founded. These were usually nonconformist in flavour and geared to the needs of commerce and science. But the power of the established Church, the need for new forms of social control in early 19th century England and the enduring power of the landed class snuffed out these 'modern' foundations. By the late 19th century the English schooling system was dominated by the Victorian public schools catering for the future leaders of society, who were becoming increasingly distanced from the world of business and industry, and the elementary schools providing for the majority of the population. Structural changes in industrial organization and employment patterns and, after 1851, a growing awareness of a lack of competitiveness with European and American manufacturers, prompted calls for radical change in this system. From the 1860s onwards educationalists and industrialists joined together in the technical education movement, which gave birth to commissions and government enquiries in an attempt to inject into the curricula of the elementary and public schools greater scientific and technological content. Despite the efforts to 'modernise' the system at every level, the liberal tradition held good. Public schools kept to their classical core curriculum and the elementary schools continued to impart religious and moral training and the three Rs.

One marked feature of the economic crisis today is the sharp decline in the traditional 'smokestack' industries of the first industrial revolution, as well as in manufacturing. The reasons for this decline are complex and involve both cyclical and structural factors, but one of the distinctive features of the British situation is that in the search for simple causes of this decline, education holds the political limelight. Three separate but related arguments are directed towards the education system. The first claims that education is a major consumer of public spending which is wealth-consuming rather than wealth-creating. The second argues that the education system encourages young people to enter occupations which are not part of the wealth-creating segment of the economy. Finally, it is claimed that when school-leavers do enter industry they are not adequately equipped in terms of skills, knowledge or attitudes. This was the argument forcefully put by the British prime minister, James Callaghan, when he launched the 'great debate' about education and the world of work in 1976.

All of these assertions are problematic. The first argument denies that education is an investment and instead makes it a cost. The second argument appears to deny the role of market forces as an allocative mechanism for jobs. The first two arguments both entail the proposition that the economy can be simply divided into wealth-creating and wealth-consuming elements, while the majority of economists maintain that the whole of the economy is interdependent (Gershuny and Miles, 1983). The final argument assumes that employers can agree amongst themselves on their requirements for youth labour, and that they can successfully distinguish needs from wants.

The increasing importance of new technology in the economy has been added to this confused mixture of arguments. Education could become an investment if young people were educated in and through new technology. The glamour of 'high-tech' industries, if they were given enough exposure in schooling, could be used to encourage young people to choose industry as a career; while finally it is argued that schools must be used to produce the skills, attitudes and knowledge required for the new industries based on new technology.

All of these new technology arguments present difficulties in the British context. As we have already argued, new technology is only gradually changing the workplace. Teachers and their students exploring their industrial hinterland are just as likely to find old technology as new. Furthermore the service industries, especially financial services, are even more likely to have seen transformed by new technology than manufacturing industry. If new technology really is seen as glamorous it is unlikely to cure the reluctance of the most able young people to work in manufacturing industry.

Studies of the economy and of the demands of employers have not produced the unequivocal results that might have been thought necessary if the school curriculum was to be transformed. In the first place it is important to distinguish between high-tech industries and high-tech jobs (Rumbhigherger and Lewin, 1984). Less than one-quarter of workers in the so-called new technology industries have jobs which require a detailed knowledge of new technology. Furthermore, this sector of the economy is small, employing only 2.7 per cent of the British work-force (Wellington, 1987) and 15 per cent of the US workforce. These proportions are unlikely to increase greatly (Rumberger and Lewin, 1984; Wellington, 1987). Although there are still shortages in these areas they are for qualified and experienced technicians and graduates. There is no labour market for school-leavers as such, although one must recog-nize that schools might need to encourage young people to go into higher education to take relevant qualifications if these shortages are to be ameliorated.

Although British industrial and commercial employers have tradi-tionally grumbled about the skills, attitudes and knowledge of school-leavers (for an historical account see Reeder, 1979; for the modern picture see Jamieson and Lightfoot, 1982), it is not clear that their views are a reliable guide to the requirements of industry. Histori-cally, British employers have been mistaken in their beliefs about their own needs. They failed to understand that the first industrial revolu-tion had created a long-term need for large numbers of people skilled in science and technology. They were content to allow the public schools to keep their classical core curriculum and indeed colluded with this anachronism by sending their sons to these schools (Weiner, 1981). They valued the hierarchical educational structure which filtered and selected children so that on leaving school they could be easily slotted into one appropriate industrial stratum, and which inculcated in the children of the lower stratum the 'right' attitudes. In evidence given to an official investigation of higher elementary schools in 1906 these were described as a good character, qualities of subservience and general handiness (Reeder, 1979).

It is not clear that the employers of the 'new age' are any better at diagnosing the needs of industry as opposed to their wants. The evi-dence suggests, for example, that many employers do not know what is required to perform jobs in their own work organizations (Townsend et al, 1982; Ashton and Maguire, 1986); that employers are more likely to prefer traditional academic subjects in their employees than subjects which have been specifically designed for industrial relevance (Central Policy Review Staff, 1980). There is little evidence that employers are requiring IT-related skills in school-leavers. Literacy and numeracy remain the key requirements alongside certain personal qualities (Wel-lington et al, 1987).

Technology panic: the response of the education system

By the 1980s a number of problems facing Britain appear to have coalesced: the long-term decline of British manufacturing industry; a dramatic rise in youth unemployment set against a background of high adult unemployment; continuing worries about the 'performance' of the British education system all set against a background of dramatic inventions in information technology which, it is claimed, were pushing Britain quickly into the second industrial revolution.

The most important reaction to this complex scenario is a plethora of central government initiatives that have as their main thrust a revolution in education and training provision for employment. One of the centrepieces of this provision is education and training for new technology. The most important initiative is a structural one: the creation of a specialized government agency, the Manpower Services Commission (MSC). This *dirigiste* arm of government is constructed to act swiftly. It does this by sidestepping the usual bureaucracy of government departments, by keeping consultation with interested groups down to a minimum, and by employing a large budget and staff. The MSC is attached to the British Department of Employment (DoE), and thus the major source of change has been outside the direct influence of the education ministry.

It is difficult even to chart the initiatives that were launched in the 1980s, so quickly did they fall from ministerial desks or those of the MSC. The major ones included the Microcomputers in Schools Programme, funded by the Department of Trade and Industry (1981–84); the Microelectronics Education Programme, funded by the Department of Education and Science (1980–86; see Chapter 6); the setting up in 1981 of Information Technology Centres to train young people who had left school in IT skills; the creation of the Youth Training Scheme (YTS) in 1982, an MSC initiative providing a one-year training programme, subsequently extended to two years, designed for the majority of students who left school at the statutory leaving age; the Technical and Vocational Education Initiative (TVEI) launched by the MSC in 1982 in a small number of schools (see Chapter 12). Its aim is to enrich the curriculum of 14–18 year olds by the inclusion of more employment-related education. It is to be gradually extended to the whole age group. In 1985–86 the Department of Trade and Industry launched schemes to provide cheap software for schools and to provide each school with a modem. Most recently of all the government has announced the setting up of City Technology Colleges. These new colleges are intended for 11–18 year olds and are to be established in inner-city areas of Britain. The capital cost of these colleges is to be met by industry and the revenue costs by government. Industry will be an important stakeholder on the board of these colleges and it is expected that the curriculum will reflect industrial interests with a strong emphasis on information technology.

It is very difficult to make sense of all these initiatives. They represent a kind of 'technological panic' on the part of government about the UK's education and training system. Surveying the initiatives and their results, insofar as we have evidence of these, it is difficult to avoid the conclusion that few of the fundamental questions raised by the second industrial revolution have been systematically posed. The first question must be what blend of skills, knowledge and attitudes towards new technology is required of school-leavers. It may be the case that much specific IT education and training is best done *after* the completion of compulsory schooling in government youth training schemes or industry itself. In favour of such an approach might be the fact that high-performing economies like Sweden and Japan place almost no emphasis on IT in their compulsory school curriculum. Further, because the rate of innovation in IT is so formidably high, the costs of supplying schools with up-to-date hardware and software are enormous. The argument against such an approach can be found in Britain's deep-seated antipathy towards technology and industry in its schools. It could be argued that unless such attitudes are confronted at an early age, students will not go on to enrol for post-school education and training courses.

In Britain it has been decided that schools should be the launching ground for education in information technology and to further this end the government has invested considerable amounts of money in microprocessors and related software. As Wellington *et al* (1987) point out, however, this has been done to the accompaniment of a 'flood of rhetoric and unreflective enthusiasm as to its vocational significance'. The minister responsible for launching the Micros in Schools Programme, Britain's first Minister of Information Technology, declared, 'I want youngsters, boys and girls, leaving school at sixteen, to actually be able to operate a computer' (quoted in Wellington *et al*, 1987, p 3).

Unfortunately it is not clear what 'being able to operate a computer' might mean in practice, and despite the large investment in IT in British schools the picture does not look encouraging. In 1985 there were on average only 0.9 microcomputers per 100 pupils in primary schools and 1.7 per 100 in secondary schools (Hansard, 13 May, col 255). Computer studies was only the twelfth most popular ordinary level examination subject in 1984 (DES, Survey of Examining Boards in England, 1984). There are currently no approved GCSE information technology courses in British schools, although some are offered by the non-traditional examination boards. There seems general agreement that large sums of money have been wasted on expensive hardware that lies underused in schools because not enough investment was put into teacher training and supporting software. Although few British teachers would go quite so far as the director of software evaluation for one of the largest school systems in the US, in concluding that 'high quality educational software is almost non-existent in our elementary and secondary schools' (Noble, 1984), it is difficult to find many teachers who believe that the software support is adequate.

The final question that might be asked about information technology in the classroom is, 'Who is to be the main beneficiary of such programmes?' Are all children to be exposed to information technology on the grounds that it will affect them all as citizens and consumers, if not immediately as workers? Or should the main emphasis be on the most able children on the grounds that the real problem faced by the economy is a shortage of highly skilled information technology technicians and technologists, and that it would be enormously expensive to provide information technology for all children? The first wave of UK government initiatives appears to have supported the comprehensive principle of information technology for all, and this resulted in successful attempts to place a microcomputer in every school. In order for this policy to have an economic payoff, however, the government has to make sure that information technology has a real impact on the most able students, because only these students have the ability to fill the shortages that currently exist in the high-technology companies that are operating at the leading edge. This is a difficult task in Britain where the most able students have traditionally opted for a liberal education that gave them access to the established professions. This shortage of able students in high-technology vocational areas of the curriculum is the major reason why there has been such recent emphasis on girls and technology in Britain. The government has realized that girls are the great untapped talent in science and technology and that the manpower (sic) shortage in high-technology areas of the economy would be solved if only more women entered these occupations. It remains to be seen whether the most important government initiative in this field, the Technical and Vocational Education Initiative will be successful in these areas. The initial evaluation reports show that the initiative is making considerable progress in attracting high ability youngsters to the vocational side of the curriculum, but that it is meeting with much less success with the girls (MSC, 1987).

Educational needs in the age of new technology

The English academic and policy maker, David Hargreaves, in his influential book *The Challenge of the Comprehensive School*, poses the question: 'What kind of society do we want to create and how can the education system help us to realize such a society?' (Hargreaves, 1982). While such questions have always been important for educators, the revolutionary potential of information technology places them much more firmly on the agenda. This is because new technology potentially undermines the established ways of organization at work and in civic and family life, and thus presents us with choices. The possibility of accessing a vast range of electronic information and of opening up networks of communication and debate through computers gives to every individual the opportunity to have a say in the future direction of society. Whether or not the individual will want to seize this opportunity and become involved in decision-making at local and national levels will depend on a set of attitudes and values concerning social responsibility which it is traditionally the task of the educator to engender. Involvement with technology *per se* will not necessarily, as Serge Mallet (1975) suggests, bring about a critical frame of mind capable of envisaging superior forms of social development. The key figure in such a process of social change is the educator.

It is possible to envisage the application and use of the new technologies leading to the creation of a divided and unequal society, the product of a hierarchical and selective schooling system. It is equally possible, however, to envisage an alternative way ahead. Brian Simon describes such an alternative, which he calls the 'democratic option' and which he believes is the socially just way forward. It is

> based on the standpoint that the scientific-technological revolution gives the conditions for, and even necessitates, raising the educational level of the whole population, with the clear aim of ensuring that *all* are capable of mastering the scientific principles underlying the new technology, of operating it and of ensuring that it be directed to realizing its full potential for human and social development. This option implies that the introduction of the new technology proceeds on the basis of social planning determined by democratic decision-making (Simon, 1984).

If Simon's vision is to be realized we believe that compulsory schooling should concentrate not so much on the technology but on accessing, manipulating and above all understanding the new richness of information that it provides. The technology itself will be subject to rapid change and this factor alone plus the cost of the equipment means that schools will never be able to keep abreast of the latest technological developments. This problem could only be overcome if the barriers between school and work were lowered so that students had ready access to the latest technology.

It is important to stress the *information* aspects of information technology and to realize that the nature of the revolution means that we will all have much more information, about a wider variety of things, presented in a wider variety of forms. Our teaching will certainly have to embrace the new skills of accessing this information, but the crucial educational issues are the traditional ones of schooling. Ironically new technology places a premium on the fundamental skills of numeracy and literacy, and on the insights into the human condition provided by the humanities and social sciences.

If education follows this conclusion then some of the difficulties facing the introduction of information technology in schools will be overcome. In Britain, as in many other countries, 'computer studies' tends to be dominated by boys. We believe that this is because of the subject's 'masculine' image, that is one that concentrates on the rational, technical and impersonal aspects of the subject. This stereotype is reinforced by the fact that it is mostly men who teach about computers and boys who study them. Elkjaer (1987) argues that in order to attract and maintain the interest of girls, computer studies 'must leave room for learning processes which contain possibilities for gaining a wider social and humanistic understanding of the applications and implications of information technology'. Choices have to be made about the uses to which the new technologies are put and these choices are made on the basis of values, feelings and emotions, not by reason and logic alone. It is important that women have a say in decisions about the place of technology in society; the feminine perspective is a life-enhancing one and should influence the future direction of society (Jones, 1982).

Giving children from all social backgrounds access to information technology in schools is another important issue. In the UK children from working class homes are already at a disadvantage because they come from households which are less likely to possess a home computer. Furthermore, it is argued that private schools, to which many of the more affluent classes send their children, will have more ready access to the technology itself, as will state schools in more affluent areas (Reinecke, 1984). All children are likely to benefit from the more active and experiential-based pedagogy that is often employed in computer-based teaching, but there is little evidence to suggest that children from disadvantaged backgrounds benefit particularly from this approach. If the current trend of using information technology across the curriculum in a wide range of subjects is developed then the benefits could be marked, but for such teaching to be commonplace in schools an enormous investment in both hardware and software needs to take place: even in a country like Britain which claims to be one of the leading countries introducing information technology into schools.

There is finally the pressing need to heal the growing rift that is developing in Western industrialized countries between technology and the humanities. In the UK despite the efforts of the Microelectronics Programme to promote computer-assisted learning in history and geography, the humanities curriculum as a whole has been affected only marginally. But the purposes of humanities teaching are essential ingredients of a technological education which is grounded in democratic and humane values. The asking of critical questions arising out of social understanding is the hallmark of the humanities. The philosopher Bernard Williams justified the connection in the following way:

> If it is right that the humanities as subjects make an essential contribution to the understanding of society and that the understanding of society is essentially connected to ways in which we can reflect on it, question it and hence try to change it; then questions of who should be taught how much of the humanities are essentially connected with questions of how open or transparent society should seek to be (Williams, 1987).

In a closed society run by an elite such questions would go unasked, the technological imperative would go unchallenged and the majority of the population, through ignorance, would fall into a 'fatalistic acceptance' of technological determinism and play no further part in the important decisions relating to the new technologies (Jones, 1982). We are, nevertheless, all members of the society in which we live and have the right and duty to share in deciding upon the future course of that society. The most important need for education for the 21st century is to find a way of integrating the values and outlook of the humanities with the logic and language of the new technologies.

References

Ashton, D N and Maguire, M J (1986) *Young Adults in the Labour Market* Research Paper No 55 DEP: London

Braverman, H (1974) *Labor and Monopoly Capital* Monthly Review Press: New York

Campbell, D and Connor, S (1986) *On the Record* Michael Joseph: London

Cane, A (1983) More expected to work from home *Financial Times* 1 September

Central Policy Review Staff (1980) *Education, Training and Industrial Performance* HMSO: London

Central Statistical Office (1986) *Social Trends* No.16 HMSO: London

Child, J (1984) New technology and developments in management organisation *Omega*, **12**, 3

Davies, R L and Howard, E B (1985) Whither tele-shopping? *ESRC Newsletter* **55**, June

DES (1984) *Survey of Examining Boards in England* HMSO: London

Elkjaer, B (1987) Are girls the problem? Gender and computer science in the Danish secondary school system. Institute of Information, Royal Danish School of Educational Studies: Copenhagen (mimeo)

Ferguson, M (1985) The family and new technologies *ESRC Newsletter* **55**, June

Gershuny, J (1986) Time use, technology and the future of work *Journal of the Market Research Society*, **28**, 4

Gershuny, J (1987) The leisure principle *New Society* **79**, 1259

Gershuny, J and Miles, I (1983) *The New Service Economy: The Transformation of Employment in Industrial Societies* Frances Pinter: London

Hansaid (House of Commons Parliamentary Debates) HMSO: London

Hargreaves, D (1982) *The Challenge of the Comprehensive School*, Routledge and Kegan Paul: London

Jamieson, I M (1986) Corporate hegemony or pedagogic liberation?: The schools industry movement in England and Wales in Dale, R (ed) *Education Training and Employment: Towards a New Vocationalism?* Pergamon Press: Oxford

Jamieson, I M and Lightfoot, M (1982) *Schools and Industry* Muthuen: London

Jones, B (1982) *Sleepers Awake: Technology and the Future of Work* Wheatsheaf Books: Brighton

Jones, B (1982) Destruction or redistribution of engineering skills? The case of numerical control in Wood, S (ed) (1982) *The Degradation of Work* Hutchinson: London

Jones, B and Scott, P (1987) FMS in Britain and the USA *New Technology and Work Environment* **2**, 1, Spring

Mallett, S (1975) *The New Working Class* Spokesman Books: Nottingham

MSC (1987) *TVEI Students and Studies — Three Years On* MSC: London

Noble, D (1984) Jumping off the computer bandwagon *Education Week* **3**, 24 October

Nora, S and Minc, A (1978) *L'Information de la Société Rapport de la Republique* La Documentation Française: Paris

Northcott, J and Rogers, P (1985) *Microelectronics in Industry. An International Comparison: Britain, Germany and France* PSI: London

Rajan, A (1985) *Recruitment and Training Effects of Technical Change* Gower: Aldershot

Rajan, A (1987) Technology in the workplace: assessing the impact *Manpower Policy and Practice* **2**, 4, Summer

Rajan, A and Pearson, R (1986) *UK Occupation and Employment Trends to 1990* Butterworths: Guildford

Reeder, D (1979) A recurring debate: education and industry in Bernbaum, G (ed) (1979) *Schooling in Decline* Macmillan: London

Illusions Penguin: Harmondsworth

Rumberger and Levin, H M (1984) *Forecasting the Impact of New Technologies on the Future Job Market* Project Report No 84-A4, Institute for Research on Educational Finance and Government, School of Education: Stanford University, USA

Rumelt, R P (1981) The electronic reorganisation of industry Paper presented at the *Global Strategic Management in the 1980s Conference:* London. Quoted in Child (1984)

Sherman, B and Jenkins, C (1979) *The Collapse of Work* Eyre Methuen: London

Simon, B (1984) Breaking school rules *Marxism Today,* September

Sorge, A, Hartmann, G, Warner, M and Nichols, I (1983) *Microelectronics and Manpower in Manufacturing* Gower: Aldershot

Townsend, C et al (1982) *London Into Work Development: Project* Institute of Manpower Studies: University of Sussex

Warner, M (1984) New technology, work organisation and industrial relations *Omega* 12, 3

Weiner, M (1981) *English Culture and the Decline of the Industrial Spirit: 1850–1980* Cambridge University Press: Cambridge

Wellington, J J (1987) Employment patterns and the goals of education *British Journal of Education and Work* 1, 3

Wellington, J J et al (1987) *Skills for the Future* HMSO; London

Williams, B (1987) Necessity disguised as luxury *Times Educational Supplement* 23 January

Williams, V (1984) Employment implications of new technology *Employment Gazette* May

2. Learning strategies: a new instructional technology

Martin Tessmer and David Jonassen

Summary: This chapter outlines the history, characteristics, issues and future directions of learning strategies. The chapter examines learning strategies' evolution in the field of instructional technology, their definition and characteristics, the types of learning strategies, the problems and questions concerning the research and utilization of learning strategies, and the directions for the future research and discussion of learning strategies in instructional technology. As a 'new', process-oriented instructional technology, learning strategies offer hope for improving student learning through student acquisition and control of their mental and emotional processes.

Introduction

Instructional technology as process and product

Technology has been defined as both process and product. The process is the systematic application of scientific solutions to practical tasks and the product is the hardware and software that results from technological processes (Heinich *et al*, 1986). Similarly, the instructional technology field involves both process and product components in its search to develop solutions to learning problems (AECT, 1977), utilizing processes such as needs analysis and instructional development, coupled with product hardware such as multimedia and interactive video.

Through the years, the changes in the product aspects of instructional technology have been widely perceived and recognized by educators and trainers. In the electronic technology age, teaching machines, video, computers, interactive video and CD-ROM have all been widely demonstrated and discussed. However, the changes in technological processes are frequently overlooked or misunderstood. For example, in the 1950s and 1960s, teachers and technologists alike thought that programmed instruction was primarily a product, such as a teaching machine or self-instructional text. Programmed instruction was seldom perceived as a behaviouristic process of instruction, encompassing its own theory base, assumptions, and procedures. As a result, there was a general lack of understanding of the process for developing programmed instruction (Glaser and Cooley, 1973).

Computer-based instruction is a current example of an instructional technology that contains both product and process aspects — the products being computer hardware and software and the process being the design and presentation of instruction that maximizes the computer's unique instructional capabilities.

Learning strategies are a new example of the process of instructional technology. Specifically, learning strategies represent a learner-controlled method for processing and recalling knowledge from instruction and instructional materials. This technology focuses on the development of generalizable mental skills in the learner, as opposed to the development of instructional features in instruction or instructional materials. Learning strategies are emblematic of the current shift in instructional technology from a behaviouristic to a cognitive view, from an emphasis on learners' external performance to learners' internal processing. As the influence of cognitive science becomes more dominant, the emphasis on the development of learning strategies is a growing emphasis in the field of instructional technology.

This paper discusses the origins, characteristics, and types of learning strategies, as well as issues concerning their research and utilization. The first section will trace the intellectual and scientific changes in instructional technology that have contributed to the growth of learning strategies and their acceptance as a learning technology. The next section reviews the characteristics and types of learning strategies, and how they are implemented to improve learning. The final two sections cover current issues about the research and utilization of learning strategies, and future directions for researching and developing learning strategies in instructional technology.

The evolution of instructional technology

In this century, instructional technology has undergone at least three distinct scientific and intellectual revolutions, what Kuhn (1962) would call 'paradigm shifts'. These shifts represent changes from the physicalist to the behaviourist view, the behaviourist to the neo-behaviourist view, and the neo-behaviourist to the cognitivist view. These paradigm shifts have affected both the theory and practice of instructional technology. Since the advent of learning strategies is an outgrowth of the current shift from a neo-behaviourist to cognitivist view, the rationale for each of these shifts clarifies the role of learning strategies in instructional technology.

The physicalist view

In the early part of this century, the visual instruction movement emerged in education. The movement focused on the non-verbal roles of audiovisual materials and devices, on machines and materials instead

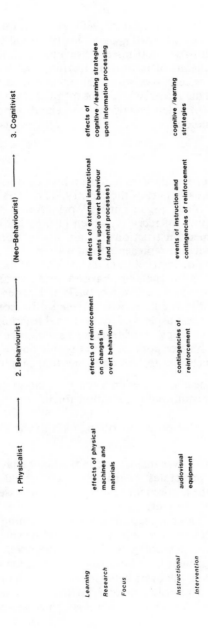

Figure 2.1 *Paradigm shifts in instructional technology*

of learning and the learner (Saettler, 1968). As such, the physicalist conception was a product-oriented view of instructional technology. The physical means of instruction (Pressey's teaching machines, for example) were the primary means of improving learning via instructional technology, and the concern was with their creation, improvement, and implementation. This materialistic concept of learning dominated the field until the 1950s, when behaviourism gained popularity as a new instructional technology.

Behaviourism

While the behaviourist paradigm had been prevalent in psychology and education since the early part of the century, its heaviest influence upon instructional technology began during World War II with the need to train massive amounts of recruits, which in turn helped promote the rise of programmed instruction as an instructional technology. Programmed instruction represented innovations in both the product and process aspects of instructional technology. It included a process approach to instruction that emphasized small steps in instruction coupled with constant corrective feedback of learner performance.

Most importantly, the behaviourist perspective contributed to the rise of two other process aspects of instructional technology, the systems approach and the conception of learning as a change in performance or behaviour. The systems approach has become one of the cornerstone processes of instructional technology, one that emphasizes:

☐ a rational procedure to design a system to attain specific objectives
☐ a logical decision-making method for the design of man-made entities
☐ a form of logical problem-solving akin to the scientific method (AECT, 1977).

The systems approach was initially developed by behaviourists according to behavioural principles. Learning was construed as a disposition to behave, so that the attainment of learning was assessed by the change in behaviour of the student.

Within the behaviourist tradition, student learning was defined in terms of student performance, a perspective that survives in today's education and training technologies. The development of instruction involved the arrangement of the external events of instruction in order to produce changes in the overt behaviour of the learner. Instructional technologists were primarily concerned with learner performance, not with the knowledge or mental processes that generated such performance.

Neo-behaviourism

As instructional technology continued to evolve from behaviourism, many practitioners found it difficult to accept its tenets wholesale. They accepted the need for empirical evidence of learning attainment and the utility of manipulating the external events of instruction to promote that learning, but rejected the notion that understanding the 'black box' of human learning processes would not contribute to the improvement of human learning.

While the neo-behaviourists made few attempts to define the 'black box' of learning and memory exhaustively, they at least acknowledged its existence. By making cognitive claims about mental processes that intervene between external events of instruction and overt learner performance, the neo-behaviourists posited learning processes as part of the process component of instructional technology: the learning process had to be considered in planning and producing instruction. Many educational technologists today take a neo-behaviourist perspective, relying on a behavioural empiricism for their methodology, yet searching for cognitive variables that can influence student learning.

The cognitivist view

Since the late 1950s, a gradual revolution in educational psychology has occurred. Learning psychologists such as Miller (1956) began to investigate the effects of cognitive variables upon learner performance. The mechanistic behaviourist model of human learning, with its view of learning as a simple, reflexive and quantifiable activity, was replaced by an active and organismic model. In this view, learners have organized knowledge bases and actively participate in the construction of their reality (Reese and Overton, 1970). By the early 1980s most instructional psychology research questions were phrased in cognitive psychology terms (Dick and Gagné, 1982). This cognitive model of learning has replaced the behaviourist model in psychology, and has begun to influence instructional technology, particularly in the instructional design processes of the field.

In a cognitive model of instructional design, the organization, processing and storage of information by the learner are all important variables in the development of instruction. Learners organize their knowledge and experience into schemas or networks (Klatzky, 1982; Anderson et al, 1978), such that the purpose of instruction is to map the structure of the new content onto the cognitive structure of the learners (Wildman, 1981; Wildman and Burton, 1981), or to support the internal processes of learning (Gagné, 1977). Analysis of a lesson or task can entail an information-processing analysis of the learner's covert thinking processes in performing a learned capability (Gagné and Briggs, 1979; Greeno, 1985). Similarly, the influence of a learner's prior knowledge upon new learning has become more widely acknowledged among instructional technologists, giving precedence to readiness-for-learning interventions such as advance organizers (Ausubel, 1960), objectives, and prequestions (Hartley and Davies, 1976).

Learning strategies have emerged as part of the cognitive science revolution in instructional tecreorganhnology. These strategies are used by the learner to control comprehension and storage of information, as opposed to a dependence on external comprehension/storage interventions contained in instruction and instructional materials. The proper learning interventions are not so much provided for the learner as generated by him, which suits the generative hypothesis of learning assumed by various cognitive psychologists (Wittrock, 1974). Learning strategies purposively provide learners with the skills to integrate new learning into their cognitive structures, and to reorganize these structures on the basis of that learning. From a cognitive view, instructional technologists should aim at activating the appropriate learning strategies in the learner during instruction, and not simply the replication of behavioural responses (Jonassen, 1985a).

Characteristics and types of learning strategies

Definition of 'learning strategy'

Learning strategies form a major subclass of a class of skills called *cognitive strategies*. Cognitive strategies are the intellectual skills that people use to control their internal cognitive processes of attending/perceiving, encoding into memory, retrieval, and problem-solving (Gagné, 1977). Learning strategies are then the information processing methods that people use to control their learning, which can involve processes of attending/perceiving, encoding, and retrieval. Simply put, learning strategies are 'the way one uses one's head' when learning.

Learning strategies vary in their quality, origin, generality, and purpose. Just as there are good learners and bad learners, so some people use effective learning strategies and others ineffective strategies or no strategies at all. Most people have acquired their learning strategies through experience and maturation, but effective learning strategies have been successfully taught to students (Derry and Murphy, 1986; Thompson, 1985). Some learning strategies are general planning skills that can be used across a variety of tasks and contents, while others are specific tactics used while performing a specific learning task (Snowman and McCown, 1984).

Most important, learning strategies can be distinguished by the way they function to control the learning process; how they affect the information processing of the learner. Some strategies act directly upon the information to be learned, reorganizing it, paraphrasing it, or imaging it. These are called *primary* strategies. Other strategies improve the general cognitive functioning of the individual by relaxation, anxiety reduction and time management. These are referred to as *support* strategies (Dansereau, 1985; Jonassen, 1985a). Both the primary and secondary classifications encompass a number and variety of learning strategies.

Primary strategies

Primary strategies can be divided into two main groups: information processing strategies and active study strategies. Active study strategies are used to improve the processing (studying) of instructional materials, while information processing strategies are used to control cognitive processes themselves.

1. INFORMATION PROCESSING STRATEGIES

There are four types of information processing strategies: recall, integration, organization, and elaboration. As indicated in Figure 2.2, recall strategies are primarily behavioural, verbal learning practices such as chunking, organization, and practice. These strategies focus on repetitive practice and organization procedures that are designed to facilitate the learning of lists of information, so the learned performance does not generally transfer to other tasks. Mnemonic strategies that create rhymes and novel images of to-be-learned information are also used as recall strategies (Paivio, 1980), and may be transferable.

Strategies that integrate and organize information are sometimes referred to as recall and transformation strategies (Dansereau, 1978; Dansereau *et al*, 1979). They are processing strategies that facilitate the transformation of information into a more memorable form. Paraphrasing and exemplifying strategies are important examples of strategies used to integrate new information into the learner's cognitive schema (Rumelhart and Ortony, 1977). In paraphrasing the learner will convert verbal information into grammar and terms of their own prior knowledge. In exemplifying the learner creates his own examples of new information, thus relating it to his prior knowledge. These strategies not only integrate new information into a learner's schema (accretion), but can also restructure or refine the schema itself (Norman and Rumelhart, 1975).

Organizational strategies are helpful in structuring or restructuring the learner's knowledge base by determining how the ideas of new information relate to one another and/or to previous knowledge. Categorization and outlining are two recognized versions of this learning strategy. In categorization, the learner may group diverse ideas into broad categories. In outlining, the learner may indicate the relationships between ideas, frequently by producing a visual or spatial map of the relationships of ideas (Jonassen, 1984; Dansereau, 1978) as well as the categories into which they can be grouped (Diekhoff, 1982).

Finally, elaboration strategies can be used to add information onto new information to make it memorable and understandable by making it more meaningful (Mayer, 1980). One recognized elaborative technique is to create sentences that incorporate separate ideas into a coherent proposition (Stein *et al*, 1982). Other techniques require the learner to generate implications or inferences about the information to be learned, to encourage deeper processing of new information.

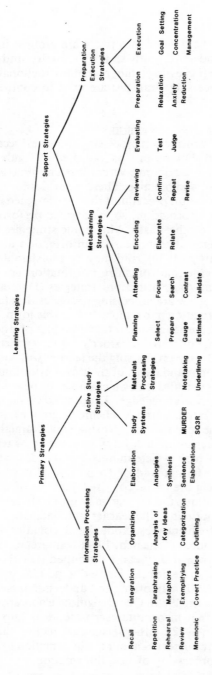

Figure 2.2 *Taxonomy of learning strategies*

2. ACTIVE STUDY STRATEGIES

While all active study strategies focus on learner processing of instructional materials, some represent an entire study system of interrelated strategies, while others are isolated study strategies that correspond to Snowman and McCown's (1984) notion of learning tactics.

Two of the most famous study systems of learning strategies are the MURDER system (Dansereau, 1978) and the SQ3R method (Robinson, 1946). Each of these systems encompasses a number of study steps the learner must follow in learning from text, different steps representing different learning strategies. For example, the steps in MURDER are: set the **M**ood to study, read for **U**nderstanding, **R**ecall information without referring to text, amplify and store to **D**igest it, **E**xpand knowledge by self-inquiry, and **R**eview mistakes (Dansereau, 1985). Each of these steps represents the use of one or more learning strategies to aid in information processing tasks of studying text.

Study tactics are specific learning activities that frequently involve overt learner activities such as writing or speaking. Underlining, notetaking and summarizing are three of the most popular study tactics used by students. While these strategies are primarily materials-based ones, they utilize primary information processing strategies of integration and organization. Underlining serves to focus the learner's attention on key ideas, while notetaking can involve both the determination of key ideas and paraphrasing of information. Summarizing requires the learner to paraphrase key ideas as well.

Support strategies

Support strategies help the learner develop and sustain a good internal state for learning (Dansereau, 1985). As a result, many support strategies are complements to primary strategies, in that support strategies can facilitate the successful application of primary strategies. There are two general classifications of support strategies: metalearning strategies and preparation/execution strategies. Metalearning strategies are strategies a learner uses to monitor his cognitive processes, while preparation/execution strategies are used to establish the proper mental/physical state for learning and to aid in the efficient application of strategies during learning.

1. METALEARNING STRATEGIES

Metalearning involves an individual's awareness, knowledge, and use of the monitoring of cognitive goals, experiences, and actions for the purpose of increasing understanding and retention of learned material (Brezin, 1980). Metalearning is based on the principles of metamemory (Flavell and Wellman, 1977) which involve the learner's self-awareness of his ability to store and retrieve information from memory. Metamemory is specific to the trait characteristics of the learner, the nature of the task, and the specific strategy that a learner uses to improve his memorization of new information. Another conception of metalearning is that it is a higher level 'executive control' mechanism that allows learners to respond to different learning tasks by selecting and implementing lower level strategies such as the 'learning tactics' just discussed in this paper. More capable and adept learners seem to be more skilled at selecting and using the monitoring activities to store and retrieve information (Flavell and Wellman, 1977; Armbruster and Brown, 1984). Thus, good learners are aware of and monitor their information processing during learning, as well as utilizing various information processing strategies.

Brezin (1980) has identified five classes of monitoring strategies (see Figure 2.2): planning, attending, encoding, reviewing, and evaluating. Planning activities include the selecting of relevant learning goals for the task at hand, preparing by activating relevant memory schemata, gauging the difficulty or depth of information processing required, and estimating the number, type, and difficulty of processing demands for the task. Attending strategies include focusing (attending) on the instructional materials, searching memory for information relevant to the new information, contrasting new information with information in memory, and validating the new information by confirming or reconciling it with information in memory.

Encoding strategies are used to clarify and elaborate new information by linking it with existing knowledge and engaging it in deeper levels of processing. These encoding strategies include many of the information processing requirements mentioned earlier in this paper. Reviewing strategies include confirming the correctness and thoroughness of new information learned, repeating learned information through recall and practice, and revising learned information as needed, based on the reviewing and repeating activities conducted. Finally, learners use evaluation strategies to judge the clarity and coherence of instructional materials, and determine the importance for learning of various pieces of information in these materials. While many of these strategies overlap with information processing strategies, their function as metalearning (monitoring) strategies is to monitor learning rather than to produce it, so that they can be used in conjunction with information processing strategies. Brezin (1980) believes that they can be embedded into instructional materials to foster monitoring processes, thereby improving memory.

2. PREPARATION EXECUTION STRATEGIES

While primary learning strategies can markedly improve student learning, their effectiveness can be diminished if the psychological state of the learner is less than optimal (Dansereau, 1985). Preparation strategies seek to establish the proper 'mood' in the learner in order to facilitate information processing. Anxiety reduction techniques (Richardson, 1978; McCombs, 1982) seek to reduce an anxious learner's debilitative tension toward learning new information. Correspondingly, relaxation techniques seek to accomplish the same end for all learners by preparing them to concentrate upon the new instruction. These preparation techniques may be incorporated into learning strategy systems such as MURDER, or used in isolation.

Execution strategies are used by the learner during the process of learning. Concentration management techniques, for example, are used to maintain deep information processing levels in students while they learn. Time management techniques enable the learner to use available learning time effectively. Similarly, goal setting and scheduling (McCombs and Dobrovny, 1982) or goal imaging (Singer, 1978) enable the learner to set up benchmarks to measure and monitor his learning performance. As with preparation strategies, execution strategies may be used as part of a more complex learning strategy system that contains a variety of primary or secondary learning strategies (Weinstein and Underwood, 1985).

Issues in learning strategy research and utilization

While the identification of learning strategies and the development of learning strategies training programmes is progressing, there are a number of practical and theoretical issues that surround this new technology. Basically, these issues deal with the questions:

1. Do learning strategies facilitate learning?
2. What learning strategies should be taught to learners?
3. How can they be taught?
4. How does this new technology interface with the 'old' technologies of instructional media and development?

Do learning strategies facilitate learning?

While it is obvious that people acquire cognitive strategies to facilitate their learning and problem-solving, it does not automatically follow that these strategies can be taught via a training or instruction programme (Gagné, 1977). While a large number of learning strategy studies have demonstrated successful use of learning strategies in experimental conditions, the question is whether induced strategies will be used outside the experimental situation. More specifically, the question is whether learning strategy instruction or training can give the learners strategies that they will both retain and transfer. These are related but separate issues, since a student can retain a skill or strategy, but fail to apply it to eligible situations (Roger, 1979).

As several researchers have indicated, two key measures of effective strategy training are the maintenance and generalization of the strategy over time (Brown, 1978; Peterson and Swing, 1983), where maintenance refers to the retention of the strategy in memory. While people's *acquired* learning strategies are part of their long-term memory if not their very persona, *induced* strategies may fail to be retained after instruction. To date, there is a paucity of experimental evidence about the long-term retention of learning strategies, since many strategy experiments fail to do any long-term follow-up to see if the strategy is retained over time (Dansereau, 1985). While long-term retention remains an open question in learning strategies research, several experimenters have found strategy retention in their studies. Ringel and Springer (1980) found maintenance of recall tactic in elementary school children who were informed of the utility of the tactic learned. Barclay (1979) found maintenance of a rehearsal tactic in tenth and twelfth grade students trained to use it. Kestner and Borkowski (1979) judged that first grade children were able to retain and use an interrogative elaboration strategy four days after instruction.

While students may retain a given learning strategy over time, they may fail to apply that strategy to new tasks (Snowman and McCown, 1984), indicating a lack of strategy transfer. The failure to generalize newly-learned skills and strategies is a persistent issue in human learning (Clark and Vogel, 1986; Sternberg, 1983). Even when new tasks seem formally identical to the training tasks, students may fail to transfer strategies in which they have been trained (Hayes, 1985).

While transfer of strategy training is problematic, there have been a number of strategy training efforts where students have successfully transferred strategies to new tasks (White and Snowman, 1985; Mayer, 1980; Peterson and Swing, 1983). However, the success of strategy transfer seems to depend in part upon the generality or specificity of the learning strategy selected for training, and the time available for strategy training. General, content-independent strategies appear to be harder to train for transfer, while content-specific strategies that relate only to a special class of tasks may be more trainable (Dansereau, 1985), although less transferable. Part of this transfer difficulty can be attributed to the time requirements necessary to learn general strategies.

Perhaps the most successful results in strategy retention and transfer have been in strategy training programmes, where a strategy or set of strategies is taught in an organized and specific manner. Programmes such as the Chicago Mastery Learning Reading Programme (Thompson, 1985), Dansereau's MURDER programme, and the Cognitive Strategies Learning Project (Weinstein and Underwood, 1985) have all demonstrated success in retention and transfer of their learning strategy goals. Programmes such as these devote a considerable amount of training time and instructional materials to the acquisition of a set of mutually supportive learning strategies (a combination of primary and support strategies) for use across a range of instructional tasks.

What learning strategies should be taught?

By now it should be obvious that there are a large number of learning strategies that can be learned, which vary in their function (primary vs support), level of generality (content-specific vs content-independent), and applicability to different learner populations (adult vs children, low ability vs high ability). As Hayes (1985) indicates, there may be several hundred plausible thinking/learning strategies for instruction.

Unfortunately, there is no acknowledged set of rules or heuristics for selecting appropriate learning strategies, other than some general criteria to use for consideration. Among these criteria are learning needs of the student, potency of the learning strategy (generalizability), available training time, characteristics and ability levels of the learners, amount of mental effort required to learn the strategy, and prior knowledge and learning strategies already possessed by the learner population. In considering these factors, the instructor may decide upon a set or entire programme of learning strategies, as opposed to any specific strategy.

Perhaps the greatest aid to learning strategy selection can be provided by the creation of a comprehensive taxonomy of learning strategies, organized according to their function and level of generality. Instructional technologists have already established categorical organizations of general learning strategies (Jonassen, 1985a; Rigney, 1978), but as yet no exhaustive compendium exists of strategies and their relationships. Once the function and generality of individual strategies are determined, technologists can more easily design strategy training programmes composed of related and complementary strategies. With a hierarchical taxonomy, technologists can also find it easier to design programmes that utilize a top-down strategy training plan recommended by theorists such as Dansereau (1985), in which students are taught a range of general strategies first, followed by more specific strategy training.

How should learning strategies be taught?

Like the selection of learning strategies, the instruction of learning strategies is still very much an open issue, owing in part to the novelty of this as an instructional technology and the number of learning strategies recently identified. In the quest to design an instructional technology for learning strategies, concerns have come up about: instructional methods for different abilities of learners, methods for different ages of learners and general instructional prescriptions that suit almost all learning strategy instruction.

1. LEARNING STRATEGY INSTRUCTION FOR VARYING ABILITIES

In this area, the main concern has been with strategy instruction for low ability learners, since this population is usually more deficient in learning strategies than middle or high ability learners. Several studies have indicated that low ability students tend to profit more from learning strategies instruction (Mayer, 1980; Andre and Anderson, 1979), and that high ability learners may in fact have their strategies impaired by such instruction (Holley et al, 1979; Jonassen, 1987).

Stein et al (1982) found that students with low language and reading test scores could be trained to acquire elaborative learning strategies, but required prompting in order to utilize them. Following this line of thought, Rigney (1978) suggests that students who lack strategy development may require *embedded* learning strategies where cues or prompts for a student to use a learning strategy are actually built into the instructional materials. To this end, Jonassen (1985b) has incorporated learning strategies into computer courseware, to aid student information processing.

2. STRATEGY INSTRUCTION FOR VARIOUS AGE LEVELS

Prior knowledge and previous possession of learning strategies are two factors which vary with the age of the learner. Both factors can affect strategy acquisition and instruction. Adults tend to have large stores of prior knowledge about a variety of subjects (Jonassen, 1987), so that learning strategies used to access prior knowledge can have more success with this age group. On the other hand, older students tend to have a repertoire of learning strategies as part of their cognitive makeup (Peterson and Swing, 1983), which can interfere with the acquisition of new learning strategies.

3.GENERAL INSTRUCTIONAL PRESCRIPTIONS FOR STRATEGY
  INSTRUCTION

While no definitive list of instructional methods has been outlined, instructional designers have concurred that several methods seem useful for most types of learning strategy instruction:

a. Students need to have the value and utility of the strategy explained to them in order to aid learning (Brown, Campione, and Day, 1981).

b. Extended and extensive practice needs to be provided in strategy use (Weinstein and Underwood, 1985; Jonassen, 1987).

c. To maximize strategy transfer, students must apply the strategy to a wide variety of applicable contexts over an extended period of time (Hayes, 1985; Sternberg, 1983).

d. Through practice or instructions, students need to access prior knowledge that is relevant to the acquisition of the targeted learning strategies (Baker and Brown, 1982; Schonfeld, 1979).

e. Embedded instructional strategies that prompt strategy usage can be used to train low ability students in strategy usage (Rigney, 1978).

Other instructional interventions will also be used during instruction, depending upon the type of learning strategies selected for instruction.

How does the new instructional technology of learning strategies relate to the old instructional technologies?

As indicated at the outset of this paper, learning strategies are a new type of process instructional technology. However, the onset of learning strategies into instructional technology will affect both the product and process aspects of this field.

In the process aspect of instructional technology, learning strategy instruction is gradually replacing some of the behavioural science aspects of instruction that focus solely on the control of external events in instruction (Jonassen, 1985a). In the design and planning of instruction and instructional materials, the learners' covert processes will deserve as much consideration as their overt behaviour. In fact, the instructional technology process of instructional design will focus more on the instructional design of learning strategies themselves, just as there are now instructional design processes for concept learning and problem-solving. This learning strategy would include the needs assessment, selection, production, and evaluation of learning strategies for students, as well as the selection of instructional activities to facilitate strategy acquisition. In this way, the new process instructional technology of learning strategies becomes a new focus for the 'old' process instructional technology of instructional design and development.

In the product aspect of instructional technology, the selection of embedded (versus detached) learning strategies for learning strategy instruction necessitates a number of media design and production considerations. Since embedded learning strategies are embedded in instructional materials, questions arise about how this embedding can take place for different strategies in different types of media. For instance, how does one properly embed information processing strategies in instructional television, or audio tape? To date, the focus on embedding learning strategies is on the media formats of CAI (Jonassen, 1985b), live instruction (Swing and Peterson, 1983), and text (Bernard, 1985; Brown, Campione and Day, 1981). These and other media formats represent important design considerations as to how product instructional technology can properly embed the process technology of learning strategies.

Future issues in the research and utilization of learning strategies

Each of the issues described in the preceding section is an important research agenda item for instructional technology. Thus, more research is needed on how students can acquire learning strategies through classroom instruction, and how strategy instruction programmes can be implemented into a schoolwide curriculum. In particular, several learning strategy issues are particularly relevant to instructional technology: 1. the role of learning strategies in instructional design and development, 2. the impact of psychotechnologies upon learning strategies and instructional technology research.

The role of learning strategies in instructional design and development

With the increasing recognition that learning strategies are an effective instructional intervention, learning strategies selection may become an important part of the instructional design process. Just as instructional events and activities are selected during the design planning process (Gagné and Briggs, 1979), learning strategies selection may become an important part of this process. Learning strategies selection may become an independent step in the overall design process, or may be a part of the overall plan for selecting instructional events and activities. The selection of learning strategies will then affect other stages of the instructional design process such as task analysis, since certain types of task analysis (such as information processing analysis) must be conducted prior to learning strategy selection.

As learning strategy selection becomes a more recognized part of the instructional design process, learning strategy implementation becomes a larger issue of the same process. An instructional activity such as 'provide feedback to the learner' takes different forms in CAI, television, and text. Similarly, the use of embedded learning strategies that are contained in the instructional materials themselves necessitates decisions about how the strategies can be embedded in different instructional materials. To implement an information processing learning strategy into media such as CAI, television or text, the designer/technologist will have to consider the media attributes of the medium (Salomon, 1979). Thus, the implementation of learning strategies becomes a technological consideration for instructional designers and media production specialists alike.

Psychotechnologies and learning strategies

David Guellette (1987) has described the potential emergence of a new type of instructional technology called 'psychotechnology'. Like learning strategies, psychotechnology focuses on the management and control of the psychological processes of the learner, and can include support learning strategies such as relaxation training, anxiety reduction and imaging. However, psychotechnology also includes biofeedback, meditation, music, and body disciplines such as yoga; techniques that at present have received little consideration as learning technologies.

As instructional technologists expand their investigation into the use of learning strategies, some of these psychotechnologies may receive greater consideration as valid instructional interventions. These 'strategies' may utilize both the intuitive and analytic capabilities of learners during learning (Guellette, 1987) to improve their information processing capabilities. While the effectiveness of these strategies is still an open issue, the increasing emphasis on the processes of educational technology for instruction (Heinich *et al*, 1986) makes psychotechnologies for learning an increasingly pertinent issue.

Conclusion

Learning strategies is an emerging aspect of the processes of instructional technology, an outgrowth of a cognitivist focus upon the internal information processing activities of the learner during learning. As an instructional intervention to improve student learning, learning strategies represent the student's control of his internal thought processes to improve learning from instruction, as opposed to the use of externally imposed instructor activities or features to accomplish the same end. While research has to some degree demonstrated that these strategies can be effectively learned and utilized, further research is needed to determine what strategies exist, which should be learned by a given learner population, and how they can be taught. As a new instructional technology, learning strategies will become a larger part of instructional design and development.

References

Anderson, R, Spiro, R and Anderson, M (1978) Schemata as scaffolding for the representation of information in connected discourse *American Educational Research Journal* **15**, 433–450

Andre, M and Anderson, T (1979) The development and evaluation of a self-questioning study technique *Reading Research Quarterly* **14**, 605–623

Armbruster, B and Brown, A (1984) Learning from reading: the role of metacognition in Anderson, Osborn and Tierney (eds) *Learning to Read in American Schools* Erlbaum: Hillsdale, New Jersey, USA

Association for Educational Communications Technology (1977) *Educational Technology: Definition and Glossary of Terms* AECT: Washington, D C

Ausubel, D (1960) The use of advance organizers in the learning and retention of meaningful verbal material *Journal of Educational Psychology* **51**, 267–272

Baker, L and Brown, A (1982) Metacognitive skills in reading in D P Pearson (ed) *Handbook of Reading Research* Longman: New York, USA

Barclay, C (1979) The executive control of mnemonic ability *Journal of Experimental Child Psychology* **27**, 262–276

Bernard, R (1985) Strategy cueing for activating students' use of illustrations in text: a report of two studies in Alloway and Mills (eds) *Aspects of Educational Technology XVIII* Kogan Page: London

Brezin, M J (1980) Cognitive monitoring: from learning theory to instructional applications *Educational Communications Technology Journal* **28**, 227–242

Brown, A (1978) Knowing when, where, and how to remember: a problem of metacognition in R Glaser (ed) *Advances in Instructional Psychology* (Vol 1) Erlbaum: Hillsdale, New Jersey, USA

Brown, A, Campione, J and Day, J (1981) Learning to learn: on training students to learn from text *Educational Researcher* **10**, 2, 14–21

Clark, R and Vogel, A (1986) Transfer of training principles for instructional design *Education Communications and Technology Journal* **33**, 2, 113–123

Dansereau, D (1978) The development of a learning strategies curriculum in O'Neil, H F (ed) *Learning Strategies* Academic Press: New York, USA

Dansereau, D (1985) Learning strategy research in Segal, Chipman, and Glaser (eds) *Thinking and Learning Skills* (Vol 1) Erlbaum: Hillsdale, New Jersey, USA

Dansereau, D, Collins, K, McDonald, B, Holley, C, Garland, J, Diekhoff, G and Evans, S (1979) Development and evaluation of a learning strategy training program *Journal of Educational Psychology* **71**, 64–73

Derry, S and Murphy, D (1986) Systems that train learning ability *Review of Educational Research* **56**, 1, 1–40

Dick, W and Gagné, R (1982) *Instructional Psychology, 1976–81* (contract no. N66001-81C-0456) US Navy Personnel Research and Development Center: San Diego, USA

Diekhoff, G (1982) Cognitive maps as a way of presenting the dimensions of comparison within the history of psychology *Teaching of Psychology* **9**, 2, 115-116

Flavell, J and Wellman, H (1977) Metamemory in Kail and Hagen (eds) *Perspectives on the Development of Memory and Cognition* Erlbaum: Hillsdale, New Jersey, USA

Gagné, R (1977) *The Conditions of Learning* (3rd edn) Holt, Rinehart and Winston: New York, USA

Gagné, R and Briggs, L (1979) *Principles of Instructional Design* (2nd edn) Holt, Rinehart and Winston: New York, USA

Glaser, R and Cooley, W (1973) Instrumentation for teaching and instructional management in Travers, R (ed) *Second Handbook of Research on Teaching* Rand McNally: Chicago, USA

Greeno, J (1985) Some examples of cognitive task analysis with instructional implications in Segal, Chipman, and Glaser (eds) *Thinking and Learning Skills (Vol 1) Research and Open Questions* Erlbaum: Hillsdale, New Jersey, USA

Guellette, D (1987) Psychotechnology as instructional technology: systems for a deliberate change in consciousness Paper presented at the annual meeting of the Association for Education Communications Technology: Atlanta, Georgia, USA

Hartley, J and Davies, I (1976) Preinstructional strategies: the role of pretests, behavioral objectives, overviews, and advance organizers *Review of Educational Research* **46**, 2, 239-265

Hayes, J (1985) Three problems in teaching general skills in Segal, Chipman, and Glaser (eds) *Thinking and Learning Skills (Vol 1) Relating Instruction to Research* Erlbaum: Hillsdale, New Jersey, USA

Heinich, R, Molenda, M and Russell, J (1986) *Instructional Media and the New Technologies of Instruction* (2nd edn) John Wiley and Sons: New York, USA

Holley, C, Dansereau, P, McDonald, B, Garland, J and Collings, K (1979) Evaluation of a hierarchical mapping technique as an aid to improve processing *Contemporary Educational Psychology* **4**, 227-237

Jonassen, D (1984) Developing a learning strategy using pattern notes: a new technology *Programmed Learning and Educational Technology* **21**, 3, 163-175

Jonassen, D (1985a) Learning strategies: a new educational technology *Programmed Learning and Educational Technology* **22**, 1, 26-34

Jonassen, D (1985b) The electronic notebook: integrating learning strategies in courseware to raise the level of processing in Alloway and Mills (eds) *Aspects of Educational Technology XVIII* Kogan Page: London

Jonassen, D (1987) Integrating learning strategies into courseware to facilitate deeper processing in Jonassen, D (ed) *Instructional Design for Microcomputer Software* Erlbaum: Hillsdale, New Jersey, USA

Kestner, J and Borkowski, J (1979) Children's maintenance and generalization of an interrogative learning strategy *Child Development* **50**, 485-494

Klatzky, R (1982) *Human Memory* (2nd edn) W.H. Freeman and Co: San Francisco, USA

Kuhn, T S (1962) *The Structure of Scientific Revolutions* (2nd edn) University of Chicago Press: Chicago, USA

Mayer, R (1980) Elaboration techniques that increase the meaningfulness of technical text: an experimental test of the learning strategy hypothesis *Journal of Educational Psychology* **72**, 6, 770-784

McCombs, B (1982) Enhancing student motivation through positive self-control strategies Paper presented at the annual meeting of the American Psychology Association: Washington, D C, USA

McCombs, B and Dobrovny, J (1982) Student motivational skill training package: evaluation for Air Force technical training (AFHRL-TP-82-31) Logistics and Training Division, Lowry Air Force Base: Colorado, USA

Miller, C A (1956) The magical number seven, plus or minus two: some limits on our capacity to process information *Psychological Review* **63**, 81-97

Norman, D and Rumelhart, D (1975) Memory and knowledge in Norman, Rumelhart and the LNR Research Group (eds) *Explorations in Cognition* W.H. Freeman: San Francisco, USA

Paivio, A (1980) Imagery as a private audio-visual aid *Instructional Science* **9**, 295-309

Peterson, P and Swing, S (1983) Problems in classroom implementation of cognitive strategy instruction in Pressley and Levin (eds) *Cognitive Strategy Research: Educational Applications* Springer- Verlag: New York, USA

Reese, H and Overton, W (1970) Models of development and theories of development in Goulet, L R and Bates, P B (eds) *Life-Span Developmental Psychology: Theories and Research* Academic Press: New York, USA

Richardson, F (1978) Behavior modifications and learning strategies in O'Neil, H F (ed) *Learning Strategies* Academic Press: New York, USA

Rigney, J (1978) Learning strategies: a theoretical perspective. In O' Neil, H F (ed) *Learning Strategies* Academic Press: New York

Ringel, B and Springer, C (1980) On knowing how well one is remembering: the persistence of strategy use during transfer *Journal of Experimental Child Psychology* **29**, 2, 322-333

Robinson, F P (1946) *Effective Study* Harper & Row: New York, USA

Roger, J (1979) Theories of the transfer of learning *Educational Psychologist* **14**, 53, 53-69

Rumelhart, D E and Ortony, A (1977) The representation of knowledge in memory in Anderson, Spiro, and Montague (eds) *Schooling and the Acquisition of Knowledge* Erlbaum: Hillsdale, New Jersey, USA

Saettler, P (1968) *A History of Instructional Technology* McGraw-Hill, Inc: New York, USA

Salomon, G (1979) *Interaction of Media, Cognition, and Learning* Josey Bass: San Francisco, USA

Schonfeld, A (1979) Can heuristics be taught? in Lockhead, J and Clements, J (eds) *Cognitive Process Instruction: Research on Teaching Thinking Skills* Franklin Institute Press: Philadelphia, USA

Segal, Chipman, and Glaser (eds) *Thinking and Learning Skills* (Vol 1) *Research and Open Questions* Erlbaum: Hillsdale, New Jersey, USA

Singer, R (1978) Motor skills and learning strategies in O'Neil, H F (ed) *Learning Strategies* Academic Press: New York, USA

Snowman, J and McCown (1984) Cognitive processes in learning: a model for investigating strategies and tactics Paper presented at the annual meeting of the American Educational Research Association: New Orleans, USA

Stein, B, Bransford, J, Franks, J, Owings, R, Vye, N, and McGraw, W (1982) Differences in the precision of self-generated elaborations *Journal of Experimental Psychology (General)* **111**, 4, 399-405

Sternberg, R (1983) Criteria for intellectual skills training *Educational Researcher* **12**, 2, 6-12

Thompson, W (1985) A practitioner's perspective on the Chicago Mastery Learning Reading Program with Learning Strategies in Segal, Chipman and Glaser (eds) *Thinking and Learning Skills* (Vol 2), Erlbaum: Hillsdale, New Jersey, USA

Weinstein, C and Underwood, V (1985) Learning strategies: the how of learning in Segal, Chipman and Glaser (eds) *Thinking and Learning Skills* (Vol 1) *Relating Instruction to Research* Erlbaum: Hillsdale, New Jersey, USA

White, M and Snowman, J (1985) Learning to remember: a memory-directed strategy that transfers. Paper presented at the annual meeting of the American Educational Research Association: Chicago, USA

Wildman, T M (1981) Cognitive theory and the design of instruction *Educational Technology* **21**, 7, 14-20

Wildman, T M and Burton, J K (1981) Integrating learning theory with instructional design *Journal of Instructional Development* **4**, 3, 5-14

Wittrock, M C (1974) Learning as a generative activity. *Educational Psychologist* **11**, 87-95

3. Developing a rationale for the new technologies in education

Jonathan Anderson

Summary: Of the many complex issues that the use of new technologies in education gives rise to, why and how the new technologies are to be deployed are the two most important, in that these constitute first-order questions. It is with these fundamental questions that this chapter is primarily concerned. How do the new technologies contribute to the education process? How does information technology relate to the rest of the curriculum? In other words, what is the rationale for using computer-based technologies in education? Particular reference is made to computers, at all main levels of education, in meeting the needs of individuals and of society.

Discussed first is the need for a rationale and the consequences for society at large if there are no clearly enunciated reasons for using computers in schools. In trying to develop a rationale, three key questions are then addressed: Who are the learners? What are they to learn? And why should they learn? From a consideration of these questions some of the major reasons advocated for using computers in education emerge. Thus a justification in the short term is arrived at, but it is also important to look ahead, and the chapter closes with a long-range view of possible computing developments in the remaining years of this century and the resulting implications for educational institutions.

Although computers receive major attention in this chapter, it is more accurate to refer to new technologies or computer-based technologies, since the discussion also centres on computer storage media, word processors, electronic message systems, videotex, communication satellites, and telecommunications generally. In what follows, the terms 'computers', 'computer-based technologies', 'information technology', and the new technologies', are used more or less interchangeably to refer to microelectronics-based technologies where computing and communications come together.

Introduction

Computers, almost universally, generate excitement and enthusiasm. These machines have been described as 'the most pervasive technology of our time'; '...nothing will be viewed by history as more significant'; '...the outcome of one of the most remarkable intellectual ferments to take place in human history'; '...historians of the future are likely to look back on the present as a turning point in the evolution of human society'. In most countries of the world, the same enthusiasm has extended to the educational use of computers: conferences of professional associations often feature computer education as a central theme;

many journals include columns on the uses of computers in education; parent bodies and school councils are enthusiastically raising funds for the purchase of computer equipment; different education systems are beginning to release policy statements on computing in schools; and some countries have established or are considering the establishment of national computer education programmes.

The need for a rationale

Such has been the unbridled enthusiasm for computers by many school communities that one government minister commented that many schools are becoming 'mesmerized by hardware'. The minister continued:

> They feel that if only they acquire a lot of new hardware...new computers and so on, suddenly all the mysteries of life will be revealed and all problems will be solved (Jones, 1984).

As is generally now recognised, computer hardware by itself will not solve any problems, educational or otherwise. What is done with computers, the quality of the software, and the preparedness of teachers to use the new technologies, are all important. If schools have unrealistic expectations of computers, disappointment and disillusionment with the technology must ensue.

A properly considered rationale for computers will help determine the role of computers in education: where, for instance, computers are deployed in schools, how they are deployed, priorities for use, what kinds of hardware to purchase, what kinds of software are needed, whether machines should be linked in networks or whether stand-alone systems are the preferred option. On the other hand, lack of any rationale leads, at best, to a waste of resources and, at worst, to an unfulfilled potential.

If teacher education programmes are to meet the needs of schools, then teachers must clearly be familiar with the new technologies and, according to how the technology is to be used in schools, be properly prepared to teach about it or with it. A rationale for the use of computer technology in schools, then, has important consequences for tertiary institutions.

Not all schools have been equally enthusiastic about the new technology, whether for economic reasons or because of reluctance to innovate. What seems fairly certain, however, is that whatever educational institutions do about computers, these machines are here to stay in the rest of society and will continue to affect profoundly the way people live and interact: another quite potent argument for carefully considering reasons for using computers in education.

Yet another reason for the need for a rationale is the presence of microcomputers in many homes. One Australian report noted that already there are more computers in students' homes than there are in the schools where these students attend (A'Herran, 1986). The home provides a larger commercial market for both hardware and software and there is a danger that the needs of the home, as perceived by computer vendors, will overshadow those of schools. If computers are powerful tools for learning, as is argued, then schools should be at the forefront in the use of the new technology and in providing directions for parents about, for instance, appropriate educational software.

Consequences of a lack of rationale

Some of the obvious consequences of not having a rationale for the educational use of computers are the reverse of those detailed above. There are a further three important, potential consequences, highlighted by Cerych (1982) in an analysis of national policy issues. These consequences apply with equal force to the present discussion.

First, there is the equity argument. In the absence of a considered rationale, and if much learning about computers takes place at home outside of school, then those students from homes which can afford computers will be advantaged while other students will be disadvantaged. Second, there are the needs of society. 'It is far from certain,' notes Cerych (1982), 'that the knowledge about computers acquired outside the formal education system will be of the kind required by the economy and society.' And, third, there is the arguable loss of potential for learning if the new technologies are not fully utilized.

Developing a rationale

To return to the questions with which this chapter started, why are we introducing computer technology in schools and across the curriculum? What are computers to be used for, and how are they to be used? In attempting to answer these questions in order to arrive at some rationale for computers in education, discussion focuses on three prior, more basic, questions.

1 Who are the learners?

This question may be answered in varying degress of specificity. One suggestion is that four groups of learners, for whom knowledge about computers and their use is necessary, may be identified:

a. all students, at all levels from kindergarten to university;
b. some students with a special interest in computers who do not wish to major in computer studies;
c. some students with an interest in the technical aspects of computers; and
d. those students who may wish to become computer specialists and engineers.

A second, broader group of categories, not directly at variance with the above, but oriented more towards adult working life after schooling, is the following:

a. the general public;
b. computer users; and
c. computer specialists.

In terms of the educational continuum, the general public might be thought of as *all* students, computer users as *some* students, and computer specialists as a *few* students. The terms *all, some* and *few* are used purely as descriptors. They may convey some indication of the numbers involved, though the actual numbers in each category will depend on a state's or nation's needs. Obviously, however, the second group (*some*) and the third group (*few*) are subsets of the first group (*all*).

Continuing with these three broad categories, we may attempt to define each group a little more precisely in terms of the needs of society and the resulting implications for schools.

A. ALL STUDENTS
Microelectronics is transforming the work and life styles of *all* people. The education that we impart today should equip *all* students for the telecommunications revolution which is changing the environment of everyone.

B. SOME STUDENTS
Some people will work closely with computers, either using them as tools or working in an environment where they interact and communicate with other skilled computer users. Schools need to provide opportunities for *some* students to develop interests and skills in information processing and computer applications.

C. A FEW STUDENTS
There is a need for a *few* people to be highly trained in the various specialisms of the microelectronics industry. The education system needs to prepare to fill these roles.

2. What are they to learn?

In considering this second question, we will continue with the three groups identified above (all, some and few) and comment briefly for each in turn.

A. ALL STUDENTS
Computer awareness/literacy/appreciation includes being familiar generally with telecommunications, of which computers are a part, and having a broad understanding of computers and their use. These are goals for *all* students.

B. SOME STUDENTS

Computer fluency implies some degree of competency in interacting with computers, not necessarily developing programming skills, but rather developing programming-like abilities. The use of applications software requires a clear understanding of computer input, data processing, and output. For *some* students this kind of knowledge of the capabilities of computers is required.

C. A FEW STUDENTS

For a *few* students there is a need to be familiar with specialist applications of computers, to be able to design new applications and better means of communicating with computers.

3. Why should they learn?

Again, an answer to this third question is sketched briefly for the three groups identified.

A. ALL STUDENTS

It is important that *all* students should be comfortable about using computers; be aware of their potential and their limitations; be familiar with the range of computer applications in society; know the implications of such applications; recognize the computer's capabilities for storing and accessing information; and be able to cope with the explosion in the amount of information available.

Implicit in these objectives is the real reason all students should be familiar with the new technologies. Computers provide new and powerful tools for storing and accessing information. Increasingly, as the world storehouse of information is held in the memory banks of computers, it is imperative that all students know how to access this storehouse.

B. SOME STUDENTS

The number of computer users will grow with advances in technological development. It is important that those who work in computer environments can communicate effectively with technologists, with programmers and systems analysts. For some people, a fuller appreciation of the capabilities of computers is thus necessary in order to distinguish between what are reasonable expectations of whatever may be the current state of technology and what is unreasonable.

C. A FEW STUDENTS

There is a need to produce a better interface between people and computers. This requires software that is designed for the general public and is easier to use. To design and produce such software requires special skills on the part of a few people.

Justification in the short term

In trying to arrive at some answer to the question 'Why use computers in education?', three first-order questions have been posed, namely:

Who are the learners?
What are they to learn?
Why should they learn?

Discussion of these questions does not, of itself, provide a rationale for computer education, although it may provide certain pointers.

To appreciate what the justification is for computers in education — a truly vital question — involves consideration of the respective roles of school and society; consideration also of the role of teachers, especially those whose primary concern is with literacy, and the development of language and conceptual development; an understanding, too, of the distinction between teaching and learning; as well as an examination of the nature of curriculum.

What follows does not pretend to cover all these aspects of the educational process. Rather, a series of points is presented, out of which emerges what are seen to be the key reasons for advocating the use of computers in education.

Equity

As a result of the explosion of information in today's world, there is the very real danger of what is referred to as the 'Matthew effect'. If general accessibility to electronic information via computers, and new information services like Prestel, Viatel, Teledon, and many others, is not to widen the gap between the haves and have-nots in our society, nor to create groups of information elite and information impoverished, then schools, as society's specific agencies for providing equality of access, have an important responsibility. To be denied the information now available from today's electronic sources is to leave people vulnerable and powerless.

There are many aspects of the equity issue which could be discussed — for example, access to computers by girls, the greater opportunities to use computers in certain subject areas, the affluence of school communities in acquiring computers, equality of access in remote areas, and so on. A fuller discussion may be found elsewhere (Anderson, 1985).

The equity issue has complex ramifications extending even to the way microcomputers are used in schools. There is some evidence to suggest, for example, that schools in higher socioeconomic areas use computers to develop problem-solving skills (ie students programming computers) whereas schools in lower socioeconomic areas primarily use computers for drill and practice (ie computers programming students).

The special needs of students with communication difficulties, the physically disabled and the intellectually impaired, have been shown to be alleviated by adaptations to microcomputer systems. In so far as microelectronic-based technologies allow communication barriers to be broken down and enable students to lead richer and more rewarding lives, here is an important justification for computers in education.

Computer literacy

Literacy is the concern of all teachers, but especially of reading and language teachers. As changing methods of storing information have progressively led us away from a heavy reliance on memory to writing so decried by Socrates, then from writing on papyrus and hides to the mass printing presses, and now from paper to the new medium of computers, computer literacy becomes a fundamental aspect of literacy.

By computer literacy is understood, first, being familiar and at ease with computers generally in the same way that literacy implies being familiar with books. The period that we are moving into is not dissimilar to the time immediately following Gutenberg. The quantity of information becoming available on the new medium requires an educated community. Schools clearly have a crucial role to play; more than ever, there is an urgent need for technologically literate teachers.

But computer literacy implies even more if predictions for the decades immediately ahead have any credence. According to one such prediction, we can expect:

(1) a diminution of the importance of the printed word in favour of electronically distributed magnetic recordings; (2) a lessening of human effort in deciding what information to record and how; (3) a smaller number of information depositories and a larger number of service institutions; (4) the disappearance of the scholarly journal as a bound, tangible entity, in favour of the 'journal' as a collection of independently published articles, individually distributed to consumers on demand (Meadow, 1979).

Less a prediction than a factual statement is the comment from the managing director of Australian Telecom (whose business it is to anticipate the information needs of the public) which says plainly:

The world has entered the information era in which ultimately all information will be stored, processed, packaged, presented, accessed, transmitted, exchanged, through the medium of computers, computer memories and electronic/electromagnetic communications (Pollock, 1983).

If we are about to enter a wholly recorded world, computer literacy becomes a vital aspect of literacy, and this leads to a consideration of how students access the new storehouses of information.

Accessing information

According to certain appraisals of the impact of communications technologies, it is predicted that not only businesses, but householders too, will be directly affected by the vastly increased amounts of information becoming available.

> We are entering a new era in communications. Before the end of the 80s it is likely that many businesses and some homes will be linked directly with computers giving access to enormous libraries of information (South Australian Council on Technological Change, 1982).

It follows that among the most pressing tasks of education will be to teach *all* students how to access the new storehouses of information, just as it has always been the task of education to make the accumulated knowledge of mankind in libraries accessible to all. In broad terms, this means that students need to know how data are organized in databases, how to interrogate these databases, and how to utilize the information once retrieved. These are not completely new skills: rather they are an extension of literacy.

It has been suggested that students who are familiar with resources such as Roget's *Thesaurus* are on their way to understanding the basic concepts of a database (Adams and Jones, 1983). In the first edition of the *Thesaurus*, which appeared in 1852, Roget explained the fundamental difference between this new work and a dictionary.

> The purpose of an ordinary dictionary is simply to explain the meaning of the words; and the problem of which it professes to find the solution may be stated thus: The word being given, to find its signification, or the idea it is intended to convey. The object aimed at in the present undertaking is exactly the converse of this: namely, the idea being given, to find the word, or words, by which that idea may be most fitly and aptly expressed. For this purpose, the words and phrases of the language are here classed, not according to their sound or their orthography, but strictly according to their *signification* (Preface to Roget's *Thesaurus*, 1852).

The principle behind the *Thesaurus*, of working from the general to the particular, is rather similar to the tree-like structure of many databases. A primary task of the new literacy might be identified then as teaching students the kind of insight that Roget so ably expounded in 1852.

Once students have some conceptual understanding of databases, a second task is to teach students how to ask questions of the data. Again, as in using a thesaurus, accessing databases requires a rather clear idea of what information is being sought. This is a vital study skill. As Adams and Jones (1983) note, 'What the computer can do is to facilitate this teaching of information skills ... Use of a computer data-bank compels the use of an effective questioning technique'. In today's world, it is less important to know the right answer: it is much more important to know the right question.

A third task of education is to show students how to utilize effectively the information retrieved as a result of the questions asked. Just as calculators freed students from intricate calculations to engage in more rewarding problem-solving, so do computerized database searches free students from the often time-consuming task of looking for information. They are freed to reflect upon the information gleaned — what has been referred to as the emancipation learning paradigm — to assess the information critically, to correlate it with other information, and to use the information thus obtained as a springboard for further explorations. This is more likely to be the basis for real learning, rather than the 'busy work' so often encountered in schools where students copy out large amounts of text with little understanding.

There are many excellent database packages now available for student use. All come with a simple query language allowing students to interrogate the stored data and to retrieve information. Not only do students thus gain familiarity with the ways that government, business, industry, science and academia store and access information, but they themselves become historians, scientists, economists or geographers, making hypotheses, confirming or rejecting these in the light of data obtained, and so increasing the total store of knowledge. The use of these databases is thus a microcosm of education's dual role to transmit knowledge and to develop skills in order to acquire further knowledge; they are also a splendid means for promoting computer literacy.

General-purpose tool

The computer is the most general-purpose tool yet invented. In emphasizing computer literacy and accessing of information, the justification for using computers in schools has been as a communication tool. The computer is also widely used as an all-purpose tool in the world of work — in business and commerce, government, transport, industry, medicine, and the arts; and students will require some general understanding of what these all-purpose tools do in these different fields, what they cannot do, and what they should not do.

Many boring, repetitious and dangerous tasks, formerly performed manually on production lines, are now being done by computer-controlled machines or robots; in banks routine money transactions are capably handled by computerized tellers; elsewhere, as in the world of newspapers, computers have eliminated completely the need for such tradesmen as metal typesetters. The computer is alternatively seen as 'a boon tool' or 'a tool of doom' in the way it is refashioning the workplace. At the very least, students should have some understanding of how computers are transforming the world of work.

Computers have also given rise to a range of new crimes. Reports of unauthorized entry into the computer databanks of financial institutions and of the military, as well as the misuse of personal and confidential information held on computer, are becoming quite commonplace. Software piracy and questions of copyright have emerged as complex legal issues. This impact of computers on society is yet another area which students should meet in schools.

Because of its impact on every facet of human life, the computer is part of the world to be explored by young learners. To learn about the limitations of this general-purpose tool, the computer, and how to direct and control it in our future daily lives, is another justification for computer education. In other words, the computer is worthy of study in its own right. But students need not only to learn about computers, they need also to learn with or from computers.

Tool to aid learning

There is some evidence that computers enhance and aid learning, providing a more interactive learning environment. Characteristic of much computer-assisted instruction (CAI) software, for instance, is that students are provided with immediate feedback; they know immediately whether their responses are right or wrong; they can progress at their own pace; the computer is endlessly patient; and the task of record keeping for teachers is greatly eased, freeing teachers for individual consultation.

While the advantages of this mode of computer use are real, the negative features of this kind of learning need also to be recognized. Much CAI material fails to utilize the full potential of the computer; it often adds little to learning that cannot be provided by more traditional, less expensive means; the learning materials, while initially motivating, frequently fail to retain the interest of students; and much computer-based learning material runs counter to the educational philosophies espoused by many teachers.

Computer-assisted instruction can take a number of different forms. It includes, for instance, the kind of instruction where the computer is used essentially for drill and practice; it includes much learning where the student is controlled by the computer; it includes computer-managed learning where the computer keeps records of student learning; and it includes what is sometimes called electronic blackboard where the computer is used to present material.

If the computer can individualize learning and, at the same time, free teachers from much of the routine of teaching so that they can help those students experiencing difficulties and if, further, the computer can motivate students, thereby making learning a less passive, more active process, then here is a further justification for the introduction of the new technology across the curriculum.

Tool to extend the mind

One of the major justifications for the use of computers in education advanced by Conabere and Anderson (1985) is that the language in which one works shapes fundamentally the manner in which one approaches problems and the thinking processes one will employ. As one example, the use of Logo in schools can be considered. Papert, the founder of

Logo, developed the language principally in response to what he saw as the misuse of computers. In computer-assisted instruction, Papert (1980) argued, the computer programs the child: his vision was for the child to program the computer.

It is claimed that children who use Logo develop better information processing and inferential skills than those who do not. Papert, for instance, asserts that children learn something of epistemology in that they learn 'to think articulately about thinking' (Papert, 1980). Assuming for the moment that such claims are valid (though evidence from transfer of learning experiments and arguments against the teaching of grammar give some grounds for doubt), such computer-centred learning experiences may fundamentally redefine the nature of intelligence. Weizenbaum (1984), who also is often critical of many uses to which computers are sometimes put, nevertheless argues that computers, like other tools, help shape people's understanding of their world and also of themselves. All children, then, should have the opportunity to explore the 'microworlds' created by computers.

A second example of the way the computer might be a tool to extend students' minds is when it is used as a word processor. Daiute (1985) expresses it in this way:

> Computers, like other writing instruments, change the nature of written communication. The computer is a dynamic instrument that accepts the writer's words, carries out commands, and offers suggestions about texts. Such a writing instrument can blur the distinctions between thinking, talking and writing in a way that the pencil and typewriter have not (Daiute, 1985).

The computer could not have arrived in schools at a more propitious time in view of the current emphasis in many countries on writing as a dynamic process. The focus today in an increasing number of classrooms is more on the means and the creative process than on a single, final, neatly written, end product.

As a dynamic tool, then, the computer has the potential to free the mind for more productive learning and, in so doing, to extend students' thinking, perhaps even changing the very nature of their thought processes. Here are further major justifications for the computer in education.

Clear and critical thinking

Key skills in computer programming are said to be the ability to define problems precisely and to think critically. Clear and critical thinking are also key educational objectives. However, when it comes to including computer programming in school computing activities, there is often controversy.

The debate on whether to teach computer programming at school usually runs along the following lines. One side contends that teaching programming to students engenders bad habits (an argument often advanced by educators at the tertiary level or specifically directed to the BASIC language). Different responses are that there are few examples of other learning which develop bad habits, that the claim is made by those wishing to preserve academic territory, or that languages like Logo, and some versions of BASIC, allow structured programming. A second contention is that learning to program will enhance a student's vocational prospects (an argument often advanced by parents). A usual counter-argument here is that a new generation of languages will very likely be in use by the time students graduate. Yet another argument is that programming skills are not required for most computer use, to which a common response is that some programming skills are required to modify programs for educational purposes.

The debate is obviously muddied by the different groups of protagonists or antagonists involved, by the fact that different programming languages are referred to, and because the identity of the learners is not clearly defined.

In the computing policies of some education systems it is sometimes stated that learning to program is not necessary for all students. On the surface this might seem a sensible approach. One difficulty, though, is how computer programming is defined. Does it refer to Logo, for example? If, as is contended by some, working with Logo microworlds develops new modes of thought (see page 58), should not all students be given the experience of learning this computer language? A second problem is that it is often difficult to distinguish applications programs from computer programming in higher-order languages. In database or spreadsheet programs, for instance, or in simulations and modelling, the kinds of skills required are rather similar to those required in computer programming.

A more sensible approach might be to advocate teaching programming-like skills to all students (not necessarily programming). To develop these skills, computer-based learning packages such as word processors, database systems and spreadsheet programs could be used since the use of these requires a degree of precision. There is input, the data are processed, and the resulting output needs to be interpreted, which is what is implied in the term 'programming-like skills'. To the extent that the use of applications packages of the kind described enhances clear and critical thinking, there is further justification for computers in education.

Recreational activity

In the debate on computer programming, the argument that learning to program will help students get jobs is highly suspect. What seems more certain is, that in a society where individuals routinely use computer-based technologies, there will be increasing amounts of leisure.

Education for leisure is a task already accepted by schools. With total time for leisure increased, even if not shared equally by those in employment and those unemployed, writers like Wellington (1985) are stressing that more time should be devoted in the school curriculum to 'the enrichment of leisure'.

Now for many students programming is an enjoyable pastime; it is a recreation that manyreason are increasingly turning to as they tire of games on their home computers; it is highly motivating; and, furthermore, it is a challenging intellectual activity. None of these reasons is peculiar to computer programming but, at a time when computers are being promoted across the curriculum, the inclusion of computer programming as an intellectual and recreational activity seems apposite. As well as this, writing programs is one of the best ways of giving students a sense of control over the machine, and a means for some of raising their self-esteem.

Tool for teachers

The justifications advanced above are stated essentially in terms of learning and enrichment of leisure from the perspective of students. The computer is equally adaptable as a tool for teachers.

To consider but one example of how computers might assist teachers, one series of programs (Baumgart, Low and Riley, 1982) allows the computer to function as a teacher's tool to analyse students' tests. Such programs could find ready application in most teaching situations. The courseware, comprising sets of slides, computer programs and manuals, was designed as a kit of materials for pre-service and in-service education of teachers.

One of the program modules produces test analysis statistics for classroom tests. The program may be used for both norm-referenced and criterion-referenced tests. Tests are scored, and percentages and a histogram of the distribution of marks displayed. Statistics which can be computed include mean test score, standard deviation, reliability coefficient and standard error of measurement. Then for each item there is a display of the distribution of responses for each alternative, facility and discrimination indices, reliability if the item is omitted, and point-biserial correlation coefficient. Two other program modules allow the teacher, in interactive mode, to enter student data into a file or add data to an existing file.

Another program module combines marks (tests, projects, and so on) within a subject or across subjects. Yet another program module is used to adjust marks so that the mean and standard deviation are aligned to those of another test. The final program module provides a Rasch item analysis.

Such programs as these, and other similar ones, are useful as tools, not only for analysing class tests but also for providing insights into topics like moderation and scaling. Here, then, is further justification for the use of computers in education.

Catalyst for curriculum reform

Yet another justification for computers in education is the opportunity provided for looking afresh at what is done in schools. Initially, the major computing activity in schools was to teach about computers and hence there were courses on computer awareness, computer studies and computer electronics. This was an almost inevitable consequence because computers were predominantly used in the secondary school with its subject-dominated, vertical curriculum. But with the introduction of computers into primary schools, and with the growing realization that here is an incredibly versatile tool that can be used across subjects, greater emphasis is being given to teaching and learning with computers.

Initially, again, the emphasis on teaching and learning with computers was to use the computer as a tool to do classroom tasks very much as they had always been done; hence the emphasis on computer-assisted instruction, much computer-assisted learning and computer-managed learning, and even the use of the computer as an electronic blackboard. Essentially, computers were used to do the 'old' things in the 'old' way.

For all tools, it takes time to discover new uses, other than those for which the tool was originally fashioned. For example, it took more than a hundred years for the stationary steam engine to be placed on a moving carriage leading, later still, to the invention of the locomotive (Weizenbaum, 1984). Similarly, with the development of newer kinds of software has come the discovery that the computer can be deployed to do new tasks, tasks which not only utilize the capabilities of the machine more effectively but also facilitate student learning and the growth and development of concepts. This, in turn, is forcing educators to examine current curricula, and especially hidden curricula: another powerful reason for computers in education.

The rationale

To summarize the discussion thus far on the justification for computers in education in the short term, no more apt words express the importance of information to educators than the following:

> Never before has so much information been available to so many, and never before have our lives depended so much on our ability to handle information successfully. We need to be able to search out what we require, to assess critically the ideas and facts offered to us, and to make use of our findings (Schools Council, 1981).

The mark of democracies is that information is available to all citizens and that no group in society should have a monopoly. Since the school is the only universally available agency that can provide equality of access, there is an onus on schools to familiarize all students with computer-based technology and to promote the kinds of skills needed to function in an information society. This is an important justification for introducing computer technology across the curriculum.

The different skills discussed above — knowing where to search for information, the kinds of questions to ask, and so on — are not new. These are the fundamental skills with which education has always been concerned. Suggesting that computers have a place in schools is therefore to emphasize traditional learning skills. But computers can greatly facilitate the search for and the retrieval of information, and learners are thus released for more productive learning tasks. This, in turn, suggests the need for a re-examination of all aspects of the curriculum, and so a further justification for computer education.

Mention has been made of the interactive nature of computer-based learning. Learning is always more effective when the learner is actively involved and motivated. Most importantly, computers have the potential to release students for more productive thinking: another justification.

The computer has been variously described as 'an imagination machine', an 'almost anything machine', and 'a one-in-several-centuries invention'. An 11-year-old from Seattle recently told me: 'Computers are our second mind.' This may well be the major justification for the educational use of computers.

On the other hand, not all the effects of computers are seen as positive. What the various impacts of computer-based technologies are on society, what its potentials as well as its limitations are, are yet further reasons for computers in education.

Looking ahead

The immediately preceding discussion relates to the current educational use of computer technology in a number of countries around the world. For educational planners it is useful to try to look ahead, perhaps to the next five years and into the next decade. However, in a field as rapidly changing as computer education, this is an exercise fraught with difficulty.

If we look back at forecasts made in the past ten to fifteen years about the use of computers in education, O'Shea and Self (1983) note that there is not a close match with current practices. In the United States, for example, there were many predictions made in the early days of computers that routine computerized drill and practice in schools and colleges would be in almost universal use by 1979 and that more sophisticated learning programs would supersede these over the next ten-year period. In Britain, by contrast, the Council for Educational Technology in 1977 did not foresee any revolution in computer education, since computers would 'remain obstinately expensive'. Even Toffler, author of that best-seller of the 1970s, *Future Shock*, not only failed to predict the impact the microprocessor would have on society but failed to mention microprocessors at all. The simple explanation is that the date of his manuscript (Toffler, 1970) predated by a year the invention of the first chip by Intel in 1971. O'Shea and Self conclude that most predictions about educational computing in the past ten years have been 'either wildly over-optimistic or over-pessimistic' (1983).

With caution, then, we look forward to the remaining years of this century. Developments that perhaps can be foreshadowed with some degree of certainty in the medium to long term are the advent of fifth generation computers, the coming of age of artificial intelligence, and the increasing sophistication of expert systems.

The 'fifth generation computer' is a concept: it is the name given to a national project of the Japanese, the main goals of which are to develop machines that are many times more powerful than today's supercomputers but, more importantly, machines that have almost human qualities of hearing, speaking, seeing and problem- solving (Feigenbaum and McCorduck, 1983). This Japanese project, announced at the beginning of the present decade with a lifespan of ten years, although reportedly on target, may fall short of its ambitious aims. Artificial intelligence (AI) includes the development of programs that are designed to make machines behave intelligently, like speaking and hearing, for example. The fifth generation computer project in Japan, and similar projects in other parts of the world, have given enormous impetus to research on artificial intelligence, since the two are closely entwined. Research in AI, in turn, has led to the development of what are called expert systems, which are programs for solving problems in narrowly defined fields where a degree of human expertise is well established.

There are some who might question the relevance to classroom practice of a dream, as yet not realized, for a new generation of computers; others like Weizenbaum (1984) have seriously questioned whether research should even be undertaken in developing programs to make what are essentially human decisions. It is significant, though, that the director of the fifth generation project, Dr Kazuhiro Fuchi, expects the results of the Japanese research will have its greatest impact on personal computers.

> The real impact will be on the computers that are readily available to people — personal computers — rather than mainframes or supercomputers. The purpose of this project is to develop basic technology. Then, using this technology, you can make big computers and you can make small computers. But it is more important for the world to apply it to the personal type (quoted in Ahl, 1984).

If Dr Fuchi is right that the impact of this national research effort will be felt on personal computers similar to the kind currently in schools, colleges and universities, then there are obvious implications for education.

Artificial intelligence is no longer regarded with the same suspicion as in earlier years (perhaps Weizenbaum excepted); and some quite sophisticated expert systems have already been developed. There can be no turning back. In some fields, such as medical diagnosis, the performance of expert systems is as good as the very best human experts. Similar embryo systems are under development for diagnosing reading difficulties (Colbourne, 1984) and research into correction of English essays is yet another application that is well advanced. According to some, AI will fundamentally affect our concept of education, especially the nature of intelligence, and will impinge on classroom practice.

It seems likely that the justifications that have been advanced for the educational use of computers will maintain their relevance in the longer term. Indeed, the possibilities offered by the technology will steadily expand and become more powerful as educators learn to exploit it more effectively. Significantly, as far as schools and other educational institutions are concerned, there is a breathing space to prepare for the arrival of the newer generation of computers. It is important not to lose the opportunity offered, for the major tasks ahead for computer education relate less to computers than to education.

References

Adams, A and Jones, E (1983) *Teaching Humanities in the Microelectronic Age* Open University Press: Milton Keynes

A'Herran, A (1986) The extent and nature of primary school children's access to computers in homes *ACE News*

Ahl, D H (1984) Progress on the project: an interview with Dr Kazuhiro Fuchi *Creative Computing* 10 (8), 113–114

Anderson, J (1985) Communication and the information age in Anderson, J (ed) *Computers in the Language Classroom* Australian Reading Association: Perth

Baumgart, N, Low, B and Riley, S (1982) *Student Assessment Project* (A set of seven modules developed for in-service use by teachers) Macquarie University, School of Education: Sydney

Cerych, L (1982) *Computer Education in Six Countries: Policy Problems and Issues* Institute of Education: Paris

Colbourne, M (1984) Computer-guided diagnosis of reading difficulties *Australian Journal of Reading* 6 (4), 199–212

Conabere, T and Anderson, J (1985) Towards a rationale for the educational use of computer technology *Occasional Paper No 8* Australian College of Education: Melbourne

Daiute, C (1985) *Writing and Computers* Addison-Wesley: Reading, Mass.

Feigenbaum, E A and McCorduck, P (1983) *The Fifth Generation* Addison-Wesley: Reading, Mass.

Jones, B (1984) Schools mesmerised by hardware *Pivot,* 11 (1), 5–6

Meadow, C T (1979) Information science and scientists in 2001 *Journal of Information Science* 1 (4), 217–222

O'Shea, T and Self, J (1983) *Learning and Teaching with Computers: Artificial Intelligence in Education* Harvester Press: Brighton

Papert, S (1980) *Mindstorms: Children, Computers and Powerful Ideas* Harvester Press: Brighton

Pollock, W J B (1983) Developing a national telecommunications infrastructure for the information era in Goldsworthy, A W (ed) *Technological Change: Impact of Information Technology 1983* AGBS: Canberra

Schools Council (1981) Information skills in the secondary curriculum in Marland, M (ed) *Schools Council Curriculum Bulletin No 9* Methuen: London

South Australian Council on Technological Change (1982) *Communications Technologies: An Introductory Summary* Technological Change Office: Adelaide

Toffler, A (1970) *Future Shock* Pan Books: London

Weizenbaum, J (1984) *Computer Power and Human Reasoning* (2nd edn) Penguin: Harmondsworth

Wellington, J J (1985) *Children, Computers and the Curriculum* Harper and Row: London

4. New perspectives on open and distance learning for adult audiences

John Whiting

Summary: This chapter discusses open and distance learning systems in a European context, and is largely based upon the author's participation in and knowledge of the European Commission DELTA project. The views expressed are those of the author, and should not be interpreted as representing those of the Commission, since he is not a Commission spokesman. The evolution of open and distance learning systems is considered from both technological and pedagogic perspectives, leading to a detailed examination of a proposed model for an advanced third generation open and distance learning system. This more fully exploits the new information technologies (computer hardware, software and telecommunications) in ways which suggest rapid implementation of a cost-effective solution of the increasing lack of education and training provision. Cost-effective development by exploitation of technologies developed for other purposes is a feature of the proposal. The prime intention of this chapter is not so much to inform, but to provoke argument, discussion and thought about an increasingly important problem.

Introduction

The educational systems of post-industrial societies such as those of the United Kingdom, the USA and most nations within the European Community are traditional, hierarchical in organization, and notably resistant to change, especially at the tertiary level. In Britain, up to 40 per cent of school leavers do not obtain any recognized qualification or leaving certificate; many of these leavers are poorly numerate and some are virtually unable to read and write. Similar problems are evident in the USA. Hence, despite vigorous programmes of post-school training in Britain, the result is youth unemployment, anomie and other even less desirable social effects. The leavers who do obtain qualifications find that their chances of employment are increased by their obtaining a graduate or postgraduate qualification from a university or polytechnic. The minority who are given the chance to do so (around 10 to 12 per cent of the UK school leavers, but usually higher elsewhere) are predominantly middle class in origin and within the upper quartile of examination performance at school. The UK government alone in the European Community has largely disregarded calls for increased funding for education and has placed great stress upon active partnership between a diminishing industrial base and badly under-funded universities.

Societies change: the rate of change and the increasingly fragmented nature of modern post-industrial societies dictate the need for educational change to accompany these societal changes to increase both productivity and the population's ability to live in such societies. Government and the educational establishment have so far signally failed to implement such changes properly. Partly this is due to traditional inertia and resistance to change. More significant than this are a cluster of factors related to what has come to be known by the collective term 'information technology' or 'IT'. Here at least, the UK government has been innovative, with its widely emulated Microelectronics Education Programme for schools, coupled to a wide ownership of home computers, higher than any other nation in the European Community. However, the production of educational software remains mostly a cottage industry, though the training community, fuelled by the need for cost-effective and cheap training, is one of the most advanced in Europe. Much activity in aspects of computer-based education and training is evident at all levels of education but there is a lack of overall co-ordination and planning leading to much unnecessary duplication of effort. During 1986, for example, the USA spent $29 billion on IT-related methods of training. Expenditure in the UK and Europe is much less per head of population.

The Commission of the European Communities, particularly Directorate General XIII, Telecommunications, Information Industry and Innovation, has been aware of these problems for some time, with particular reference to the development of the new information technologies. In a climate of rapid technological change, the need for periodic retraining and upgrading of skills amongst the European population has never been greater. It has been estimated, for example, that the average person will require retraining between three and five times during his or her career. In addition, the economic responsibility for the non-working population falls upon a diminishing workforce. Today's retired people form 13 per cent of the European population, but will reach 25 per cent by the year 2020. For living standards to be maintained at their current level, let alone improved, manpower productivity has to be increased. Application of the new information technologies to enhance and extend the provision of education and training is the most feasible complement to their application to industry, and by far the only practical and cost-effective solution to the retraining problem. Given that the majority of the effort is to be directed at adults, many of whom will be in employment, then traditional, institution-based education and training systems (either full- or part-time) cannot meet the expected demand. In any case, disruption of employment by course attendance and the high costs of traditional education and training both vitiate the success of such methods. While application of the new information technologies to institutional education and training will undoubtedly lead to improved productivity and quality, it is unsatisfactory because of these factors. The European Commission estimates that around 80 per cent of what they term the 'economically active' population of the Community is locked out from traditional education and training, either because of restrictions upon release or inconveniences of provision. Many of this large majority are in any case poorly motivated toward further education and training because their school or college experience often acts as a positive disincentive for more of the same. The solution is easy to discern but difficult to design and implement in a cost-effective and economic manner. The precedent set by the UK Open University, now widely emulated elsewhere, and the Open Tech for more applied vocational training as a more recent example, show this to be utilization of the ideas of open and distance learning. The solution advocated in this chapter relates to new concepts for open and distance learning, arising from the factors mentioned above.

Evolution of open and distance learning

Open learning can be defined as a system or collection of processes and procedures which permit anyone to learn at times and places of their own choice, in ways and at speeds which are suited to them. Distance learning can share this definition if it is appreciated that geographical separation is a major factor in the education or training process. The major emphasis in open and distance learning has therefore always been placed upon the learners themselves in the physical absence of human tutors. This has meant that a greater degree of structure has been required in the philosophy and design of open learning courses and their associated instructional materials.

The most usual approach has been to produce instructional materials in a linear sequence of units or modules of study, based upon largely textual resources. Each unit or module is designed to be complete in itself within its membership of one or more instructional sequences, leading toward an examinable qualification. Supporting materials are usually textbooks, course and unit documents plus references to background reading. Some systems also provide audio, video or computer-based materials and some are supported by the broadcast of radio and television. In nearly all cases, the latter are only a minor component of the courses, though American video courses broadcast either through conventional or satellite-based systems are an exception. Most systems have some form of tutor consultation mechanism built into them. Assignments, essays and self-assessment questions and revision exercises are also featured.

Before considering the two current generations of open and distance learning systems in more detail, it is worthwhile to examine some ideas about such designs and the learning strategies which they adopt.

Learning strategies and designs

Current open and distance learning systems work and result in high levels
of learning when measured by summative assessments. The pedagogic
model most often used to design them is closely related to the school
experience, ie the 'classroom-teacher' model where there is a serial
mixture of exposition, practice, study, assessment and remediation followed by examination and, for some, qualification. The greater degree
of structure applied to open and distance learning instructional materials
is intended to compensate for the lack of a human teacher capable of
instant response and other tutorial functions. The sequence and topics
of open learning are also closely related to the curricula of institutionally based courses of full- or part-time instruction. This is so because
they are well established and understood, easily examinable in conventional ways, and their qualifications accepted by employers and external
qualifying bodies. It is also true that it is easier to develop an open and
distance learning course from existing full- or part-time courses.

There are two very important factors which influence the success of
open and distance learning systems designed in these ways. First, the
higher motivation of open and distance learners in comparison to institutional students, particularly full-time students who go to college or
university direct from school. Second, the quality and presentation of
the instructional materials produced for open and distance learning
courses, which is generally higher than those produced for institutionally based courses of similar or identical content. One has only to look
at the excellent materials produced for the UK Open University to see
a good demonstration of this point. However, the quality (in terms of
both presentation and pedagogic structure) being high has led to the
belief that the independence of the learner is catered for by the higher
quality of the materials in the absence of direct human tutorial support.
To extend this point a little further, it is probably true to say that this
pervasive belief has also led to a concentration upon the technological
means at the expense of the human needs of the individual students.

However well-motivated any individual learner may be, current open
and distance learning systems do not attempt to cater for variation in
learning styles or preferences. Whilst the speed of learning is left to the
individual, this is often constrained in practice by assessment and examination schedules, which are seen by many as a motivating factor in
themselves. This cannot be denied, but it does mean that traditional
practices and habits of thought are perpetuated instead of being adapted
to newer, more potent modes of education and training. Partly this is
due to educational inertia, in the sense that the learning topic, curriculum and sequence of instruction are held to be either immutable (the
syllabus is sacrosanct) or self-evident in the topic of instruction itself.
Partly too, it is organizationally inconvenient to diverge too far from
traditionally established patterns of instructional design. These factors
mean that the selection of open learners will be oriented toward those

who fit such patterns both in the initial selection process and later when those less suited to them drop out. This may be one reason why open and distance learning courses suffer from higher dropout rates than institutionally based courses in addition to the disincentives induced by previous educational or training experiences. A further factor which receives scant attention is that of the learner's purposes in wanting to undertake an open and distance learning course. The major purpose, and virtually the only purpose recognized by educators iand trainers, is said to be self advancement towards personal or employment-related objectives such as promotion or increased qualifications and salaries. A more realistic consideration of requirements shows that there are two dimensions by which learners can be better categorized for the purpose of designing open and distance learning systems:

a. expressed or implicit learner requirements
b. learner (user) models.

The second of these dimensions is considered in more detail in a later section of this chapter, since it is directly relevant to the design of an advanced, third generation open and distance learning system. The first of these can be put into a taxonomy as below:

1. *Curiosity*
   Obtaining information or knowledge almost by chance without any definite objective or need.
2. *Carousel*
   Being interested in a wide variety of topics, but seeking information only when time is available, or when briefly or marginally motivated to do so.
3. *Information-seeking*
   Here there is a need for specific information and knowledge which is sought for, obtained and used. The information is often thereafter disregarded and forgotten.
4. *Informal learning*
   Learning undertaken for personal satisfaction which may or may not lead to a recognized qualification, award or new set of skills.
5. *Formal learning*
   Learning for a particular, externally set objective such as satisfaction of summative criteria for a course leading to an award or skills qualification.
6. *Study and scholarship*
   Discovering new knowledge for personal or altruistic benefits; research.

Levels 4 and 5, particularly Level 5, are the ones which current open and distance learning systems are designed to satisfy. Level 6 is marginally accommodated. Level 1 is not catered for at all. Level 3 is typified by users of institutional databases. Level 2 is the one most commonly utilized by the poorly motivated majority of potential open and distance learners, and also by continuing education programmes. It ought to be, and sometimes is used to feed Level 5 courses. This taxonomy can be used as a means of tactical planning (and strategic design) in the development of open and distance learning courses, particularly those which will exploit the new information technologies.

At this stage, it is necessary to outline a self-paced learning strategy that will not only be suitable for most levels of this taxonomy, but will also be suitable for the advanced third generation open and distance learning system which will fully exploit the new information technologies. The strategy is not new, having first been proposed in 1922 by Washburn. Later developments were made by Bloom (1968) and Block (1971). Its most common descriptors are 'mastery learning' or 'competency based education'. The principle of the strategy is simple: since individuals differ in their preferred modes, speeds and styles of learning, then in order to optimize learning the instruction should be individually tailored to accommodate these requirements. The practicality of such individualized tuition in today's mass market education and training for the 200 million economically active adults in the European Community might appear quite impossible because of the lack of human resources. However, if instructional material is designed to cater in parallel for a majority of known learner requirements, this may partially substitute for the lack. In this scenario no attempt is made to match individuals with precisely tailored learning strategies. Instead, the strategies are made diverse enough to account for a range of learner styles which, between them, will cater for a majority of learners. This paper is not the forum to present the arguments and evidence for such an approach to mastery learning, but some experiments have been reported elsewhere (Whiting, 1984; 1985; 1986) in undergraduate education and training in biology. In these studies the students used multimedia instructional materials, including a high proportion of computer-based learning in an institutional setting and achieved high levels of mastery. Summative assessments produced distributions which were lognormal, ie significantly skewed toward the higher percentage scores. Exploitation of such an approach for open and distance learning systems based upon the new information technologies is suggested as fruitful in the light of later discussion.

Existing types of open and distance learning system

Open and, in particular, distance learning systems can be categorized in terms of the means of transmission of the instructional materials to and from learners, and in terms of the types of materials supplied. Both these can be mapped on to the taxonomy of learner requirements given in the previous section, which will demonstrate two current types for satisfaction of informal and formal learning (levels 4 and 5) and a cluster of similar ones which satisfy the carousel and information seeking modes (levels 2 and 3).

A combination of two-way postal transmission and the use of entirely textual instructional materials characterizes the 'correspondence course' pattern which has been in use for many years. Here, there is little if any direct (face-to-face) interaction between tutors and learners. The textual materials are often in the form of notes, *aides-mémoire* and supplementary material relating to a set course textbook, supplemented by sets of study instructions and schedules, assignments and occasionally, short self-test questions for formative assessment. Such a pattern parallels the same course of instruction given in institutional formats, including formal examinations. Such systems utilize little if any tutorial assistance though most have some form of query mechanism which is designed to solve what learners feel are intractable study problems. Systems such as these are termed 'first generation' open and distance learning systems in this chapter, and satisfy formal and (less successfully) informal learning needs.

Second generation systems are typified by the additions which they make to first generation ones. Whilst postal exchange of textual materials remains the basis for the majority of second generation systems, the instructional materials are supplemented by two types of additional media of transmission, either alone or in combination. The first of these is tuition distributed by the mass broadcast media, radio and television. The second is distribution via the postal system of instructional material in other forms than text on paper, such as audio tapes, slide sets, film and, increasingly, videotape. More recently computer-assisted learning software has been added to the list in a minority of cases. However, outside of technologically developed nations even the use of broadcast media is somewhat uncertain, let alone distribution of instructional materials other than in textual form.

One of the most well developed second generation open and distance learning systems is the UK Open University. Its textual materials are of very high quality, as are its radio and television broadcasts. Some of its course units are capable of entirely independent study, thereby satisfying some carousel and informal learning requirements, though most are still designed to satisfy formal learning toward graduate qualification. The Open University pattern also utilizes local and regional study centres, studies advisors and tutors as well as summer schools. These additions are implementations of tutorial and study support systems, considered in the next section.

Support systems

Open and distance learning systems have always required some means whereby learners can receive support. The usual interpretation of this has been to provide well structured modular instructional media in the expectation that their sophistication, coupled with good pedagogic design, will be enough to compensate for the lack of direct human tutorial support which is available in institutional settings. The high dropout rates for open and distance learning courses and the higher motivation to learn of the remainder in comparison with institutionally based courses tend to obscure the need for support beyond that offered by the instructional materials themselves. That such need for support does exist beyond the materials themselves is evidenced by the introduction of the Open University tutors, study centres and summer schools. Recent evidence (Hodgson, 1986) shows that even when such support systems are provided the support needs are not wholly met.

Many experiments have been made to provide support through technologies such as existing telecommunications, audio conferencing and interactive or semi-interactive computer information systems, but with variable success (Laaser, 1987). In most cases, technology has been the major consideration, with little attention being paid to the human aspects of sophisticated support systems. The limited nature of available technologies and the relative lack of human resources are mutually reinforcing problems. Current telecommunications and computer technologies are too slow and expensive to provide the levels of support that are necessary in an advanced third generation open and distance learning system. Without much more sophisticated hardware and software systems it is virtually impossible for the available human resources to cope with the current demand for open and distance learning, let alone any extensions of it to the wider markets now becoming evident.

The new information technologies

Information technology has been hard to define, like all new ideas which accrete around a totally new concept or collection of disciplines. When attempting to make a definition, ideas remain diffuse and conclusions reached by different people are confused. Rather than produce another definition here to confuse the issues further, it is more useful to state here that, in the author's view, the new information technologies consist of a fusion between computer hardware, software, telecommunications and human concepts related to them. Particular humans will arrive at different syntheses of views most often related to their particular areas of knowledge and expertise. People interested in educational and training matters will produce a cluster of concepts and descriptors which resemble, but differ from, those which arise from discussions between psychologists and cognitive scientists. People involved in computer science or those involved in commerce will have their own versions which differ again both within and between these groups. However, all will share a requirement to base their clusters of IT — related concepts around hardware, software and telecommunications. In terms of advanced, third generation open and distance learning systems of the kind envisioned by the European Commission and its DELTA programme, this is most certainly true. One reason for this is because the Commission sponsors research and development in related areas, as witness the ESPRIT, RACE, BRITE programmes and the DG V COMETT proposals. The UK Alvey project is an example of a national initiative, and the multi-national EUREKA program is an example of a programme initiated outside of the European Commission. Another reason is because the Commission, as well as most European nations, recognizes that traditional educational systems are inadequate in the face of new education and training needs, and that the new information technologies are capable of exploitation to promote more cost-effective and more widely acceptable and available solutions.

However, whilst both these reasons are valid and compelling in themselves, they tend to encourage purely technological solutions which take little account of human factors. The analogy here with the computer industry itself is striking. The manufacture of more and more powerful and diverse hardware configurations has not been matched by the software systems to exploit them to their full extent. One has only to consider the complex and idiosyncratic nature of proprietary operating systems such as MS-DOS or UNIX for evidence of this point. Even the iconographic, mouse driven (WIMP) interfaces are still very far from ideal when compared to natural spoken or written language between humans. Many of the most successful software applications packages used for common business functions such as word processing or spreadsheet calculation still require considerable time investment from their users before they can be fully exploited. Most users of such packages rarely go beyond a stage at which they make use of what they perceive to be the most useful subset of commands and procedures which the applications package provides. Another striking analogy implicit in what has been presented in earlier sections of this chapter is the poor development of support systems for open and distance learning in comparison with the better developed instructional materials.

Computer hardware

The speed of progress in computer hardware does not need reiterating here. It is already at the stage where any person with a mid range wage or salary can purchase a powerful and versatile home or business microcomputer without financial burden. By 1990, if not before, $2,000 will suffice to buy a desktop machine as powerful as a minicomputer, such as a DEC VAX 11/780. The point of this brief comment is to demonstrate that the kind of computer hardware which can be configured to act as a personal learner workstation in an advanced third generation open and distance learning system is almost available at a price that a majority of the employed population (and, by subsidy, the unemployed population as well) can afford relatively easily. Since such hardware will be produced to satisfy increasing demand in the business environment, amongst others, there is little if any need to devote research and development funding to production of a unique hardware configuration to act as a dedicated learner workstation.

Before considering the software developments specific to the adaption of such hardware for educational and training purposes (where much of the research and development expenditure will be needed) an outline of the hardware specification for a learner workstation and its peripherals is given below. This will serve to indicate the likely areas for software development in the use of the workstation in an advanced open and distance learning system.

Current (1987) personal computers have up to 4 Mb of main memory and about 10 to 20 times this as offline storage on integral Winchester hard discs. A learner workstation will eventually require a 500 Mb/5 Gb configuration, but it is difficult to predict when such a configuration will become necessary since a lot will depend upon related software developments. In the short-term future, however, a 32-bit computer with 8 to 10 Mb of main memory and 250 Mb of offline storage will serve as a development vehicle, as long as it is readily interfaceable to the wide variety of peripherals which it will need to act as a learner workstation. The processing speed of the prototype workstation will need to be between 5 to 7 MIPS in order to provide acceptable response times for the complex programs needed to control and monitor the system. Peripherals which will be needed include input devices such as keyboard, mouse, scanner (for text and diagrams), touch screen, concept keyboard, analogue and digital user port and simple forms of single word speech recognition. It will also need a communications I/O port for remote site messaging and a satellite receiver. Its output devices will include a high definition RGB computer display with the capacity to display video separately or in combination with superimposed computer output. Other outputs will include speech, printer and plotter and high speed communications via the modem. One other peripheral will necessarily be a laservision device, which will act as both an optical memory device and video storage and display device. A CD-ROM (ie compact disc) peripheral will also be useful for encyclopaedic information resources.

Operating system software

The purposes of a learner workstation dictate the kinds of software needed to implement them on the hardware outlined in the previous section. The overall control of such software relies upon some form of operating system which makes it simple to exploit both the power of the hardware and its associated peripherals plus the particular software elements specific to the functions of the learner workstation. The issue here is whether to utilize existing operating systems, which are not designed for pedagogic aims, or to design and implement one to accommodate these aims more easily.

Earlier discussion made it clear that the most cost-effective means of producing a learner workstation was to exploit hardware constructed for other applications, most probably business data processing. Whilst this may be interpreted as a compromise, it is both sensible in terms of expenditure and in terms of the high power and versatility of the likely hardware specification of such advanced machines, for which development costs are very substantial indeed. The brief hardware specification for a prototype learner workstation, given in the previous section, is enough to permit cost-effective pedagogic exploitation. Exactly the same arguments apply to the selection of operating system software with even more force, since software development costs are at least one order of magnitude higher. It therefore makes sense to select an operating system which is well supported by both hardware and software producers. There is little point in selecting one which will only run upon one restricted hardware configuration, since this will place severe limits upon both its availability and use, no matter how well it is suited to pedagogic aims. This rules out operating systems which are not virtually industry standards, and dictates that the choice be made from a relatively small selection. Prominent amongst these are MS-DOS and, more likely, the family of wholly or partially compatible operating systems under the UNIX name. Whilst most of its users would readily admit that UNIX is a difficult operating system with which to come to terms, particularly those who are not computer scientists or skilled computer users (ie most of the developers and users of a learner workstation), it is an operating system which is implemented upon a very wide range of computers, it is more capable of extension than most other systems and, lastly, it has gained worldwide acceptance. Its refractory nature in use does not recommend it but there are few, if any, others which are any better.

The development problem peculiar to the learner workstation which utilizes a version of UNIX as its operating system therefore becomes one of 'protecting' the educational, training or learning user from the complexities and obscurities it contains whilst preserving and exploiting both its flexibility and extendability. Experience with the use of microcomputers utilizing the Motorola 68000 processor (Apple Macintosh, Commodore Amiga and the Atari ST) indicates the simplest way to achieve this objective. The WIMP interface which these machines possess is simple and straightforward to use and also conceals the complex nature of the operating system behind such ease of use. There are already some WIMP interfaces to UNIX available, so the main work will be in writing and implementing the particular pieces of software required for pedagogic purposes. Operating system software exists after all to permit more things to be done, and to permit them to be done more quickly and easily by an expanding community of users.

Pedagogically oriented software

Having outlined the hardware and operating system software of the learner workstation, this section presents some information on the types of software systems which will be needed to fulfil its pedagogic purposes as part of an advanced, third generation open and distance learning system. There are four broad areas of software development:

a. computer-based instructional materials;
b. software systems to assemble the materials;
c. programs and routines to permit their use;
d. pedagogic control and monitoring systems.

Each of these is outlined in the subsections below, before going on to examine the design of a third generation open and distance learning system of which they will form an important part.

INSTRUCTIONAL MATERIALS

A common term used to describe computer-based educational or, more usually, training software is 'courseware'. Most courseware consists of screen-based presentations of text, diagrams and animated graphics through which the learner interacts via a keyboard or, less often, other input devices. Most of the current courseware is serial in design, with varying degrees of branching structure to accommodate variation in speed of study. The commonest type of interaction is in pressing a key to advance the material, followed by either menu selection (multiple choice) or free format text entry by users attempting to answer questions posed by the courseware. A variable amount of textual support is provided for expansion of the courseware. Some patterns of instruction are entirely serial, tutorial exposition, whilst others are more advanced, using simulations or gaming. Not very many are open-ended.

The limitations of such courseware lie in the single channel of information transfer (keyboard-screen) and the imposition of a single pedagogic structure. In the light of earlier discussions, this is quite unsuitable, despite the general success of such courseware in achieving training objectives in limited fields of expertise. For an advanced learner workstation and the sophistication of the open and distance learning system to which it contributes, much more is needed. The instructional material (so called to distinguish it from the term 'courseware') will have to be multi-media in both presentation and pedagogic structure. This will mean that its interaction with a learner will be via a variety of concurrently initialized means besides the keyboard, including mouse, touch, speech and concept keyboard. It also means that the instructional material is configured to a variety of tuitional paradigms, eg textual tutorial, graphical demonstration, explorable microworld or simulation. The power of the learner workstation and its associated peripherals, like the laservision and satellite reception facilities and the communications facilities, will add to the diversity of provision. Such a multimedia approach is designed to create an educational and training environment that will satisfy most of the requirements for mastery (competency) learning and training.

MEANS OF ASSEMBLY

Courseware is written by means of proprietary authoring languages or systems which tie the material to both their own system or language, and to a specific hardware configuration. A good source of information and review of the field is given by Barker (1987). Whilst such fourth generation software tools have much to recommend them, mostly that they make courseware authorship easier and quicker, it is usual to expend between 100 and 300 hours of time in the production of one hour of finished courseware. This accounts for the high cost of the product. Another factor which increases the cost is that the market for courseware is a bespoke one; the emerging courseware industry does not yet serve a mass market except in the production of generally useful non-educational software tools, most often to serve the business market.

The multimedia nature of the instructional material advocated in the previous subsection may therefore be considered even more difficult to construct. That is why the term 'assembly' is used instead of authorship. This is taken to mean the putting together of existing resources with newly created instructional strategies and structures to provide pedagogic coherence. The three elements in such a process are:

1. the resources themselves;
2. the means to identify, acquire, create, rearrange and store them in an easily accessible and computer addressable form;
3. the existence of pre-defined instructional strategies and pedagogic structures stored on the same computer system.

The resources are those which would be utilized for more traditional instruction in institutional settings, and include text, diagrams (most usually found in textbooks and lecture notes), pictures, film, video, data, and conventional software. A quite large proportion of the resources required would have to be created in any case, but the utilization of existing materials, and the careful selection of knowledge domains for which a large training and education market exists already, will keep the amount of creation needed as low as possible. The problems inherent in obtaining permission to utilize existing material may, however, force the creation of large amounts of new material with the consequent increase in both time and cost. It is to be hoped that such a problem can be overcome, but the political climate is not hopeful.

The need for storage of information and knowledge in computer addressable form should be clear. Only in this form can the various materials be manipulated into coherent arrangements in a common control environment. The problems of producing a software structure to allow this are quite difficult since they will involve some means whereby the software can 'understand' the information and knowledge it holds. The current state of the art as far as artificial intelligence is concerned is not sufficient to provide a generalized interpretative system for this purpose (Self, 1987). While current rule-based expert system tools may suffice for creation of limited domains of expertise, the creation process is slow, too complex and insufficiently flexible to permit people who do not have a clear understanding of the process and the supporting algorithms and language to make sensible use of it for pedagogic purposes. These are precisely the people who will need to create in order to serve the expected large market for a third generation open and distance learning system. This argument therefore points to the need for the conceptualization and development of a sophisticated set of software tools to allow such creation, which is one of the most urgent needs at present.

As far as pedagogic structures and instructional strategies are concerned, much is already known from learning theory, training procedures and pragmatic experience to attempt a categorization of suitable self-paced learning strategies, of which mastery (competency) learning is one which appears particularly suitable in an open and distance learning context. The problem here is not one of knowledge, but one of adaption of it to the multi-media, computer-based approach to tuition. The interleaving of several different strategies (thus permiting adequate matching to a majority of learner preferences and styles) around a body of described knowledge based upon the resources and their assembly discussed above is not simple to solve. Links between elements of the knowledge are important here because the strategies must 'understand' them in several different ways in order to provide for a variety of means of approach to them by learners, and also a variety of possible pathways toward learning which they are encouraged to adopt. The best initial approach is probably a pragmatic one. Here, several explicitly devised strategies are applied, used and assessed through a prototype system which lacks 'understanding'. The experimental data obtained in terms of learner performance, attitudes and ways of use of the material may well provide sufficient information to build a more sophisticated and intelligent system.

USE, MONITORING AND CONTROL

In an open and distance learning system, the use of the instructional materials is at the discretion of the individual learners; whether they use it or not cannot be so easily controlled when compared to an institutional setting. However, with the type of instructional materials outlined above and the generally higher degree of motivation possessed by open and distance learners (also encouraged by the more sophisticated nature of the learning materials themselves) this may well be a small problem. Much will depend upon the support systems offered internally by the materials themselves (which will be in advance of current courseware and other resources) and those offered externally via high-speed telecommunications facilities (of which more is discussed below) exploited by the advanced open and distance learning system itself. The purposes for monitoring and control must be carefully defined in order to avoid being regarded as obstrusive and smacking too much of 'Big Brother'. Since the learner workstation will be connected to the open and distance learning system through advanced telecommunications facilities, the possibility of very close monitoring of use and progress is a real one, though open to abuse from both the learner and the system. The software control system in the learner workstation, for example, could be made to provide very detailed interaction records of learner usage. If such information is used for the benefit of the learner in pedagogic terms, and if the disclosure of such information is left at the discretion of the learner, not the system, then there should be few problems. Following this argument leads to two main purposes for monitoring:

a. monitoring learner progress and learning performance;
b. attempting to model the learner.

The first of these should be self-evident for both formal and informal learners, though the means whereby it is achieved are open to discussion. A need for formal examinations and other measures of objective achievement is axiomatic if education and training objectives are to be met to the satisfaction of employers and qualifying bodies. The need for formative assessment in any self-paced learning system, particularly one which is an open and distance learning system, is also axiomatic. Whether any combination between these is possible is unknown. A further factor will be the amount of cross-validation and acceptance of units of study between qualification awarding institutions and authorities. American experience has shown that such mechanisms can be operated successfully provided a high degree of cross-consultation takes place in the design of units of study and their assessment. A similar precedent is being set in the UK between the Open University and the Council for National Academic Awards (CNAA) which is still the validating body for graduate and postgraduate degrees awarded outside of the universities.

In human-to-human teaching and tuition, teachers develop some sort of informal model of each person they teach in terms of personality, performance, ability, motivation and other pedagogic factors. Such models act as effective guides to teachers in adapting their teaching to take account of individuals. Most often such models are intuitive and rarely expressible in other than subjective terms. The ways in which they are developed are mostly inaccessible to categorization and analysis. One aspect of the application of artificial intelligence is the modelling of users of computers, often described as 'user modelling' or 'human computer interface' (HCI) research. The educational and training importance of this lies in finding ways in which a software system can be built which replicates all or part of the human teacher's user modelling activities. The problems are extensive (Self, 1987) but their solution for an advanced open and distance learning system is essential in order that it can optimize the learning performance of its users in the relative absence of human contact. The major problems are twofold; first to build an understanding of what reliable procedures and parameters are necessary in order to build a reliable and predictive user modelling system, and second, to discover a way or ways in which the advanced open and distance learning system can acquire and analyse enough information upon which to base an analysis. Whilst one way forward is by pragmatic experiment with non-intelligent systems that generate data from which experimental systems could be built, it is a long process. The use of full interaction records of learners with their instructional materials and support systems will need to be supplemented by more formal studies into the individual psychology of the users, and also their attitudes of mind, aptitudes and other parameters which cannot as yet be predicted from educational assessments. A further problem lies in the no doubt considerable influence of the disciplines and subjects which users are attempting to learn.

The need for telecommunications

Learners participating in any open and distance learning system require external support. Current practices have been described in an earlier section. In an advanced open and distance learning system, where each learner makes use of a sophisticated learner workstation, it makes sense to provide a telecommunications-based support system, since the speed and power of these facilities will increase almost as fast as the power and flexibility of computer hardware. The use of the national and international telecommunications networks for learner support is at present minimal. There are two reasons for this. The first is the limitations of the technology available to individuals through the telephone system. The second is the lack of experience and ideas for their use for supporting open and distance learners.

Many local area and wide area networks (LAN and WAN) exist. LANs are devoted to linking microcomputers and other, larger computers together in order to communicate and share resources. Speeds of transmission are high in comparison to those of WANs, being in the range of kilobits to megabits per second. Typical WAN speeds are between 75 and 2,400 bits per second for the individual home user, though obviously higher for the network's internal transmission links. This WAN speed limitation therefore inhibits all but the smallest amounts of information transmission between individuals because of excessive time on line; a typical piece of courseware used for an industrial training programme will be around 200 Kb in size. Transfer of this via the existing telephone system, using error checking to avoid data corruption, will take nearly three hours to transfer at 1.2 Kbits per second which means excessive telephone bills for the individual. Hence the continuing need for traditional postal systems. Advances in the provision of higher speed public access telecommunications over the next few years will be dependent upon the size of national and international investment and research and development programmes such as the European Commission RACE proposals. Much of the stimulus for such improvements will spring from the business market and should lead to the provision of narrow band integrated system digital networks (ISDN) by the early 1990s. These will have speeds of between 64 and 200 Kilobits per second which will permit much more rapid transfer of data. Further broadband extensions of ISDN into IBCN (integrated broadband communication networks) are unlikely to be established much before the end of this century. While ISDN speeds will be suitable for some of the purposes discussed below, the transmission of real time, high-definition video between individuals at home will not be realized in the medium-term future. Hence the necessity to make use of broadcast communication facilities, and the need to establish satellite broadcasting for the distribution of such materials to a large community of open and distance learners. That is the main reason for including a satellite receiver in the hardware specification of the learner workstation. Satellite transmission facilities at the disposal of individuals are impractical in the short- to medium-term future on the grounds of both expense and the availability of satellite channels, whereas satellite receivers will soon be in the financial reach of anyone.

Given such constraints, the use of telecommunications facilities for open and distance learning support systems may seem limited. However, this is not so if closer consideration is given to the types of support to be provided. The limitations above apply only to the distribution of data-intensive instructional materials such as long computer programs, documents, CD-ROM and video material. The conventional postal system can quite easily and cheaply cope with the distribution of these. The types of support which can be hosted on existing and proposed telecommunications networks fall into three groups:

1. learner-to-learner, learner-to-tutor communications;
2. information provision and conferencing;
3. data and information base access and searching.

Each of these is outlined in the subsections below. It should be realized here that a fourth area of use for such communications links will be the transmission of data related to user modelling, performance and assessment to some central open and distance learning centre, but this will be discussed later in the context of establishing a third generation system.

LEARNERS AND TUTORS

The problem of the isolation of the distance learner has already been discussed. Lessening of this problem can be achieved by encouragement of electronic communication between them. Current business oriented computer networks hosted on national PSTN systems such as the UK Telecom Gold and international Dialcom networks are accessible via local telephone calls, and provide quite sophisticated facilities for the exchange of textual messages. These may be prepared offline and 'uploaded' at the full available speed of the network or, of course, prepared online at greater expense. Once stored on the central system, the message can be sent to single individuals or groups of them with equal ease. Typical delays between sending and receipt are less than ten seconds. Single sender-multiple recipient messages can be sent with ease. Files of messages can be stored or downloaded to local storage media and messages received by one person can be forwarded to others with or without comments attached. Central information files can be set up and interrogated by those who are given access to them via passwords. Messages can likewise be either protected by mutually agreed passwords or by encryption. Gateways from one network to another are available, making multiple network subscriptions unnecessary, though additional charges may be incurred by their users.

The point of suggesting such facilities for open and distance learning systems is to encourage frequent learner-to-learner communication and the pedagogically valuable peer group interactions such facilities will engender. Contacts with and queries to appointed subject tutors also act to reinforce learning. Though speeds of transmission are slow, small documents and files can be exchanged as can some online assessment and other types of test. The tutors have the additional facility of mainframe power attached to their versions of the learner workstation to be used for CPU intensive tasks, though this facility might not be offered to the learners. Communication between tutors is also made relatively easy and quick. When there are large numbers of learners, however, some form of pre-formatted enquiry system may be needed to assist tutors to cope with the volume of queries, unless it becomes possible to interpose a natural language parsing and information extraction system to put queries into sets which share answers which can be input to the identified group by the tutor, or, at a later stage, by domain-specific artificial intelligence programs.

INFORMATION PROVISION AND CONFERENCING

Every user of an open and distance learning course will need some information about it other than the supplied instructional materials and contacts with other learners and assigned tutors. Typical of such types of information are assessment schedules, general course information, course noticeboards, directions to other sources of information, notice of amendments or changes which affect the course and some ancillary pedagogic information and news. Such information is most economically provided via an online information system hosted on the same network as the electronic mailing system outlined in the subsection above. The techniques and software for doing so are already in use and are well understood so there is no problem in establishing such an information system. The justification for it is twofold. First, it provides a central and easily updated source of information freely available to registered learners; and second, it provides a common course focus with which the learners can identify and thereby feel less isolated. Such a system would also satisfy the curiosity, carousel and information-seeking levels of the taxonomy of learner requirements given earlier, as well as contributing to informal and formal learning requirements.

Computer conferencing is a relatively new idea which has found most expression in the United States. It differs from electronic mail in being a directly interactive and more disciplined form of communication between people who are logged on to a computer network all at the same time. Each participant in a conference can submit messages to a queue which, from a participant's point of view, is sequentially displayed in order of receipt. Users can also move up or down the queue to or from the most recent message. The participants in a conference of this nature in an open and distance learning system would be discussing a topic of direct relevance to their course of instruction, and one for which such discussion would be beneficial, eg problem-solving activities or case studies. The conferences can be run at specific times, or made more freely available over longer periods depending upon their nature and topics. While most will probably need direction from an open and distance learning system tutor, there is no reason why groups of learners cannot establish their own conferences upon other topics of interest, thus forming a very powerful peer group discussion forum. The primary purpose of such conferences in an advanced open and distance learning system is of course to provide an electronic and distributed version of the classical tutorial system. This will satisfy the higher levels of formal learning in the requirements taxonomy.

DATA AND INFORMATION BASE ACCESS
It is unrealistic to expect that all the information requirements of individual learners can be satisfied by the instructional materials and the telecommunications-supported facilities outlined above. While, like current generations of open and distance learning, reference to other printed resources can be made in the expectation that the learners will use them, it is increasingly true that databases and 'information' bases are being established on computer systems all over the world. It would be foolish not to take these into consideration as a resource environment for users of an advanced third generation open and distance learning system. Online services can be accessed via the PSTN networks already, though given the speed and availability problems extant today, it will be immediately obvious that there are serious problems to be overcome. Permission for access, expense and the variety of different networks or LANs upon which these resources exist at present mean that use of the resources will be difficult if not impossible in a coherent and cost-effective manner for some time to come. However, the biggest problem of all is one of information resource management. There is as yet no accepted standard for database access or enquiry, nor one which is universally accepted for description of information or data held upon these systems. The enquiry systems and protocols differ from one to another, which means that no sooner does a learner get familiar with one mode of access and enquiry than he or she will need to become familiar with another, and then another. The requirement for simplicity of operation of the learner workstation and the open and distance learning system itself to which it is connected rule out the diversity of means of access and enquiry.

There are two ways of solving this. First, to replicate (and translate) relevant data and information from a variety of sources on to one central store under the control of the open and distance learning system. Second, to develop a multidatabase access and enquiry system to act as a 'front end' through which any resource can be consulted by use of the same command and enquiry system. The first solution is a short-term one, and is not very cost-effective, since the translation process will require much time and human effort. It will also mean that the learners are restricted to what the open and distance learning system controllers regard as relevant. The benefit will be that a single access and enquiry system is needed, and it can be designed to be simple and easy to use in comparison with the bases upon which the data and information were previously held. The interface could also be transformed gradually into the multidatabase system if sufficient correlation between the two is established during development. Such research and development is far from simple, particularly the multidatabase concept. However, it is likely that such developments will be made externally to the development of any advanced open and distance learning system, since the business environment as one example is already reaching a state where such facilities would be cost-effective solutions for their information requirements. The application of artificial intelligence techniques to the development of natural language enquiry systems is one current pointer to the achievement of such an objective.

Establishing a system

What has so far been discussed in this chapter are the components of a third generation advanced open and distance learning system based upon proper exploitation of the new information technologies. The three most important concepts are clearly the learner workstation and its software, the nature and creation of the instructional materials and the exploitation of telecommunications for modern and diverse support systems for open and distance learners. The integration of these into a third generation open and distance learning system will require a fourth component, alluded to but not yet made explicit in the previous sections. This is the necessity for the control and management of the system itself.

When the likely market for a third generation open and distance learning system is to be a proportion of the economically active section of a nation or group of nations such as the 200 million people in this category within the European Community, for example, the scale of the proposed system is very large indeed. In practice, during the first stage of its development, the market will be much smaller than this. At this stage therefore the separation between formation of the policies to be adopted and their practical implementation will not be necessary. The preliminary work will most probably revolve around the establishment of a relatively small pilot system which acts as a microcosm or test-bed for the gradual implementation of a more widely available and sophisticated open and distance learning system. At any stage of development the system requires a focus to which all its contributors (authors, programmers, tutors, administrators and learners) can be stably related. This has been termed elsewhere (Whiting and Bell, 1987) as an 'access station', interpreted to mean a central facility possessing the resources and links to support the contributors. The areas of responsibility within this access station are:

a. acquisition and assembly of instructional material
b. teaching, tutorial and advice systems
c. monitoring and modelling activities
d. database and telecommunication links and storage
e. administrative and data processing systems
f. external links and relationships.

Each of these areas have already been discussed in preceding sections, though not precisely under these headings. Each should be equally represented upon a management committee, which will manage the centre. The management of the centre should be a mixture of system evaluation, policy and planning and solicitation of data, information and advice from the major contributors to the activities of the centre. The analysis of these data will be carried out by the administrative and data processing systems under direction from the access centre administrator. Representatives of the learners using the system provided by the centre should also be included in the management committee, as should representatives from external bodies which contribute to the centre financially or otherwise. The centre's management committee will be answerable to the prime source of its original establishment, such as, for example, the European Commission and its appointed evaluators. Rapid evolution of such centres based upon their own and other centres' experience will have to be a feature of their development, partly because rapid solutions are required to an increasingly acute training and education shortfall and partly because of the speed of progress in the new information technologies. This role of the management committee should be regarded, in the early stages at least, as the most important.

Establishment of one or more access centres will require substantial funding, since research and development of its components and their integration into a prototype system of third generation open and distance learning will require much effort on the part of a wide and disparate community of developers over a period of two to five years. A recent estimate (Report, 1986) suggests that the development of this component of any European system will require in the region of 4,000 to 5,000 man years of effort over seven years as well as the necessary capital expenditure on equipment, accommodation and other facilities, including trial implementations to test the prototype systems which are to be developed. Such a scale of expenditure is less than might be expected because of the stress placed upon exploitation of existing facilities produced for other purposes, but it is nevertheless not at a level which national governments could reasonably be expected to devote to education and training. However, one of the key concepts in the philosophy of the European Commission's funding for research and development is that of 'additionality'. In short, this is the idea that the Commission will preferentially consider research and development programmes that are beyond the resources of a single nation within the Community (hence JET and fusion research) or those where the perceived objectives and results are likely to benefit all, or a majority of Community nations, rather than just one. A European third generation open and distance learning system fulfils both of these requirements.

For cost-effectiveness, it has been stressed throughout that development of such a system has to take maximum advantage of developments relevant to the system which will occur for other reasons, such as the introduction of progressively more powerful and flexible computers into the business environment. This will not only make the development of such a system more economic (and hence more attractive to funding bodies such as the European Commission) but will also largely ensure that the system remains compatible with the audience which will make use of its facilities. The pragmatism of such an approach will do much to gain its acceptance by those who will provide the finance to develop it, and its acceptance by the community of users to which the services will be sold.

Conclusions

This chapter has attempted to set out some ideas and speculations about what will be needed for the development of a large, modern and expandable open and distance learning system which will complement and extend existing education and training provision. It has also been written to provoke argument, discussion and disagreement in the hope that a wider sharing of views will result in the specification and development of something resembling the advanced system which this chapter advocates for European open and distance learning. However, whilst such interaction and argument as the paper contains may demonstrate a very pragmatic and objectively based analysis of one author's view of the ways forward, it has yet to put forward a human viewpoint, and more importantly, the viewpoint of a user of such a system. Accordingly, a short scenario of one likely user's experiences is presented below.

The learner lives in a post-industrial society and has a job in the lower managerial levels of a company which has offices in three other EC nations. He (or she — choose your own orientation) speaks two languages; that of his own nation and another with a wide currency within the Community. He has a flat in a small town within one hour's commuting reach of a provincial capital, but his visits to the nation's main capital are infrequent because of the distance and expense involved. Besides which, his income is lower than he likes and he wants to obtain either promotion within his current company, or move to another company. He thinks that the second alternative is better because promotion in his own branch is slow. Besides that, he would like to move to the capital because of its greater opportunities and beause of its cultural life. His local university runs few part-time courses and both it and the two local colleges of further education do not provide courses which are entirely relevant to what he wants to do. At the end of a day's work he also doesn't want to stay in the provincial capital to go to evening classes since he's tired and in any case he has a young family and his partner works full time as well. He has asked his company for day release to attend a course but the company training committee have ruled against it because they don't consider it relevant to his position or status within the company. However, one member of the committee happened to mention the address and electronic mail number of the community open learning centre. He has access to an information system at work and sends the centre an enquiry. In return he receives a screen form to complete, together with some further information by conventional post. This tells him that for a little more than twice the fees for his day release course he can enrol on an open and distance learning course which can be tailored to his requirements, delivered to a powerful computer which he leases from the open learning centre and uses when he likes at home. The centre is even willing to assist him in persuading his company training committee to disburse some financial support, the prime arguments being that the course he will undertake is more relevant to his company than any which he could attend within his local area, and the study time will not involve any more than minor loss of time at work.

The training committee agrees to meet half his expenses and he enrols on the course. He takes delivery of the learner workstation and the local engineer spends an evening with him showing him how to access the main system to get initial guidance about the nature and use of the open and distance learning system. The next post brings him several documents, a videodisc and a set of discs to install, complete with an automated installation program suite. Within one week he is thoroughly familiar with the ways and means of using the system, both on- and offline, and has already been contacted by over 40 other learners who are enrolled on the same course as he has chosen. Most of them are within his own country but 11 of them are not and he thinks it will be quite interesting to communicate with these, since he has not visited their own countries at all. Two of them are not very proficient in the languages in which the course is offered, and since they know he is bilingual (he permitted the open learning system to publish electronically a short, mutually agreed 'contact' biography on the course electronic noticeboard) they have asked him for help in understanding the course material. Soon he is fully involved (to the dismay of his partner, who finds that he has less time for their social and domestic life) and progressing well. Though he can type, he finds that use of the mouse WIMP interface is quicker and much more convenient. His telephone bill doubles, though this is partially compensated for by the decrease in his social life. His children get used to seeing less of him too. His supervisor at work is sometimes surprised by his increase in knowledge and ability to make decisions. Reports to the company training committee (which he has agreed that the open learning centre may submit to his employer) on his progress are generally favourable. The training committee begins to realize that other people in the company may well benefit from the same system of training, but decide to wait and see what the result of the first course is upon their employee.

A year or so later he takes some professional examinations in the provincial capital and passes them. His company takes note of his success and offers him a higher-level job in the capital. Meanwhile other people in his company, and one or two of his friends have enrolled on open learning courses which they think will help them. He finds that he is acting quite often as an adviser and helper of others making use of the open learning system, some in his own area but others who live elsewhere. His advice is now being sought by the open learning centre on matters to do with both helping new users and the design of the open learning system. His main recommendation to them is to the effect that there is a lot of youth unemployment in the provincial capital and environs, and that the centre should do something about it.

At this point almost anything could happen; he might take the better job in the capital or he might get involved in attracting the local unemployed people to the open learning system, or he might enrol on another, higher-level course. Certainly he will have more opportunities than he had before and will be better experienced and trained to take advantage of them. What actually happens is left for the reader to imagine.

This is only one scenario; many others are possible, some of which will not be so optimistic. However, the system which he experienced is already directly achievable within two to three years from now, given the will, the finance and the encouragement of a market to use it. The gap between existing educational and training provision, on the one hand, and the need for more, on the other, gets wider every year and only a distributed and flexible system, such as the one advocated here, has any chance at all of meeting the need for a better trained and educated population to maintain and increase the standards of living to which the members of post-industrial societies have become accustomed. One final point, however: whilst such an objective may seem laudable, there is another even more so. Not all nations are as well-endowed as those which can afford to develop and implement such a system. It makes excellent sense (as well as fulfilling a moral imperative) to ensure that the system is implemented rapidly in less well-favoured nations in order that they might also make use of it as part of a means to develop an equivalent standard of living in their own individual societies. Education and training should not be restricted to the privileged few; it has to be made truly open and available to all who wish to make use of it. Open and distance learning is the only way to see that this happens.

References

Barker, P G (1987) *Author Languages for CAL* Macmillan Education: London

Block, J H (1971) *Mastery Learning: Theory and Practice* Holt, Rinehart and Winston: New York

Bloom, B S (1968) Learning for mastery *Evaluation Comment* 1 (2), 1-13 CSEIP-UCLA: USA

Hodgson, V E (1986) The interrelationship between support and learning materials *PLET*, 23 (1), 56-61

Laaser, W (1987) Effective methods for meeting student needs in telecommunications-supported distance education in Whiting, J and Bell, D A (eds) *Tutoring and Monitoring Facilities for European Open Learning* Elsevier/North Holland: Amsterdam

Report (1986) *Draft Final Report to the European Commission on Phase II of the DELTA Proposals* Directorate General XIII Telecommunications, Information Industry and Innovation Commission of the European Communities: Brussels, Belgium

Self, J (1987) User modelling in open learning systems in Whiting, J and Bell, D A (eds) *Tutoring and Monitoring Facilities for European Open Learning* Elsevier/North Holland: Amsterdam

Washburne, C W (1922) Educational measurements as a key to individualizing instruction and promotion *Journal of Educational Research* 5, 195-206

Whiting, J (1984) Cognitive and student assessments of a CAL package designed for mastery learning *Computers and Education* 8 (1), 58-67

Whiting, J (1985) The use of a computer tutorial as a replacement for human tuition in a mastery learning strategy *Computers and Education* 9 (2) 101-12

Whiting, J (1986) Student opinion of tutorial CAL *Computers and Education* 10 (2), 281-292

Whiting, J and Bell, D A (eds) (1987) *Tutoring and Monitoring Facilities for European Open Learning* Elsevier/North Holland: Amsterdam

Part 2:National perspectives

5. Information technology and education in the UK: a survey of recent developments

Rhys Gwyn

Summary: The author examines the lessons learned from developments in recent years in the uses of information and communication technology in schools in the UK. He outlines the achievements of the national Microelectronics Education Programme, but does not see government support as motivated by educational considerations alone.

Grassroots movements, particularly the demand from the primary sector, have helped to develop an awareness of the importance of content-free or 'tool' software. A framework for analysis of the educational potential of such software is provided, but there are also wider perspectives, drawing upon technologies such as electronic mail, video storage and satellite transmission. As yet, we are only at the beginning of potential change, and we must anticipate major re-orientations in our thinking about the teacher-learner relationship and about the institutional structures of education.

Introduction

This chapter attempts to summarize some recent important developments in the educational takeup of the new information and communication technologies NICT) by schools in England and Wales; it also attempts to extract certain key learnings from the summary and to suggest that it is now possible to see identifiable developmental paths emerging from what was at first a very open-ended and unstructured situation.

Inevitably, any such statement about the picture in England and Wales has to rely on an element of generalization, since national bodies — notably the Department of Education and Science (DES) — can only guide the education systems of the UK; they cannot dictate curriculum practice. Thus the kind of statement which it is legitimate to make about parallel developments in France, under a central Ministry of National Education, simply cannot be made about the UK. Instead, one has to trace what appear to be the patterns to be found in the different approaches adopted by the separate local education authorities, acknowledging that what is true of a great many may well be quite untrue of a significant minority.

Nonetheless, there is a picture that can now be identified. What is more, it is an appropriate moment at which to do so, and this for two reasons.

The first is that schools in England and Wales have by now had well over half a decade of experimenting with the NICT. Indeed, many schools have a far longer record of using computers, in some cases going back as far as the mid-1960s. What we have come to know as 'computer studies', though it is no longer typical of educational use of the NICT, has been on the syllabus of some schools for over 20 years, and inevitably a great deal has been learned from that experience. But it is nonetheless true that, so far as the generality of schools are concerned, it was the availability of microcomputers (and of one micro in particular) from the early 1980s that really initiated the surge of interest and of activity that has as one of its outcomes our present state of understanding.

The second reason for the timeliness of this stocktaking is that it was not only schools that found the availability of the then new microcomputer to be of interest: so also did government. One of the manifest indications of this interest was the decision to set up the Microelectronics Education Programme, a scheme which, along with that operating in France, has rightly been seen as one of the most important attempts made by any government to give a lead (within the context of the constraints on government intervention to which I have already referred) in the educational takeup of the new technologies. The Microelectronics Education Programme (MEP) generated a great deal of interest, both at home and abroad; it provided a focus for developmental activity on a wide scale and, like all good government schemes, it has now (1986) drawn to a close, having run its allotted course. It would be quite impossible, in fact, to attempt any review of the use of computers and related technologies in schools in England and Wales over the past few years without focusing, at least initially, upon MEP. It seems appropriate, therefore, to take stock relatively soon after the demise of the programme, and to try to see just what has been learned from the experience of the 1980s.

This is not to say that MEP encompassed the totality of development in England and Wales: far from it. I shall seek also to identify those areas of more recent, and also still imminent, developments which go far beyond the remit of the MEP concept and which point the way ahead. It is my personal belief that some of these developments may yet prove to be quite revolutionary for our established patterns of thinking about education.

It may help to put the remarks which follow into perspective if I set out at once one article of faith about the role of the new technologies in education. It is that they are important, not as technology *per se*, but as tools with which the processes of learning and teaching can be enhanced, and I see it as quite essential that educationists view them in this light. I believe that the pattern of development since 1980 or so has been, in fact, one that has taken us to at least this level of understanding, and the chapter will attempt to argue this interpretation. In examining the uses of the new technologies of information and communication in schools, the concerns we are addressing are pedagogical and not technological; our targets are determined by the learning needs of children and not by hardware or software design. The technology, like all technology, is unimportant in itself. What is of the utmost importance is the use we choose to make of it.

The Microelectronics Education Programme

MEP — a brief survey

The national Microelectronics Education Programme (MEP) for England, Wales and Northern Ireland was announced in 1979 by the then (1974–79) Labour Government of James Callaghan, rethought by the newly-elected administration of Margaret Thatcher in 1979, had its Director appointed late in 1980 and finally produced its strategy paper in April 1981 (Fothergill, 1981). The Programme, which was never intended to be institutionalized on a permanent basis, was finally brought to a close in 1986 and its structures dismantled; this was a process sometimes misconstrued by observers abroad as an adverse reflection on MEP but it was, of course, perfectly normal practice in respect of a short-term project of this kind.

It is important to stress that MEP operated in only two of the three education systems of the United Kingdom, ie those of England and Wales and of Northern Ireland. In Scotland, a quite separate scheme, the Scottish Microelectronics Development Programme (SMDP), operated from 1979 onwards, and did so quite independently from MEP although there was a considerable synergy between the two. Within SMDP, for example, there was at the outset a rather greater emphasis on the production of software than was initially characteristic of MEP. Given that the two schemes and their settings were so different, this chapter focuses on MEP only.

At no time was a formal evaluation of MEP envisaged, though recently Her Majesty's Inspectorate (HMI) published a retrospective summary of the achievements of the programme. The overall judgement of their report (DES, 1987) is even-handed and impartial in the best traditions of the Inspectorate. Their main conclusions are positive in respect of materials development and much of the in-service teacher training which was developed, but negative in respect of some factors, notably communication difficulties and the difficulties of avoiding duplication and of ensuring delivery of a final product.

This is not the context in which to offer any alternative to the perspectives of HMI, and an individual perception must be, in any case, subjective. In the preparation of this chapter, however, I have found it interesting to re-read a study which I undertook for the European Cultural Foundation in 1982 and which examined the then still-embryonic MEP in the context of emerging policies for information technology and education (Gwyn, 1982). In the paragraphs which follow, where I attempt to identify what seem to me to be the salient features of the MEP experience, I have looked back to some of the — slightly sceptical — views to which I found myself drawn already in 1982, and have found that hindsight tends to justify much of my scepticism.

MEP and hardware provision

It may be as well to dispose briefly of one point at the outset and to make clear that, whatever else MEP was meant to be, it was not a scheme for placing hardware in the schools. In this respect, it differed from SMDP and, perhaps more markedly, from the strategy adopted by the Ministére de l'Education Nationale in France, where development was postulated upon a programme of steady provision of hardware to schools.

Where support for hardware provision came from in England and Wales was not the Department of Education and Science but the Department of Trade and Industry (DoTI) which offered to all schools subsidized purchase of one microcomputer per school. An interesting sidelight on this provision is that the subsidy applied only to an identified (and very small) range of machines. In that all of these were of British manufacture — insofar as that can be said of any micro — the DoTI was quite possibly acting in breach of European Community law. The French government acted in precisely the same manner.

The DoTI scheme was an important catalyst to the introduction of hardware into the schools, but its eventual importance should not be over-emphasized. The first machine apart, schools — ie their local education authorities (LEAs) and their parent-teacher associations — have had to provide their own hardware. Many are indeed impressively equipped, others very poorly, but not even those schools with relatively impressive provision come anywhere near a level of true adequacy. There is still a very long way to go in the UK, as elsewhere, before schools may be said to be properly resourced for the NICT.

There exists in fact a double problem. One aspect of this problem is that the expenditure that has been incurred in respect of hardware often seems to be viewed as a 'one-off', with no thought on the part of providers for the inevitable replacement of machines as they become worn out. The other dimension is that the need for replacement does not stem from wear and tear alone but also from obsolescence. One sees no evidence that authorities recognize the need for total replacement of hardware over, at the very least, a seven-year cycle, yet this is probably what is required. There are more senses than one in which the world of education is far from realizing the implications of the new technologies, and this is potentially a major problem. However, it is not a problem that ever fell within the remit of MEP; I return later to the way in which the fortunes of hardware manufacturers influenced educational development in England and Wales.

The emphasis on regional structure

One of the key features of the MEP, when the scheme was finally implemented, was its regional structure. In order to participate in MEP, the 104 local education authorities in England, Wales and Northern Ireland were required to group themselves into 14 regions, 12 of which were in England. Only co-operation on such a regional basis would allow the authorities to bid for MEP funds. Regional centres were set up, each with its director and staff. This regional structure dominated the whole MEP operation.

At the time, the regional strategy immediately aroused doubt on two counts. The first was its artificiality in terms of existing structures, in that it imposed upon LEAs a form of co-operation for which there was essentially no precedent, and which indeed ran contrary to the tradition of complete independence of LEAs from one another. In the event, the processes of agreeing on regional groupings and of deciding precisely what activity should be located in any one authority or institution did give rise to a fair amount of quite inevitable jockeying for advantage, though the process was completed surprisingly quickly. In some cases — not all — the groupings worked well; indeed, in the former MEP region in which my own institution is located the computer education advisers who formed the core of the MEP regional management committee have continued to work in voluntary association after the demise of the programme, and there is widespread acceptance that the heavy demands of development make inter-LEA collaboration highly sensible.

The second doubt entertained about the regional strategy was perhaps better founded. My concern in 1982 was that the MEP laid a 'high emphasis on ...."operationalization", the process of getting the thing to work' (Gwyn, 1982) and hindsight suggests that this concern was justified. It was inevitable that once the regional strategy had been decided it would account for a very high proportion of programme budget. In those regions where the regional centre was both active and effective (the two qualities are not necessarily synonymous) such expenditure was perhaps well incurred, but informal consensus suggests that only half of the centres, and this at a generous estimate, could be said ever to have fallen into this category. The question has to be asked, then, whether overall the regional strategy upon which MEP was based was the most effective means of delivering the necessary innovation.

To say this is not to undervalue the great deal of work done on some regions; nor, particularly, should the contribution of the central directorate team be overlooked. The work of the directorate, under Richard Fothergill, was highly motivational, and amongst other things did much to promote the national and international visibility of the programme in terms both of making known many of the lessons learned from development and, more prosaically, encouraging a takeup of British hardware and software in a number of countries. Further, if one is critical of the way in which the MEP infrastructure soaked up much of the budget, one has to acknowledge that it is difficult to envisage what a workable alternative might have been. There remains nonetheless a judgement that is of relevance to innovation strategies generally and not just to those concerned with information technology, namely that the medium can all too easily become the message — that there was a sense in which MEP as a programme, with all that that entailed in organization and administration, overshadowed what MEP was supposed to achieve.

Materials production

This is by no means to deny the importance of the programme. One area, for example, in which the impact of MEP was beneficial was that of materials production.

This production did not happen immediately; in the Scottish programme, as I have remarked, the production of software was earlier highlighted as a priority. But what did begin to happen, sadly rather late in the life of the programme, was production of a series of resource materials targeted essentially at the training of teachers — a key point, to which I return below. These packs contained, typically, a certain amount of software and of program notes and instructions, backed up with appropriate readings; in some cases — for example, materials connected with the educational use of viewdata and viewdata simulations — such support enabled innovative areas of work to be introduced. In addition to this centrally supported activity, many LEAs and institutions were grant-aided by MEP to produce packages specific to given subject areas. Much of this material — to take one example, the steady stream of resources developed on Humberside — was of first-rate quality. Finally, other packages, produced commercially, received considerable publicity through the MEP grapevine (each regional centre served as a resource centre where teachers could browse through currently available software before committing scarce school resources to a purchase) and this did much to disseminate good practice.

But what did not emerge from the programme was as revealing in a sense, as what did. With hindsight, one is astonished that MEP did not stimulate production of the one item which would have been invaluable, namely a standardized database program that could have been used across the secondary curriculum; such a program was in fact produced for the primary school. This one item alone would have done a great deal to promote classroom use of the new technologies, but it was not to be. Neither, for that matter, did either a spreadsheet or a secondary word processing package emerge from MEP, though all these products were available in one form or another from commercial sources.

What was, however, the most intriguing phenomenon of all was that the best of these support materials were produced for an area which, at the outset, did not fall within the remit of MEP at all. This area has been hinted at already; it was the primary sector. I return on page 105 to the quite fascinating issue of the momentum generated in primary use of the new technologies; suffice it to say for the moment that much of the credit for the primary support work carried out under the MEP banner can be put down to the effect of the committed leadership of Anita Straker and of a great deal of hard work by her small team. Certainly the stream of resource packs that were produced — on primary language work, on the micro and infant teaching, on problem-solving, Logo and on mathematics — did a great deal to promote development at this very important level of education, and this output has to be regarded as one of the outstanding successes of the programme.

Teacher training

One weak element in the performance of MEP related to the provision of teacher training.

From a very early stage in the process of introducing the NICT into schools it has been apparent that an important barrier to progress has been the lack of appropriately trained teachers. Indeed, this has been a major dilemma, because the problem is in fact a three-cornered one: it has been difficult to provide adequate training for teachers because applications of the new technology appropriate to the classroom, on which training might have been based, have not been available. Appropriate classroom applications have not been available because it has not been easy to arrive at a clear picture of what the eventual goal is thought to be: how, in short, the NICT might best contribute to the processes of teaching and learning. It has been difficult to construct this clear picture because we have not had teachers trained in an understanding of the potential of the NICT — and so the argument continues.

In fact, of course, each of these three factors — the supply of teachers who have been appropriately trained, the ready availability of suitable classroom applications, and an overall conceptual structure within which to locate developmental activity — is a necessary component of the total picture; they do not follow in sequence one from another. But what has been important, not just in England and Wales but also elsewhere in Europe and in North America, is that the cost element relative to each of these three components is not equally balanced. A conceptual framework may be developed, in fact, at virtually negligible cost by a relatively small group. Providing material resources, whether hardware or software, is clearly far more expensive, and much has been made by national governments in, for example, the UK and France, of the supposedly vast amounts — 'supposedly' because in both countries the sums in question have been totally inadequate — spent on hardware provision and software development. But even this expenditure seems trivial when compared with the true costs of training teachers.

Much can be done through initial or pre-service teacher training. However, it has also to be recognized that this is a very long-term form of investment in renewal of the profession, since the new teacher emerging from initial training is seldom in a position to make a major impact on practices in the school in which he or she begins work. Moreover, the speed of response demanded in respect of the introduction of the NICT into schools virtually pre-empted the question: whatever might be achieved via initial training, it was clear that a major thrust was required in respect of the re-training of teachers already in service. The need for a strategy in this area has been recognized by every country where a serious attempt has been made to come to grips with the educational implications of the new technologies; France has led the way in the adoption of such a strategy at the national level, and has done so since the 1960s.

It is, of course, a very expensive strategy indeed since, if it is to be implemented properly, it calls for a massive expenditure on teacher release and replacement time. Moreover, it presupposes expenditure on one of the other elements, namely hardware and software resources.

The MEP plan identified teacher re-training as an important component of strategy, and considerable efforts were made to mount short-term 'awareness' courses, of which much was made. However, the 'short' in 'short-term' was all too accurate, with the courses in question typically lasting some two days. This is a generalization, and it is certainly true that, within the context of MEP, longer courses were mounted, and mounted successfully. But what was never remotely possible, given the very limited financial and human resources which were available to the MEP regional centres, was that the programme could make a serious impact on massive in-service demands generated nationally by the new technologies.

We touch here on one of the basic problems with which MEP was confronted. At the time of the introduction of the scheme, no one could have pretended that the existing institutions responsible for training teachers were geared up to take on a special training role for the NICT in schools. Consequently, there was an argument for establishing the completely separate network of regional centres, but with hindsight it can also be argued that the relatively large amounts expended on staffing and running the centres — which, by their definition, had only a temporary lifespan — might have been better directed towards bringing the permanent training institutions to the point where they could in fact make the contribution required of them. In the event, these institutions had to develop their capacity to train teachers for the NICT with only a modicum of support from MEP or, for that matter, from central government.

But we have also learned from the experience of the 1980s that the importance of the involvement of teacher training goes beyond what I said earlier about the insights that teachers can bring to bear on the development of appropriate classroom uses of the new technologies. There is also a question of attitude which must also be acknowledged, and this is of critical importance.

The NICT emerged as a new factor to be taken into account by schools and teachers in the early 1980s. As it happened, this was also a period of considerable upheaval in schools, certainly in the UK. Classroom rolls were falling, closures and amalgamations were proceeding apace, and the political debate surrounding education, involving accountability on issues such as racism and gender, grew in intensity. The resources available to schools, measured in even such basic terms as funds for textbooks and materials, were steadily cut back, while the teaching profession itself became involved in a bitter and protracted dispute over pay and conditions of service with a government from which the profession felt increasingly alienated. This situation, of course, has persisted to the time at which this chapter is being prepared. In this climate, the time required for professional renewal *vis-à-vis* the NICT was often not available and the constant promoting of the new technologies was seen by many as yet another demand on an already burdened profession; during the industrial action undertaken by the teacher unions, participation in formal in-service work was ruled out. There was resentment also of the fact that relatively large sums could be invested in the new technology at a time when it was not possible to buy such basic items as textbooks or materials.

What has been remarkable, in fact, is that such a great deal has been achieved by the teachers and those who train them despite the generally unfavourable climate. Indeed, one has no hesitation in saying that the fact that we have reached even our present state of understanding of what the NICT may bring to education is due in very large measure to the enormous reserves of goodwill and professional commitment that ordinary classroom teachers are prepared to bring to any development which is seen to contribute positively to the learning of their pupils. It is in this sense that attitude has been all-important: attitude which rejects fear of the unknown technology and which is prepared to make a commitment to its largely unexplored potential. But the key to this commitment is the provision of training which is seen to be appropriate. Experience has demonstrated time and again that most teachers, if shown applications for which they can see a classroom use, are very ready to commit themselves to the further training needed to enable them to make full use of the technology offer. It in here that teacher training holds the key to progress.

Certainly MEP achieved some measure of success in respect of teacher training, especially in terms of introductory or 'awareness' courses, but that was as far as it went. The real task of training teachers to understand and use the new technologies to their full educational potential lay far beyond the resources made available to the programme. That is a task that continues, not only in England and Wales, but in all countries seeking to introduce the NICT into schools, and it is likely to do so for the foreseeable future as training seeks to catch up with the technology offer and our improving capacity to exploit that offer.

International visibility

An area which may be dealt with briefly, but in which MEP was remarkably successful, was that of achieving international visibility for its activities and for the UK approach generally.

On the entrepreneurial side, MEP and British manufacturers collaborated in concluding quite large-scale agreements with more than one government abroad. While activity of this sort related more to questions of exports than to the educational issues which are the proper concern of the *World Yearbook of Education*, there is a point here which cannot be ignored. It is that — and again both the French and the British examples will serve — the support given by national governments is by no means motivated by purely educational considerations, and I return to this point on page 105. For the moment it is perhaps sufficient to note that MEP enjoyed a considerable success in promoting abroad a takeup of British hardware and British software, and that this perhaps helped to establish a myth of a national programme that was successful in all its aspects. The DES Report already referred to, however, does point out that this activity was by no means central to the remit of MEP.

There was, however, another and more valuable — from the educational point of view — dimension to the international exposure of MEP. During the period of MEP activity, the Commission of the European Community mounted a series of important conferences, at the European level, on the educational implications of the NICT, the first being held at Marseilles in 1984. These conference provided a forum for debate at a critical time in the development of national policies, and it was clear, on each occasion, that the input of MEP representatives was highly valued by participants from other countries. Indeed, one of the most successful of these conferences was held in the UK, in Newcastle upon Tyne in 1986, with a heavy emphasis on UK software and classroom strategies. Given the quite marked cultural differences that do exist between the education systems of Europe, it was highly interesting to observe the very positive response shown by many participants from other member states of the Community in the materials shown. Contact at this level has led to practical co-operation in respect of more than one project, but what was more important still was the opportunity of sharing perspectives on challenges which, despite cultural differences, remain remarkably similar from one country to another. In this area, MEP made a significant contribution.

Observations

These are but a few observations on a scheme which quite certainly did much to promote, in the UK, the concept of 'computers for schools'. There is no intention here, as I made clear at the outset, to offer any kind of evaluation of MEP, and no one clear picture of the programme in fact ever emerged. What was perhaps most important about the programme was that it did convey a message, namely that the new technologies which were so much in the news for a variety of reasons actually did have something to offer to education. The scheme generated a climate in which teachers felt, rightly or wrongly, that if they did not somehow acquaint themselves with the potential of the NICT, they would be missing out on an important development; this feeling was of course strengthened by the fact that so many pupils were so evidently computer-literate, thanks to the hobbyist approach by which so many parents were captivated. The scheme did provide a great many teachers with a supportive environment in which to take their first steps towards conversancy with the new technologies, and admittedly rather late in its life, it produced some materials which proved to be quite invaluable.

The Microelectronics Education Programme was by no means an undiluted success, but it gave an impetus to the introduction of the new technology into schools which was, at the time, quite invaluable. The fact that we have now moved beyond what MEP was trying to do is just one measure of its value.

The state supported approach

Political and economic motivation

There are, however, other dimensions to a scheme such as MEP. MEP was an example of the state supported approach: a scheme initiated and supported at government level. As we have seen, the French government was also early in the field with a national plan for the insertion of the new technologies into the school system; some of the reports associated with the French plan, notably Nora and Minc (1978), are key documents in the development of our understanding of the importance of the NICT. In both countries the level of investment has been relatively high — quite inadequate, but high relative to what was being done elsewhere, which as often as not was nothing at all. But also in the case of both countries, it has been abundantly clear that the introduction of the new technologies into schools has been as much motivated by economic as by educational concern. In other words, the attraction for governments has been that of producing a computer-literate workforce able to support the move towards a post-industrial economy; there are references in plenty to 'keeping ahead of the Japanese' (or French, or Americans, or British, depending on the national context in which one happens to be writing) to support this interpretation. I have dealt with these issues at some length in a report prepared for the FAST Programme of the Commission of the EEC (Gwyn, 1987) and do not propose to retrace the ground here, but it is certainly my firm conviction that the idea of improving the quality of education through the introduction of computers, as a worthwhile end in itself, has been relatively low on the list of governmental priorities. There is nothing unduly surprising about this; in fact, one would be surprised if the reverse were the case.

What has been at the heart of the 'computers in schools' movement, however, has been an intriguing paradox. The new technologies, and all that they mean in terms of automation of process and increased economic efficiency, are seen as the key to the future economic well-being of Europe (see, for example, Mackintosh, 1986) and it is therefore highly desirable that pupils in schools acquire mastery over them; this is the external motivation. But the technologies are, by their very nature, ideally suited to educational use, so that what is imposed on schools from the outside offers, in fact, solutions to many of the problems with which schools are normally faced. The essential point is that the NICT are precisely that: technologies of information and of communication. As such they engage directly two of the skill areas basic to education, namely the processing of information and the act of communicating. This is not to say that school does not also deal with other areas, such as inter-personal and creativity skills (though here too the technology can contribute) but merely to point out that information and communication are certainly central components of the educational process. To take concrete examples: databases and word processing applications have rightly been central to the takeup of NICT by the world of commerce and of management generally. But the reasons which make these applications central in those instances are paralleled precisely by reasons which make them equally central in the classroom: they are efficient tools for mastering the welter of 'information' with which we are confronted, and for communicating that information.

This point is developed further on page 109. The particular aspect that needs to be drawn out here is that governments may have some realization of the future economic importance of the new technologies they have so assiduously promoted in the schools. It is very much to be doubted whether any government has a full appreciation (or indeed any appreciation at all) of the educational revolution that they may unwittingly have released by promoting the use of the technologies in schools. There is a very great deal of educating to be done at the political level before this point is grasped.

The extent of investment

Another point which has yet to be grasped fully is the extent of the investment required at national level if innovation is to proceed and proceed effectively. We have seen already that this investment must touch upon a number of areas, which include everything covered by the umbrella term 'resource provision' as well as teacher training and re-training. Each offers problems of different kinds and at different levels of demand.

Resource provision is indeed an all-embracing term. It would be easier to quantify if the technology were static, but of course it is not. A few examples must suffice.

As we have seen already, hardware provision cannot be regarded as a 'one-off'. It is not merely a question of the need to replace machines as they wear out. It is necessary to accept that any given microcomputer, for example, will become obsolete before it physically wears out; this is not a reflection of the longevity of the machines but of the speed of their obsolescence. The classic example is Acorn Computers' BBC micro, which has been at the centre of developments in UK schools: this machine is no longer available in the form in which so many teachers learned to use it. What is even more to the point, even in its present form, it represents an outdated technology. Many will argue that it is, and will remain for some years, perfectly usable in schools, and this is certainly true. What is also true is that this very usability risks fossilizing development at a relatively primitive stage. The machine in question is one generation behind the *de facto* standard that dominated the mid-1980s, namely that of the IBM PC, while that standard itself has been surpassed by the same manufacturer's new standards, announced in 1987.

Issues such as these remain to be faced, and a failure to face them invites wastage at best and disaster at worst. An example that comes to mind is that of the Domesday Project, an imaginative experiment in the development of a highly innovative video resource. The Domesday discs offer classrooms a sophistication of resource hitherto unheard of, but the price at which the hardware is on offer, despite a generous government subsidy, puts it way beyond the reach of all but the best-endowed of schools. It is a classic illustration of the conflict of motives, educational and economic, underlying so much thinking at the national level.

The irresistible momemtum: primary education

A movement from the grassroots

What has been particularly fascinating in the UK, as has been remarked already, has been the spontaneous generation of activity at the primary (five-ten age range) level.

In the original strategy for MEP there was no mention of primary education, and it was quite common, as recently as 1983 or even 1984, to hear considerable scepticism expressed as to whether the NICT had any contribution at all to make to teaching and learning at this level. Similarly, planning at the national level in France was entirely directed at the secondary level, while in many of the West German *Länder* the prevailing attitude seemed to be that there existed, at the upper-secondary level, the subject area 'informatics', and little else.

Against this background, the veritable explosion of innovation which has taken place at primary level in England and Wales is nothing short of astonishing. Children at junior level use databases and word processing; they communicate — even internationally — using electronic mail, they build viewdata simulations, use control technology and download pictures from weather satellites. Even at infant level (ie five to seven-year-olds) pupils use simple word processing packages and even databases, as well as the more obvious computer-aided learning packages. And the use of Logo at this level is so much a classic case of the apt use of the new technology in education (Goodyear, 1984: Lawler, 1985) that there is no need to elaborate on it here.

What is astonishing about these developments is their spontaneity. The drive for computers at primary level came entirely from interested and enthusiastic teachers, from a few enlightened authorities prepared to experiment and, very often, from parents — sometimes with computer industry links — who felt convinced that their children could benefit even at an early age from experience of the new technologies. This enthusiasm led to a rapid penetration of the technology into primary schools, very much on an *ad hoc* basis, it has to be said — indeed the actual spread of machines is still both inadequate and uneven — and at the same time to a great deal of developmental work in which MEP and other bodies had perforce to participate.

What is not astonishing about this phenomenon, or at least not to anyone with any first-hand knowledge of the primary schools of England and Wales, is that the primary school should have provided the perfect testing-ground for innovation and development, so much so that it is quite reasonable to claim that more has been learned about the true potential of the NICT in the classroom through work at this level than through work at secondary level. There are sound reasons why this should be so, and it is worth examining them.

The cross-curricular approach

The secondary school lays a number of constraints upon innovation. One is the demand of preparation for public examinations, the pressure of which is often hostile to any innovative approach. Another is the compartmentalization of school activity in terms of curriculum 'subjects' with little chance for cross-fertilization. It is no coincidence, and certainly a matter for grave concern, that in many secondary schools NICT provision is seen still as the province of the mathematics or sciences departments.

The primary school presents a totally different environment, and one which in many ways is educationally superior. The absence of examination pressure allows for an emphasis on the development of learning, creative and inter-personal skills (though recent policy announcements at government level may put this climate at risk). The absence of subject divisions institutionalized along departmental lines means that the primary teacher can relate a number of different disciplinary approaches to a common theme. Shared activity and collaborative project work is part and parcel of the normal primary school day. Above all, the emphasis of the primary school is pedagogical — that is, on creating conditions for learning appropriate to the needs of the children — rather than, as is too often the case at secondary level, instructional, ie where the exigencies of external factors such as the existence of a recognized 'body of knowledge' or the demands of an examination syllabus determine what is taught.

What this has meant, almost from the outset, is that the new technology has been experimented with in the primary classroom for its potential as a tool for teaching and learning. It is true that clear answers did not appear overnight, and that much early software was of a rather elementary form of computer-aided learning, often simplistic exercises designed to test very limited skills. But what emerged very rapidly was a rejection of this simplistic approach, as teachers quickly realized that there was no argument for using the computer for teaching tasks which could be approached far more effectively by other, traditional, means. Instead — and here the influence of the primary team within MEP was invaluable — attention very quickly shifted to more content-free tools which could be used across large areas of the primary curriculum. Primary database programs were very soon available, as were word processing packages suitable for young pupils. One highly important device has been the concept keyboard, a touch-sensitive and programmable device which allows the teacher to configure overlay sheets, placed on the keyboard and to which the keyboard is programmed to respond by producing, on the screen, text generated by a pupil's key-press. Such overlays are designed to meet the learning needs of a particular class or even of an individual child; this has been a major advance in the teaching of reading and writing skills and has meant that, in many schools, children are in fact using technology from the earliest possible age.

Thus what has come out of the primary school has been a highly important emphasis on the new technologies and their pedagogical value as a classroom tool. This is so critical to our understanding of the role of the NICT in education that it merits a section to itself.

Learning — the tool approach

Technologies of information

The importance of the 'tool' approach has been one of the most important lessons learned from the experience of recent years, demonstrating as it does the remarkable degree of fit between the new technologies and the needs of the school.

There is, of course, nothing new about the idea that technology development has implications for education. The most obvious example is the invention of printing, which made possible a degree of educational provision hitherto unthinkable; that the possibility was not immediately taken up to its full potential, in terms of universal education, was a matter of cultural and social constraints, not technological ones. But it is clearly the case, to take just one example, that the mass education movement of the 19th century would not have been possible without the printed book.

There have been false dawns. The best known is Edison's famous claim that the invention of the phonograph would revolutionize education. Nor — fortunately — did the 'teaching machines' of the 1960s and early 1970s ever prove to be the panacea they were thought to be.

The links between technology advance and education are as often, and more importantly, indirect than they are direct. That is to say, for example, that the nature of school in the 19th century (its division into work units, adherence to a programme of learning, the emphases on timetables, obedience and work-oriented values, its characteristically urban setting) was entirely determined by the demands of a society founded on technology advance, though the technology itself found relatively little place in the school.

But what is especially interesting about the implications of the NICT for education is that they are both indirect and direct. They are indirect because of the impact — widely accepted — of the NICT on the socioeconomic bases of Western society and particularly because of their impact on the nature and availability of employment. Thus the NICT are an essential contributory element in the current development of the social and economic context in which school exists. But the implications are also direct, for reasons identified already: that the NICT are by definition to do with information and with communication, two of the essential components of the educational process.

The indirect implications of the NICT for education are a fascinating topic of investigation. It is possible that, within a lifetime, they will bring about radical changes in the nature of school. But this speculation is one that takes us too far away from the scope of this chapter. Moreover, there is more than enough to occupy our thinking as we attempt to analyse the more direct classroom implications of these challenging technologies.

A framework for analysis

In looking at these implications, we have at least managed to see further than the undifferentiated mass of 'computer-assisted learning' software with which at first we appeared to be confronted. This much has been learned from the experiences of the past few years.

More than one attempt has been made at providing a framework through which to analyse the different ways in which the new technologies can be offered in the classroom: here I draw upon that of the Information Technology Group of the Association for Teacher Education in Europe. The analysis focuses essentially on the use of the computer as such, and I look later in more detail at other aspects of the technology.

The important thing, according to this analysis, is to see the potential of applications in terms of a spectrum of possibilities ranging from a support for learning, at one end, to the discharge of a quasi-teaching function at the other. When we view the potential in this light, we are not only given a convenient set of reference points against which to measure specific packages; we are also enabled to see that different applications of the technology in fact invoke quite different pedagogical approaches. A brief summary, which is all that is possible here, will illustrate the range of this spectrum, taking six points along the range.

1. At one end, there are what the analysis refers to as 'tools for thinking and learning'. By this is meant applications which are

completely content-free, which can be used across a number of curriculum areas, but which have as their dominant characteristic the fact that they deliver into the hands of the pupil the full power of the technology in an easily utilizable form. The language Logo is the example *par excellence* of this kind of application; Prolog, if it can be exploited properly, is likely to fall into the same category.

2. Second, we have what are perhaps the most generally useful applications of all, identified as 'tools for organizing knowledge'. These follow the pattern of the classic applications of management and business: database, word processing, spreadsheets and graphics output. These are, like the first category, entirely content-free, but they constitute a separate category inasmuch as they determine more closely the kind of uses which they allow. It is at this point, as much as any, that the critical point about the new technologies being technologies of information can be seen to apply.

3. The third and fourth categories in this analysis display the steady progression from the open-ended, learner-centred, approach, towards the emphasis on teaching. First, there are applications of the simulation or game kind, which are still relatively open in that they do not dictate outcomes precisely, but which are nonetheless relatively specific to given kinds of learning (often the discovery or guided learning approach). There is much excellent primary software of this kind. Then there are applications which do not set out to teach as such, but which provide electronic resources specific to given areas. The new resources becoming available on videodiscs, with their hitherto unimagined speed of access to visual resources, are a case in point.

4. The fifth category identified is what is called 'tutorial software', that is to say, programs which have been written specifically as means of imparting instruction on given topics. This is perhaps the area to which the term computer-assisted learning is most appropriately applied. As an aside, one might remark that the extent to which this approach is or is not found acceptable may be an indicator of certain cultural differences between the British and Usalian view of education. The new videodisc technology may also be quoted in this context, in that it can be used as an excellent instructional — in the sense of training — device for situations where tightly controlled behaviour responses are required; we need to be clear, however, that this is training and not education, an important distinction.

5. The final category, according to this analysis, is that of drill-and-practice applications which do nothing much more than test learning retention. These applications are not to be despised. Used appropriately, they can provide a teacher with valuable information about pupil achievement in certain areas, but it is essential

to remember that this is possible only in a very limited range of areas, and that there would be a great danger in reducing pupil assessment too readily to what can be done by computer.

A preferred choice

The bias of the above analysis is probably clear. In the eyes of those who prepared it, the exciting potential of the new technologies lies in the first categories: in open-ended software that allows children to explore concepts or to organize their knowledge, drawing the while on the full resources of the most powerful tool yet invented. To move in this direction is to place the emphasis on the learner rather than on the teacher, on the process rather than on the outcome, on the development of intellectual skills rather than on the retention of fact. Paradoxically, to use the technologies in these ways is to exercise a humanizing influence on education.

An emphasis at the other end of the spectrum, however, leads to a far narrower concept, based on instruction, on repetition, and on conformist, convergent thinking rather than on thinking which is creative and divergent. This approach is not without its place, but to allow it to dominate our uses of the NICT in education would be disastrous. If we have learned anything from the experiences of the past few years in England and Wales, it is that the future in education lies with the exploitation of the NICT for far more dynamic forms of implementation.

This is not to say that the way ahead is easy to map out: far from it. In the last section of this review, I shall return to the question of the scale of the challenge ahead.

New technologies, wider perspectives

The technology offer does not stand still. The analysis of the last section referred essentially to the NICT in the form of the classroom computer or computers, that is, to a technology used within the constraints of an existing framework for education. We have to recognize also that the technology may affect the framework itself.

There were hints of this already in the previous section: the video-disc provides an interesting focus. With this technology, on present day standards — ie at approximately ten per cent of the standard of five years hence — an active play disc can contain the equivalent of 55,000 still frames or, to refer to a technology more familiar in the classroom, 55,000 transparencies. Any one of these can be located with total accuracy within a second or two, even on a front-to-back search (that is, looking for frame 49,999 when the disc head is positioned at frame 0). The availability of such a resource in the classroom is clearly a development from what is already known, but the size and speed of the resource goes immeasurably beyond what has hither-to been imaginable, and introduces into the classroom a totally new dimension of resource. (We have not yet succeeded in making full use of this resource, but that is another matter and not essential to the argument.) Effectively, resources at this level begin to open out the walls of the classroom and to introduce new windows on the world.

These windows become very much more open once we begin to consider the potential of communications technology. This is an area in which truly remarkable progress has been made, and it will suffice perhaps to point to two examples.

Electronic mail

Electronic mail has been used in classrooms, on a relatively wide scale, for over two years. In the UK, the best known example is that of the Times Network for Schools, which allows classrooms to communicate easily and instantly with each other.

Already a fascinating range of experiments has opened up. At one end, we have very young primary children dialoguing with the spirit of Merlin (who just happens to have found his way into the network) and being led into far-reaching exploration of the lost legends of Arthur — the spirit of Merlin being, of course, a friendly collaborator on another mailbox in the network. At another extreme, I will refer to a project on which I am currently engaged, which involves trainee teachers and school pupils in Manchester and Copenhagen exchanging data for comparative study of the environment in their two countries, the work involving them in the construction of shared databases, in file transfer, in the exchange of language materials and in co-production of 'desktop' newspapers, each group acting as the other's 'foreign correspondent'; at the time of writing, this link is being extended into a veritable network of eight different European countries.

What this kind of project — coupled with, for example, the availability of information bases such as DIALOG or even national viewdata services — does is to open up the classroom to the world. What there is to be learned is no longer constrained by the books available or the knowledge of the teacher; pupils can learn from each other and each other's experience. The possibilities are boundless.

Satellite

Electronic mail, of course, may well travel by satellite, though if it does, the fact is transparent to the user. What has also proved exciting has been the work done by a few enterprising schools and teacher training establishments in downloading information from weather satellites.

A few years ago, activity of this sort would have been unthinkable. Now, there are primary schools involved. The ecosphere has become the context in which the school operates.

These are just examples of applications of the technology which offer
to schools completely new dimensions of resources. Beyond them lie
other possibilities of which we only begin to have a glimmering; the
kind of distance learning networks postulated by the European Community DELTA project is just one example of the potential offered by
the NICT. The takeup — or failure — of this potential, of course, will
be determined by political and economic considerations, and not on
educational grounds, but we are at least in a position to formulate some
first impressions of the scale of change in our educational structures
which may be invoked, and we need to look briefly at this issue.

The challenge to established practice

The potential challenges come on many fronts. There is no doubt, for
example, that the growing importance of the information industries has
already brought about important changes, of more than one kind, in
the nature and extent of employment opportunities available to young
school leavers, and we may expect to see emphasis on information, communication, and, above all, life-long learning skills feature even more
prominently in future curricula.

We may also anticipate that the NICT will contribute to a significant degree to changes at deeper levels, on the cultural and philosophical
planes. Writer after writer, too numerous to mention but among them
Bolter (1984), Evans (1931), Jennings (1985), Ladurie (1978) and
Mandrou (1973), has sketched the extent of change that takes place in
social and cultural patterns over time, and has shown how the thinking
behind technical and scientific advance, as well as its outcome, contributes to such change. In the UK, even reports commissioned at
government level (Bessant, 1988; 1986) point to the extent of social
change brought about by the new technologies. New levels of affluence
and the new working conditions which produce them, for example, are
directly traceable to the uses of the NICT by the international money
markets; if we say this, of course, then we must equally trace the social
divisiveness of such affluence to the impact of the new technologies as
much as to a political climate which is supportive of both affluence
and its social consequences.

It is dangerous to ignore the fact that developments on both these
levels — that of employment and that of sociocultural change — have
important implications for education, since they affect, directly as well
as indirectly, the context within which school functions. As society
changes, as culture evolves, so must school attempt to adapt to its changing environment. But these are issues which it is not possible to address
directly here. What we have to do is to identify, albeit briefly, those
areas of larger-scale change which are amenable to exploration and,
very importantly, to the research and development activity which is
urgently needed if our schools are indeed to adapt to the challenges of
the new technologies. I suggest that it is important to view these from

an educational, and not a technological, standpoint, and that there are, in fact, two such areas about which at least something had been learned from recent experience. They are, first, the nature of the teaching — learning transaction and, second, the way in which learning is institutionalized by the school. Both suggest fascinating possibilities for change, and I shall here deal very briefly with each in turn.

The teaching-learning transaction

The classroom transaction between teacher and pupils, over as many centuries as the school has existed, has been weighted heavily on the side of the teacher. That is to say, the role of the teacher has been that of mediating and transmitting to the pupil a given body of knowledge and a given range of skills.

This is not to say that the teacher has always transmitted blindly what society has required. That happens, certainly, but what has been very important in the development of the teaching profession has been the exercise, by individual teachers, of their right and responsibility to act as a filter mechanism for what their pupils learn often even in defiance of what authority expects. But conformist or non-conformist, the teacher has been the arbiter, possessed not only of authority status, but also of more knowledge, more skill and more experience than the pupil and, as a consequence, in a position of advantage.

It is scarcely conceivable that this position of advantage will ever be, in itself, overturned. But what is emerging quite clearly is that the use of the new technologies does introduce into the classroom transaction a new element which produces a radical shift in the teacher-pupil relationship. When pupils have access to a computer, they have access to a processing power which is greater than their own, greater than that of the teacher, and greater — over its narrowly defined range of activities — than the capacities of teacher and pupils together. The introduction of this 'third partner' into the classroom is still only a recently noticed phenomenon, but it is an important one. Since it means, in effect, that children can not only carry out enquiry which they themselves propose and construct but also enquiry in respect of which the teacher may be very hard pressed, if capable at all, of prediciting the outcome, there is here an important shift of emphasis from the teaching process to that of learning; consequently, there is shift in the balance of classroom power between teacher and pupil.

We are still very far from knowing just where this may lead us, and it will be obvious that the traditional teacher-pupil relationship will continue to permeate the classroom situation; children cannot be expected, for example, to plan out their own educational needs *ab initio*. Nonetheless, the shift is an important one, about which we shall discover more as databases, spreadsheets and other tools — including expert system shells, which so far have been the subject of limited exploration only — continue to find their way increasingly into the curriculum.

School as institution

Our earlier observations about the communications aspects of the new technologies beg important questions about the nature of school.

Hitherto, school has been an enclosed world, largely self-contained in respect of its resources, though important advances have been made in the post-war period with, for example, educational television. But where such external resources have been available to the learner, they have been available on a one-way, transmitted, basis. Educational television itself, for example, is distance teaching, not distance learning. There are two important dimensions to the change being wrought by the NICT.

The first is that distance access of resources of the learner's own choice becomes a possibility (at present, that is all that it is). Bibliographic databases such as DIALOG already point the way, while the concept behind the EEC DELTA project is that of a European network of learning resources, available to learners anywhere the necessary access facilities are installed. This is a concept that still has very far to go before it reaches maturation, but it is one that clearly has very considerable implications for the notion of school as a self-contained learning resource. Furthermore, it is once again a concept that places an increased emphasis on the role and the autonomy of the learner at the expense of the directive role of the teacher.

A second aspect of change in this area is that it makes possible a change in kind of the learning resource itself. This becomes especially interesting at the international level, where the potential opens up for classrooms in different countries to become resources for each other. In the developmental work to which I referred earlier, for example, classrooms will provide each other with environmental and other data, on a comparative basis; they will also act as partner resources for languages learning. This idea is still under active development, and its potential is best illustrated by the notion of, let us say, a class in Manchester 'correcting' the English of a class in, say, Montpellier, and vice versa. It is a concept that offers exciting prospects for authentic language learning while at the same time raising many challenges related to standards and notions of correctness. Here, the idea is offered as illustration only; its implications for school as organization and for the role of the teacher will be apparent.

There is perhaps enough in such illustrations to indicate some likely lines of development, and some of the implications of such development. It is impossible to predict the extent of change which will in fact take place over the coming decades, but enough is known — enough has been learned from the few short years of full-scale experiment in the UK and elsewhere — to indicate that such change could be very exciting indeed. However, enough also is known to make us realize how much is not known, and how important it is that a thorough-going research and development activity be maintained in respect of the new technologies and education.

Whatever the eventual impact of the NICT upon education, one thing is already established. What will be important about the changes that take place is that they will be pedagogic, as well as social, cultural and political. The technology in itself is only a means to an end, and that fact must be retained as a guiding principle throughout the developmental work in which we must continue to engage. Within the general context of that work, the task of educating teachers for their role in a school possibly much transformed by the educational takeup of the new technologies will remain a major priority.

References

Bessant, J et al (1985) *IT Futures: What Current Forecasting Literature Says about the Social Impact of Information Technology* National Economic Development Office: London

Bessant, J et al (1986) *IT Futures Surveyed: A Study of Informed Opinion Concerning the Long-Term Implications of Information Technology for Society* National Economic Development Office: London

Bolter, J D (1984) *Turing's Man: Western Culture in the Computer Age* Duckworth : London

DES (1987) *Aspects of the Work of the Microelectronics Education Programme* Department of Education and Science: London

Evans, H (1931) *Cwm Eithin* Gwasg y Brython: Liverpool

Fothergill, R (1981) *Microelectronics Education Programme: the Strategy* Department of Education and Science: London

Gwyn, R (1982) *Information Technology and Education: the Approach to Policy in England, Wales and Northern Ireland* in *European Journal of Education* 17, 4

Gwyn, R (1986) Technological Advance and Educational Change, in Johnston and Sasson (1986)

Gwyn, R (1987) *Vision and Scenarios for Education and Teacher Training* Commission of the European Community FAST Occasional Paper 138: Brussels

Jennings, H (1985) *Pandaemonium: The Coming of the Machine as Seen by Contemporary Observers* Andre Deutsch: London

Johnston, A and Sasson, A (1986) *New Technologies and Development* Unesco: Paris

Ladurie, E le Roy (1978) *Montaillou: Village Occitan de 1294-1324* Editions Gallimard: Paris

Mackintosh, I (1986) *Sunrise Europe: the Dynamics of Information Technology* Basil Blackwell: Oxford

Mandrou, R (1973) *Des Humanistes aux Hommes de Science: XVIe – XVIIe Siecles* Editions du Seuil: Paris

Masuda, Y (1981) *The Information Society as Post-Industrial Society* World Future Society: Washington DC

Nora, S and Minc A (1978) *L'Informatisation de ia Societe* la Documentation Francaise: Paris

Van Weert, T J (1984) *A Model Syllabus for Literacy in Information Technology for all Teachers* ATEE: Brussels

Vian, J (1977) *L'Ecole CAP 2001* Editions ESF: Paris

Watts, A G (1983) *Education, Unemployment and the Future of Work* Open University Press: Milton Keynes

Weizenbaum, J (1984) *Computer Power and Human Reason* Penguin Books: Harmondsworth

6. Education for the new technologies: current developments in Bulgarian schools

Mikhail Draganov and Raina Pavlova

Summary: The paper outlines the current state of utilizing new technologies in Bulgarian schools and the preparedness to introduce such technologies on a mass scale in schools.

The general characteristics and the structure of Bulgaria's educational system are described, as well as the factors determining the specifics of introducing new technologies in education. Special attention is paid to using computers in schools. The developments, goals and tasks of computer-aided learning are discussed together with the respective progress plans and programmes. The current position is illustrated and details given about the future development of the material facilities and the training of teaching staff. The objectives and tasks of education are enumerated, and the contents of the 'Fundamentals of Informatics and Computer Science' subject introduced in Bulgarian schools are presented.

The various aspects of the mass introduction of computer-oriented information technologies in Bulgarian schools are considered in detail. The choice of computer-oriented technologies has been substantiated. The nature and the contents of the new technologies as well as their goals and tasks are set out; the methods and methodologies of their development and large-scale introduction are outlined.

The major goal of introducing the new technologies in education is to raise the quality and efficiency of learning. Basic requirements in this respect are their mass scale introduction, unified approach, efficient use of computer facilities, correct understanding of the role and place of the new tools depending on the objectives and the components of the process of learning.

Introduction

In our age science and practice have always gone together. On the one hand, practical demands are conducive to the development of science and, on the other, quite often a scientific discovery or achievement has changed current practice and created new demands for scientific products. This is especially true of the relationship between engineering science and industry. This phenomenon was initially termed techno-scientific progress, and then techno-scientific revolution, to stress the qualitatively new level of science-industry interaction both in terms of outcome and as a means of production. The 20th century was termed the technology age and rightly so.

At the basis of each production stands some process, a technique, which should constantly be improved in order to improve production itself. This process, however, has its limits. From a certain point on, further development is possible only in case technologies which are introduced and are new in essence. For some 10 or 15 years now we have increasingly been calling our age not so much the technology age, but the high technology age. This fact is indicative of the dramatic development of technologies. High technologies first appeared in industry, and soon covered all other aspects of our life — management, business, communications, everyday life. Education was not to lag behind.

High technology and education

The reasons that brought into existence and boosted the new technologies in education are closely related to the appearance and development of the new technologies outside it. Since its major goal is to equip young people with life skills and habits for work in a specific social environment, education has to comply with the need to prepare young people for life and work in the age of rapidly advancing high technologies. This is true of each and every country, Bulgaria included. The rate at which these technologies develop is so high that many people who finished their education 10 or 15 years ago proved incapable of working under the new conditions and had to take further qualifications. The new technologies in industry and the non-productive sphere are most diverse. The goal of the school in this context is to provide for a fundamental training in the general specifics of these technologies. Although diverse, they have similarities, largely in that they are realized by means of a complicated control process. This fact in itself is very important.

It is common knowledge that control is an information process related to collecting, processing, storing and transmitting data. Each one of these activities constitutes an individual class of information processes, characterized by their own specific characteristics, means and methods of realization. The advancement of these means and methods in control processes, as well as of the data processing proper, gave rise to the information industry and information technologies. The information technologies proved to be fundamental technologies of a kind. It is for this reason that Bulgarian schools began paying special attention to the methods and means of realizing these information technologies, concentrated in two major directions. Two needs were recognized:

☐ studying the methods and means of realizing information technologies;
☐ making use of the information technologies for managing the educational system.

Simultaneously, it became evident that the very process of instruction was in need of new teaching technologies, and information technologies at that. Thus three aspects of the information technologies in education were delineated.

Factors determining the introduction of new technologies in the educational system

In Bulgaria the experience of many countries was studied and analysed in using new technologies in education and postgraduate training. Resting on this analysis and on our own experience, respective decisions were taken at government level and projects were set up to introduce new information technologies in education.

Preliminary research showed that the new technologies in education are in essence information technologies, making use of computers, video systems and combinations of the two (with or without communicative systems — interactive video, video-text, teletext). Of significance is the use of some hardware systems (video and optical discs), as well as software systems (eg expert systems) and knowledge bases.

The analysis showed that the introduction of the new information technologies in the individual countries had been characterized by specific factors such as:

- [ ] structure and specificity of the educational system;
- [ ] the country's general level of development;
- [ ] home production of computers, video systems, etc;
- [ ] the country's need of trained personnel;
- [ ] government and industrial support;
- [ ] organizational and other factors.

As listed above, these factors are not arranged in any significant order, but rather present some specific requirements in developing and introducing particular information technologies in the educational system of a given country.

Currently, the presence and use of new technologies in our educational system are regulated both by these factors and by our unceasing effort to promote further education and the country's development in general, to give everybody a chance of self-expression and development. In order to gain a better understanding of our attitude and policy regarding the presence of new technologies in education, and of current developments, we are going to give some details concerning the general characteristics, the specifics and structure of the country's educational system.

General characteristics and specifics of Bulgaria's educational system

Obviously, the main goal of the Bulgarian educational system is to give young people adequate life skills and habits, ie:

- [ ] to provide them with the respective level of general education, upbringing and general culture;
- [ ] to teach them the necessary general knowledge in the natural sciences and in the humanities;

☐ to bring them up as industrious and good citizens of their country;
☐ to supply them with a vocational training in diverse subjects.

The major tasks facing the educational system are oriented towards the attainment of the main goal in its several aspects and some of them are directly related to the introduction of new information technologies:

☐ to provide young people with knowledge of a wide range of subjects and with skills to apply this knowledge in practice;
☐ to prepare them for the conditions of life and work in our age — the age of informatics and computers;
☐ to provide them with modern vocational training and general polytechnical education.

Our secondary education comprises also compulsory vocational training. The problem of vocational training is one of the paramount issues of the country's educational policy. What is aimed at is that each school leaver should have some kind of professional qualification. This would be impossible to achieve without making use of the new information technologies in education.

Bulgaria's educational system rests and operates on several major principles:

☐ schools, universities and all educational establishments are state-owned;
☐ education is free;
☐ secondary education is compulsory;
☐ all young people may receive the type of education they want and are capable of receiving, in accordance with the country's needs;
☐ education has central management and is plan-based;
☐ the curricula, syllabuses and textbooks are unified nationally for one and the same type of educational establishment;
☐ one and the same type of learning establishment provides equal opportunities for the leavers and equal training;
☐ education is based on democratic and humanitarian principles and keeps the spirit of the national traditions;
☐ it is closely related to practice and keeps pace with the new achievements in science and technology;
☐ education is closely associated with the needs of industry;
☐ the educational system is state-funded;
☐ industry is involved in funding the system of vocational training and planning the needs of trained personnel (industry being state-owned);
☐ part of the vocational training is being conducted in industrial conditions.

As far as the introduction of new technologies in education is concerned, it is of great importance that education is state-funded and centrally managed and that curricula, syllabuses and textbooks for one and the same type and level of school are unified.

Some principles of postgraduate training are also of significance:

☐ teachers update their knowledge, upgrade their qualifications and take new qualifications at special institutes, universities and other schools of higher learning;
☐ workers do the same at vocational education centres, owned by the industrial enterprises, outside the educational system;
☐ higher education graduates upgrade their fundamental and professional training at the schools of higher learning, and get special qualifications at learning centres within industry.

The system of secondary and higher education is managed by the Ministry of National Education.

Structure of Bulgaria's educational system

The general structure of Bulgaria's educational system is shown in Table 6.1.

Age	Level	Note
3 – 6	pre-school	kindergarten non-compulsory
6 – 9	I-III grade	compulsory
9 – 14	IV-VIII grade	compulsory
14 – 17 (18)	IX-XI (XII) grade	compulsory
18 and over	semi-higher and higher	non-compulsory

Table 6.1 *Bulgaria's educational system structure*

The first to third and fourth to eighth grades constitute the primary education, which is unified countrywide. As for the secondary education, there are three types of high schools:

☐ technical colleges;
☐ secondary vocational technical schools;
☐ unified secondary polytechnical schools.

The duration of a technical college course is four years. It provides students with general educational, technical, special and vocational training. It prepares executive and managing staff with secondary education. A technical college usually offers several subjects. There are technical colleges in electrical engineering, mechanical engineering, construction work, motor transport, mechanization, economics, etc.

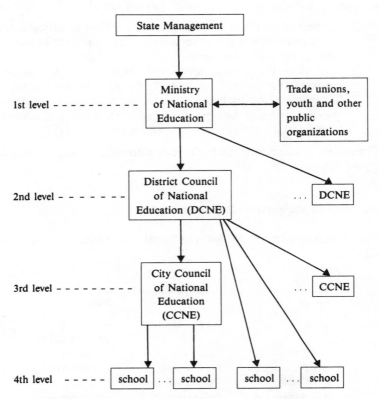

Figure 6.1 *Bulgaria's educational system: general
management structure*

The course of study in a secondary vocational school is three years.
It too provides general education and technical qualifications, special
and vocational training, preparing executive personnel. Such schools
are usually industry-oriented.

The unified secondary polytechnical school, as a rule, includes a
primary school as well. Specific in this case is the secondary level. Its
first two years (ninth and tenth grade) are devoted to a general education. There follows a course of study at a vocational educational centre,
the latter being either associated with the school or not. Secondary education is finished when students leave the vocational centre course. The
purpose of this course is to provide them with a vocational training.
Its duration is either one or two years, depending on the subject. It comprises also some obligatory general instruction and technical subjects
and certain optional subjects.

The overall course of study in a unified secondary polytechnical
school (both primary and secondary levels) includes also some classes
to form student skills and habits for work and to get them acquainted

with the fundamentals of modern industrial production and technologies. In order to provide conditions for work close to industrial technologies, the so-called inter-school centres have been set up, operating with regular industrial equipment. In them students both learn about and turn out some industrial products.

There are also mathematical and foreign language unified secondary schools, as well as sports and arts schools.

Figure 6. 1 illustrates the general structure of the management of the educational system.

The structure of the educational system's management corresponds to the structure of the country's administrative management. The country is divided into districts, consisting of towns and villages. Usually methodological guidance of education is directly effected by the district educational councils. Only some cities have methodological bodies of management of their own, as they are divided into city districts with the status and managerial structure identical to that of the country districts.

Bulgaria's educational system and the new technologies

Just as everywhere else, the introduction of new industrial technologies made it necessary to train personnel with higher and secondary education to handle them. Hence, high technologies first appeared in secondary schools as a subject of study. Some specialized schools (technical colleges) and separate classes in other schools were set up, mostly in microelectronic technologies, microprocessing equipment, biotechnologies, information technology, etc, equipped with the respective facilities. Thus the means of effecting the new technologies became tools of instruction. From an educational viewpoint high technology has two major aspects: it is both a subject of study and a tool of instruction. And if the majority of new technologies are of parallel importance to the educational system as a whole, information technologies (as was pointed out) proved in a sense to be fundamental ones. They, just as the others, should be considered in the context of the educational system in their two aspects: as an object of study and as a tool for instruction. As control processes are effected by means of information technologies, a third aspect should also be mentioned: that they are a means of effecting the management of the educational system. This will not be considered here but it should be noted that computers are used for automating informational and control activities both on the ministerial level and on the district and school levels.

The new technologies in our education system are in essence computer-oriented technologies. The wide application of microprocessor and microcomputer systems and the possibilities for their application in all spheres and activities made it necessary to make them a subject of study for the secondary schools. Simultaneously, work began on using micros as a teaching tool.

Our schools have at their disposal a number of video systems , too, but so far they have not been used actively in instruction. The use of interactive video in education is still in an experimental stage.

Microcomputers in Bulgarian schools

The managerial bodies of Bulgaria's Ministry of Education were quick to assess the enormous significance that microcomputers were going to acquire in all spheres of life, and hence in education, too. Back in 1981 a decision was taken to equip schools with computers, even if the possibilities and efficiency of their usage were not as clear as they are now, but were rather intuitively felt. Some requirements concerning the computers to be introduced in schools were formulated; the major ones being that they should be similar for all schools so as to allow the exchange of software. Some specific conditions in this country made it necessary for them to be Bulgarian-made. Their number was expected to be about 1,000. In 1981 Bulgaria did not produce microcomputers. The Ministry of Education placed an order with the industry to develop and begin the production of an educational personal computer. In order to allow the use of ready-made software it was decided that the Bulgarian educational personal computer should be compatible with the most common computer at that time — the Apple II.

By the end of 1981 the first 200 computers were supplied to schools and aroused great interest. By that time certain experience had already been gained in using the Apple II. In 1982 regular production was launched of the Apple II compatible Bulgarian educational personal computer, and thus a beginning was made.

Microcomputers, the youth and the state

The Bulgarian highest state management appreciated the strategic significance of the task of teaching young people using computer technology. In 1984 the government passed a special regulation providing all necessary conditions for conducting instruction by using computer systems. Material facilities and servicing staff were provided, organizational and other problems were solved. The Ministry of Education, the youth organizations and industry were the factors involved in implementing this policy. Efforts concentrated in three directions:

- ☐ supplying personal and professional computers and peripheral devices needed for the teaching of children and young people;
- ☐ promoting work on developing software to be used by young people in learning, and also in other fields and activities;
- ☐ scientific, methodological and organizational backup both of the process of instruction and self-learning, and in applying the experience amassed in practice.

Special attention was paid to studying and introducing computers and the means for their utilization in learning and in extra-curricular activities at all levels and types of schools and universities.

The government put the Ministry of Education and other ministries under an obligation to allot annually considerable funds for buying computers for schools. Our schools were supplied with micros and peripheral devices according to a planned scheme. Outside the system of education, youth and other organizations and industrial enterprises set up computer youth clubs. All the necessary conditions were at hand for teaching young people how to use computers. The major role in these activities, of course, was that of the Ministry of Education.

Comprehensive programme, 1985-1990

In implementation of the government's decision, the Ministry of Education drew up and adopted, in early 1985, a comprehensive programme for the 1985-1990 period. It had the following major social and economic objectives:

☐ to meet the needs of the industry and the national economy of specialists with secondary education in the field of programming and computer systems production, utilization, maintenance and servicing;

☐ to introduce computer systems and their uses to secondary school students so as to provide them with sufficient knowledge for using computers in future;

☐ to arouse in them an interest in computers and create habits for future work with them;

☐ to raise the efficiency and innovatory character of teachers' work;

☐ to improve the quality of instruction, intensify and individualize learning;

☐ to develop automated systems for informational backup and control, to improve the quality of control;

☐ to provide an occupation for young people in their free time, by means of computer games, problem-solving tasks for developing their thinking, etc;

☐ to provide conditions for expanding the integrative processes in learning and cognition through the possibility of graphically presenting the material, making calculations, accessing information databases, and achieving integration of the instruction in various subjects and scientific branches.

These were the tasks as seen from the perspective of 1984. The programme contained four basic goals and parts.

1. To provide the theoretical knowledge about computer systems and practical experience in using them (computers as a subject of study).

1.1   To train secondary education specialists for the production, programming, utilization and maintenance of computer systems.

1.2   To provide students with a broad knowledge of the possibilities of utilizing and the social uses of computers, to enable them to acquire systematic knowledge and skills and promote their technical and constructive thought in the field of informatics, broad as it may be.

2.   To ensure efficient utilization of computer systems in the process of upbringing and learning (computers as tools of instruction).

2.1   To provide pedagogical and methodological support of computer-aided learning.

2.2   To provide the necessary software for CAL.

3.   To introduce computers in the management of the educational system.

4.   To provide facilities and servicing staff for introducing computers in schools.

4.1   To train teachers to employ computers in instruction.

4.2   To ensure the facilities needed.

In implementation of item 1.1 of the programme (personnel training) it was planned to:

☐ make an analysis of the types of subjects to be studied in personnel training courses in computer production and usage, and to update the former, if need be;

☐ update the professional qualification characteristics of the respective professions;

☐ develop or update curricula and syllabuses;

☐ analyse the existing teaching materials and write, translate and publish textbooks and manuals;

☐ assess the needs of executive personnel in the respective professions and set a network of schools to meet these needs.

In implementing item 1.2 of the programme (to provide all students with knowledge for the computer uses in society) 13 tasks were to be carried out, among them being:

☐ to determine the place of informatics and its syllabus in secondary schools (aspects, methods and means of using computers as information devices);

☐ to update curricula and syllabuses;

☐ to write and publish textbooks and other methodological literature;

☐ to conduct some experimental courses, etc.

The implementation of item 2.1 envisaged 15 major tasks, related to various methodological and pedagogical problems of computer-aided learning (computers as an instruction tool). Two of them are of paramount importance:

- ☐ determining the goals, the place and spheres of application of computers inside and outside classes for the respective age groups, types and forms of education and subjects;
- ☐ analysing and complementing the CAL-oriented subject-matter of the school subjects.

Item 2.2 (providing educational software) comprised five tasks, the major of them being:

- ☐ to develop system software for the purposes of education;
- ☐ to develop applied software (courseware) in the various subjects.

The third part of the programme remains outside the sphere of education.

In implementing item 4.1 of the programme 15 major tasks were envisaged, such as the working out of a module system and qualification characteristics for the modules, for upgrading the qualifications of all teachers. To this end a comprehensive plan was drawn up for the period up to 1990 to upgrade teachers' qualifications in programming and using computers in schools. We shall give this plan a more detailed consideration further on.

It was decided also to compose unifield syllabuses and curricula for the module qualification courses and a time-schedule for them. Textbooks were planned to be written too.

For the implementation of item 4.2 (providing material facilities) 11 main tasks were mapped out, the most important concerning the funds for buying computers, establishing a software library for educational purposes, etc.

Terms, executive personnel, funds and financing organizations were set out for each of these tasks.

We discussed the programme in greater detail as it was the major document, mapping out the directions of work for six years ahead. At present (July, 1987) there is active work on reviewing its implementation and it is about to be updated. Its new version is to be endorsed by the end of this year.

Teachers' qualifications upgrading plan

As mentioned before, the Ministry of Education adopted a plan for raising teachers' qualifications concerning computer programming and uses in learning. It has four goals:

- ☐ to train qualified teaching staff for theoretical and practical classes in programming, computer usage and informatics in schools;
- ☐ to give teachers theoretical knowledge and practical experience in using computers in class;
- ☐ to provide the managerial staff of the system of education with a basic awareness of computer uses in learning and management;

☐ to provide the material facilities, financial and personnel backup needed for carrying out the qualification courses.

Fifteen tasks are to be carried out to implement the programme. The institutes and universities which are to hold these courses are being fixed and time-schedules are being set for the various courses, etc. A qualification module scheme, composed of four modules, has been worked out and is being implemented as shown in Table 6.2.

Module	Duration	Destination	Goals (1) and Results (2)
1st	1 week 36 hours	School managers and teachers in all subjects	(1) To provide basic knowledge about computers and their uses in teaching; (2) Some skills to use computers in teaching
2nd	1 month 144 hours	Teachers in all subjects	(1) To provide a better training and enable teachers to acquire skills to use ready-made software; (2) An expanded training and skills for using ready-made software
3rd	3 months 432 hours	Teachers in mathematics and physics, economists and engineers — teachers in appropriate subjects	(1) To expand the training in informatics, programming and using computers; (2) The graduates may become teachers in informatics and programming
4th	1 year	As in module 3	(1) To provide teachers with fundamental knowledge and skills to develop educational software; (2) Graduates may become teachers in postgraduate courses

Table 6.2 *Qualification module scheme*

There are curricula and syllabuses for all the four modules.

Implementation of the Ministry of Education programmes and plans

A review of the programmes and plans of the Ministry of Education has shown that most of the tasks are being implemented in the scope and content required, and on schedule. All prerequisites to this end are in hand:

- [ ] the organizational prerequisites and managerial units have been set up;
- [ ] special research centres for scientific and methodological support of the process of employing computers in education have been set up;
- [ ] numerous research teams and experts from universities and institutes of higher learning have been enlisted to solve methodological problems and to carry out the qualification upgrading scheme.

Positive results have been obtained, such as:

- [ ] students show an increasingly pronounced interest in computer technology and a growing skill in operating it. A number of regular and extra-curricular educational sessions were introduced in programming and computer literacy;
- [ ] teachers' qualification courses were a success. There are, among the teaching staff of each school, teachers in various subjects who are able either to develop or use educational software;
- [ ] schools have been fitted with a large number of computers;
- [ ] numerous pieces of courseware have been developed and are being made use of, and computer-oriented methodologies have appeared for a number of school subjects;
- [ ] a large number of textbooks have been published, together with special literature and periodicals on the subjects; a number of research teams conduct experimental and research work in schools;
- [ ] most diverse competitions in programming and computer usage have been organized on district, national and international levels;
- [ ] many workshops, conferences and symposia have been held.

Conditions for applying computers in education: current state and developments

There are at least three necessary conditions for employing computers in education:

- [ ] technical facilities;
- [ ] trained teaching staff;
- [ ] educational software.

Technical facilities

The majority of the computers have been supplied to secondary schools. At present, we have at our disposal some 15,000 educational micros, Bulgarian-made, mostly 8-bit Apple II-compatibles, called Pravets-8. Their configuration is usually of two floppy discs and 48 or 64 K RAM. We also produce the IBM PC-compatible Pravets-16, which is now being introduced in schools. At the moment, they are to serve the purposes of professional education. Plans for the near future involve both an increase in the number of computers produced and in the types of configurations, so as to supply existing computers with more printers, plotters and digitizers, as well as to connect them in local networks of greater capacity drives.

Bulgarian schools differ in size, and so do the numbers of computers in them. Small schools have five to ten micros, and there are some large schools which are equipped with over 100 machines. The average school can be said to have about 15-20 microcomputers. Practically all secondary schools in the country have been furnished with computer labs. A total of about 1,500 micros have been installed in primary schools. Another 3,000-4,000 have been supplied to the computer clubs of youth and other organizations − most used by secondary school students, too. In the secondary schools the ratio is 1 micro to 35-40 students. The same ratio for the primary schools (first-eighth grade) is very small. At the present stage of the schools' preparedness to use computers, they will need at least another 10,000 8-bit and some 5,000-6,000 16-bit machines. As evident from the 20-year-long experience of our universities, however, the number of specialists able to use computers in learning grows more rapidly than the number of computers available, so that an increasing lack of computers may be expected in the near future, which will become even greater when they begin to be employed on a large scale in various subjects.

Results of the teachers' qualification scheme

The results from the implementation of the programme for upgrading teachers' qualifications can be seen in Table 6.3.

Duration	Number of graduates		
	1985	1986	1987 (planned)
1 month	239	752	258
3 months	200	176	171
1 year	40	55	49

Table 6.3 Results of teachers' qualification scheme

At present there is at least one teacher in each secondary school who has taken at least a month's qualification course. It should be borne in mind that this year the first graduates in informatics and computer applications and uses with teaching qualifications will leave the University of Sofia.

The number of teaching staff who have taken a month's qualification course (Module 1) amounts to some 14,000, mostly secondary school teachers, which is about 10 per cent of the country's entire teaching staff, the percentage for the secondary schools being much higher and for primary much lower.

The Ministry of Education decided to organize first module courses (one week) in all schools, engaging as lecturers the teaching staff who have already taken computer literacy courses. Thus, by the end of 1989, almost all Bulgarian teachers are expected to have passed the first module courses.

Educational software

This is the most complicated problem from both the scientific and the methodological point of view, and it is related also to the problems of the feasibility and efficiency of computer-aided learning, the mode of utilizing computers, etc. The educational software must answer a number of specific requirements in terms of the educational system, organizational considerations, methodological and pedagogical demands, and much else.

The first attempts were naive, merely a simple transference of the textbook material to the computer. The futility of such an approach was soon perceived: still there followed a period of stumbling in the dark. The majority of software available was not fit for educational uses or had numerous shortcomings. This period covered three or even four years, yet it was both objectively determined and indispensable, for experience was being gained. Many experts from universities and institutes were enlisted in developing educational software, together with experienced teachers. It may be said that we were quite clear about the type of software needed in education only in 1986 or even 1987. In order to develop it, however, to its full scope and content, a lot of time will be needed. The Ministry of Education drew up a programme, comprising 33 research projects on the methodological and practical problems of developing educational software. It is being implemented jointly with some other countries and will be completed by the end of 1990.

Informatics and information technology in schools

In order to allow students to study informatics, computer technology, and the methods and means of its usage, a new compulsory subject, termed 'informatics', was introduced in secondary schools in the school year 1986-87 in the tenth grade (the second year of the technical colleges). It continues to be studied in the 11th grade, with a total duration of 102 academic hours.

What were the reasons for that? In our age informatics — a notion of a fundamental nature — has acquired enormous significance. In the context of the informational boom the ability to be oriented in the increasing flood of information becomes an especially valuable one. The same holds true for the ability to discover the inherent hierarchical relations between information units in the information arrays. The various activities in handling data fall roughly into four major groups

— collecting, processing, storing and transmitting. The various combinations between these activities make up the various information processes. The need to automate these processes promoted the development of respective methods and theoretical media and established informatics as an independent, fundamental discipline. The principal technical device for automating information processes proved to be computer and microprocessor systems. The term 'algorithm' came to the fore as a major one in realizing any information process. Among the vast majority of information processes one of them definitely stands out: control. Control processes underlie any activity. Computer-based technologies for the control of machines, technological processes, production lines and various production activities have become the hallmark of our century. Microprocessor systems, microcomputers, computer-based control technologies have made their advent in all areas and activities, even in everyday life. They have become an objective reality, an element of the environment in which people live and work. Hence the necessity to prepare the coming generations for this environment. Life has made it necessary for young people to master the fundamentals of informatics, algorithms, the methods and means of computer science and of realizing information activities and processes and acquiring skills and habits for work with computer systems.

From the causes that made it necessary to introduce informatics in schools, its objectives and tasks may be formulated.

The first main objective is to teach students the properties of information, the methods and means of collecting, processing, storing and transmitting it. Each of these activities is in itself a separate branch of informatics, with its own subject matter and facilities. These comprise knowledge about algorithms and algorithmic structures, about the way of organizing and structuring data, etc. The goal is to develop in students a specific, algorithmic manner of thinking, as the way of thinking reflects on the manner of action, and actually, the two of them are at the basis of the technological manner of thinking and work. The attainment of the first main goal does not require computers. However, when studying information processes and activities and the functional specific of computers as information machines, it becomes necessary to study the basic algorithms, simulating these processes and activities, and after that to study the methods of communicating with computers, ie programming methods and languages.

Grasping the fundamentals of programming is the second main objective of informatics as taught in schools. This does not mean that every student is to become a software developer. It is a matter rather of acquiring basic knowledge and habits by using a programming language in practice. BASIC was chosen as an appropriate and easy one. Studying programming, students gain a better insight into the methods and means of informatics and their knowledge becomes more comprehensive and lasting. Writing programs, they become better aware of algorithmic and information structures, and form habits which pose practical tasks correctly and present problems in a formal manner. They learn about modelling methods and are able to compose simple mathematical models. The psychological barrier to computer-assisted work is overcome and students become more confident and are able to grasp problems in depth and check on the correctness of their decision in practice. Mastering the fundamentals of programming and the practical skills students acquire will enable them to use computers during instruction in other subjects. These are first and foremost the natural sciences and the technical (specialized) subjects in vocational education, ie they will be able to use computers in doing calculation problems, simulation and modelling some processes and phenomena, for automating some engineering tasks, etc. Many of these can be accomplished by using ready-made software. This is the third major objective of the subject — to teach students to make use of ready-made software. Besides, they should be able to interpret the results obtained correctly and apply them in practice. It is very important that the third objective should be attained, as practically the use of ready-made programs and the work with control systems (also using ready-made programs) is the most common case. Some experts are of the opinion that the third objective is so important that instruction in informatics should be reduced only to its attainment. This is a somewhat extreme view, but it is a case in point of how important it is for students to have practical experience of using some of the most common applied software, such as:

- text editors and word processing systems;
- electron tables;
- information systems;
- computer-aided design systems and others.

It is fairly obvious that all typing work in the near future will be carried out using universal word processing systems for microcomputers. School leavers therefore must have some practical experience and abilities in this field.

Parallel to the three basic objectives of the informatics course in secondary schools, there are two others — quite important ones, too.

First, students should obtain a general idea of the purpose and functions of operational systems and some practical skills for employing the major functions of the basic operating system of the school computers.

Second, they must be given a general idea of the computer's and microprocessor's systems makeup and principles of operation. These two goals must not become an end in themselves, but should be given their due anyway.

The curriculum in informatics is composed of the following basic parts:

1. Introduction to informatics; nature, significance and characteristic features; information activities and processes.
2. Introduction to computers; nature and general principles of construction; work with the school computers.

3. Algorithms and programs.
4. Programming in BASIC.
5. The module principle in programming; subprograms.
6. Data arrays, basic data structures and processing algorithms.
7. Operational systems.
8. Computer-aided problem-solving.
9. Computer uses.
10. Work with the most commonly available applied software and systems.

The entire course of instruction is both theoretical and practical. There are a couple of considerations regarding it.

☐ It is considered that the school subject informatics as presented above should be studied in earlier grades (the ninth, for instance).
☐ The curriculum for practical classes should be enlarged.

Together with the regular informatics classes, experiments are being conducted on studying elements of it even in the fifth, sixth and seventh grade, using LOGO. Attempts are being made and experiments are under way to integrate the course in informatics with instruction in mathematics. One can judge the results of the introduction of informatics in secondary schools roughly from the level of training of the new enrolment of students at the higher institutes and universities. Our personal observations have shown that so far their level is not very high. It should be noted, however, that the students who were the first to study informatics as a school subject will enrol in institutes of higher learning in the academic year 1988–89. So far there have been students able to do programming in several languages even in their first university year. Usually they have learned BASIC, FORTRAN, Pascal or Assembler under the guidance of some of their teachers or professional programmers.

Forward to computer-oriented information technologies in Bulgaria's educational system

We consider this part of the chapter to be the most important one for the topic ('Education for the new technologies' and most closely related to it. From the point of view of chronology and for the sake of presenting as complete a picture as possible, the preceding sections were just as indispensable, for this is the only way to grasp our understanding of the matter correctly and assess it objectively. In this country a project is under way for introducing new, computer-oriented information technology in education, which should comply with the specific conditions and the goals of our governmental educational policy.

So — computers as a tool of instruction! What is their place? How are they to be used? With what objectives? How are they to be attained? By what criteria should they be judged? These and numerous other questions have long been asked. It is only in 1986–87 that the answers began to emerge. The process of introducing new, computer-oriented technology in education was termed, for brevity's sake, the computerization of education. The authors of this chapter came forward with a comprehensive conception concerning the strategy, methods, approaches and mechanisms of computerizing secondary education in Bulgaria for the 1987–1992 period. It met with some criticism, especially with regard to the mechanism of achieving computerization, which only helped clarify it. Its underlying tenets were proved to be right. Its salient feature is that it complies with Bulgarian reality and the goals of the educational policy of the state.

Why computer-oriented, and not computer-based, information technology?

Let us first discuss the two terms.

They both imply that computers are made use of in instruction. The difference lies, however, in the role and the place of computers in learning. Computer-oriented technology, as the term is understood in this country, allots the teacher a leading place in instruction. Both the teacher and the students use computers actively, but just as an ancillary aid. Powerful as the computer may be, it is still a tool in the hands of both teacher and students. Computer-based technologies, however, do not necessarily require the presence of a teacher. With them the role of teacher is taken over by the computer, which is the main teaching aid, without which instruction becomes impossible.

It is assumed that computer-based techologies offer greater potential in terms of individualizing and intensifying learning, enhancing its quality and efficiency. From the viewpoint of methodology and facilities, however, we consider them not to be very advanced worldwide. The computers by which they are effected are still not sophisicated enough, not cheap enough.

A major requirement in choosing the particular type of computer-oriented technologies for the conditions and objectives of the country is the possibility of introducing it on a mass scale throughout the country. There is more than one approach to the matter, given that consideration. For us, the choice was predetermined. What do we mean by this?

The first prerequisite for a large-scale introduction of computer-oriented educational technology is a sufficient number of computers to be made available at schools. When their number is not sufficient, but is nevertheless considerable and keeps growing, the objective is to achieve the highest social efficiency. This is an extremely important task of great social significance. The means of buying computers for Bulgaria's educational system are provided by the state, ie by society. Therefore it has the right to expect them to be utilized in the most effective way. This can be achieved only if the education effect of computer-aided learning is greatest for any given period of time. Our scheme is aimed at achieving exactly that.

The observance of these principles is thought to underlie the introduction of computer-oriented educational technology in Bulgaria.

1. Using computers in the process of instruction to enhance the quality and efficiency of learning.
2. To ensure highly efficient, all-round utilization of the computers available.
3. To provide conditions for a large-scale introduction and unified approach in employing the computer-oriented learning technology.
4. To determine the place of computers in education, depending on the goals and the components of the process of instruction.
5. To adopt a differentiated approach (setting a priority for the subjects in which the new technology will be introduced, and among their separate parts) in the introduction of the new technology, and to effect it in stages.
6. To retain the existing tutorial system of education, preserving or even increasing the role of the teacher in the classroom.
7. Computers should be an ancillary aid, a tool for both students and teachers.
8. In introducing the computer-oriented learning technologies, the subject matter of what is studied is not to undergo significant changes for the time being.
9. It is considered at this stage to be more expedient to introduce computer-oriented technologies in the natural sciences and technical subjects.

How are these principles to be interpreted and what are they determined by?

Enhancing the quality of learning should be expressed, above all, in a more profound and lasting acquisition of the material taught, some reduction of the time needed (intensification of learning), promoting the curiosity and interest of the students and developing their thinking.

The highly efficient and all-round utilization of the existing microcomputer facilities is an extremely important, socially significant task. The micros now available make possible instruction in informatics; time is alloted for students to visit the computer labs and work by themselves on what they have been taught in the informatics classes, extra-curricular classes are held there and sometimes these labs are used in regular classes. All-round utilization of the computers would actually mean their all-day-round utilization. A highly efficient one would mean that computers were used in such subjects and methodological units and in such a way as to achieve better effect as compared to traditional instruction. As the amount of computers introduced in schools keeps growing, their all-round utilization will be achieved if they are involved as widely as possible in the instruction of various subjects.

Highly efficient and all-round utilization of mirocomputer technology will be effective only if achieved throughout the country on a mass scale. The current practice of writing courseware for individual units in individual subjects and using them in individual schools should be encouraged, yet it must be made clear that this is 'piecemeal' work and inefficient for society as a whole. It is useful in that experience is amassed in this way, and experimental work is done, which is, of course, an inevitable stage that has to be passed through, but efforts should be concentrated on doing work on a mass scale: mass introduction of micros and courseware for one and the same methodological units throughout the country. Hence the need for a unified approach. This means that the fashion in which the computer is to be employed in the particular methodological unit must be the best, the most appropriate one, and the courseware developed in the best manner possible. In order to introduce such a programme on a mass scale, country-wide, the respective teaching aids, methodological guides, etc, must be provided. They, together with the courseware, should become part and parcel of the learning documentation.

The role of computers in instruction should be determined with a view to the goal and components of instruction. Therefore, when talking of computer-aided learning, it must be clear what type of learning is meant — regular school classes or extra-curricular classes, tutorial, drill or laboratory classes. It is extremely important what type of instruction will be employed — tutorial or individual learning. In the two cases the computer's role, purpose and place are different. When calling the computer an 'aid', it should be clear whose aid it is — teacher's or students'. These are different aids with different uses.

In the coming years microcomputers in our schools could be made efficient use of in the following directions:

- ☐ in theoretical and applied learning of informatics, programming and the technical subjects;
- ☐ as a universal computing device in the natural sciences and technical subjects;
- ☐ for mathematical modelling and graphic illustration in studying the nature of some processes and phenomena;
- ☐ numerical methods and optimization procedures software;
- ☐ for computer-aided design and drawing;
- ☐ as word processors;
- ☐ for automating laboratory experiments;
- ☐ for illustrating processes and phenomena, using other devices and experimental equipment attached to them;
- ☐ in using instrumental tools and learning media;
- ☐ in appointing specialized classrooms and laboratories in physics, chemistry, electrical engineering, electronics, etc;
- ☐ in vocational training — for simulation and modelling of mechanisms, machines and systems, industrial lines and production;
- ☐ automatic teaching systems for individual work.

It is considered that computers should not be used as an electronic textbook or drawing board. It is believed also that using computers as an end in itself is damaging not simply because it is inefficient, but also because this creates in students a distorted idea of the computer's role, its nature and possibilities. Computers should be used in such a way as to bring about a new quality of education, an educative effect. Otherwise their use is unjustified.

We also offer a method of implementing computer-oriented technologies in secondary schools. Its main points are the writing of textbooks and developing courseware. We believe that the most appropriate approach in this respect is to make an in-depth analysis of the subject matter for the respective subject for each grade so as to determine the expediency, the possibility, the place and manner of using micros for each methodological unit. The requirements of the courseware should contain a full list of the functions of the software, its major points, objectives, tasks, etc. When fully formulated, the courseware may begin to be developed.

To enable the mass introduction of computer-oriented technology in education throughout the country we think it necessary for each student and teacher to be supplied with the respective sets of learning aids. Such a set should contain a textbook, diskettes with the courseware and software documentation for teacher or student. The place, the goal and manner of employing each courseware unit should be pointed out in the textbook.

Conclusions

If we have to define the current stage of development and large-scale introduction of computer-oriented learning technology in Bulgarian secondary schools, we must say it is at the initial stage. The major problem is to effect this on a nationwide scale, otherwise the results will not be worthwhile. In our opinion it will take five or six years to develop in full and introduce on a mass scale a relatively complete computer-oriented learning technology in secondary schools. If it is a matter of separate schools and individual subjects, we have already obtained quite good results.

At the same time it should be borne in mind that at present active work and experimentation is going on in Bulgaria in the field of interactive video systems, which will also be introduced on a large scale. Evidently, the computer-oriented learning technologies are to be integrated with the interactive video, which will considerably expand their possibilities.

The introduction of computer-oriented educational technologies, integrated with interactive video, videotext and teletext systems will bring about a qualitative improvement in existing teaching systems. It is our surmise that active work in this respect will begin in this country after the year 1992.

7. Educational informatics; some Romanian initiatives

Horia D Pitariu

Summary: Romania makes computer equipment and has acquired positive experience in the training of data processing personnel. It is estimated that informatics will in future become part of the general knowledge of every individual. Thus, notions of informatics are taught in high schools; the curricula of informatics high schools allot 42 per cent of teaching activity to subjects in this profile and to computer work. The informatics high schools function as units of production, being self-financed. Higher education includes informatics as a subject in most colleges; therefore any graduate can become a data processor. A system of post-high school and postgraduate classes can be added to this; they are supplemented by periodically organized classes for improving professional training in informatics.

There is a history of educational informatics in Romania, marked by many transformations and creative syntheses. A positive aspect of this activity is its integration within the national economic system, which is a benefit to our economy by its socioeconomic implications. At present, Romania produces all types of computers, considered commonplace in science, technology and schools.

The quality of the workforce used in informatics is a factor of vital importance, as it has to meet the requirements of the national economy. On a parallel plane, informatics appeals to the wider public who must learn that the new computer science implies a new interdisciplinary approach.

In parallel with the implementation of computers in the socioeconomic life of Romania in the late 1960s, the organization of a national network for training data processing specialists was begun. Postgraduate courses were first organized and the informatics high schools were established. The informatics educational system is co-ordinated by the Ministry of Education and by the regional computer centres. The necessary technical means for an efficient instruction has laid a scientific basis for education. The manpower is rigorously planned in accordance with the demands imposed by the progress of technology.

Figure 7.1 shows the structure of the educational system in Romania. It should be mentioned that the minorities can study in their own native language, the number of schools being in proportion to the population in question; this privilege is extended to higher education as well.

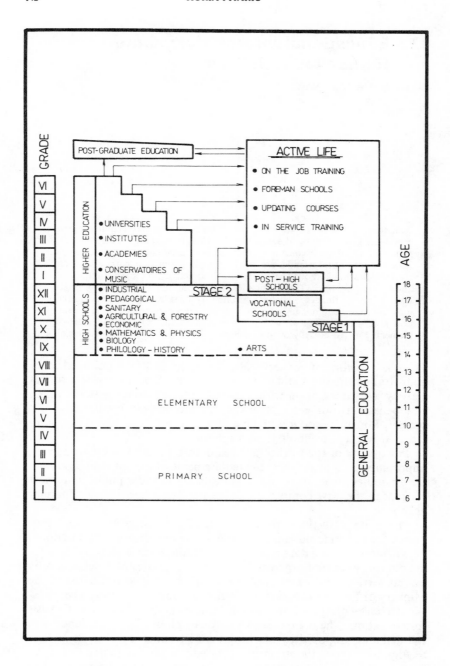

Figure 7.1 *The Romanian educational system*

With regard to primary and elementary education, it guarantees the instruction of children between the ages of six and fourteen through eight years of schooling (the pupils who show aptitude for sports or arts can develop them in classes set up for the respective profiles). The high school training is meant to develop general cultural and technico-professional knowledge; it is organized as full-time education and as evening courses. It comprises two stages: the first stage (grades 9–10), which includes all elementary school graduates (graduates of the eighth grade) and forms part of the general education, which takes ten years; and the second stage (grades 11–12). The high school system comprises nine school types and 34 school profiles:

a. industrial, with 12 profiles (mechanics, electrotechnical, metallurgic, chemistry, etc);
b. agro-industrial and forestry — 3 profiles (agricultural, agricultural mechanics, forestry);
c. economic — 2 profiles (accountancy and commerce, catering);
d. sanitary;
e. mathematics and physics — 6 profiles (informatics, electronics, mathematics-mechanics, etc);
f. nature sciences — 3 profiles (physics-chemistry, chemistry-geology, geology-geography);
g. pedagogical — 2 profiles;
h. philology-history — 2 profiles (philology-history, history-geography);
i. arts — 3 profiles (music, graphic arts, performing arts, ballet).

The tenth grade graduates have three choices: to pursue their studies in the second stage; to take up vocational training in vocational schools; to be employed as practitioners. The high school studies are concluded with a graduation examination which also includes a diploma project; the graduates can pursue their studies in the system of higher education. Vocational schools train skilled workers. Higher education (three to six years) is organized in accordance with the main branches of socioeconomic activity. The forms of instruction are:

the universities — they train teachers as a rule, but also research and production personnel;
the polytechnic institutes;
the institutes of medicine, agronomy, theatre, etc;
the academies — a form of instruction typical of business administration and the training of management personnel;
the conservatoire, a music school of higher education.

Postgraduate courses are organized by the institutes of higher education, and take from 1–12 months. This type of instruction is meant to update the specialists' professional knowledge in keeping with the law, to raise continually the standards of personnel. Within the economic units on-the-job training can be organized, as well as post-high school

courses, schools for foremen, in-service training for the entire personnel (every five years) (Dancsuly, Ionescu, Radu, Salade, 1979; Pitariu,
1979; Lăscuş, 1986).

Admission to the various types of education shows some peculiar
features. Thus, with regard to the tenth grade instruction, the entrance
from the eighth grade into the ninth grade is based on the certificate
of graduation from the elementary school. If the number of candidates
is higher than that of places available in the ninth grade, knowledge
tests are administered. Entrance into the ninth grade is guaranteed, in
such cases, by the grade average, and is dependent on the number of
places available. The candidates whose grade averages are below the
entrance grade average are directed towards other schools, dependent
on their grades. With regard to the 11th grade (the second stage of high
school), about 60 per cent of the graduates of the first stage are admitted, by taking an entrance examination regardless of high school profile.
The rest of the graduates can pursue their studies by taking evening
classes in high schools or by going on to vocational schools. Admission to higher education is based on an entrance examination. The
subjects in which the candidates are tested at high school level are Romanian language and literature, mathematics and physics. With regard to
higher education, they reflect the profile of the field in question.

As regards the curricula, a general cultural training is guaranteed in
primary and elementary schools. Dependent upon aptitudes and
interests, the pupils can go more deeply into various artistic and technical fields within school and pioneer circles. In the high school the
general theoretical training is supplemented with a vocational training.
The ratio between the respective number of classes is approximately 2:1.
The pupils complete their technico-professional knowledge by attending classes in the basics of the vocational field in question (734–836
hours per year) and by taking 1,620 hours per year of production activities in enterprises and school workshops.

The educational system of Romania has included informatics in the
curriculum of mathematics — physics high schools as well as in higher
educational institutes. Informatics is bound to become part and parcel
of the cultural and professional background of each individual regardless of specific professional training. The great popularity of personal
computers (eight types are made in Romania at present) has required
young people and youth organizations to set up a series of circles and
summer camps where children of all ages learn about computer programming, under the guidance of specialists. The magazines for young people
have also carried feature articles on informatics. Thus, people have
familiarized themselves with notions of informatics, with programming
languages outside the school system proper; pupils from diverse schools
take part in informatics quizzes. As a result, the interest in and recep-
tiveness to informatics have grown; from this point of view, we can speak
of the existence of a positive motivation for this achievement.

Training in the field of informatics started with the implementation of computers in the country's socioeconomic life, when the need for trained personnel was great. Thus, postgraduate and post-high school analyst programmer courses were organized at first, then informatics high schools and higher education institutes were set up. Lately, the in-service training system has been introduced.

Post-high school and postgraduate courses on informatics

This training was the initial variant adopted when implementing the first computation centres, prior to setting up an educational system of informatics (after 1967). They are meant to provide a rapid supply of skilled personnel. This form of learning is still in effect at present, its objective being to supplement the necessary personnel and attract experienced specialists towards informatics as an opportunity of professional reorientation. Training is performed exclusively by specialists in the specialized profile departments included in the regional computer centres or in some ministries. The training process develops in two stages: a period of intensive courses attended by suspending the usual employment activities in production (10-15 weeks), followed by practice at the workplace (14 weeks). The final examination consists in defending a project undertaken during the practical training period, the topic of which is selected from among the range of problems specific to the enterprise financing the student. Finally, the students obtain a certificate enabling them to work in the job they have been trained for. Because of the great influx of the candidates of various professional profiles, admission to this type of course was initially based exclusively on a psychological examination. For this purpose a test battery consisting of six tests, meant to appraise aptitudes for informatics, was validated (the gain achieved by using the psychological tests is 20 per cent for analyst programmers and 30 per cent for junior programmers) (Pitariu, 1984). Thus, it was possible to organise homogenous classes of students with an aptitudinal potential for informatics, which facilitates training at superior parameters of efficiency. At present, the psychological examination has a limited influence, being supplemented by a knowledge test in the field of specialization.

High schools of informatics

These were set up in 1971 with the purpose of training average personnel for data processing. Studies are programmed for a term of four years (age 14/15-18/19), covering two stages: the first stage for the ninth and tenth grades and the second stage for the 11th and 12th grades. Admission is based on a knowledge test including mathematics and Romanian language together for the first stage, and an entrance examination conducted in mathematics and physics for the second stage. The graduates of these informatics high schools can work as operators for data collecting, transfer, and primary processing. Generally, 80 per cent of the first stage graduates are selected for the second stage and then, after the final graduation exam, they are considered skilled for junior analyst programmer, computer operator, and data control jobs. The graduates of informatics high schools can also take entrance examinations for any higher education institute.

Besides these high schools of informatics, all the mathematics and physics high schools include in their curriculum applied mathematics for computation technique, enabling the students to acquire knowledge of mathematical logic and Boolean computation, automatic data processing systems, programming languages and numeric calculus.

The educational system in high schools of informatics evinces some peculiarities. Generally, high school education comprises three forms of instruction: basic, specific, and practical. Basic subjects, with insignificant changes, are common to all schools, regardless of profile. They include mathematics, physics, chemistry, biology, Romanian language and literature (the schools for minorities also teach the respective nationality's language and literature), history, geography-geology, elements of social and political sciences, political economy, philosophy and modern languages. The specific subjects include economy, organization and administration of enterprises, mechanical drawing, and technological subjects specific to each vocation (technical calculus, programming and operation of calculus systems, information systems). As a whole the basic subjects make up 58 per cent of the classes, the informatics subjects are 11 per cent, while the practical training makes up the remaining 31 per cent. A graduate of the first stage in high school attends 1,021 classes (one class = 50 minutes) aimed at training him as a specialist, and the second-stage graduate has to attend 1,082 more classes. The practical training is organized so that each high school of informatics is provided with the specific equipment of an average capacity computation centre. The high school can be considered as a production unit. The school has a series of contracts with various enterprises, and it has a plan for production, the income of which enables it to support itself financially. There are, for instance, enterprises that do not have a computation centre, so that the current estimates of the administration of their material supplies or the computation of wages are done by the informatics school computation centre. Contracts are also concluded as regards not very difficult project topics. From a motivational point of view, this approach mobilizes the pupils, stimulating them towards achieving high quality professional performances. We must emphasize the correlation between teaching the specific subjects of informatics and the production practice, ensured by the double responsibility of the teachers who are also the production practice instructors.

Recently, owing to the increased interest in computer-assisted instruction (CAI), the high schools of informatics have become involved in this activity, both as beneficiaries and as creators of computer-assisted lessons. Though CAI is still in an experimental exploration stage, its penetration into the educational system is already manifest, especially in the education institutions aimed at training automatic data processing personnel.

Higher education informatics

Departments of informatics were first set up in 1971, offering three possibilities of training students in informatics:

a. sections of informatics within various universities;
b. departments/sections in polytechnical institutes;
c. the Faculty of Economic Planning and Cybernetics at the Academy of Economic Studies.

Students are admitted to attend these higher education institutes on the basis of a selection examination. Graduates are qualified for analyst and programmer as well as system engineer jobs (polytechnic graduates). Nevertheless, basic notions of informatics are taught with few exceptions in all higher education institutes. Thus, the future specialists, eg in medicine, learn about applications of informatics in their field of activity.

Higher education takes from four to six years, graduation being certified by a diploma paper which is supposed to be personal research. Graduates are guaranteed a job, which they can choose according to their performance at the university (the grades obtained during the course).

In-service courses in informatics

These are at present a much praised activity which is being developed under the legal framework established by law 2/1971. The law provides that each individual with a job attends an updating course every five years. These courses are organized without suspending normal employment. As a rule, the topic of the course is quite diversified, since it is established in accordance with the problems specific to the enterprise in question. In this global framework, informatics courses are also organized. Usually, the informatics courses are organized when an enterprise introduces the calculus technique and the staff needs to be trained, when new problems in informatics appear, or when the staff of an industrial unit request a series of lectures on certain topics in informatics (robotics, presentation of a programming language, etc). The attendance at such a course is concluded by taking an examination or defending a project. The attender has various advantages with regard to his promotion and the course itself is also considered a reorientation activity.

Staff holding management jobs in informatics or another area are also supposed to attend these courses.

The wide application of computers in Romania has its direct consequence in an outstanding enlargement of the educational basis with a flexible instructive content enabling a rapid integration of informatics in the educational system of Romania.

The Romanian experience in the field of informatics started as a result of social requirements. The modelling of future generations in the spirit of the ideas set by the informatics revolution is also a basic aspect (Drăgănescu, 1987). In the near future, informatics will be part and parcel of the people's general education.

References

Dancsuly, A, Ionescu, M, Radu, I, Salade, D (1979) *Pedagogie* Editura Didactică şi Pedagogică: Bucureşti

Drăgănescu, M (1987) *Informatica şi societatea* Editura Politică: Bucureşti

Lăşcuş, V (1986) The principle of permanent orientation Studia Universitatis Babeş-Bolyai, Philosophia, **31**, 2, 66-69

Pitariu, H (1979) *Dictionar de Pedagogie* Editura Didactică şi Pedagogică: Bucureşti; pp 425-427

Pitariu, H (1984) Psychological selection of personnel for data processing professions in van der Veer, G C, Tauber, M J, Green, T R G, Gorny, P (eds) *Readings on Cognitive Ergonomics — Mind and Computers* Springer-Verlag: Berlin

Radu, I T (1974) *Sisteme de învătămînt general-obligatoriu* Editura Didactică şi Pedagogică: Bucureşti

8. Informatics in Danish schools

Lise Fogh

Summary: Informatics is introduced in the Danish school system in order to provide the pupils with skills for applying and assessing the new technologies and also to benefit from the educational opportunities inherent in the new media.

So far informatics is an optional course in primary and lower secondary education, and an integrated part of curriculum in upper secondary education.

Currently much research and development work is done in Danish schools to determine the best way to introduce education for the new technologies into the curriculum.

The Danish educational system is characterized by a decentralized development, with the result that there is no national plan as regards curricular matters, in-service education of teachers, purchase of hardware and software, or development of educational software.

Recently the Danish Centre for Education and Information Technology has submitted a proposal for a national plan, suggesting a development and enlargement of the activities over three years. The plan suggests the development of the local centres and national co-ordination of activities.

Reasons for introducing informatics in Danish schools

Informatics is being introduced into the curriculum of Danish schools for at least two reasons.

One is the necessity of providing the pupils with skills which will prepare them for a society in which computers and the use of new communication and information technology become more prevalent. It is a question of the pupils' future skills and their understanding of the environment and context, in which technology, informatics, and data processing are being applied.

The aim is to make them computer literate and to make them capable of taking part in the development and assessment of the information society by means of a knowledge of the implications and consequences of the new technologies.

The educational system cannot send students without knowledge of the new information and communication technologies out into a modern society which relies to a great extent on these technologies.

Another reason for introducing informatics in the Danish schools is the educational advantages and opportunities which the new media imply for the learning process. This might either be the use of general tools like spreadsheets, word processing or databases in various subjects, or it could be special computer-aided learning programs, for instance a program simulating population growth or an interactive video program for learning a foreign language.

However, genuine computer-based instruction programs and tutorials, based on a rigid route through the subject matter of the program with a fixed series of questions and answers, have never met with great success in Denmark, since the pedagogical tradition here is opposed to this kind of learning style. Instead the best programs are considered to be those designed to help the learner with some tools for learning, letting the learner pose the questions and the program provide the answers.

Current practice

Since 1984 computer literacy has been an optional course in the lower secondary schools in eighth-tenth forms (pupils 15 to 18 years old). It is not yet in the curriculum in primary schools. About 90 per cent of the lower secondary schools offer computer literacy and it has proved to be a very popular optional course, attended by more than a third of each cohort. There is a slight dominance of boys in the classes. On an average there are four micros per school.

The aim of the course is to give the pupils insights into electronic data processing and its areas of application. The pupils gain experience in problem-solving using computers and the instruction contributes to the pupils' ability to assess and evaluate the pros, cons, and consequences of the use of computers.

The upper secondary schools are better equipped with micros, having about ten in each school. Since 1984 informatics has been taught in upper secondary schools as a compulsory course of 30 lessons in the first form. During the last two forms it is integrated in other subjects. This Danish model for introducing informatics in upper secondary education is remarkable, in that most other countries started out with specialized (optional) courses in computer literacy. The Danish model is meant to ensure that all pupils, regardless of sex and line, will learn about information technology and microelectronics as a tool.

The 30 lessons course in the first form gives a general introduction to the subject, including some practice at the computers, demonstration of programs and tools, discussions of the social implications of information technology, and a visit to a company or institution using the new technologies. This introductory course is planned and carried out by a team of teachers, usually made up of teachers from natural science, the social sciences, and the humanities. This is to secure a wide spectrum of approaches. If possible both female and male teachers are in the team.

During the following two years the pupils will apply computers in various subjects when appropriate.

Since 1987 computer science can be studied in upper secondary education as an optional, specialized course, which includes the more technical parts such as algorithms, programming languages, and programming.

Styles of learning

Computer literacy taught only as an optional course in lower secondary education is meant as a temporary measure while research and development work is done to investigate its future role in the curriculum. The question is whether computer literacy ought to become an independent subject, a special course taught during a couple of weeks, an integrated part of the curriculum in a number of subjects, or whether it should constitute part of a new science subject. There is also the question of how early in the educational system to introduce the issue.

Although the intention for the present optional course in computer literacy is to give a broad introduction to the use of computers, the actual teaching has to some extent been characterized by some initial difficulties, such as a lack of hardware and appropriate software, and insufficient training of teachers. Instruction was also made a difficult task because of a very uneven basis of qualifications among the pupils, some of whom have their own computers at home. In the beginning too much time was spent teaching the pupils a programming language.

Research and development

Currently much research and development work has been done to gain experience. In Horsens, a municipality in the peninsula of Jutland, a project has been carried out in 1985 and 1986 offering computer literacy as a compulsory course of two-weekly lessons for all fifth forms in the area (that is pupils of the age of 10–12). This implied that the fifth forms had two additional lessons every week, which had been accepted by the local education authority. It was decided that these lessons should be taught by the ordinary teachers teaching the classes, rather than by teachers already specialized in the field. This decision had two implications, one being that the new topic would be taught by those teachers who had the best knowledge of the individual pupils, and the other being that in this way supplementary education of teachers would be more widely spread among the teachers. The teachers involved in the project had an introductory course of 12 workdays. The project has been followed by a group of researchers from the Danish Educational Institute who have submitted a report, as has the project management. It appears from these reports that the project has been a success. The pupils have been very interested and motivated, and their age is considered appropriate for learning and working with computers. It also appears that part of the success was due to the fact that the ordinary teachers taught the courses.

The aim of the compulsory computer literacy course in fifth form is very similar to the directions for the optional course in eighth-tenth form. That is, to give the pupils a knowledge of computers and electronic data processing and to let them use the computer as a tool in problem-solving. It is also an aim to show them where and how new information technology is applied in various work processes in society.

All classes started out with a sequence of operating instructions. Then followed a number of different sequences, some lasting several weeks.

In this project much attention was paid to make the use of computers in various work processes obvious for the children. When working with for instance registers, the pupils were asked first to make a register by using old-fashioned index cards. Then they would make one by using a file program on the computer. The difference in retrieving information from the two systems became evident. A similar process was used for looking up telephone numbers. First they used the printed telephone directory, then they made their own little database of relevant numbers and finally they found numbers by using the online telephone information service.

To make the children grasp the historical development of technology, an example within production was selected, for example the woodworking industry. The pupils spent a full day at a museum with workshops demonstrating the technology of the last century. Later they visited a modern factory where a machine was programmed to produce a special item in only a fraction of the time spent in the manual process.

From interviews with the pupils after the first year, it appears that the majority find that the course has been exciting and interesting, and that they prefer using the computer as a tool. When asked, for instance, which of the topics they found most exciting, 'making a class newspaper' got a higher score than did 'word processing'.

Integration in the curriculum

The integration of informatics in various subjects in upper secondary schools has been successful, although some initial difficulties arose, especially a shortage of relevant software. The integrated use of computers in the classroom is also made difficult by the fact that in most schools the computers are assembled in a special 'data-room', which has to be booked in advance. In some schools the data-room is open for the pupils during the day. This makes it possible for the teachers to give assignments which have to be solved by use of a computer. However, some schools had to stop this open-door principle because of theft.

At an upper secondary school in Herlev, in the outskirts of Copenhagen, one class carried out a project using word processing in connection with the writing of papers in small groups.

Evaluating the project the teacher is certain that the use of word processing was conducive to the process, not least to the process of defining and structuring the material. Since the writing was visible on the screen for the whole group all the time, and since corrections and alterations were easily made, the work in the group was more concentrated on the subject matter in question than on the form. And the part of the teacher changed from correcting the final product to a discussion of a product in progress. Undoubtedly the students became more aware of the actual writing process.

The teacher made a couple of other interesting observations. The ordinary data-room was useless for this kind of teaching. Two rows of computers leaving space for one or two at each machine did not work. Each group needed lots of space and tables around the computer for books, notebooks, and coffee cups. And unlike other instances of work with computers, the girls had in this case an advantage, since some of them already knew how to type. They had only to learn the special functions in the word processing program, whereas the boys were unfamiliar with both typing and word processing, and their additional knowledge of bits and bytes was of no use.

In Denmark educational programs are most prevalent in the field of natural science and also the social sciences. The programs within social sciences tend to be comprehensive and open-ended, and they serve as a tool more than as a medium for teaching. Some schools have modems and access to information retrieval in various databases. The formation of a special school data bank with a simple command language and relevant data is being considered.

Programs for teaching foreign languages tend to be simple drill and training programs exercising grammatical inflections, and for that reason are mainly used with beginners. However, it seems obvious to use word processing also in this connection. Likewise experiments are set up to allow communication with classes in a foreign country via electronic mail systems.

Some very recent experiments with interactive video suggest that this medium has many advantages in the teaching of foreign languages. The combination of video strips and sound provide a more complete notion of the language and the cultural context. It is possible to see what the country looks like, and see the body language used when speaking. In addition the video disc provides a chance of repeating even small sequences of speech, a full transcript of the text as well as quick access to grammatical and lexical information.

A decentralized system

The Danish educational system is different from the system in other countries in a number of aspects. In this connection it is relevant to mention that about 90 per cent of all Danish children attend the public schools providing education free of charge. The first nine years of school, that is primary and lower secondary education (pupils from the age of six-seven to the age of fifteen-seventeen), are compulsory and take place at a *folkeskole*. Included in the *folkeskole* is an optional tenth year. The additional three years of upper secondary instruction are optional and take place at a *gymnasium*. Currently approximately 35 per cent of a birth cohort attend *gymnasia*.

The *folkeskole* is a comprehensive municipal school. With regard to syllabuses and teaching methods, the individual school and local education authority have a high degree of autonomy. Parliament sets the general aims of the *folkeskole* while the Minister of Education is responsible for objectives and guidelines for individual subjects, but it is up to the local education authorities and the individual schools to decide the content of the subjects.

The *gymnasia* are managed by the counties. In comparison with the *folkeskole*, the instruction at the *gymnasia* is more centrally administered, eg the Ministry of Education sets the aims for the individual subjects and issues detailed regulations governing the content and number of teaching hours for each subject in the various branches.

So far there has been no comprehensive national plan regarding the introduction of informatics in the Danish school system as regards not only curricular matters but also teacher training and purchase of hardware and software. There is a long tradition for decentralized development in Danish schools, the result being that some of the *folkeskole* schools still have not purchased any equipment and consequently do not offer the optional course, whereas others have several micros and have gained much experience in applying computers in various subjects.

Similarly many courses within informatics and computer science have been offered teachers, but many *folkeskole* teachers still have very little or no practical knowledge of computers and their use in education. The Royal Danish School of Educational Studies is in charge of supplementary teacher training and education for *folkeskole* teachers, and since 1984 many courses have been arranged in the local departments all over the country.

In the *gymnasia*, where informatics is a compulsory course, all teachers have attended at least an introductory course of 40 hours. Furthermore each *gymnasium* has selected one teacher to be in charge of the equipment and to support colleagues when using it. More specialized, subject-oriented courses are arranged by the teachers' professional associations.

Hardware and software

Another consequence of the decentralized development is that the individual school authorities have decided which type of computers to purchase, with the result that a number of different machines with incompatible operating systems are disseminated in the schools. The most prevalent machine is a Danish computer, Piccoline, produced by Regnecentralen a/s, covering about 30 per cent of the market. The Piccoline uses the CCPM operating system, but has recently been enlarged with a concurrent DOS system as well. Many schools have a number of Piccoline computers connected in a local network. The Danish programming language, COMAL-80, is predominant and can be used on most of the computers. PASCAL and PROLOG are also being used.

The many different machine types in the schools have made the development of educational software a difficult task. Since the educational market is already a small market, it becomes even less attractive for publishers and software houses to develop programs for a diversity of machines. Accordingly, many teachers complain of the lack of appropriate programs, and instead of larger, professional programs, the need for materials is met with many small, 'home-made' programs developed by enthusiastic teachers. However good some of these programs might be, they are often designed for a specific situation and thus difficult for others to apply.

In fact about 100 publishing and software houses on the Danish market develop programs for the educational sector. The majority are either textbook publishers or small firms comprised of a couple of teachers and perhaps one programmer, and with only a small number of products each.

National and regional organizations

The National Institute for Educational Media has two departments dealing with information technology. One is a technical department and the other is a software department. They are in charge of testing and documentation of hardware and software.

Moreover, each county in Denmark has a local centre for educational media which services the schools by distributing educational software. Some counties and municipalities have in addition established specialized resource centres to support the schools and teachers in questions of new technology. These centres are also in charge of teacher training within informatics and local research and development projects, and often they develop software in co-operation with teachers.

Besides, a number of regional collaboration projects exist with the purpose of funding development of software or larger research and development projects, for instance testing the use of databases in the classroom.

In 1984 the Danish Centre for Education and Information Technology (CPI) was established on the basis of a private grant. It is a non-profit institution under the auspices of the Danish Ministry of Education, with the purpose of supporting a comprehensive application of information technology in primary and secondary education. CPI is also the Danish Euryclee Centre, responsible for many international contacts and projects, especially among the EEC countries.

The main activities of CPI deal with information, education, and research. CPI arranges and takes part in workshops and conferences, and the staff give lectures and advice to teachers and school authorities on the choice of educational hardware and software and their application. To promote the production of educational software, CPI develops suitable programming tools and software, and gives technical and educational consultation.

Recent proposal for a national plan

CPI has recently submitted a proposal for a national plan, with the intention of obtaining some unity in the aims and endeavours and co-ordination of the many activities.

The plan suggests a development and enlargement of the activities over three years, in order to avoid waste of time and money already spent to introduce informatics in the schools.

Since the most important part of the system is the teachers, the plan suggests more supplementary education and in-service courses for the teachers, so that all teachers gain experience in working with a computer as a personal tool. Additionally, 20 per cent of the *folkeskole* teachers and 50 per cent of the *gymnasia* teachers should have a general knowledge of informatics and be able to apply different types of programs. The courses could to a large extent be shorter courses dealing with software packages. A small percentage of the *gymnasia* teachers, teaching computer science, need supplementary education at university level.

The plan also suggests an increase in the number of computers, so that an average *folkeskole* has 10 computers and a *gymnasium* 20 computers. Until now the equipment in schools has been paid for by the counties and municipalities, but CPI suggests that the state takes on some of these expenses.

To secure an active market for the development and production of educational software, the plan suggests a funding so that each school annually has a sum of 15,000 DKK (=appr. £1,300) at its disposal for the purchase of software.

In recognition of the decentralized tradition in Danish education, the plan suggests a structure for co-ordination, which as its backbone has the activities of the teachers, supported by the local centres. To gain the needed unity and co-ordination, CPI proposes that a national council is set up to advise the Ministry of Education and the local authorities. At present (Summer 1987) the plan is being debated by the involved parties, that is at ministerial, county and municipal levels.

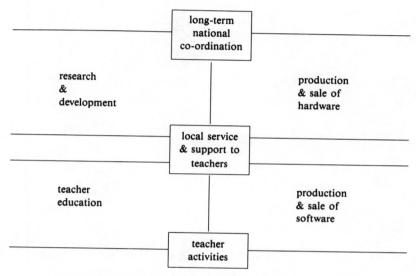

Figure 8.1 *The organization of activities suggested in the proposal submitted by CPI (1987)*

References

Christensen, G (ed) (1987) *Datalære i 5.klasse 1985/86* Horsens Kommune: Horsens, Danmark

Dylander, B *et al* (1987) *Education, skills, and informatics* – a Danish contribution to the EEC FAST-programme *TWE 3, network 2* CPI: København, Danmark

Forslag vedrørende informatik og edb i folkeskolens og gymnasiets undervisning i treå rsperioden 1987-90 (1987) CPI: København, Danmark

Hansen, K F and Jacobsen, J (1987) *Datamaterne i skolerne* Skolen NU: Gyldendal, Danmark

Hansen, K F and Jensen, P E (1986) *Informationsteknologi og skole* Status og udviklingslinier Danmarks Paedagogiske Institut: Munksgaard, Danmark

Jensen, P E and Klewe, L (1987) *Undersøgelse af datalære 1* Danmarks Pædagogiske Institut: Danmark

Part 3:Specific initiatives

9. Staff development and microcomputers: an Australian case study

Peggy Nightingale

Summary: Academic staff of a large Australian university with an orientation toward science and technology were surveyed to determine what academic tasks they were performing with the assistance of microcomputers. Responses suggest that a surprisingly low percentage of this university's staff were using microcomputers in their academic work. The survey also asked what training users and non-users of the technology would most like to receive. The survey identified a number of difficulties in attempting to meet the perceived needs of academic staff, including an organizational problem within the university — that is, that no one had been assigned responsibility for conducting staff development activities in academic uses of computers. The case is argued that without appropriate training for academic staff, any university's goal of computer literacy for all graduates is very distant. A proposal is offered which would allow training to proceed with limited resources. The model is of a strong central co-ordination of local services which draw on the expertise of enthusiastic users of the technology.

Introduction

During the past several years, staff of an educational research and development unit at a large Australian university have recognized changes in their own work patterns and in those of their colleagues throughout the university as microcomputers appeared on more and more desks. Occasionally something would appear in the literature on higher education about academic uses of microcomputer technology — most often about applications in teaching (eg Mikhelson and Carswell, 1985) but sometimes about other uses, such as in class administration (Denholm, 1983), in writing for academic purposes (Thomas, 1986), or in management of large quantities of information, be it verbal or mathematical data (Hopkin, 1986). Most authors were as enthusiastic about the possibilities of increasing 'productivity in academia' through the use of microcomputers as was McKenzie when he wrote for academics in the field of geology (1984).

The educational research and development unit is one of the sections of the university charged with offering training and development activities to the staff of the institution (among other roles such as maintaining a programme of research and conducting various investigations for the university). The focus of activities is on the institution's educational

role, but policy and process in higher education is the broad area of
the unit's interests and responsibility. As has been explained in some
detail in another publication (Nightingale, 1987b), there can be some
difficulties for units like this in trying to do too many different things,
particularly in the professional development area, and in establishing
who should accept responsibility for training in some specific areas. The
use of microcomputers is one of those problematic areas.

In the annual cycle of workshops and seminars, the unit started to
offer intea, evthe assroductory sessions on how to choose equipment,
the use of microcomputers in teaching, word processing for academic
writers, and so on. Such sessions were well attended and appreciatively
evaluated, but the unit was very conscious of the extremely limited
programme it could offer in this area, even with the assistance of staff
from the university's computing services department. The unit's staff
themselves were in phase one of the computer literacy curve (Haeckel,
1985), the stage in which one may use the technology to increase efficiency and convenience of doing jobs one must do anyway, but they
were not innovating or developing new applications. Until 1986 a unit
of the computing services department offered training in the use of some
popular software packages and other support to academic users of
microcomputers, but limited resources resulted in a decision not to offer
any more staff development programmes on microcomputers through
the user services unit. It thus became necessary for the unit to consider
very carefully both what was most needed and what it was possible to
do to meet at least some of those needs.

However, there was no solid information about the extent to which
academic staff were using microcomputers or for what purposes. Obviously, if 90 per cent of academics were already users, there was little
point in continuing to offer introductory programmes; on the other
hand, if there were still substantial numbers of staff in some areas not
making use of the potential of this technology, introductory sessions
should probably be continued. In addition, if some individuals who
were doing clever things with their microcomputers could be identified
and persuaded to share their discoveries with their colleagues, the unit
might be able to help fill the gap in development activities for academic
staff in this area. It was decided to survey all academic staff to find
out what people were doing with microcomputers and what they wished
to learn about them.

The following is an abridged report of that survey, focusing on what
was learned about the uses of microcomputers in academic work and
academic staff's perceptions about their training needs at a large university with a science/technology orientation in 1986. Omitted is data about
the most commonly used types of hardware and software, and similar
data of local interest. (This is available in Nightingale, 1987a.) The paper
concludes with a discussion of the implications of the findings as regards
development of student computer literacy and the need for staff development activities to promote the use of microcomputers in academic work.

Primary response[1]	No. of responses	% of response group	Faculty staff no.[2]	% faculty response
Applied Science	46	9	132	35
Architecture	22	4	69	32
Arts	37	8	127	29
Biological Science	31	6	96	32
Commerce	36	7	145	25
Engineering	56	11	179	31
Law	11	2	47	23
Medicine	55	11	137	40
Professional studies	23	5	61	38
Science	44	9	178	25
Graduate School of Management	10	2	40	25
Defence Forces Academy	50	10	142	35
Unknown/other	65	13	–	–
Total primary	486	100	1364	36
Secondary response[3]				
Not using; don't want to learn	97	62		7
Use larger computers	26	16		1
Interested but with reservations	22	14		1
Other	11	7		–
Total secondary	156	99		11
TOTAL RESPONSE	642			47

1. Primary response — full questionnaire returned.
2. Includes 'research only' as well as 'teaching and research'.
3. Secondary response — chose 'not interested' optional statement or gave other reason for not answering full questionnaire.

Table 9.1 *Survey response rate*

Method and response

In July 1986, a questionnaire (see pages 175–179) was sent to all academic staff of the university, approximately 1,350 persons. Every effort was made to keep the form simple and quick to answer, building in short cuts for people who were not currently using microcomputers. Those persons with no interest in microcomputers whatsoever were given an opportunity to avoid the questionnaire completely; in the covering note was a statement beside which such people could place a mark: 'If you aren't using a microcomputer and have no interest at this time in learning anything about microcomputers, please tick this box and return this sheet to...'

After a disappointing less-than-40 per cent return of full questionnaires and cover-sheets combined, a follow-up letter was mailed. It explained once again why it was important to the unit to have the information sought after, asked people to try to find the questionnaire or seek a replacement form, offered the statement for uninterested persons again, and finally asked anyone who was unwilling to fill out the full form and who felt the alternative statement was not applicable to send a brief note explaining why they were among the non-respondents. It was anticipated that some would be such skilled users of the technology that they were not interested in training, some might not be interested because they saw no prospect of purchasing equipment, and some might just be too busy to take time to learn about microcomputer uses.

After the follow-up mailing and allowing for staff members away on study leave, a response rate of just over 50 per cent was achieved (Table 9.1). 486 full questionnaires were returned, and 156 other responses were received. It was concluded from the comments received after the follow-up letter that the non-respondents were most likely not particularly interested in microcomputers, or in training activities on their use.

Of the 156 secondary responses (cover sheet or reminder returned), 97 chose the option statement that they were non-users and not interested in learning anything at the moment. Most of the rest commented either that they use larger computers and so are not especially concerned with micros (26), or that they are interested but only with reservations since they see no hope of getting a micro or are too busy to learn, etc (22).

Thus, about 36 per cent of all academic staff at the university showed enough interest in microcomputers to answer the full questionnaire about their use and about necessary training for staff (primary response rate). Of these, 77 per cent were users of the technology; that is, 27 per cent of all academic staff (see Table 9.2).

The primary response rate for faculties ranged from 23 per cent in Law to 40 per cent in Medicine.

	No.	% response group	% total response	% university staff
Primary				
User	374	77	58	27
Non-user	102	21	16	7
Unknown	10	2	–	–
Secondary				
User	26	17	4	2
Non-user	119	76	18	9
Unknown	11	7	–	–
Total Response				
User	400		62	29
Non-user	221		34	16
Unknown	21		3	–

Table 9.2 *Microcomputer user versus non-user response*

Use of microcomputers

Respondents to the questionnaire who identified themselves as users of microcomputers were given a list of 16 possible applications of microcomputer technology in academic work and asked to tick those tasks for which they used a microcomputer.

The five most common uses were:

Word processing (69 per cent of questionnaire respondents)
Administrative tasks (39 per cent)
Scientific computing (31 per cent)
Graphical presentation of data (29 per cent)
Linking to mainframe (26 per cent)

Most of the other uses identified in response to an open-ended question in this section could be included in one of the 16 categories; for instance, writing in word processing, or overheads in designing graphics, including preparation of teaching materials. Most of the microcomputer users who responded to the questionnaire use the equipment for many tasks: over two-thirds for three or more; 40 per cent name five-ten tasks.

Users tend to be enthusiastic, making comments such as:

(An engineer recollecting seeing a microprocessor for the first time in 1976) 'As I looked at that black chip, I said to myself, "This is it; this is a turning point in my life." '
(Arts faculty person who uses database, spreadsheet, project planner, graphics, and publications programs, as well as word processing) 'There are many things that I do that I just couldn't do without them.'

Even those who have used the technology less, or for fewer tasks, are equally enthusiastic:

'[I use the micro] almost entirely for word processing work of all kinds, for which I find it extraordinarily useful, especially for composing written work of any length.'

The questionnaire on microcomputers in academic work also included a section about what the respondents' students used computer technology to do. Twenty-eight per cent of the primary response group say that their students do not use this technology in the subjects they teach. Respondents replied that the most common student use of computers was for computation/data processing, with 21 per cent saying students would typically use a university microcomputer and 27 per cent saying they use mainframe computers; word processing was the next most common student use of computers, but only 16 per cent of respondents reported students using their own micros and 19 per cent reported students using university micros. (Note that there is probably overlap in these groups as respondents could tick more than one box.)

Academics' views on training needs

Training most wanted by microcomputer users

Eighteen possible applications about which people might like to learn more were listed on the questionnaire. The five topics most wanted by respondents who were already using microcomputers were:

Currently available educational software (27 per cent of primary response group)
Update on new software or applications (27 per cent)
Graphical presentation of data (24 per cent)
Teaching by computer-aided learning (23 per cent)
Handling bibliographies (20 per cent)

143 respondents ticked five or more boxes in this section. Open-ended responses did not suggest any other topics which were required by a number of users.

Training most wanted by non-users

A slightly different list of 20 applications was offered to non-users to try to ascertain what were their preferences for training programmes. The five topics most wanted by non-users were:

Word processing (14 per cent of primary response group)
Administrative uses (9 per cent)
Handling bibliographies (9 per cent)
Introduction to what a microcomputer can do (9 per cent)
Graphical presentation of data (8 per cent)

56 respondents ticked five or more boxes in this section. Again open-ended responses did not suggest other topics which might be much in demand.

Who should provide the training?

The survey asked people what sources of information/guidance they had found most useful in learning about microcomputers. The most favoured sources were: consultation with friends/colleagues (22 per cent), manuals (19 per cent), and magazines (12 per cent), with *Byte* being named specifically by 4 per cent of respondents.

The survey also tried to find out what type of training activities would be most popular. Hands-on sessions were favoured. The questionnaire tried to distinguish between sessions where there would be instruction and guided practice ('training sessions'), and sessions where participants might be left to experiment on their own with less guidance ('workshops'), but this distinction may not have been appreciated by respondents. Each of these options was ticked by 40 per cent of respondents; 34 per cent expressed interest in newsletters; 30 per cent in seminars; and 24 per cent in user groups.

However, when a small number of staff members were interviewed after the survey, there was a recurring theme in their discussions stating how helpful it would be to be able to locate other people with similar interests or with expertise one could borrow. More experienced people especially seem to value exchange with others very highly and expect that to be the most productive learning experience.

On the other hand, inexperienced people feel they need an introductory course of some kind before they can benefit from exchanges with users. One interviewee who was very anxious to learn to use a word processing program said that his school has a computer consultant who is too busy to give such basic instruction, that there are meetings run by the school's experienced users which are too advanced for him, and that even the school secretaries could not spare the time to instruct him. Almost all non-users suggest brief courses: for instance, an hour and a half every week for five weeks during session, or classes every day for a week out of session.

When the university's computing services department decided not to offer staff development on microcomputers, they argued that such training was available commercially and that academic staff could hire instructors or enrol in courses outside the university. The survey asked how many respondents would be willing to pay consultants if groups of interested people were formed to reduce the costs to individuals: 48 per cent said they would not pay their own costs, 33 per cent said they would participate if they received some assistance from their schools, and 10 per cent said they would pay their own costs. A typical comment on this section of the questionnaire was: 'I consider this to be part of the University's responsibility for staff development'; or, with less restraint, 'a typical bureaucratic solution to difficult problems'.

Discussion

In considering the responses to this survey of staff about their uses of microcomputers in their academic work, it was somewhat surprising to discover that there is apparently a fairly substantial majority of university staff who are not yet using microcomputers. One would have predicted at least widespread use of microcomputers as word processors, since so much of academic life revolves around writing, but response to the survey would put the percentage of academics using word processing at somewhere around 25 per cent of the staff (and this was the most common use of the technology).

There is comparable information from the University of Western Australia (University Uses of Microcomputers Project, 1984). There, 32 per cent of staff reported using microcomputers for word processing, the most common use (p 19). When asked about the frequency of use of micros, 40 per cent of UWA respondents said 'never', and 22 per cent said 'rarely'. In addition, when the UWA report considers responses to another question on expertise with microcomputers, it comments, '...a large group have no knowledge of microcomputers at all' (p 18).

Why, when academic users of the technology are enthusiastic about its benefits, have not the colleagues of these users leapt on the bandwagon? Other than simple technophobia, one answer may lie in the response of a non-user to the questionnaire. This individual, who ticked six applications as things he/she would like to learn about (including scientific computing), commented:

'The use of microcomputers is of interest and potential value to me but my academic commitments are so relentless and unavoidable that I cannot find any time at all to learn about them.'
'All computations in my subjects are formulated to be done with pocket calculators — I cannot find the time to change this system and am not sure that changes are desirable.'
(and finally) 'Most courses and manuals are prepared by enthusiasts for enthusiasts — there seems to be little help for resistant learners who cannot devote much time to such an intrusion. There are probably a number of university people in these circumstances but they won't respond to this questionnaire.'

The low level of use of a technology which has such a large potential for assisting academics in many of their tasks suggests that there is, indeed, a serious need for staff development activities to encourage the en incuse of microcomputers in academic work. However, this case study reveals many difficulties in delivering such a programme. The first is deciding where the responsibility for such training lies. At this time, the university's computing services department has withdrawn completely from training microcomputer users, but the department does accept a role in user education regarding the central computing system. The university's staff development unit (which is mainly concerned with offering training to general staff of the university) offers training for word processor operators (many of whom use microcomputers rather than dedicated word processors); some academics have been included in 'safe practices training' concerning the use of keyboards and they may enrol in a touch typing course the staff development unit offers; there is a user support network for keyboard clerical staff but no such network exists for academics. The unit has, as described previously, offered a few seminars on various topics concerning microcomputers in academic work. The unit sees its primary developmental role on campus as supporting the teaching and learning functions of the institution; consequently, the unit should be most interested in applications of microcomputer technology that are directly related to education. Clearly, no one is at present charged with responsibility for overseeing, co-ordinating or providing staff development in academic uses of microcomputers.

In making the decisions about what support will be offered to academic users and potential users of microcomputers, there are other issues which must be addressed — issues which the survey of staff made obvious.

In the first place, there is apparently no overwhelming interest among the academic community in seeing such a programme developed. The response to the survey was, to put it mildly, disappointing (though no less than the response to the University of Western Australia's similar survey). The 27 per cent of questionnaire respondents who chose the most wanted topic for development activities (currently available educational software) are only 10 per cent of the academic staff of the university. So we must ask whether, given limited resources at present, there is enough demand at this university to invest time in developing programmes for training academic staff in the use of microcomputers to accomplish academic tasks. The training programmes will have to begin by creating a demand. Is the benefit of employing this technology in academic work great enough to do so?

Secondly, some of the items on the 'most wanted' lists of development activities are the most difficult to offer. To keep abreast of developments in educational software in even a few disciplines would be an enormous task, requiring constant monitoring of specialist literature as well as commercial producers. It is not just a matter of listing available software; it must be evaluated by someone, and few academic staff would have time to conduct proper evaluations of a number of programmes while they were discharging the rest of their duties. There is no way the unit can take on the job of finding and recommending educational software in the multitude of teaching areas covered at the university. The best the unit can do is to try to put similarly inclined people in touch with each other, but at this stage of little knowledge and use of microcomputers in teaching, there is not a reasonable sized group of people to lead the others. So, at least for some time, it will probably not be possible to provide much leadership in the area most wanted by the respondents, which is also the area in which the unit would most like to lead education applications.

There are, however, some areas where the unit has found it possible to offer assistance. The programme of workshops and seminars in the past few years has included sessions on word processing packages, including more advanced instruction on Microsoft Word, on data management packages and bibliographical work on microcomputers, on computer-aided instruction, on choosing hardware, and so on. The survey has helped with decisions about what introductory sessions to offer in future which will be most useful to the greatest number of staff members. It has also identified many of the members of the university community who may be willing to share their expertise with others, so there is a place to start when seeking seminar leaders for particular topics.

Implications of the case study

Learning to use a microcomputer and/or a mainframe computer is important to students as well as to academic staff. Baldridge, Roberts and Weiner (1984) are probably right about the importance of the microcomputer in higher education in the next decade, but their predicted percentages should probably be reduced and their target dates extended if one were brave enough to make the sort of predictions for Australian conditions that they do for American. Their 'guesses' are listed below:

Guess one: Truly powerful computers will be developed to fit in your coat pocket and go to work with you.

Guess two: The primitive 'electronic mail' links of today will be as sophisticated as your telephone within this decade.

Guess three: Massive research and information libraries will be at the fingertips of every citizen in the country within the decade.

Guess four: By the end of the decade, every child in the United States will be computer literate at some minimal level by the time he or she is eight years old.

Guess five: By 1995 at least 50 per cent of the jobs in the United States will require an active working knowledge of computers.

Guess six: In 1995 almost every course in every college and university will use computers to some extent. (p 3)

Baldridge *et al* are absolutely convinced that there is no parallel between fads for various audiovisual aids in teaching and the use of the microcomputer; they believe that a better comparison is with the telephone (p 4). Despite their predictions, they estimate that at the time of writing their book, some 50 per cent of American university undergraduates had never touched a computer keyboard.

Offering more recent data, the Centre for the Advancement of Learning and Teaching at Griffith University (Queensland) surveyed the 1986 first year student intake to assess their computer literacy (Bond, Landbeck and Trigwell, 1986):

'Over 80 per cent of new first year students in the university and in all degree programmes except humanities (part-time) have used a computer. Computer use in this sense means the use of any computer for any purpose, including computer games, at any period of their lives.

'...37 per cent of the sample of entering students own, or have regular access to, a personal computer.' (p 2)

The Griffith data also give some idea of what students can do with computers: 36 per cent can write computer programs (p 2); 70 per cent had used computers for computer games; 40 per cent had used learning packs; 35 per cent had used data management packages; 32 per cent had used word processing packages; 25 per cent had accessed data banks; 20 per cent had used graphics packages; and 11 per cent spreadsheets (p 4).

Similar data on the experience of undergraduates at the university under consideration are not available, but one would expect their experience to be at least as extensive as the Griffith students'. However, response to the survey suggests that not a great many students are using microcomputers (or mainframes) in their day-to-day tasks as students. Assuming that those who answered the full questionnaire include most of the more computer aware and interested members of academic staff, this response does suggest that a fairly small percentage of students are, in fact, becoming computer literate as a result of their study at this university.

It would seem that the university is not yet approaching the goal of computer literacy for all graduates as envisaged in the Report of the Computer Teaching Working Party, December 1985. Whether students are gaining experience with the technology is not unrelated to the subject of this survey of academic staff uses of microcomputers. Both Baldridge *et al* (1984) and Bowden (1984) make the connection between achieving computer literacy for students and the need for staff development in the use of computers. Baldridge's recommendation is that 25 per cent of any budget for computing resources be allocated 'to a faculty/staff/administrator training programme' (p 98). He and his colleagues also write:

> One reason we stress the need for a full training programme for faculty as opposed to individual learning is the need for curriculum innovation. When a whole group of faculty are learning together, a 'snowballing' of expertise is likely to occur. Group learning triggers interest among faculty to experiment with curriculum changes.
>
> There are many innovative ways in which computers can be used in the curriculum, far beyond the traditional research uses for graduate students and computer science for undergraduates. The possibilities now exist for fruitful, productive use of computers throughout the curriculum, spreading even into the previously non-computer oriented liberal arts. (p 19)

As has already been intimated, curriculum development is not the only pressing reason for seeking to encourage academics to develop skills in using microcomputers. Holligan (1986) outlines the benefits of wide-area academic networks, naming applications such as electronic mail, conferencing, remote searching of databases, machine-readable texts, accessing library catalogues, and checking bookshop stock. However, he stresses that the utility of networks will not extend beyond enthusiasts and adepts if information services are not a first priority; others have trouble finding out what is available, what one can do and how one goes about doing it. In the end, most simply shrug and say how nice it would be but... Zinsser's (1983) attempt to introduce the principles and appeal of writing with a word processor, or Daiute's (1985) description of how her work patterns include transferring manuscripts from

New York to California by a touch of a button, so she can have immediate editorial comment, would similarly be enough to convince academic
writers of the possibilities that the technology could be of great assistance
to them. But once again, without readily available support and
assistance, the whole idea may seem unobtainable pie in the sky.

Institutions must reconsider their commitment of resources for staff
development in this area. Self-instruction is inefficient and extremely
wasteful of the time of academic staff, who already have teaching and
research programmes to maintain. Most of the persons whose need for
training is now being considered are not non-specialist users of computers, such as the people the university's computing services department
assists with the central system. That is, their need for assistance is very
different from that of a group of mainframe users, who may be expected
at least to know how to frame the questions to solve their problems.
They face a very difficult and frustrating task if they are to be expected
to initiate themselves into the world of the microcomputer; the learning curve for such persons engaged in this enterprise is notoriously 'flat',
and it is not surprising that many just give up. Even those who have
been initiated often report terribly frustrating experiences in trying to
teach themselves to operate complex software.

A proposal

A model for provision of training which might be considered is that
proposed by Coutts-Stern (1985) in her report on the education and
support of non-specialist computer users at Macquarie University (New
South Wales). Although she was considering all computer usage, not
just microcomputer usage, she identified the same resource constraints
at that institution as are operating throughout higher education. Her
model is of a strong central service, linked to strong local services:

> 'The central service would be a technically proficient service which
> concentrates on higher-level expertise for problem solving, 'train
> the trainer' programmes and strong communication channels to
> schools and departments. This service in turn would support local
> services or subject-specific services (eg a social sciences data centre)
> which would cater for the users' area-specific needs. Currently at
> Macquarie users turn more frequently to their friends and col-
> leagues for advice than to the existing services... Drawing these
> local users into local support services by training and supporting
> them and then allowing them to train and support their colleagues
> would be an effective, relatively low cost way of helping to meet
> local needs.
>
> 'Both central and local services would take the form of infor-
> mation centres... The central and local services would need to be
> very closely co-ordinated and the necessary overhead cost of such
> co-ordination must be planned for.'

Coutts-Stern follows Baldridge *et al* in recommending budgeting for education and support whenever equipment is purchased. She envisages using casual staff and internal secondments to provide the people to run at least some computer-related courses for non-specialist users. In her model the strong centre would clearly be in the university's computing centre; the local centres would be built around existing professional and technical officers within the schools (faculties) of the university. Most important for consideration is her vision regarding capitalizing on existing resources.

'The support which most suits the type and volume of usage in universities should have as its objective the greatest possible self-sufficiency of the users. Anything which users can efficiently learn to do for themselves and subsequently pass on to other users should be taught to them. Matters which are too complex or specialized for the non-specialist user should be the responsibility of a (usually central) specialist group... User enthusiasm should be used as a resource for support. Key innovators in computer usage should be identified and support specifically directed to them on the assumption that well supported non-specialist enthusiasts in turn become a source of considerable help to their colleagues...'

This suggests that there should be tangible support for those academic users of microcomputer technology who are willing to develop and pass on academic uses of hardware and software. That support might take the form of grants to encourage specific projects or time released from teaching responsibilities. Similarly, technical or professional officers might have their duties redefined to include responsibility for conducting training for academic staff or supporting the development of a microcomputer teaching programme. However, there must be central co-ordination, and there must be a clear and specific decision about the responsibility for that function.

Conclusion

In conclusion, if the enthusiasm of academic staff users of microcomputers is any measure of the usefulness of this technology, then microcomputers can contribute substantially to efficient and effective academic work. In addition, responsibility to students who will be expected to have reached a basic level of computer literacy before graduation demands that they be initiated into the use of the technology as part of their university education. However, too few members of staff are willing or able to invest the substantial amount of time necessary to teach themselves to use a microcomputer and various software packages, nor are they willing to invest their own money in training programmes. Institutions which find themselves in positions comparable to that in this case study should reconsider, in the light of this survey of staff needs and interests and the demonstrated benefits of this technology in academic work, various approaches to offering a co-ordinated programme of training and support to academic users of microcomputers.

Acknowledgements

The questionnaire used in the survey was prepared with the assistance of David Boud, Lee Andresen and Helen Simpson. Data was analysed with the assistance of Helen Simpson and Peter Furnell; the latter also interviewed some microcomputer users and non-users to supplement data collected by the questionnaire.

References

Baldridge, J V, Roberts, J, and Weiner, T (1984) *The Campus and the Microcomputer Revolution: Practical Advice for Nontechnical Decision Makers* American Council on Education, Macmillan Publishing Company: New York

Bond, D, Landbeck, R and Trigwell, K (1986) *Computer Literacy: The Intake Characteristics of First Year G U Students* Centre for the Advancement of Learning and Teaching, Griffith University: Brisbane

Bowden, J (1984) Applying new technology to tertiary teaching: possibilities and problems in the large-scale introduction of computers in Anwyl, J E and Harman, G S (eds) *Setting the Agenda for Australian Tertiary Education* Centre for the Study of Higher Education, University of Melbourne: Parkville, Vic

Computer Teaching Working Party (1985) *Report of the Computer Teaching Working Party* University of New South Wales: Sydney

Coutts-Stern, A (1985) *The Education and Support of Non-Specialist Computer Users at Macquarie University* Internal report: Macquarie University

Daiute, C (1985) *Writing and Computers* Addison-Wesley Publishing Company: Reading MA

Denholm, R (1983) Computer managed learning as a pilot project in TAFE Victoria *Proceedings of the Conference on Computer-Aided Learning in Tertiary Education* University of Queensland: Brisbane

Haeckel, S (1985) Some view! *Information Processing (IBM)*, **4** (2), 12- 13

Holligan, P (1986) Patchwork academe *The Times Higher Education Supplement* 27.6.86, pp 20-21

Hopkin, D (1986) Back to the future *The Times Higher Education Supplement* 27.6.86, p 24

McKenzie, G (1984) Using microcomputers to increase productivity in academia *Journal of Geological Education* **32**, 171-175

Mihkelson, A and Carswell, D (1985) The microcomputer as a teaching aid in tertiary chemistry *IUPAC International Newsletter on Chemistry Education* **23**, 7-9

Nightingale, P (1987a) Microcomputers and academic work: survey of academic staff at the University of New South Wales *Research and Development Paper No 66* Tertiary Education Research Centre, University of New South Wales: Sydney

Nightingale, P (1987b) Multiple and conflicting expectations of 'units' in higher education *PLET*, **24** (1), 55-61

Thomas, G (1986) Writing and thinking: some effects of a new technology *Teaching News* **28**, 2

University Use of Microcomputers Project (1984) *Interim Report* University of Western Australia: Nedlands

Zinsser, W (1983) *Writing with a Word Processor* Harper and Row Publishers: New York

Appendix 9.1 : Questionnaire

UNIVERSITY OF NEW SOUTH WALES
TERTIARY EDUCATION RESEARCH CENTRE

Microcomputers and Academic Work

* You may not need to answer all of the questions. Watch for the short-cuts that apply to you.

* Please return your completed form by 28 July 1986 to:

MICROCOMPUTERS AND ACADEMIC WORK
Tertiary Education Research Centre
Kensington

* Any enquiries or additional information to Dr Peggy Nightingale, x4934.

---

1. Do you currently use a microcomputer for any of your academic tasks (teaching, research, administration, writing, etc.)?

No.	%			No.	%	
102	21	☐ No		374	77	☐ Yes

If yes, go to question 2.

If no, what do you wish to know about? (You may tick more than one box.)

No.	%			No.	%	
43	9	☐ An introduction to what microcomputers can do	31	6	☐ Selecting equipment for purchase
28	6	☐ Currently available educational software	25	5	☐ Evaluating software
21	4	☐ Teaching by Computer-Aided Learning	27	6	☐ Data management
3	-	☐ Teaching students to use microcomputers	37	8	☐ Graphical presentation of data
45	9	☐ Administrative uses, eg. class records, exam scores, filing	28	6	☐ Designing graphics, including preparation of teaching materials
69	14	☐ Word-processing	29	6	☐ Accessing databases, eg. Dialog, Medline
24	5	☐ Electronic mail/ computer conferencing	31	6	☐ Creating databases
45	9	☐ Handling bibliographies	20	4	☐ Scientific computing, eg. solving algorithms
17	3	☐ Desk-top publishing	17	3	☐ Interfacing with research equipment
20	4	☐ Spreadsheets	32	7	☐ Linking to mainframe computers

Other - please specify_____

Please comment on your particular interests in microcomputers._____
_____
_____

Please go to Question 10.

---

2. You have identified yourself as a microcomputer user, for what tasks do you presently use a microcomputer? (You may tick more than one box.)

No.	%			No.	%	
50	10	☐ Teaching by Computer-Aided Learning	119	25	☐ Data management
73	15	☐ Teaching students to use microcomputers	142	29	☐ Graphical presentation of data
187	39	☐ Administrative uses, eg. class records, exam scores, filing	87	18	☐ Designing graphics, including preparation of teaching materials
334	69	☐ Word-processing	36	7	☐ Accessing databases, eg. Dialog, Medline
29	6	☐ Electronic mail/ computer conferencing	69	14	☐ Creating databases
82	17	☐ Handling bibliographies	147	31	☐ Scientific computing, eg. solving algorithms
57	12	☐ Desk-top publishing	106	22	☐ Interfacing with research equipment
103	21	☐ Spreadsheets	125	26	☐ Linking to mainframe computers

Other - please specify_____

We would welcome elaboration on how you use microcomputers._____
_____
_____

No %

3. How often do you use a microcomputer?   No   %

☐ Daily (or almost daily) 256   53   ☐ Fortnightly   13   3

☐ Weekly   66   14   ☐ Monthly   8   2

☐ Infrequently (This may include concentrated periods of use which occur at infrequent intervals.)
33   7

4. What machine(s) do you use? (You may specify more than one.)

☐ Apple II, IIe   104   22   ☐ Olivetti   20   4

☐ Apple Macintosh   113   24   ☐ President   17   3

☐ IBM PC (AT or XT)   110   23   ☐ Datamax   9   2

☐ NEC APC or APC III   63   13   ☐ Other - specify _____
123   26

Do you use a modem?

☐ No   208   43   ☐ Yes   83   17

                  missing 190   40

5. Who owns the machine(s) you use? (You may tick more than one box.)

☐ I do.   166   34   ·   ☐ University   313   65

☐ Other - specify   35   7

6. Where are the machine(s) you use located? (You may tick more than one box.)

☐ At home   204   42   ☐ UNSW research laboratory   83   17

☐ UNSW own office   191   40   ☐ UNSW other laboratory   41   8

☐ UNSW School office 85   17   ☐ Elsewhere at UNSW - specify 30   6

☐ UNSW computing laboratory 56 12   ☐ Other - specify   17   3

7. What software do you use? (You may tick more than one box.)

A. Word processing

☐ MS Word   99   21   ☐ Word Perfect   11   2

☐ Wordstar   94   20   ☐ Macwrite   84   17

☐ OK Editor   13   3   ☐ Other - specify 169   35

B. Database, file management, spreadsheets, integrated packages

☐ Dbase II 56 12   ☐ Visicalc 22 5
☐ Dbase III (or III+) 30 6   ☐ Multimate 7 1
☐ PFS File 24 5   ☐ Excel 12 2
☐ Lotus 1-2-3 47 10   ☐ Symphony 8 2
☐ Open Access 6 1   ☐ Other - specify 92 19

C. Data analysis

☐ SPSS (or SPSSx) 55 11   ☐ Other - specify 70 15

           No %

D. Graphics, publications packages   No %

☐ Macpaint 74 15   ☐ Visigraph 6 1
☐ Pagemaker 13 3   ☐ Print Shop 16 3
☐ Other - specify 91 19

E. Communications

☐ Kermit 74 15   ☐ Crosstalk 20 4
☐ Other - specify 49 10

F. Scientific computing, languages, etc.

☐ Turbo Pascal 41 8   ☐ Fortran 84 17
☐ Cobol   ☐ Other - specify 132 27

G. Please add any category or program we might have missed. _____

_____

8. What uses of microcomputers would you like to learn (more) about? (You may tick more than one box.)

☐ Currently available educational software 131 27   ☐ Up-date on new software or applications 128 27
☐ Teaching by Computer-Aided Learning 112 23   ☐ Data management 72 15
☐ Teaching students to use microcomputers 41 8   ☐ Graphical presentation of data 117 24
☐ Administrative uses, eg. class records, exam scores, filing 85 18   ☐ Designing graphics, including preparation of teaching materials 93 19
☐ Word-processing 71 15   ☐ Accessing databases, eg. Dialog, Medline 91 19
☐ Electronic mail/ computer conferencing 51 11   ☐ Creating databases 56 12
☐ Handling bibliographies 98 20   ☐ Scientific computing, eg. solving algorithms 44 9
☐ Desk-top publishing 85 18   ☐ Interfacing with research equipment 69 14
☐ Spreadsheets 59 12   ☐ Linking to mainframe computers 65 13
☐ None 21 4   ☐ Other - please specify 6 1

Please elaborate: what particular aspects of these uses do you wish to explore? What level of knowledge do you require?

_____

_____

_____

9. As a potential purchaser, what would you be interested in learning about?

☐ Selecting equipment for purchase *148* *31*   ☐ Evaluating software *130* *37*

☐ Nothing *63* *13*   ☐ Other - please specify_____ *7* *1*

10. Do you expect in the foreseeable future to link a microcomputer to a University mainframe computer via

☐ modem and telephone line *123* *26*   ☐ direct lines *83* *17*   ☐ not at all *140* *29*

Dual options
47 *10*

Missing
88 *18*

11. For what do students use computing technology in the subject(s) you teach? Please indicate what equipment they would use for each application by ticking the appropriate box.

☐ My students do not use this technology. *137* *28*

	Own micro		Univ. micro		Mainframe		Other (specify)
Word processing	☐ *77*	*16*	☐ *95*	*20*	☐ *30*	*6*	
Computation/data processing	☐ *34*	*7*	☐ *99*	*21*	☐ *133*	*28*	
To learn programming	☐ *13*	*3*	☐ *61*	*13*	☐ *80*	*17*	
CAL - computer acts as instructor	☐ *2*	*-*	☐ *23*	*5*	☐ *18*	*4*	
Interfacing for collection of data and control of equipment	☐ *6*	*1*	☐ *74*	*15*	☐ *9*	*2*	
Simulation	☐ *11*	*2*	☐ *58*	*12*	☐ *50*	*10*	
Information retrieval (access bibliographies, other databases)	☐ *3*	*-*	☐ *28*	*6*	☐ *29*	*6*	
Communications - electronic mail/ computer conferencing	☐ *5*	*1*	☐ *10*	*2*	☐ *25*	*5*	

Other - please specify *27* *6* _____

12. What types of activities focussed on microcomputer technology would interest you? (You may tick more than one box.)

☐ Seminars, including demonstrations *143* *30*   ☐ Workshops, mainly hands-on experience *191* *40*

☐ Training sessions, including instruction *193* *40*   ☐ Participation in specific software or hardware users group *114* *24*
   and hands-on practice

☐ Newsletters *168* *35*   ☐ Other - specify_____ *14* *3*

Comments_____

13. The University's Computing Services Department will no longer offer any training workshops. If groups of interested people were formed to reduce the costs to individuals, would you be willing to pay consultants to conduct training programs on hardware or software?

☐ No   ☐ Yes, if my School met some of my costs   ☐ Yes, even if I had to pay my own costs
232   48   158   33   50   10

14. What sources of information/ guidance have you found most helpful in your learning about the use of microcomputers in your work?   (Please name particular journals, manuals, books, or seminars, etc. and specify for what they have been useful.)

consultations	22%
manuals	19%
magazines	12%
(BYTE 4%)	

Identifying yourself below is entirely optional. We ask to know who you are because we would like to be able to bring people with similar interests together, and because we would like to let you know when activities in which you have expressed an interest are scheduled.

Name_____

Faculty_____

Thank you very much for your time.

Please return by 21 July to: MICROCOMPUTERS AND ACADEMIC WORK
                               Tertiary Education Research Centre
                               Kensington

10. Practising education with the new information technologies

Chris Bell

Summary: Various agencies are encouraging the introduction of new information technologies (NIT) into all courses at post-compulsory level in the United Kingdom. This has wide-ranging implications for all teachers, designers and administrators of these courses. Whilst some are knowledgeable and aware of NIT, many are not. This chapter explores some of the reasons for widely introducing the basics of NIT to all staff, some of the problems in facilitating and disseminating innovations within a context of professional development and describes an attempt to help provide basic awareness training, support and encouragement for those staff in post-compulsory education who claim to be 'NIT naive' and wish to gain knowledge of the implications and potential of NIT in education.

Introduction

'Innovations in education have criss-crossed the sky like Roman candles, and most spluttered out quickly, leaving only the smell of disenchantment in the air' (Marilyn Ferguson, *The Aquarian Conspiracy*).

New information technology (NIT) is a wide-ranging and increasingly frequently used term at all levels of education and training, and throughout industry, commerce and research. The emphasis on just what constitutes NIT varies. For example, two frequently quoted 'definitions' of NIT indicate rather different emphases:

'Information technology means the collection, storage, processing, dissemination and use of information. It is not confined to hardware and software but acknowledges the importance of man and the goals he sets for this technology, the values employed in making these choices and the assessment criteria used to decide whether he is controlling the technology and is being enriched by it' (Chatland and Morentz, 1979).

'[Information technology is] all items of electrical and electronic equipment which incorporate microprocessors or transistors, and items of equipment which operate in conjunction with them but independently. Thus, microprocessors, microcomputers, word processors, are included in the definition, as is all equipment peripheral to these devices (such as printers, disc drives, automated typewriters etc).

[It is also] the academic discipline concerned with the study of the application and development of the underlying principles involved in their use' (FEU, 1984a).

The 'technological' vs 'applications/uses/implications' distinction is one which certainly exists in post-compulsory education. Side by side (although perhaps often not communicating too well) are those who are engaged in NIT innovations, pushing the limits of knowledge forward at an ever increasing rate; and those who are applying NIT to facilitate the learning of their students, their own administration, or are introducing the fundamentals of NIT to learners (perhaps colleagues). Unfortunately the spectrum extends to include the many who do not use NIT, have not really come to terms with its applicability or utility, and often express concern at lack of understanding:

```
─────────────────────────────────────────────▶


        NIT                    NIT                    NIT

    'researchers'            'users'                'naive'
```

Although the 'NIT message' is loud and clear from many directions, the necessary infrastructure for what is basically a staff professional development issue often does not exist to provide very basic awareness training, support and facilitation for the many staff who find self-motivation in this direction difficult or who, possibly correctly, consider NIT a low priority amongst the increasingly multifarious pressures to which they are being subjected.

Notwithstanding this, all predictions are that NIT is here to stay. It will become an increasingly important part of everyday life, work and education. In the post-compulsory sector within the UK, various agencies have indicated the importance of NIT for all, at all levels. For example the Computer Board for Universities and Research Councils has suggested a wide range of educational uses of NIT (UGC, 1983); the Council for National Academic Awards (CNAA) has pressured for an NIT element in all of the courses for which it is responsible (CNAA, 1982); and the Further Education Unit (FEU) has produced various documents and policy statements (eg FEU, 1984b) concerning NIT.

The utility of NIT in education

One of the factors that sets NIT aside from other innovations in education is that the technology, and its applications, are all-pervasive. They are also multifarious (unlike say, the programmed learning 'revolution'). A recent Council for Educational Technology publication stated:

'Indeed, there is no part of the FE curriculum which can be unaffected by information technology, whether because the 'traditional' FE courses are subject to technological change... or because teachers are finding 'non traditional' uses for new technologies... or because of pressures to introduce all students to IT... as students, parents and employers see links between IT and economic change' (Donovan, 1986).

The new information technologies are not, obviously, just a tool of education. They encompass one of the few developments which is in one way or another permeating practically every aspect of work and life in the majority of developed countries. It is unlikely that anyone reading this will not have come into contact in the recent past with something that has directly or indirectly drawn upon NIT: monetary transactions, television or radio, transportation, to name but a few of the many possibilities.

Within all areas of education and training, NIT can be applied to enhance the learning process, help organize and manage learning, provide evaluative feedback on learning undertaken, be used as a device of display and demonstration, collect experimental data, control devices, aid design, be useful in all areas of administration and enhance communication.

Aspects of NIT at a basic level are various but have been identified by the Computer Board for Universities and Research Councils (UGC, 1983) as comprising:

- the use of applications packages (eg statistics, computer-aided design)
- teaching about the basics of computers
- continuous assessment (eg using multiple choice questions)
- electronic blackboard (eg computer output of diagrams, notes etc)
- databases
- electronic mail, telesoftware and telecommunications
- computer-assisted learning
- monitoring problem-solving activities
- simulations and modelling
- management of learning (eg electronic diaries to track work done and problems encountered)
- aids to open access of learning.

Donovan (1986) identifies the following additional aspects:

- word, data and information processing
- broadcasting: cable and satellite
- video, tape, film and disc
- administration.

And Gibson *et al* (1986) add the following aspects:

☐ teletutoring and teleconferencing
☐ graphical display of information
☐ computerized record keeping
☐ authoring systems
☐ interactive video
☐ control technology
☐ computer networks.

The range is wide; many of the other chapters extend and explore it.

A rationale

Within post-compulsory education, there are a number of training and educational foci to be considered when analysing the NIT content of an institution's activities. At least three broad areas of focus can be identified, although in practice there will be overlap:

1. Learners, largely within the disciplines of computing and technology, who are, or will become, the practising NIT professionals. These require a highly sophisticated level of knowledge of computing, the associated technologies and applications.
2. Learners in a variety of disciplines who will be expected to have a good knowledge of those aspects of NIT directly relevant to their work areas. For these, NIT will be used primarily as a tool to support particular needs (for example data collection and manipulation, control, statistical analysis, design).
3. All learners who do not fall into one of the above categories need to have a basic awareness of, and sensitivity to, NIT. For this group, NIT must be very much wider than computing alone. It is likely to involve the applications of computers and associated peripherals, but generally in the form of 'black boxes' to facilitate that which needs to be achieved. Knowledge of what happens inside the box is generally unnecessary. The use of communications, word processing, spreadsheets and databases may fall into this category.

'Learners' in the above context could equally well be 18 years plus students, mature students, students undertaking continuing education or indeed the staff of the particular institution engaging in professional development.

In the majority of institutions within the post-compulsory sector, any learners and researchers involved within the first category are well catered for, although as always, human and material resources are often scarcer than would be ideal! Staff are generally well trained and knowledgeable in their field. Initiatives which characterize this category are, in Europe, the European Strategic Programme for Research and

Development in Information Technology (ESPRIT) (see for example O'Farrell, 1984), and in the UK, the Alvey programme (see for example Department of Industry, 1982). Both initiatives have aimed to focus on basic research and design in pre-competitive activities. Areas of work represented include:

> very large scale integration (VLSI)
> man-machine interfaces
> intelligent knowledge-based systems
> software engineering
> advanced information processing
> computer-integrated manufacture.

Learners in the second category are also generally well catered for. Within most departments, there are some staff interested in specific applications of NIT who are willing and able to update and enhance their knowledge. In turn these staff often become involved with the teaching of NIT applications specific to their department and may become agents of change within their department or further afield.

It is the third of the above categories where there appears to be little work reported or occurring within many of the post-compulsory institutions with which the author is familiar. If indeed elements of NIT are to be introduced into all courses at post-compulsory level, then all staff involved with these courses need to have an awareness of, and sensitization to, the basic concepts and applications. As time passes, the need for specifically focused professional development in this area is likely to decrease, but at the present time this need is apparent.

An approach to raising staff awareness of NIT

Building upon the foregoing, this section describes the ways in which one part of one institution involved in post-compulsory education is attempting to facilitate and support professional development in NIT for staff who claim to be 'NIT naive' or who would like to explore further the basic concepts and applications to their own work environment.

The strategy adopted has been developed over some three years of organizing and evaluating staff development activities in NIT, working with staff from one institution undertaking professional development and staff from outside attending various short courses and other activities. Staff have included academic, technical and secretarial. The approach continues to develop in the light of feedback and knowledge gained.

There is little new or revolutionary in the strategy developed; however, it appears to be having some success. Undoubtedly there is a variety of alternatives being pursued by others; some are likely to be more effective, others less so.

Some problems

Within education, new information technologies have the potential to be widely adopted and adapted, not only influencing teaching methods and methodologies and being a subject worthy of study in their own right, but also having the potential to modify administrative systems, methods of reporting, of assessment and evaluation radically. They have the potential to help staff in many areas of education: administration, teaching and technical. They also have the potential to hinder these staff in achieving personal or institutional goals.

Any organization subject to innovation is likely to have some staff motivated and knowledgeable in the area of the innovation. These may become agents of change or may prefer to become deeply involved with the innovation rather than to encourage or facilitate its wider adoption. It is likely that a large proportion of staff will not be knowledgeable, not able (or willing) to spend much time investigating and learning about the innovation and may well be sceptical, hostile or ill at ease with the ideas. Introducing basic awareness of NIT to these staff needs to be undertaken in a way which is effective, efficient and treated sensitively.

Gross *et al* (1971) have indicated five major barriers to the adoption of innovations.

1. A lack of clarity among staff about the innovation;
2. Staff lack of skill and knowledge to perform a new role;
3. Unavailability of required learning materials;
4. Lack of staff motivation;
5. Incompatibility of organizational arrangements.

In the context of introducing NIT to staff in educational institutions, it has been noted that attitudes towards the adoption may well include:

1. The ostrich: ignore it and it will go away.
2. The Luddite: NIT is going to take over from the teacher or administrator, so refuse to use it.
3. The fatalistic: NIT is here, there is nothing that can be done about it; it will destroy education or will it be its saviour?
4. The co-operative: NIT has useful applications. Use it where appropriate but if a job can be done better without it, then be prepared to use other techniques.
5. The imaginative: adapt 'traditional' uses of NIT for new applications. (YHAFE, 1982)

There are many pitfalls possible in facilitating staff awareness in basic aspects of NIT. John Cowan (1987) listed the 'seven deadly sins' to be avoided:

1. aimlessness;
2. ineffectiveness;
3. inefficiency;

4. narrowness;
5. shallowness;
6. lack of inspiration;
7. an impersonal approach.

These pitfalls are applicable to any teaching/learning situation, but if they occur alongside insecurity and possible reticence in coming to terms with NIT, then motivation and learning can be very low indeed.

At a more pragmatic level, a major problem in providing the sort of staff development aimed for lies with the lack of suitable 'change agents' in many institutions. Those who have high expertise in NIT are often not the best at motivating and communicating with the 'NIT naive'; and those with responsibility for professional development often do not possess the necessary knowledge. This problem has very often been cited as the single major reason for the lack of suitable basic NIT professional development (personal communications to the author).

Some solutions.

There are no definitely right or wrong answers to providing and promoting professional development, particularly in an area changing as fast and as value-laden as the new information technologies. A study of the literature of the dissemination of innovation and professional development will quickly reveal a variety of strategies, each with differing underlying philosophies. Indeed, Black and Ogborn (1977) note:

'Discussions... soon reveal deep differences about almost every matter at almost every level, for the vital need for rigor as opposed to the need for student's views, reactions and problems, to differences about how, when and what to teach. Passionately held positions are struck and defended...'

While few actual professional development or dissemination processes follow just one strategy, consideration of various researches into this area provides identification of the possible approaches, and serves a useful role both when developing strategies and subsequently when evaluating and modifying them.

Chin (1970) suggested various strategies used in educational change, deriving a threefold classification: empirical-rational, normative re-educative and power-coercive.

The empirical-rational approach involves appeal to the intellect, convincing people by rational means of demonstrating increasing effectiveness or efficiency of some new practice or idea. Often, information derived from basic research is utilized. The normative re-educative approach involves attempts to change ideas, attitudes, skills and values. The power-coercive approach is based upon the application of power — political, economic or legal — to bring about change directly.

Havelock (1968) developed a similar threefold classification including an alternative strategy, social interaction, which relies upon informal
networks of information. Although it has similarities to the empirical-
rational approach of Chin, less emphasis is placed upon formal means
of dissemination.

Havelock has suggested that there are three main forces which affect
the reception, diffusion and adoption of new educational ideas: how
ideas are initially received by individuals (personal factors), how these
ideas are communicated via networks of individuals (interpersonal
factors), and the effects of the structure of the institution (institutional
factors).

Personal factors include:

☐ personality traits (openness; persuadability)
☐ situational needs (satisfaction or dissatisfaction with the current
   situation; clarity of aims; past experiences of change; amount
   of pressure applied; personal gain/satisfaction)
☐ adaptive demands (types and amount of change needed).

Interpersonal factors include:

☐ direct factors (leadership; continuity; credibility of information
   passed on)
☐ indirect factors (cohesiveness of group; support for change; group
   norms; homogeneity of group).

Institutional factors include:

☐ structure (types of hierarchy; openness of hierarchy; reward and
   'punishment' structures)
☐ functional (perceptions of need; perceptions of aims; stability).

Finally in this brief analysis of dissemination and professional development, Eraut (1972) has provided a framework indicating the relationships
between what he terms 'modes' and 'levels of discourse' in dissemination of innovation/professional development. This framework (Figure
10.1) indicates those methods of provision (modes) which are likely to
satisfy various developmental aims (levels of discourse) best.

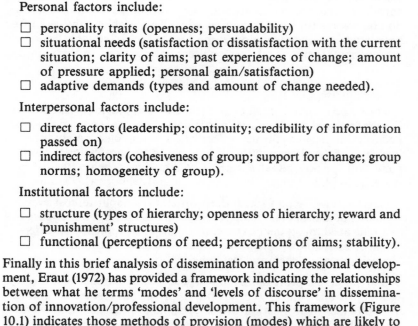

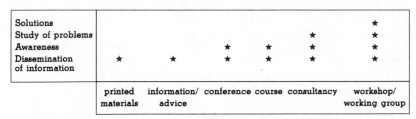

Figure 10.1 *Relationships between modes and levels of discourse in
the dissemination of innovation*

Taking account of the various problems and pitfalls likely to be encountered, and the various ideas emanating from dissemination and communication theory, a strategy is being developed to provide, facilitate and disseminate basic awareness in educational aspects of NIT.

The target audience to be addressed included those staff in education who claim to have little or no expertise in the field of NIT (although staff claiming some expertise are not actively discouraged from participating in any of the staff development activities). The numbers of staff falling within this category is estimated to be several hundred within the one institution, drawn from academic, secretarial and technical. In addition, staff from a number of other institutions (including the compulsory sector) have taken part in many of the activities and have helped formulate approaches and strategies.

Those organizing and tutoring the staff development activities include members of the institution's learning resources centre (educational services and library services), computing department, and computer services. In addition, the expertise of individuals from outside the institution has been drawn upon both to tutor and provide ideas/support. The group is very much an *ad hoc* one. All have many other responsibilities and come together in various combinations as and when the need arises.

The broad aims of the programme of staff development in NIT include:

1. To introduce the basic concepts of NIT
2. To provide 'hands-on' experience with a variety of computer applications apposite to the work of participants
3. To explore ways in which NIT may be applied within education
4. To develop a critical awareness of the utility of NIT within education
5. The development of openness and flexibility in attitudes towards NIT and change in general.

The strategy adopted is eclectic both in terms of its approach and underpinnings. Although overall aims, directions and strategies have been identified, many of the development activities are responsive, arising from needs (either expressed or felt). For example, groups of both 'learners' and 'teachers' are brought together for specific activities, enquiries are often followed up culminating in some planned activity, a short course is organized in response to a local need, a department wishes to introduce some basic aspects of NIT and seeks advice.

The staff development activities engaged can be broadly divided into the following, although in practice there is overlap:

☐ courses of varying length;
☐ individual and small group consultancy;
☐ problem-centred groups;
☐ self-sustaining networks;
☐ demonstrations of specific applications;
☐ 'open days';
☐ provision of information and ideas 'on demand'.

COURSES

The term 'courses' is being used here to include all those activities which draw together a group of people for some planned learning. Most courses involve much independent hands-on experience, discussion, problem-solving and workshop activity in addition to more formal teaching.

Courses offered thus far range from those lasting about ten hours, generally designed to provide a 'general awareness overview' of NIT or to concentrate upon a specific topic (eg word processing) to those lasting some 60 hours designed to provide a more comprehensive overview and allow greater experimentation. Numbers accommodated have ranged from about 5 to 25, depending upon demand and equipment availability.

Details of such a 60-hour module are given in Appendix 10.1 in the form of course members' initial notes. These should provide a 'flavour' of the content offered and approach adopted. It should be noted that, in the example given, the distribution and discussion of the notes is preceded by one or two contact sessions where a brief demonstration of each of the topic areas is given and discussed. In this way course members are introduced to a range of NIT applications and can focus more easily upon those which are considered to be of utility in their own work situation.

Shorter courses are often organized in a similar way but with a narrower focus; or their aims, content and approach are negotiated to satisfy particular needs.

It is considered that the teaching/learning approach adopted is of utmost importance as noted in the previous section. A 'hidden' aim is to encourage course members to participate actively, develop new skills, become open to modifying attitudes and experiment within a friendly, responsive and supportive milieu, leaving sessions with a desire to learn more and adapt knowledge gained to their own particular situations. To this end, an 'autonomous learning' approach is adopted where possible, with adequate tutor support, often at the expense of staff-student ratios.

Most of the basic applications of NIT noted in Appendix 10.1 (see pages 195-198) have various levels of paper or disc-based tutorial notes including:

☐ a general overview of an application of NIT, what it can do, how it can be useful, some ways in which it can be integrated into 'normal' work (curriculum and administration) and can be linked with other applications. Here, as in group and individual discussions, emphasis is not upon the technology, but upon its applications and adaptations to the work situation of the course participants.

☐ a basic tutorial, often adopting a 'cookbook' approach giving clear and simple instructions. The main aim of this approach is to help ensure that those using the tools of NIT have some initial success at achieving results, therefore encouraging motivation.

☐ more advanced notes, ideas and prompts for those who have mastered the basic concepts and skills.

An approach which draws heavily upon tutorial resource material allows a more individualized approach, aiming better to satisfy the often diverse needs of the course members, and giving the tutors more freedom to solve the inevitable problems which arise, and to provide personal support and encouragement where necessary.

Groups are periodically drawn together to discuss and explore topics of common interest (for example the integration of NIT into the curriculum or administration, problem-solving, the implications for education and society of NIT).

INDIVIDUAL CONSULTANCY

With any change or innovation, there is generally a need to provide support and advice to those coming to terms with, or applying, the innovation. This is particularly true where initial awareness and familiarity may be low. Whilst courses can effectively and efficiently help develop many skills, there is often a need to provide support to individuals using a consultancy approach. In general the characteristics of this approach include:

- client-centred analysis of the individual's needs and problems
- problem-solving activity aimed at satisfaction of needs.

Although individual consultancy is time consuming, the benefits, both in terms of process and product, are usually considered to be worthwhile.

PROBLEM-CENTRED GROUPS

Frequently a number of individuals have the same 'problem' or need at the same time. Where such is identified an attempt is made to bring together the individuals into what could be described as a 'problem-centred group'.

Groups may be drawn together as a subset of those gathered for an organized course, or may form as a result of knowledge of several individuals having the same problem. Wherever possible, an attempt is made to bring into such a group one or two people who have experienced a similar problem and have started to investigate solutions, preferably not experts, rather people who are a few jumps ahead. Again, this approach is found to increase motivation and participation of those who may otherwise not feel happy at learning new skills or modifying attitudes.

A particularly successful (judged by comments of participants and observations of organizers) type of problem-centred group is the one which helps a small number in troubleshooting, problem-solving and sharing ideas about a particular aspect with which they have been involved. For example, course leaders and secretaries engaged in the recording of student achievement using a spreadsheet; academic staff with experience of a particular word processing package.

SELF-SUSTAINING NETWORKS
There are several instances where self-sustaining networks of individuals
have been facilitated with the aim of providing mutual support and
problem-solving. A brief description of the development of one such
network will serve to illustrate.

A new word processing package adopted by the institution resulted
in a series of training courses being offered to secretarial staff who would
be using the package. The organized course sessions aimed to provide
basic skills training, a set of reference material and increased personal
confidence in use and application of the package. As an individual's
use of the package increased, greater emphasis was placed upon both
peer group and tutor-provided problem-solving.

After the organized sessions were complete, groups continued to meet
during lunch-hours for several weeks to discuss problems encountered,
new knowledge gained and provide mutual support. At this stage the
tutor was present, providing decreasing support as the expertise of the
group increased. Indeed, it was not very long until the roles of teacher
and learners were reversed!

Following informal sessions, the staff distributed a list of their phone
numbers to keep in contact on an *ad hoc* basis as and when needs arose.
In addition, one or two of the more adventurous staff have found ways
of adapting the package to their specific requirements, and have distributed notes of these to other group members.

A situation has thus developed where a group of some 20 staff have
moved from formal teaching, through informal problem-centred groups
towards a self-sustaining network providing advice, support and
problem-solving expertise.

DEMONSTRATIONS
Demonstrations have proved to be a cost-effective way of disseminating information about particular innovations, and of increasing
awareness. They are either undertaken by staff from within the institution in question, or the expertise of staff from other institutions or
commercial concerns has been called upon. The range of topics
represented is wide, from the use of various authoring systems to simple
databases in administration; from CD-ROM to audioconferencing.

Wherever possible, staff 'at the chalkface' are encouraged to share
their expertise and ideas rather than to call in an expert. In this way,
those attending the demonstration leave with higher motivation to apply
the ideas themselves than if they had watched a highly polished performance by a protagonist.

Several of the topics of demonstrations have resulted in follow-up
work being undertaken, perhaps leading to course activity, the formation of a problem-centred group or informal dissemination networks
being established.

OPEN DAYS
Unlike demonstrations, open days tend to be less structured and cover

a wider range of NIT applications. As in the case of demonstrations, invitations to attend are widely distributed and it is hoped that the day is not too oversubscribed (although on one memorable occasion, some 250 people passed through the door of the venue in a day!).

Open days have been arranged in a large room with areas set aside for particular activities (for example, databases, word processing, authoring systems, graphics, videotex, audioconferencing, individual consultancy, a range of videotapes on aspects of NIT). Participants are free to come and go as they wish, dipping into those aspects which interest them. Help and advice is available for those seeking it, although care is taken to avoid the hard-sell approach, emphasis being laid on allowing people to experiment, make mistakes and discoveries of their own.

An active attempt is made to record details of the interests and needs of those attending, thus allowing subsequent follow-up where this is considered appropriate, and to add to the database of knowledge about who is doing what.

INFORMATION ON DEMAND

Many of the requests for help and advice can be satisfied by paper-based resources: manufacturers' catalogues, reviews, notes about software, etc. To this end, a large collection of such resources is held and is available for use in the institution's learning resources centre.

Other requests require a knowledge of who within the locality is interested in, or has expertise in, a particular aspect. Two computer databases are currently being developed to help satisfy this requirement, one holding details of known individuals' interests and expertise, and the other comprehensively detailing the software existing within the institution.

Conclusions

This chapter has attempted to describe an approach to facilitating an awareness of NIT amongst those staff who claim to be NIT naive and providing continuing support for those staff. The approach adopted is eclectic, drawing upon various models of dissemination and professional development. The practical aspects of provision have formed the focus; institutional costs and political issues have not been examined in any depth although, in actuality, little can be achieved without much time and effort spent in engaging such aspects.

The strategies described have developed over a period of time, and continue to develop in the light of formative feedback from all those concerned. An active attempt is made to evaluate all activities. Courses have built within them frequent opportunities for feedback and usually end with a formal course evaluation. Less formal activity is evaluated through discussion with those involved, and feedback via various committees and interested parties, etc. The team of staff engaged in the professional development activities frequently discuss possible improvements and changes; emphasis in provision and strategy often changes in response to needs.

It is difficult to provide comprehensive evidence about the success or otherwise of the activities yet. Professional development in NIT as described is a long and ongoing activity; the benefits are likely to be realized over a period as changes in attitude, greater adoption and adaptation of the technologies and the gradual incorporation of appropriate NIT into course documents and syllabuses occur.

The interest shown by the previously NIT naive is in many cases amazing, in others minimal. As each activity generally leads to calls for further support, one fact that constantly comes to the forefront is the need for a more consistent, organized and funded unit comprising aware educationalists, computer literates and technicians who can draw upon sufficient resources to provide the professional development and support necessary, if the aims of the agencies noted at the start of this chapter are to be realized in any meaningful way, and the gap between those staff who are NIT aware and those who are not is not to widen still further.

References

Black, P J and Ogborn, J (1977) Inter-university collaboration in methods of teaching science *Studies in Higher Education* **2**, 2, 149–59

Chatland, R L and Morentz, J W (1979) *Information Technology Serving Society* Pergamon Press; Oxford

Chin, R (1970) General strategies for effecting change in human systems in Benn, W G and Chin, R (eds) *The Planning of Change* Holt Rinehart & Winston: New York

Cowan, J (1987) Learner-centred learning: the key issues (or seven deadly sins which frustrate facilitation) in Percival, F Craig, D and Buglass, D (eds) *Aspects XX: Flexible Learning Systems* Kogan Page: London

CNAA (1982) *Implications of the Development of Information Technology for CNAA Undergraduate Courses* CNAA Publication 2a/27: London

Department of Industry (1982) *Programme for Advanced Information Technology* The Alvey report HMSO: London

Donovan, K (1986) *Management of Information Technology in Further Education* CET: London

Ellington, H and Harris, N D C (1986) *Dictionary of Instructional Technology* Kogan Page: London

Eraut, M (1972) *Inservice Education for Innovation* Occasional paper no **4** NCET: London

FEU (1984a) *Information Technology in FE* FEU: Stanmore

FEU (1984b) *A Framework for Action in IT* FEU: Stanmore

Gibson, D G and Gray, P D (1986) *Pedagogic Skills in IT: An Analytical Framework* St Andrews College: Bearsden

Gross, N Giaquinta, J B and Bernstein, M (1971) *Implementing Organizational Innovations* Harper and Row: New York

Havelock, R G (1968) *Planning for Innovation through Dissemination and Utilization of Knowledge* University of Michigan: Ann Arbor

O'Farrell, J (1984) The European strategic programme for research and development in information technology *Journal of Information Science* **8**, 3, 31–35

UGC (1983) *Report of a Working Party on Computing Facilities for Teaching in Universities* UGC: London

Yorkshire and Humberside Association for Further and Higher Education (1982) *FE Staff Development in the Use of Microcomputers* PAVIC Publications: Sheffield

Appendix 10.1 Sample course description for a 60-hour module in basic new information technologies

Overview

These notes are intended to introduce the New Information Technologies Module and to give you some indication of content and how the module is likely to be organized.

1. AIMS

To help you develop a broad-based experience in using a range of new information technologies and a critical awareness of their applications and implications in the context of education, training and everyday life.

2. TIME

There are approximately 35 hours of contact time. In addition, you are expected to spend some 25 hours in guided self-study.

Contact time will be spent in four main ways:

☐ hands-on practical work
☐ discussion around pre-prepared topics/issues
☐ more formal teaching
☐ visits.

Guided study will be used both for the preparation of the module exercise and assignment (see below) and in preparation/learning connected with the module.

3. ASSESSMENT

To encourage you to develop your own work and to satisfy the course there will be a short 'module exercise' and a larger 'module assignment'. These may both be on one theme or on different themes; may be individual or undertaken in small syndicate groups; may be practical or written.

The topic of an individual's assessment will be negotiated, as will the deadlines; more details later in these notes. The main criterion must be that the work you undertake is of some real value to you in a work situation.

4. METHODS

4.1 Introduction

New technologies are wide-ranging and diverse. In no way can you expect to become an expert during the time allowed in the module. Two learning strategies at the opposite ends of a continuum are:

☐ a 'surface approach' where many topics are covered in little depth
☐ a 'deep approach' where few topics are covered in greater depth.

Both strategies have their advantages and disadvantages. Which is adopted (or what mixture you choose) really depends upon your own needs and learning styles. For example, you may wish to use the time to learn a word processing package in fair depth so that you may introduce it to others, or to undertake a needs analysis within your department, or to get a taster of a whole range of applications.

4.2 Negotiation

Because of differing needs of individuals, each member of the group can work out and negotiate with me their own programme of learning and assessment. If people wish to work together on topics of common interest, this may prove most beneficial.

I would like us to undertake the initial negotiation in the following way:

a. Before the contact sessions start, try to identify your main needs. Note these down in approximate order of importance to you.
b. Bring your notes to the first session, where we will spend the first 60-90 minutes discussing as a group what it is each member wishes to achieve. Modify your notes if necessary during these discussions.
c. At the end of the first session, I will take away with me a note from each of you identifying what learning you wish to achieve over the term.
d. At the second session I will feed information back to you about your proposed learning and we will come to a joint conclusion about what you wish to achieve and how you are going to do it.
e. Although assessment will be negotiated later, it is worth keeping it in mind at this initial planning stage.
f. Although I would like to have a 'learning contract' with each group member, in no way does this imply that we cannot renegotiate as time goes on.

4.3 Record of work

I would like you to keep an ongoing diary of what you do, problems that you meet and needs that you have. In this way both you and I can keep track of what is being undertaken. A suggested pro-forma is shown below.

New Information Technologies

PERSONAL DIARY

Name:
Page:

Date	Brief note of work undertaken	Comments, problems, needs etc

Figure 10.2 *New information technologies personal diary*

5. SOME POSSIBLE AREAS OF LEARNING

The topics below are a suggestion. You may have other needs (however, we may not have the equipment/expertise to satisfy some aspects) The lists are not comprehensive!

5.1 Hands-on learning

General awareness/ use of various equipment:	BBC; IBM; Atari; Mac
Word processing:	BBC: View, Wordwise IBM: Displaywrite III Mac: MacWrite
Databases:	BBC: Viewstore, Masterfile Beta-Base IBM: Reflex, DBase III, Lotus 123
Spreadsheet:	BBC: Viewsheet IBM: Multiplan, Lotus 123
Graphics/drawing:	BBC: AMX Mouse, Novocad, Paintbox, Logo/turtle graphics IBM: Paint, Execuvision Mac: MacDraw, MacPaint
Authoring System:	BBC: Microtext, Top Class IBM: Microtext, Top Class
CAL:	BBC: Various programs in most subjects
Communications:	Prestel, online databases, TTNS, audioconferencing
Presentation:	BBC: Edfax IBM: Execuvision Mac: FileVision
Administration:	BBC: Options, system developed locally Many of the above applications (eg databases, spreadsheet)

Note: a 'surface approach' may enable 4–5 of the above to be studied, a 'deep approach' 1–2.

5.2 More theoretical topics

Implications of new information technologies in your department/institution.

The utility of new information technologies; needs analysis in part of your department/institution leading to a specification for implementation.

How to integrate new information technologies into the curriculum.

5.3 'Taught' topics will probably include

Social, educational and training implications
Audioconferencing and satellite communications
Strategies for introducing new information technologies
The role of change agents
Administration systems
Computer graphics.

11. Computer conferencing in teacher in service education: a case study

David McConnell

Summary: This chapter describes a trial in the use of the CoSy computer conferencing (CC) system as part of an educational technology course taken by M Ed students at the University of Bath, England. A seminar on student learning was conducted over CoSy during the 12 weeks of the course. Student perceptions of the effectiveness of CoSy in this teaching and learning environment were collected, and the trial was closely monitored throughout in order to evaluate the experience so as to provide information about future possible uses of computer-mediated communications within the School of Education.

CoSy computer conferencing: overview

Computer conferencing provides a way of carrying out a discussion without physically having to meet the people you are having the discussion with. The discussion may be a seminar on a particular topic; a tutorial; a feedback session, or indeed a 'full-blown' conference. Participants take part in computer conferences by typing their dialogue into the conference via a computer terminal, or microcomputer linked through the public telephone system to the computer. Each typed message or statement is stored sequentially in the computer and the name of the person who 'sent' the message is automatically attached to the message so that everyone knows who is saying what.

Unlike face-to-face meetings, computer conference members do not 'meet' at the same time to type in their statements. They 'meet' asynchronously, that is at different times, and the conference usually takes place over several days, weeks or months (perhaps even years). Participants join the conference at any time of the day or night, any day of the week. They can enter 'freestanding' statements related to the conference theme, or comment on statements made by other participants. The conversations continue and the computer keeps a record of it all for everyone to see. The full power of the computer can be used to manipulate what is essentially a large database of messages. For example, participants can search conferences to follow subthemes which have developed round freestanding statements (see Figure 11.1). A conference leader or moderator often takes responsibility for overseeing the conference and its participants.

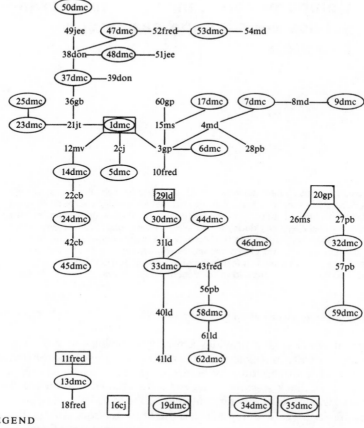

Figure 11.1 *Plot of LEARN topic*

Fuller details of computer conferencing can be found in Hiltz (1984); Kaye (1985); Emms and McConnell (1987) and McConnell (1987a).

The context of this trial

I think it is important to mention the context in which this trial was carried out so that any factors unique to our use of the system can be acknowledged. Using CoSy in a different context may well produce different outcomes and conclusions.

Our trial use of the CoSy system as a form of teaching and learning within an on-campus in-service course in educational technology for practising teachers emerged from several different concerns about the use of CC in formal educational settings.

1. It was an opportunity to try out CoSy with students prior to the Open University introducing it as a form of student support in a new course to come out in 1988. Our use of CoSy at Bath University would be evaluated, and the findings made available to the Open University to help them in their future plans.

2. Our use of CoSy within an M Ed degree course at Bath offered the students taking the course an opportunity to experience a novel medium of teaching and learning, and to reflect on the possible uses to which such technology could be put in their own professional practice. The use of online facilities, including Email, is slowly increasing in Britain. CoSy was being used at a time in the course when we were considering the educational uses of such facilities, and as such provided a concrete example of a 'state of the art' system.

3. It allowed the School of Education at Bath University to evaluate student perceptions of computer conferencing and assess their attitudes to the experience so that we would be better informed of the issues involved in introducing computer-mediated communications into our courses, both on-campus and off-campus.

Background to the trial

CoSy within the overall course structure

CoSy was to be used within the course only as one of several participatory methods of learning. I discussed our proposed use of the system with the students, suggesting that we might view the CoSy conferences as achieving at least three aims:

a. to give students the opportunity to experience teaching and learning electronically, using computer conferencing;
b. for us to address one aspect of the course via the system: we would discuss 'student learning' via CoSy;
c. to look at user perceptions of computer conferencing and consider the strengths and weaknesses of CoSy within an educational setting.

The course lasted for one term of 12 weeks. During this time, the students also studied two other courses.

The students

Some background information about the 18 students was collected in order to locate their existing computing skills and attitudes within the context of the use of CoSy in this trial.

Evidence suggests that typing skill is not a factor in determining the success of computer conferencing (Hiltz, 1984). When asked to rate their typing skills prior to this trial, most students rated them as 'hit and miss' or 'casual, but good enough'. Nobody rated them as non-existent, so there seemed to be no need to be concerned that they were being asked to begin to develop new skills in this respect, although I was concerned to give every encouragement to those at the 'hit and miss' stage if necessary.

Another factor that seemed worthy of consideration was the extent to which any of them had previous experience of using online facilities such as Prestel, computer databases and so on. The results are given in Appendix 11.1, page 215. Suffice to say that very few of them had more than occasionally used such facilities, and when they had it was usually within the context of a trial demonstration during an in-service training session. This in itself did not indicate any potential problems in our proposed use of CoSy; but it did suggest that the training session would have to allow the students time in which to become familiar with logging in and out of a mainframe computer and in using CoSy itself.

Finally, their attitudes to using computer conferencing as part of their course of study indicated that, on the whole, they were all 'excited' by the prospect, 'looking forward to it' and they felt relatively 'at ease' about the prospect of being involved in using CoSy in this way.

Briefing and training

A half day was given over to briefing the students in computer conferencing, and in training them in logging into the mainframe and in using CoSy. The version of CoSy being used was that held at the Open University in Milton Keynes, and we accessed it via the British Joint Academic Network (JANET). This link proved, on the whole, to be very good throughout the trial.

In addition each student was given a copy of a handbook on the CoSy computer conferencing system (McConnell, 1987a). This handbook was based on the official Guelph University CoSy handbook, but was presented in a more involving, lively manner with icons to help the students understand and remember the commands and facilities offered on CoSy. During the training session, and throughout the trial, I tried to follow much of the advice given by Kerr (1986) and Brochet (1985) about setting up and moderating computer conferences.

All students initially joined the CoSy 'getting started' conference for newcomers, posting and reading messages at will. They then moved onto setting up their resumés and finally moved onto a closed conference called 'hello' which was intended to provide them with the opportunity to greet each other, exchange notes on their feelings about CoSy and generally 'play around' with the system.

Evaluation of this training session indicated that it was sufficient and that the handbook was a great help when the students came to use CoSy later on. No one felt they had not been given sufficient briefing, although one or two students did comment that another brief session a couple of weeks after the initial one would have been helpful in explaining some of the more 'advanced' functions, such as editing, workfiles and so on.

Our use of CoSy

All but one of the students were able to use CoSy from the training session onwards. The student who could not was introduced to the system some ten days after everyone else, and I feel never really got to terms with the system, or participated in the conference, to the same degree as everyone else. It is clear, as Brochet (1985) points out, that latecomers are at a disadvantage, especially when the conference is well under way when they join.

The conferences

Three closed conferences (ie open only to those taking the Bath University course) were set up throughout the trial.

An initial (closed) conference was set up by me to allow students to sign into the system, share greetings and generally become familiar with using CoSy as a means of communication. To this conference was eventually added a news topic to provide details of the course and any news about changes in the course programme throughout the term; and a feedback topic where all of us could provide ideas about our use of CoSy, feedback on the usefulness of facilities and so on.

The second conference was devoted to our discussions of student learning. The first topic in this conference ('learn') was introduced by me online and initially involved the students in reading an article on student learning by Ference Marton (Marton, 1975) as a means of helping us focus on some of the research in this area. The second topic, which emerged later as a consequence of discussions about the students' own learning experiences, was called 'you', and was used as a vehicle for students to discuss experiential learning.

The third conference was for 'relaxation' and was set halfway through the course. It was made up of a game of 'I Spy' and a topic called 'frustrations', in which participants could 'sound off' about anything they wanted. The purpose of this conference was to introduce a lighthearted opportunity to play with the system, and see what emerged.

A brief outline of these conferences with details of the number of comments or statements added is given in Table 11.1.

In addition to the shared learning and communications afforded by the group conferences, we all used the personal mail facility on CoSy for sending memos about individual class work, meetings and other personal details.

Conference: Bathuni	
Topic	*Number of 'Comments'*
Hello	31
News	21
Feedback	11

Conference: Bathlearn	
Topic	*Number of 'Comments'*
Learn	61
You	12

Conference: Bathgames	
Topic	*Number of 'Comments'*
1 Spy	29
Frustrations	6

Table 11.1 *The conferences*

Evaluation

The trial of CoSy was evaluated in several ways:

a. by a pre-use questionnaire distributed to students to gather some
    background information about their previous uses of, and atti-
    tudes to, computers and online services;
b. by discussions with participants throughout the trial;
c. by online feedback about uses of CoSy;
d. by a post-use questionnaire to gather information about attitudes
    to the experience, perceptions of the role of CC in education and
    so on.

Previous research into CC (Hiltz, 1984; Brochet, 1985), and teleconferencing generally (McConnell, 1986) was consulted in the design of the questionnaires. What follows is a discussion of some of the findings of the evaluation, in particular those concerned with the users' perceptions of the medium.

Evaluation findings

Factors limiting the use of CoSy

Five main factors (from 14 possible factors, see Appendix 11.2 page 216 for details) appear to have limited the students' use of CoSy in this trial. The main factor was the lack of time for the students actually to use the system. Our use of CoSy was only one part of the overall course process, and we were addressing only one aspect of the course via the medium. It would seem that the time allotted to this aspect was insufficient for the students to feel they could address it effectively via a CC medium. More time than I had anticipated was required for the students to begin to feel at ease with the technology and with addressing educational issues via CC.

Secondly, the apparent difficulty of re-reading messages in conferences appears to have discouraged some student use, despite the fact that all the students claim to have used the re-read facility on CoSy. Without a hard copy or a scroll facility on the micro or terminal being used, re-reading items can be tedious. During the trial I accessed CoSy using the equipment the students had to use (a BBC machine with terminal emulator and medium resolution screen) and via a Macintosh micro from my home. The experiences were qualitatively different. I am sure that the provision of Macintosh equipment for student use would have increased the quality of their experiences.

The increasing length of time these conferences take is another limiting factor for students. Compared with other CoSy conferences, none of the Bath ones is particularly long; the longest topic is made up of 62 messages (conferences at the University of Guelph, for example, extend to over 200–300 statements). However, in a teaching and learning context the length of any one topic in a conference may be crucial, especially if participants join the conference at different times — as some of these students had to — and are faced with a dozen or so messages to assimilate. It may be that these students did not use the search facility to follow through discussion themes, which is one way of making sense of topics with many messages in them. Their lack of time to exploit the medium fully in this way may have been an important factor here. Nevertheless, there is a feeling that the topics approached a critical level and perhaps I should have been more aware of the potential inertia this could introduce.

The fourth limiting factor is the inconvenient access to the computer terminals. Within the School of Education there are two terminals for student use. The rooms in which they are situated are often used for teaching, so there are occasions when students have to wait for the room to be vacated before being able to go online to CoSy. Although there are many other terminals available in the computer unit, which is housed in the same building, there seems to have been a reluctance to use them. It is possible that the students feel somewhat unsure of themselves in using such facilities outside the supportive environment of the School of Education.

Finally, there is some indication that the inconvenience of having to make notes while online — in order to keep abreast of developments in topics, as *aides-mémoire* in reflecting upon items and so on — caused some irritation. The provision of a facility for making hard copies would obviously help here.

These are the main factors rated by the students as limiting their use of CoSy in this trial. One other factor limiting use, but about which there is some equivocation, is the way in which the technology itself gets in the way of the learning process. The students are divided on the importance of this factor in limiting their use of CoSy. But clearly for some students, there is a barrier imposed by the technology which gets in the way of their participation in educational conferences. This phenomenon is worthy of further investigation.

Some of these limiting factors could clearly be dealt with if computer conferencing were to be introduced as an important and much used medium within the School. More terminals could be made available, with facilities to scroll, download and make hard copies, and upload from offline processed word documents. The time given to the use of CC could also be increased in order to facilitate effective use of the medium.

Decisions about the optimum length of conference topics are more difficult to make. A strength of computer conferencing is the storing of messages over time, so allowing conferences to evolve and amass a database of interwoven dialogue which can be read and re-read and reflected on at will. Putting a limit on the total message length of a topic could be like restricting participants in a face-to-face seminar to one or two comments only. Clearly, that would be unacceptable in a face-to-face session, yet the potential complexity of an evolving CC seminar where there are no such restrictions leaves some students wilting! In our experience, breaking topics into sub-topics does not always help since the problem then becomes one of both keeping abreast of new topics and dealing with the limitations of conferencing software which requires you to quit a conference in order to join another topic in the same conference. If there are three or four *evolving* topics in a conference all of which are 'active', quitting and re-joining some becomes frustrating. Besides that, our topics were not exceptionally long nor was there much in any of them to warrant dividing into sub-topics. Clearly within CoSy, the facility to move at ease from one conference topic to another would help in this respect.

Using the search command to weave through the topic helps reduce the sense of too much data — yet for many students this would not coincide with their perception of the discursive role of a seminar where the focus is on following all participants' comments. The unique characteristics of computer conferencing require a shift in the perception of the role of discussion in seminars away from linear discussion paths to that of many branching paths which have to be considered and dealt with simultaneously. This point will be considered below.

Overall reaction to CoSy

Overall reaction to CoSy as a means of communication, and teaching and learning, indicates a mixture of attitudes. In a semantic differential given in the post-use questionnare, CoSy is perceived as being 'good', 'easy to use' and 'great fun' (see Appendix 11.2, page 216). It is, however, thought to be 'time wasting' (cf time saving) and marginally 'frustrating' to use (cf Brochet, 1985, whose students thought CoSy time saving).

Time wasting here refers to the process of logging into the computer, checking conferences for new items, re-reading items and so on. In addition, some students commented that they spent an inordinate amount of time on CoSy in relation to the role of CC within the course overall. There was a strong magnetic force compelling them to log in more often than they felt the role of CoSy in the course warranted! Some students could be seen attached to a computer terminal literally for hours! Clearly they were hooked — but they were also aware that time online meant less time for other aspects of their studies.

On other issues there is less of a clear attitude to CoSy. Equal numbers of students see it as stimulating and boring; productive and unproductive; friendly and impersonal. Follow-up interviews with the students would help illuminate these issues further.

Social presence, process and outcomes of CoSy seminars

Previous research into audio-teleconferencing (Short et al, 1976) and into shared screen teleconferencing (McConnell, 1986) has focused on user perceptions of the media. In particular, perceptions of 'social presence' (eg the degree to which users feel 'close' to each other), the process of such meetings, and the eventual outcomes of the meetings have been examined in an effort both to compare these technology-mediated meetings with more conventional face-to-face meetings, and to examine the unique characteristics of the media involved.

These three characteristics of meetings will be discussed below, with reference to the outcomes of the students' perceptions of them as collected in the post-use questionnaire.

Social presence

Social presence can be characterized by such attributes as feeling close to other participants in a meeting; the level of anxiety during the meeting; the amount of interaction, and so on. The students were asked to rate whether such attributes were 'high' in CoSy meetings, or 'low', or somewhere in between. The full results are given in Appendix 11.2, page 216.

The feeling of satisfaction after each login to CoSy is high and the level of anxiety as an online seminar participant is low. These outcomes of our use of CoSy are promising in that they indicate that CC can offer a satisfying educational experience, and one which produces relatively low levels of anxiety for students as participants.

However, the other indicators of social presence as measured here give some cause for concern. Students do not feel 'close' to other participants; they think the degree of formality in CC sessions is high (presumably compared with our face-to-face classes), and they think the amount of student-to-student interaction is low (again, compared with our other classes). All of this is undoubtedly true in our case. The course within which the CoSy seminar took place is run on a co-operative basis, with students making significant inputs to course design, assessment procedures, face-to-face sessions and so on. The class as a whole functions informally, the focus being on student involvement. So the use of CC within this context could perhaps only be seen as the introduction of a rather formal method of group discussion.

It is possible that such perceptions of CoSy as these may be more highly influenced by the intervening effects of face-to-face meetings than would be the case, say, in a distance teaching context. Once again, further research would help in illuminating this issue.

Process

The process of a meeting is defined by such attributes as the ability to raise points, follow the discussion, participate and so on. Once again, full results of the students' perceptions of the process of CoSy meetings are given in Appendix 11.2, page 216.

The question of who 'controls' discussions in a CC seminar is important in the context of adult education. The educational technology courses in which these students were involved were run as democratic meetings in which the students played a full and active role (McConnell, 1987b). Our meetings were characterized by student-led sessions and discussions in which I, as the lecturer, was no more than another participant. One of my aims was to try and transfer this andragogical approach to our meetings on CoSy.

The students' perceptions of who 'controlled' our CoSy discussions indicate a degree of uncertainty over the question. Seven students think moderator control was low, four think it was high and seven are unsure. More students felt that the amount of student control was high (eight students), but seven of them also thought it was low. Interestingly, of those rating student control 'high', several are students who are rather shy about taking control in our face-to-face sessions. This would suggest that CC could offer such students the opportunity to participate more fully in discussions. This phenomenon also appeared in a similar study into the use of the Cyclops shared screen technology at the Open University (McConnell, 1986), and is a phenomenon worthy of further research.

Student control of the learning process is also characterized by several other attributes. A small majority of the students think that the ease of raising points and posing questions in CoSy meetings is, in general, high (eight students). When compared directly with face-to-face meetings, nine rate the opportunity to raise points greater on CoSy, five rate it the same and only four think it is more difficult. The chances of being able to argue and extend points is also rated high in CoSy sessions by 11 students, while five think it low and two are unsure. Similarly, perceptions of the quality of discussions on CoSy suggest that for a small majority it is seen as being 'high' (eight students), while five students rate this aspect low, with another five 'rating' unsure.

The students were also asked about the chances of deviating from the point in CoSy meetings: ten thought this was 'high', five were unsure and four thought it 'low' Similarly, 11 students thought the probability of losing attention and interest in CoSy sessions was 'high', five thinking it 'low'. There was uniformity over the degree of concentration needed in a CoSy conference: no one thought it 'low', five were unsure, but 13 students thought a high degree of concentration was needed. Finally, perceptions of the 'pace' of discussions in CoSy meetings are divided nearly equally between those rating this aspect 'high', 'low' and unsure.

An analysis of the plot of the main conference topic 'learn' in the Bathlearn conference provides another viewpoint of the process of these meetings (see Figure 11.1, page 204). The plot was derived using Ellis and McCreary's (1985) method. Although this plot does not indicate the content and quality of the discussions, it does throw some light on students' perceptions of what happens during CoSy meetings.

Of the eight so-called 'freestanding' comments, four were initiated by me, four by students. Three of mine were information messages which did not require comment from anyone, and perhaps should have been placed more correctly in the 'news' topic of the other conference. The initial introductory message outlining and defining the conference and beginning a discussion of the paper selected for prior reading resulted in four student 'comments', three of which led onto threads of discourse between the students and myself, but all directly related to the topic theme. These, I think, were reasonably satisfying discussions. During them I was concerned to try and respond to student comments as much as possible, both in my role as moderator (in which I was concerned to facilitate discussion and encourage everyone to participate) and as an active participant wishing to take part on an equal basis with everyone else. This strategy led to what at first glance may appear to be a disproportionate number of items from me — 16 out of 35.

However, on reading through the topic transcript this does not appear out of place since, in effect, three separate but related discussions were evolving, each one demarcated from the others by the population of students taking part in them. I had hoped for, and had anticipated, all students participating in all themes of the conference, yet what was emerging was a series of branching paths to which subsets of students were contributing. In a face-to-face situation this clearly would not be possible. Each 'theme', and the students participating in it, would have to be taken in turn, those not actively interested listening and waiting for the opportunity to move onto an area of interest to them. However, the asynchronous nature of CC supported several discussions at the same time and, as the students noted themselves, allowed them to raise points and argue and extend these points to a higher degree than might usually be possible in face-to-face classes.

This I found exciting educationally, yet it really only became truly apparent to me on examination of the topic transcript after the conference was closed. During the conference I was less aware of it, and tended to see the discussions developing linearly and not as a series of branching themes attended by subgroups of participants. I suspect the students saw the conference topic in this way also, ie as one long topic rather than several subthemes. Using the search command would of course have helped in organizing the emerging discussions in the topic, but the evidence of student use of this facility (11 never used it, seven used it 'occasionally') indicates this was not done. The time required to achieve the level of managing the conference data in this way is perhaps greater than was available during this trial. Indeed, of the 18 students in this trial, ten felt they were only at the basic level of knowing the mechanics of sending and receiving messages by the end of the trial. The other eight felt they had achieved a higher level of feeling 'comfortable' communicating with others over the medium. No one felt they were at the level of knowing how to use the more advanced features of CoSy. Perhaps more help with using the more 'advanced' features is necessary midway through a conference — but there has to be a balance between the time spent on training and that spent on actually using the system for educational purposes.

Of the three other student-initiated 'freestanding' statements in the topic, two achieved clusters of five or more comments, and proved to be interesting discussions for those participating in them.

Outcomes

Finally, the students were asked to rate the outcomes (amount learned, ideas picked up, and so on) of CoSy meetings (see Appendix 11.2, page 216).

None of the seven items offered as outcome attributes for the students to rate was thought to have been satisfactorily achieved in our CoSy seminars. Only four students thought that the amount of work covered was 'high'; most (nine) thought it low, five being unsure. Similarly, despite indicating that they were generally interested in the topics being discussed and in communicating with other people on CoSy (see Appendix 11.2, results of Question 1), the majority of students felt that the amount learned while using CoSy, and the number of ideas picked up from our discussions, were low. The level of stimulation felt by the development of the topics in the conferences was also rated low by nine students, although ratings of the feeling of satisfaction at the level of response received to their contributions indicates a higher degree of satisfaction with the system. The ability to take notes for future reference during CoSy sessions is also rated low by most students, while the ease of assimilating information in the conferences is given a low rating by all but three of the students.

Brochet (1985) presents similar findings to these in her use of CoSy with adult learners. Previous work carried out by myself into user perceptions of Cyclops shared screen teleconferencing (McConnell, 1986) also indicates a high degree of dissatisfaction with the educational outcomes of such meetings. The gauge or yardstick by which users rate new technologies such as CoSy and Cyclops seems to be that of face-to-face meetings. The rich complexity of face-to-face meetings, although not always meeting everyone's needs, certainly offers the possibility of satisfying the eager learner.

It is early days yet to be sure of the full potential of computer conferencing in educational settings. Considerable thought has been given to the introduction of CC into education (eg see *Canadian Journal of Educational Communication*, 1987). Much more research needs to be carried out into the design of online courses, especially into ways of making them stimulating, exciting and worthwhile educational events for all participants.

From the findings of this small case study, CC appears to offer educational experiences which are satisfying in many ways. The process of such meetings appears to be acceptable to many students. Students are often unaware of the importance of process in learning; they look too readily for concrete examples of learning outcomes. More detailed research into the process and outcomes of CoSy seminars would help advance our understanding of these issues.

The future

This chapter has considered a trial use of the CoSy conferencing system with a taught M Ed in-service education course. Before considering the implications of this trial for future practice, it is worth asking if we achieved the aims of the trial. The three aims of the use of CoSy in this educational technology course were:

   a. to give students the opportunity to experience teaching and learning electronically, using computer conferencing.
   b. to address one aspect of the course via the system. We would discuss 'student learning' via CoSy.
   c. to look at user perceptions of computer conferencing and consider the strengths and weaknesses of CoSy within an educational setting.

Our use of CoSy has certainly achieved the first aim. We used CoSy throughout a 12-week term as an integral part of the teaching and learning in the course, considering (aim b) one particular aspect of the course theme via CoSy, ie student learning. We were able to sustain discussion of student learning at a reasonably acceptable level.

With the co-operation of the students in the trial it has been possible to obtain some very detailed information about the perceived strengths and weaknesses of computer conferencing within one particular educational context. The students have helped identify some of the factors of educational importance in using CoSy, as discussed earlier in this paper.

So, the aims of the trial with the students have been successful. It will be recalled that there was also a more general concern about the use of computer conferencing, from the viewpoint of our use of CoSy at Bath University. This was to allow:

> 'the School of Education at Bath University to evaluate student perceptions of computer conferencing and assess their attitudes to the experience so that we would be better informed of the issues involved in introducing computer mediated communications into our courses, both on-campus and off-campus.'

There are widespread changes in the provision of in-service education for teachers in Britain at the present time. A recent government paper outlines new national priorities for in-service work, and gives guidelines as to the ways in which local education authorities should begin to provide access to courses leading towards the achievement of skills and knowledge in these areas. The changes in provision of in-service courses indicate a radical shift from the existing situation where teachers attend courses on-campus, such as M Ed degree courses, to one where much of their in-service education may take place outside of university campuses, often in the schools and colleges in which they work. This change in location offers the opportunity to begin to introduce new technologies, such as computer conferencing, into our courses, as means of teaching and learning and student support.

This would require radical changes in the way we design such courses, and in the way in which teachers view themselves as learners. In addition, the hardware needed to support such a venture would have to be readily available for teachers to communicate with us and each other over CoSy. Most schools already have microcomputers and at least one modem supplied by the Department of Trade and Industry as part of their schools support programme. This would be a beginning, although hardly sufficient given that this equipment is often located in locked rooms, out of the reach of thieves! At a recent national seminar on the educational uses of electronic mail (ESRC Seminar) a group of teacher educators and researchers devised a policy document on teacher use of electronic mail which, among other things, outlined our concerns about the existing provision of communication equipment, and costs of telephone charges. It is hoped that this document will be considered by research funders and the Department of Trade and Industry in an effort to widen and strengthen this important means of teacher education.

Within the School of Education at Bath University, we are considering the needs of our local teachers and how we might provide links between them and ourselves in support of their in-service education. We envisage setting up a network of teachers in the region by providing, at the very least, modems for those enrolled on our higher degree courses for use with their own home computers where possible, or their school or college computer. Students will then be able to link into one of the University mainframe computers via the British Telecom packet switch stream, which provides local-rate calls from anywhere in the country. A decision has yet to be made about the most appropriate conferencing software for our uses. We have been trying out several different packages, among which CoSy is clearly the most attractive so far.

We would not envisage computer conferencing being the only form of support and communication for our students. Several scenarios are possible. For example, some courses could have a combination of face-to-face meetings in schools and at the University, supplemented by computer conferencing. Other courses could be delivered mainly by CC. These scenarios would seem to meet the expectations of our target audience. In the CoSy post-use questionnaire, the students were asked how appropriate they thought computer conferencing was for teaching and learning. Four replied 'highly' appropriate; 13 thought it 'somewhat' appropriate and only one thought it 'not appropriate'. They were also asked under what conditions they would be willing to enrol on a course using computer conferencing. The results are given in Table 11.2.

Under what conditions would you be willing to enrol on a course using computer conferencing?				
Would you enrol if: (*check all statements*)	Yes	Possibly	No	Can't Say
1. Computer conferencing was the only method of teaching and learning?	7	6	4	1
2. There was computer conferencing plus a FEW face-to-face sessions	9	7	0	2
3. There were MAINLY face-to-face sessions supplemented with computer conferencing	12	4	1	1

Table 11.2 *Questionnaire on computer conferencing*

There is very little resistance to the prospect of computer conferencing being used as a method of teaching and learning for these students. Even if CC were the only method of contact, these results indicate that many students would definitely register on the course, while many others would possibly do so. When computer conferencing is offered along with face-to-face meetings, the number of students definitely willing to enrol increases. No matter what the particular scenario, these results suggest that computer conferencing will be a viable medium of teacher in-service education in the future.

This trial of CoSy has indeed helped us understand some of the issues involved in educational computer conferencing, and has provided us with data on which we can begin to build future uses of the medium into some of our courses. The next stage is to provide the correct environment for using CC and to consider the design issues of teaching and learning electronically.

Acknowledgements

I would like to acknowledge the co-operation and participation of the students who took the Educational Technology 2 Course, 1987, in the School of Education, University of Bath.

This chapter is based on a presentation given at the Second Guelph Symposium on Computer Conferencing, University of Guelph, Guelph, Ontario in June 1987.

References

Brochet, M (1985) *Computer Conferencing as a Seminar Tool: A Case Study* Workshop on Computer Conferencing and Electronic Mail, January 1985 University of Guelph: Guelph, Ontario

Canadian Journal of Educational Communication 16 (2), *Spring 1987* A special issue on computer mediated communication in education

Ellis, M L and McCreary, E K (1985) The structure of message sequences in computer conferences: a comparative case study *Computer Conferencing and Electronic Messaging* University of Guelph: Guelph, Ontario

Emms, J and McConnell, D (1987) *An Evaluation of Tutorial Support Provided by Electronic Mail and Computer Conferencing* Paper presented at the ETIC conference, University of Southampton, April 1987, to be published in *Aspects of Educational Technology XXI* (forthcoming)

ESRC Seminar (1987) *Document on Teachers' Use of Electronic Mail* ESRC Funded Seminar on the Role of Electronic Mail in Education: Southampton, England, April

Hiltz, S R (1984) *Online Communities* Ablex Publishing Co: Norwood, New Jersey

Kaye, T (1985) *Computer Mediated Communication Systems for Distance Education; Report of a Study Visit to North America (Project Report CCET/2)* Open University, Institute of Educational Technology: Milton Keynes

Kerr, E B (1986) Electronic leadership: a guide to moderating online conferences *IEEE Transactions on Professional Communications* PC 29, No 1 (March)

Marton, F (1975) What does it take to learn? in Entwistle, N and Hounsell, D (eds) *How Students Learn Readings in Higher Education, 1* Institute for Research and Development in Post-Compulsory Education: University of Lancaster, England

McConnell, D (1986) The impact of Cyclops shared screen teleconferencing in distance tutoring *British Journal of Educational Technology* 17 (1), pp 41–74

McConnell, D (1987a) *A User Guide to the Open University CoSy Computer Conferencing System* (Prepared for students taking the Educational Technology 2 Course in the School of Education, University of Bath) School of Education, University of Bath: Bath, England

McConnell, D (1987b) *Student-tutor Co-operation in the Design of an Educational Technology and Development Course* Paper presented at the ETIC conference, University of Southampton, April 1987, to be published in *Aspects of Educational Technology XXI* (forthcoming)

Short, J, Williams, E and Christie, B (1976) *The Social Psychology of Telecommunications* Wiley and Sons: London

Appendix 11.1 Results of pre-use questionnaire

University of Bath: Educational Technology 2, 1987 $N=18$
CoSy Pre-use Questionnaire   *YOUR NAME:*

Answers

1 How would you describe your typing skills.

None	1	0
Hit and miss	2	7
Casual, but good enough	3	9
Good (can do 25 wpm error free)	4	1
Excellent (can do 40wpm error free)	5	1

2 Comparing your writing skills with your speaking skills, would you say you are MORE persuasive when you are

Writing	1	7
Speaking	2	8
Equal	3	3

3 How would you rate computers? Circle ONE number:

① ① ⑨ ⑤ ⑥ ⑨ ⑨
1 2 3 4 5 6 7
Wonderful   Terrible
+1 +1   +1

4 How often (if at all) have you used a 'computer before?

Never	1	0
Occasionally	2	12
Frequently	3	6

5 How often (if at all) have you used any of the following:

	Never	*Occasionally*	*Frequently*
PRESTEL	1 14	2 3	3 1
TELETEXT	1 10	2 5	3 3
TELECONFERENCING	1 18	2 0	3 0
ELECTRONIC MAIL	1 15	2 3	3 0
COMPUTER DATA BASES	1 5	2 12	3 1
TTNS	1 16	2 2	3 0

6. How do you feel about using computer conferencing as part of this course?

⑥ ③ ④ ② ① ⑥ ⑨
1 2 3 4 5 6 7
Excited /5 2   1   Disinterested

⑨ ② ⑤ ③ ① ⑥ ⑨
1 2 3 4 5 6 7
Looking /4   3   1   Dreading it
forward to it

③ ⑥ ④ ② ② ① ⑨
1 2 3 4 5 6 7
At ease /3   2   3   Anxious

7. If you would like to say anything else about our proposed use of computer conferencing in this course, please use the space below to do so *(continue on back if necessary)*.

Appendix 11.2 Selected results of post-use questionnaire

University of Bath, School of Education : Educational Technology 2,
CoSy Post Use Questionnaire, March 1987

1. Please indicate the IMPORTANCE of the following factors in LIMIITING your use of CoSy.
(5=Very Important; 4=Important; 3=Neutral; 2=Unimportant; 1=Very Unimportant)

(Check all statements):

	Important 5	4	3	2	*Unimportant* 1
1. Inconvenient access to terminals	0	4	1	3	3
2. Had some 'bad' experiences	0	3	2	6	8
3. The manual was too difficult to read/follow	0	1	3	2	11
4. I don't like typing	0	2	2	5	9
5. No one on CoSy I wanted to communicate with	0	2	2	5	9
6. I was not interested in the topics being discussed	1	1	6	7	3
7. There wasn't enough time to use CoSy	7	7	2	1	1
8. I couldn't see the point in using CoSy	1	2	3	3	9
9. The technology kept getting in the way	1	7	3	5	3
10. Messages were too difficult to read on screen	4	1	4	5	4
11. It wasn't easy to go back and re-read messages	5	8	5	0	0
12. The conferences became too long	6	6	5	1	0
13. I had to keep making notes on paper	2	6	5	2	3
14. I couldn't think on-line	0	6	8	3	1

Others (please specify):

15. ....

16. ....

Which of the above were THE MOST SIGNIFICANT factors for you?
(please list the numbers below.)

*University of Bath, School of Education : Educational Technology 2,
CoSy Post Use Questionnaire, March 1987*

2. Below are indicators of social presence, process and outcomes of learning via CoSy. Please indicate your response to each on the 5 point scale.
(5=Very High; 4=High; 3=Neutral; 2=Low; 1=Very Low.)

	High				Low
In general when using CoSy:	5	4	3	2	1
1. Feeling of satisfaction after each login	2	8	4	3	1
2. The degree of formality	2	7	5	2	2
3. The amount of student-to-student interaction	0	2	5	9	2
4. The level of anxiety while on-line	0	5	4	7	2
5. The degree of 'strain'	1	7	2	6	2
6. The degree of feeling 'close' to others	0	1	5	6	6
7. Amount of moderator 'control' over discussions	2	2	7	5	2
8. Amount of student 'control' over discussions	1	7	3	4	3
9. Chances of deviating from the point	5	5	5	3	1
10.The quality of discussion	0	8	5	4	1
11.Ease of raising points/posing questions	2	6	5	3	2
12.Degree of concentration needed	6	7	5	0	0
13.Chances of arguing/extending a point	1	10	2	4	1
14.The level of student participation	0	5	8	4	1
15.The 'pace' of discussion	3	3	5	5	2
16.Probability of losing attention/interest	3	8	2	5	0
17.The amount of work covered	0	4	5	9	0
18.The ability to take notes	0	1	6	5	6
19.Ease of assimilation of material	0	0	3	10	5
20.The amount learned	1	1	5	8	3

(Continues)

*University of Bath, School of Education : Educational Technology 2,
CoSy Post Use Questionnaire, March 1987*

	High				Low
	5	4	3	2	1
21. The number of ideas picked up	1	2	5	9	1
22. Feeling of satisfaction at level of response received to your contributions	0	5	9	3	1
23. Level of stimulation felt by the development of topics in conference	0	4	5	7	2

3. The following relate to your overall reaction to CoSy as a means of communication and teaching and learning. Please indicate your attitude to the system on each scale by circling the appropriate number.

I find using CoSy to be:

1. 1 (1) 2 (2) 3 (6) 4 (6) 5 (1) 6 (2) 7 (0)
    Extremely Good   Neutral   Extremely Bad

2. 1 (2) 2 (3) 3 (6) 4 (0) 5 (5) 6 (3) 7 (1)
    Stimulating   Boring

3. 1 (0) 2 (6) 3 (7) 4 (4) 5 (5) 6 (2) 7 (0)
    Productive   Unproductive

4. 1 (1) 2 (4) 3 (5) 4 (5) 5 (2) 6 (5) 7 (5)
    Great Fun   Unpleasant Work

5. 1 (0) 2 (6) 3 (3) 4 (4) 5 (3) 6 (1) 7 (1)
    Time Saving   Time Wasting

6. 1 (0) 2 (1) 3 (4) 4 (6) 5 (0) 6 (3) 7 (0)
    Not Frustrating   Frustrating

7. 1 (1) 2 (3) 3 (4) 4 (5) 5 (5) 6 (2) 7 (1)
    Friendly   Impersonal

8. 1 (0) 2 (10) 3 (2) 4 (4) 5 (1) 6 (1) 7 (0)
    Easy   Difficult

12. Hillingdon TVEI project: a case study of a national initiative in curriculum development

Richard Ewen

Background to TVEI

In November 1982, the Prime Minister of the United Kingdom invited the Manpower Services Commission (MSC) to launch a major new education initiative, the Technical and Vocational Education Initiative (TVEI). The first 14 TVEI projects in England and Wales began in September 1983 and were known as round 1, TVEI. A further 48 projects started in September 1984: round 2, TVEI. A further 12 started in September 1985: round 3, TVEI.

On 12 November 1984 the government announced that it was ready to provide further support to allow all interested education authorities not currently participating in TVEI to commence projects in 1985 or 1986 on condition that the criteria and guidelines agreed for the initiative still applied and the quality of projects was maintained.

Thus a further 28 proposals were submitted to the Manpower Services Commission for projects to start in 1986. Hillingdon's TVEI project is one of these 28 round 4 TVEI projects. Hillingdon's TVEI project is based on three school centres and a technical college.

The four schools are all 11–18 comprehensive schools: one single sex boys, one single sex girls and two co-educational.

The aim of the Manpower Services Commission through TVEI projects is to work in conjunction with local education authorities to explore and test ways of organizing and managing the education of 14–18 year old pupils across the ability range so that:

a. more of them are attracted to seek the qualifications/skills which will be of direct value to them at work and more of them achieve these qualifications and skills;
b. they are better equipped to enter the world of employment which will await them;
c. they acquire a more direct appreciation of the practical application of the qualifications for which they are working;
d. they become accustomed to using their skills and knowledge to solve the real-world problems they will meet at work;

e. more emphasis is placed upon developing initiative, motivation and enterprise as well as problem-solving skills and other aspects of personal development;

f. the construction of the bridge from education to work is begun earlier by giving young people the opportunity to have direct contact and training/planned work experience with a number of local employers in the relative specialisms;

g. there is close collaboration between local education authorities and industry/commerce/public services so that the curriculum has industry's confidence (MSC, 1982a).

The pilot projects selected represent a variety of approaches to the provision of full-time general, technical and vocational studies, which are adapted to the varying abilities and interests of young people aged 14–18. Vocational education is interpreted as education in which the students are concerned to acquire generic or specific skills with a view to employment. Projects should cater for students across the whole ability range. Project courses should lead to nationally recognized qualifications. The balance between what is offered for different ability levels is expected to vary between projects. Consideration should also be given to accommodating some students with special educational needs. Thus TVEI developments are clearly intended to cater for the whole ability range of the secondary school's annual intake. To this end the criteria of TVEI are quite clearly stated by the Manpower Services Commission.

'Each project should comprise one or more sets of full-time programmes with the following characteristics:

a. Equal opportunities should be available to young people of both sexes and they should normally be educated together on courses within each project. Care should be taken to avoid sex stereotyping.

b. They should provide four-year curricula, with progression from year to year, designed to prepare the student for particular aspects of employment and adult life in a society liable to rapid change.

c. They should have clear and specific objectives, including the objectives of encouraging initiative, problem-solving abilities and other aspects of personal development.

d. The balance between the general, technical and vocational elements of programmes should vary according to students' individual needs and the stage of the course, but throughout the programme there should be both a general and a technical/vocational element.

e. The technical and vocational elements should be broadly related to the potential employment opportunities within and outside the geographical area of the young people concerned.

f. There should be appropriate planned work experience as an integral part of the programme from the age of 15 onwards.

g. Courses offered should be capable of being linked effectively with subsequent training/educational opportunities.

h. Arrangements should be made for regular assessment and for students and tutors to discuss students' performance/progress. Each student, and his/her parents, should also receive a periodic written assessment, and have an opportunity to discuss this assessment with the relevant project teachers. Good careers and educational counselling will be essential' (MSC, 1982b).

These then are the criteria upon which the TVEI project development is undertaken. The national criteria suggest that each project should cover 800–1,000 students during the lifetime of the project (ie between 200–250 students per year group). In Hillingdon the project aims to recruit 75 students per TVEI school centre per year group and started such recruitment from September 1986, with a total intake of 225 TVEI students in September 1986, with further cohorts of 225 being recruited each subsequent September until 1991.

Project management and organization

The project management group comprises the head teachers of the schools involved in the project, the vice-principal of the technical college, the project director and two education advisers, and is chaired by the assistant director of education. It is this group that meets once a month and decides project policy, which is implemented on a day-to-day basis by the TVEI project director. It is important that further education is represented even at the early stages of the project's development in the planning and organization of project policy, as without this close involvement it would be impossible for further education to plan and develop courses by the time the project reaches the 16–18 phase of development. (See Figure 12.1.)

Central to every TVEI project is a project director, whose role is to manage the project and to form the link between the MSC and the local education authority. The project director is broadly responsible for the following areas of work:

a. ensuring that courses are successfully established and that arrangements exist for monitoring and evaluating them, both at institutional and education authority level;

b. co-ordinating the approach taken by institutions involved (common themes emerge);

c. assessing and providing for the in-service and training needs of staff;

d. promoting and developing new and existing links with industry and the wider community;

e. ensuring that mechanisms exist to provide sufficient and suitable work experience placements;

f. leading and encouraging curriculum development in the institutions involved and disseminating good practice;
g. keeping schools not involved in the scheme informed of progress;
h. reporting progress and the development of the scheme to the local project steering group;
i. managing the project's resources — £2,000,000 over the five academic years of project development;
j. liaising with MSC staff.

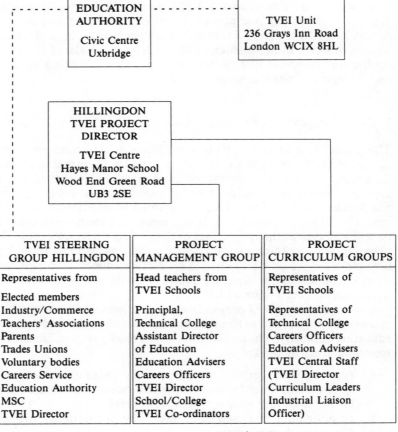

Figure 12.1 *Project management and organization within Hillingdon*

Project steering group

The national criteria require each project to bring together all the relevant interest groups to support and guide the project locally. The size and representation of a project steering group varies considerably between projects. All groups including teachers, parents, representatives from industry and commerce, and from MSC are included on the project steering group. In some cases the local project steering group includes elected council members who may also chair the group. In Hillingdon both the chairperson and vice-chairperson of the steering group are representatives of large industrial firms which are located within the borough.

Project curriculum groups

Curriculum groups have been established for curriculum development purposes, comprising one or sometimes two representatives of each TVEI school and Uxbridge Technical College. The groups meet under the guidance of TVEI central staff and/or education advisers as appropriate. The purpose of the groups is to look at existing provision across the project and to identify developments that are required. Much has been gained from the pooling of ideas, expertise and resources from colleagues in the four schools and Uxbridge Technical College. There are curriculum group meetings four times per term (half-day sessions) at the TVEI centre for the nine GCSE courses. These represent the key parts of the 14–16 curriculum, together with groups which operate for the four cross-curricular developments involved in the TVEI project, namely; equal opportunities, work experience, life studies and assessment. These curriculum groups are essential to TVEI developments in the project as they enable teachers to meet together on a regular basis to discuss the main developmental issues within the project and also provide a forum for the exchange of information between course teachers and the project management group.

The project is run on a day-to-day basis from a newly created administrative base at one of the TVEI schools — the TVEI centre — which also serves as a key part of the project's in-service provision. As well as the project director, the project is also staffed by four curriculum leaders, who represent the key areas of TVEI curriculum development, namely, technology, information technology, business studies, industry/education liaison.

The main aspects of the role of the four curriculum leaders are as follows:

1. To appraise curriculum provision and resourcing in each TVEI school and the technical college, *vis-à-vis* accommodation, equipment, staffing, syllabuses.
2. To examine national developments in agreed curricular areas and to assess their implications for the project.
3. To identify the in-service requirements for curriculum development, staff development purposes and purpose strategies for meeting these requirements.

4. To make recommendations to the project director and the project management group to facilitate staff development and curriculum development in each TVEI school and the technical college.

In each TVEI school there is also a school-based TVEI co-ordinator. The role of the school TVEI co-ordinator is very new and involves a considerable administrative load, together with trying to ensure an overview of curriculum development within the school.

The main aspects of the role of a school-based TVEI co-ordinator are as follows:

1. To liaise with the head teacher, TVEI project staff and the TVEI course teachers to achieve the appropriate resourcing of TVEI courses in line with the agreed procedures of the borough and Manpower Services Commission.
2. To maintain an inventory of all TVEI equipment.
3. To produce information as required by the borough and the Manpower Services Commission about the TVEI project in the school, regarding finance, curricula, students and staff related to the TVEI project.
4. To recommend to the project director and head teachers ideas for curriculum and staff development in connection with the TVEI project in the school.
5. To assist in implementing curriculum policies as decided by the TVEI management group.
6. To monitor and develop through the appropriate institutional channels the personal and social development of the TVEI cohort over the life of the project.

Curriculum development in TVEI

Taken as a whole, TVEI projects nationally have tended to attract rather more boys (58 per cent) than girls (42 per cent) — although this varies between projects. In several cases girls represent less than 30 per cent of the cohort, but there are two examples where more girls than boys have been recruited.

The MSC has consistently reported that where projects offer clearly differentiated option choices there is a tendency for boys and girls to choose courses along traditional lines, with boys predominating in the technology areas and girls in business and community studies.

Within TVEI education authorities have been eligible to receive financial support only to deliver those identifiable elements in the curriculum that are different from what was on offer previously.

The new programmes introduced as a result of TVEI must be seen in the context of existing curricular structures. Most schools now constrain, in different degrees, the extent to which students can choose what they study at age 14. They require all students to continue in certain core subjects, usually English, maths, some science, humanities, religious and physical education, but allow some relatively free option choice following individual counselling.

Within the school curriculum structure, the new programmes must be an optional component, since the criteria for the initiative require entry to the programme to be voluntary. That choice made, the projects are free to test a variety of curricula designs involving the new elements only, or extending the structure of a student's total curriculum.

Examples of the types of curricula patterns emerging

A. Students select a number of new options in addition to the list previously offered by the school. Such options may be *linked* (for example, a double option in business studies and commercial languages); *blocked* (so that students must choose balancing options); or *free*, following individual counselling. In some cases the subject area for development is entirely new to the school; in others it has been offered before, but in a different form.

B. Students select a number of new options as above, plus a number of common (or core) elements. These are in addition to whatever the school may be prescribing by way of core in its general education programme. These elements may be timetabled separately, or taught as an integral part of the options offered.

C. Students may focus on a particular theme involving a predetermined set of options (for example, a business studies theme may involve a package of economics, law and commerce, with some components varied according to the ability of the students).

D. Students may select an integrated *course* which spans more than one option block (for example, a personal services/community care course which includes food and nutrition, child care, biology, sociology).

E. Students may follow a common programme for up to a year. This may comprise a series of *taster* courses, where they sample a number of vocational areas in rotation. In all cases, this leads to their choosing more specialized options later.

All the approaches described above may be designed on a modular basis, that is, with short units of learning, allowing students to select different combinations of units to build up a personal programme over their first two years of the TVEI curriculum to meet their individual needs.

All programmes must include careers and educational guidance and counselling, and planned work experience. In addition, most TVEI programmes include residential education, designed among other things to encourage initiative and the ability to work in a team. In many projects, personal and social effectiveness, economic awareness and computer literacy and information technology are included as the core elements of the curriculum (MSC, 1985).

Hillingdon's TVEI curriculum pattern is most closely related to example A above, which centres upon a core course of personal and social development entitled 'life studies' and three linked option choices, which are offered to General Certificate of Secondary Education (GCSE) standard for all students. Each TVEI course comprises 4 out of 40 student periods per week in Hillingdon. Thus the TVEI curriculum constitutes 16 out of 40 student periods per week, ie 40 per cent of a student's curriculum.

Each TVEI school centre therefore offers the same curriculum structure and choice for its TVEI students. In September 1986 this curriculum package (see Figure 12.2) was represented as follows: a life studies course as a compulsory core part of the TVEI curriculum and three GCSE option courses from the following nine which were on offer:

     Business studies
     Modular technology
     Manufacturing technology
     Information technology
     Food studies
     Industrial chemistry
     Community studies
     Robotics
     German.

The curriculum (40% of a learner's timetable)

1986-87

core + 3 from outer ring

Figure 12.2 *1986–87 Curriculum package*

Inevitably such freedom of choice (three from nine courses available) tended to produce sex stereotypical choices and major difficulties arose in attempting to recruit girls into science and technology courses within TVEI.

This being the case and also acknowledging the degree of overlap that existed among the option course choices available, it was decided by the TVEI project management group that the TVEI curriculum on offer to the new cohort recruited for September 1987 would be organized differently to try to overcome these problems. For September 1987 the TVEI curriculum consisted of four courses times four periods per week, ie 16 periods out of a 40 student period week. Three out of the four courses are GCSE courses and the fourth is a compulsory course in personal and social development entitled life studies (see Figure 12.3). All TVEI students are expected to choose business studies and modular technology as two out of their three GCSE courses. The third GCSE course will be chosen from one of the following:

Information technology
German for business and commercial use
Industrial chemistry
Community studies
Food studies
Manufacturing technology.

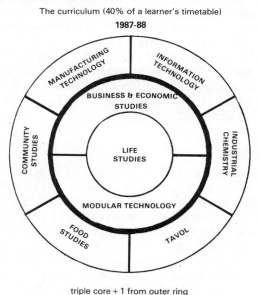

The curriculum (40% of a learner's timetable)
1987-88

triple core + 1 from outer ring
(although some learners will
follow the 1986-1987 pattern)

Figure 12.3 *1987–88 Curriculum package*

The life studies course is a course which embodies the main principles of TVEI and which seeks to develop a student's personal and social qualities through a problem-solving approach to issues which are fundamental to adolescence, adulthood and parenthood in a highly technological society in the 1990s and 21st century.

The life studies course forms a central focus for personal and social issues, as well as forming a focus for careers education and guidance and the preparation for work experience, residential experience and the evaluation of student performance as recorded in the TVEI formative profile of student achievement, which has been developed within the project during its first year.

Clearly there is a relationship between the issues in the life studies course and the two other major components of the TVEI curriculum, namely business studies and modular technology, and the opportunity for cross-curricular work between these three courses is great.

Business studies

It is expected that all new TVEI students in September 1987 will choose business studies as part of their TVEI curriculum, and this course gives a general understanding of the background of an industrial society, the wealth creation process and the part that industry plays in our society. This is obviously a fundamental part of the TVEI thrust to make students aware of the relationship between industry and education and industry and society at large, and within this course the opportunity for 'enterprise' as an educational process and the preparation for and follow-up to work experience as an educational process are available.

The business studies course offers the opportunity for students to develop keyboarding skills which are central to the use of a computer as an aid for teaching and learning.

Modular technology

This course is the application of the principles of science to everyday life. It is in fact quite difficult to give students an idea of the nature of the technology course for GCSE purposes as many of them, when making choices for fourth and fifth year study, have little or no technological experience in years one to three in the secondary curriculum. This is particularly so for girls and to this end, to demonstrate to girls in particular the nature of technology in a modern industrial society and the nature of technology within a GCSE course, extensive use has been made of a mobile technology laboratory available from the British Schools Technology Project at Trent Polytechnic entitled 'Women Into Science and Engineering', which visited each of the TVEI schools for a two to three day period during option choice time to try to demonstrate to the girls some aspects of the work involved in the GCSE course. A major point of emphasis was the work that students do as part of their project work for GCSE technology, and the relationship between that work and the social aspects of life. Technology has interesting social appplications of particular relevance to adolescents, and it is through the human and social applications of technology that many girls are being successfully brought to technological studies.

It has also been important to emphasize that technology is a valid third science choice for many students, and those students wishing to take three sciences for a strong academic basis may do so within the TVEI curriculum by choosing physics as part of their general education, and industrial chemistry and technology within TVEI, thus providing a strong trio of science GCSE courses.

The inclusion of technology as an obligatory part of the TVEI curriculum is reinforced by the thinking of Her Majesty's Inspectors of Schools (HMI) who in *The Curriculum from 5-16* (1985) state that the curriculum of all schools would involve pupils in the 'technological area of learning and experience'.

Hillingdon's interpretation of this 'technological area' of the curriculum was based on the promotion of problem-solving. The Assessment and Performance Unit studied work in technology and concluded that:

'Technological capability is seen as that which enables a person to enrich the quality of life by using technological skills, knowledge and value judgements in the development of man-made environments and man-made things.' (APU, 1981)

Technology therefore demands that for young people to become fully capable by means of education, that education should not only give opportunity in the *resources* of knowledge, skills and experience, but should also call for *action* in demonstrating these elements.

Thus amongst the participating schools consensus was established for this task-action — capability model of technology. In retrospect this agreement on a common definition and approach was particularly significant. It allowed from the outset a degree of commonality of planning, which in turn accelerated the curriculum development process.

The agreed definition of technology served as a benchmark against which the suitability of examination syllabuses could be measured.

The final choice was the London and East Anglian Group CDT technology syllabus. The rationale for selecting a syllabus submitted under the national criteria for CDT was interesting, in that it was felt that this kind of course best suited our needs when appraised against the task — action — capability model. The two most significant features of the CDT syllabuses were that the major project had to involve 'significant constructional work' and that they included a formal design examination paper. The characteristics were felt to be particularly significant in the context of the development of problem-solving capability.

The advantages of common planning across institutions was also of value in the formulation of teaching strategies. Expertise was shared and the preparation tasks were divided amongst participating staff. It was decided that the delivery of the course would be based on a 'low tech' approach to ensure that large amounts of capital were not tied up in small amounts of high cost equipment. This would allow the resources to be spread more widely to promote broader usage. This strategy has also proved to be of worth in allowing schools to cope more readily with the envisaged increase in student uptake.

The shared preparation of detailed teaching material facilitated by a common approach is also significant in terms of staffing. The increase in the total number of groups will necessitate the involvement of teachers who may be new to technology courses. The availability of proven teaching material will greatly support the in-service training provision for such staff.

Other points to emphasize about the nature and distinctiveness of the TVEI curriculum in September 1987 are as follows.

Firstly, TVEI courses wherever possible and wherever appropriate use modern computer technology as part of the teaching and learning process. For those students who wish to pursue an interest in computer technology to a specialist level, an information technology GCSE course is available as a third option choice within TVEI. All TVEI courses, however, seek to use the computer as a vehicle for teaching and learning and this is a very important feature of the distinctiveness of the TVEI curriculum in terms of teaching and learning methods.

Secondly, work experience is an essential part of the TVEI curriculum and all students are guaranteed at least one week of work experience in the 14–16 phase of the project, and also a further week in the 16–18 phase. The social advantages of work experience are well catalogued and this is an important and exciting development within TVEI with an increasing emphasis upon looking at ways in which curricular objectives for GCSE courses can also be delivered through work experience placements.

Thirdly, residential experience is an important and essential part of the TVEI curriculum and all students are guaranteed the opportunity of at least one week of residential experience within the 14–16 curriculum. Much experimental work is being undertaken by the TVEI schools at present to judge both the nature and effectiveness of the kind of residential experience which might be offered to students in the 14–16 stage of the curriculum.

Fourthly, all students have a personal record of their achievements, which is again currently being developed and will be available for all students from September 1987. This record of student achievement will include assessment of a student's personal, social characteristics and her/his cross-curricular skills, together with a record of the student's academic developments across the three GCSE courses.

Conclusion

Thus it is that in the relatively short space of 18 months this national initiative in curriculum development has taken root locally and begun to thrive.

The curriculum itself is now unfolding out of its original planning stage and issues are emerging regarding both the content and process of this curriculum. These can be identified and categorized in a variety of ways, but the following may provide some insight on those frequently identified:

1. Management issues relating to the planning, presentation and delivery of different curriculum emphases in a consortium of comprehensive schools and a college;
2. Management issues relating to the allocation of resources in a consortium of comprehensive schools and a college;
3. Professional development among teachers relating to different styles of teaching and learning;
4. Inter-institutional co-operation for the delivery of a changed curriculum emphasis;
5. The need to involve other social partners in these developments — students, parents, employers, higher education;
6. The constant challenge of ensuring equality of opportunity in terms of both access to and outcome from a different curriculum;
7. The need for in-service support to the profession to meet the demands of the new curriculum emphasis.

It is only through the commitment and professionalism of the teachers involved in the project schools that it is possible to move forward on these issues, and it is pleasing and heartening to be able to report that the profession is responding in such a typically positive manner to the challenges of TVEI and the 1990s.

References

Assessment of Performance Unit (1981) *Understanding Design and Technology* Assessment of Performance Unit: London

Department of Education and Science (1985a) *Education and Training for Young People* (Command 9482) Her Majesty's Stationery Office: London

Department of Education and Science (1985b) *Better Schools* (Command 9469) Her Majesty's Stationery Office: London

Her Majesty's Inspectors (1985) *The Curriculum from 5-16* Her Majesty's Stationery Office: London

Manpower Services Commission (1982a) *The Aims of the TVEI* Manpower Services Commission: Sheffield

Manpower Services Commission (1982b) *The Criteria of TVEI* Manpower Services Commission: Sheffield

Manpower Services Commission (1985) *TVEI Review* Manpower Services Commission: Sheffield

13. Education in new technologies for those in employment

Clive Hewitt

Summary: People will need to change their skills and attitudes frequently in post-industrial society, but there are no coherent education or training systems for this. The UK in particular lacks provision and training awareness at managerial level, and many erroneously believe that new technology will decrease training needs. UK provision is patchy at best and the initial training at colleges is not flexible or relevant enough, even when accessible, for updating existing employees. Manufacturers' or suppliers' courses do not provide adequate background.

New provision of industrial short courses by colleges is limited by lack of true incentives and relevant resources. But government initiatives have been positive, despite an overall policy that industry should provide its own training. Training grants for employers, Open Tech, PICKUP and Skillcentres are all contributing. Much interest in industry has been aroused by open or distance learning which can provide flexible modules and practical training at the workplace.

The new worker

In most advanced post-industrial societies the number of people employed is declining and it is by no means clear whether this is a permanent adjustment. It may be that combinations of government action, private entrepreneurism and further changes in market forces will lead to a return to full employment. But even if this happens, it seems inevitable that the skills and attitudes needed by people in employment will be very different from those of the earlier 20th century.

The qualities of post-industrial workers will be those shown below (in brackets are more traditional qualities still often found):

- [ ] Overall knowledge of technology sufficient to understand its current effects and likely future development (specific knowledge of a particular limited skill area);
- [ ] Relevant technical skills, and eagerness to acquire new ones at frequent intervals (concern to retain current narrow band of skills and fear of training);
- [ ] A positive attitude to change in the work situation, and the ability to adapt quickly to new roles (resistance to and fear of change and concern to retain and protect existing role);

☐ Willingness to take considerable responsibility for own development and for personal effectiveness in the work situation
(conviction that any change or view of future needs or improving work situation is someone else's business).

Now that the machines can do the calculation and drawing, the cutting
and forming, the assembly and transporting and many other manufacturing jobs, far fewer people are needed, and very few whose role is
to carry out a previously defined routine task, however skilled. Those
who are left in traditional industries will need to be the problem-solvers
and creative gap fillers who can fix and improve the systems that do
the work. Alternatively they will be working in increasingly small firms
and units which carry on trade in goods and services too small and
specialized to justify technological investment. But even this will be a
shrinking sector in manufacturing, production and servicing as machines
become cheaper and more flexible still.

So the need to educate people in new technologies while they are in
employment is large already, and will continue to grow. But the educational and training need is as much to create positive and flexible
attitudes to change as to provide specific new skills. It is, of course,
an even more urgent need for the great majority of people now passing
or about to pass through the formal education system, in which openness to change and the habit of creative response to new situations is
by no means endemic.

But coherent systems for education for change and new technologies in the workplace are few and far between, even in advanced
economies. In the United Kingdom there has been a debate in the past
ten years as to whether this is a responsibility that should be shouldered
by the public education system, by the employers, or by government
acting directly. This debate has been set against a growing mass of evidence that, prior to employment, employees in the UK receive
substantially less industrially relevant initial education and training than
those in other industrial countries, and that during employment their
employers provide them with much less in-service training. The reasons
for this are probably deeply rooted in British culture and social structure. The general position seems to be that managers and business
leaders in the UK are not as aware as their counterparts in other countries of the dominant importance of the skills, attitudes and commitment
of the people who work with them. It is commonplace nowadays in
British industry to hear managers welcome new technology as something that will reduce their dependence on the workforce. With this
perception comes the view that new technology will also bring about
the de-skilling of the workforce and that the requirement for skilled
and well-trained staff will decline. This seems to be wishful thinking,
because in other industrial countries such as Germany, Japan and the
US, exactly the opposite view is taken. While fewer people are necessary to achieve a given level of production under new technology, it is
generally recognized in these countries that each person now employed

is much more crucial to the success of the enterprise. So in these countries increasing efforts are being made to train, motivate and retain the loyalty of employees as an essential underpinning to the effective use of techology.

The effects of new technologies

It has already been seen that a new general type of worker will be needed in the post-industrial economies. However, there are some immediate effects of new technology which are already specific and observable within traditional industry. The first of these is the blurring of traditional boundaries. This is both in respect of the levels of skill and the range of skills, and is partly a function of the reduction in workforce that often results from new technology's introduction.

In the operation and support of electronic and micro-electronic based production equipment it is increasingly necessary for the operator to have some knowledge of fault diagnosis and even first line maintenance procedures. With the capital cost of equipment and the added value from it both being high, emphasis is upon rapid repair and short downtimes. Similarly where maintenance and technical staff are concerned the range of maintenance tasks to be carried out is often considerable, from simple electrical faults to the location and correction of software faults, sometimes needing correction of programming. Thus it becomes increasingly difficult to distinguish levels of skill clearly in the traditional levels of operator, craftsman, technician and engineer. One person may need to practise at least two if not three of these levels during a working day.

A second way in which blurring of traditional boundaries is taking place is in respect of distinctions between different trades and crafts. Initially in process industries, but more and more in manufacturing too, multi-skilling is the target. Many larger companies and groups are striking deals with their unions which allow electrical and mechanical maintenance personnel to be used interchangeably if suitable cross-skilling training can be given to both groups. Usually these agreements can only be implemented once the company has provided the agreed training. However, the result of these agreements is to produce a much more flexible worker able to cope with a much wider range of situations and making a significant step away from the rigidity of the traditional industrial employee.

A further and specific effect of new technology is to create a new industrial sector known as data communications. In part this is a growth in the scope and functions of existing services provided by PTT networks such as British Telecom. In part it is an enhancement of in-company communications systems used by organizations such as banks and travel services. But whole new areas of use are springing up, such as retail point of sale cash transfer systems, electronic mail order and home banking. In fact the changes in this field are likely to be the fastest and most revolutionary because they are aimed often at the consumer and because they allow a range of new services not previously on offer.

The pattern of this sector or industry is still being formed, but it is one of very high capital investment, high volume and sophisticated software-based systems. It is likely that the number and range of third party installation and maintenance contractors will grow rapidly and the skills needed to support and extend these systems are already in short supply. Training for people working in this sector will be in very high demand within the next five years and there will be strong pressure to update people already in electronics employment with specific skills in data communications.

One final point is that the general impact of the new technologies has been to bring home the need for a constant updating and revision of skills for those in employment. It is no longer enough to have a good and relevant initial training; this must also be refreshed frequently during the working life. But how far are existing training systems capable of this recurrent updating?

UK provision for traditional training

In the United Kingdom there has been a mixed traditional provision set against the relatively low level of in-service education and training for those in employment. In more traditional slow-moving times the provision has been aimed at helping people in work to top up and achieve qualifications and levels of skill they did not get through initial training. This was based on the static view that once an appropriate level was achieved this would be adequate for the rest of a working life. At most it would only need enhancement if promotion or career advancement was sought. The provision consisted of courses at technical college which were available as evening classes or night school for those in employment. The industrial impact of this provision was greatly reduced in the 600 further education and technical colleges in the UK as a result of the 1964 Industrial Training Act which introduced day-time release and block release for initial technical training for young people between 16 and 20. As a result, evening classes became day classes and were no longer available to older people working during the day who were beyond the age range in which employers would release them for initial training.

A second element in this mixed provision was a network of 60 government training centres set up in the 1960s to give unemployed people opportunities to gain relevant (but traditional) skills which would enable them to get jobs again. These tended, for obvious reasons, to be located near traditional industrial centres.

The pattern of change

It is clear that existing educational systems devised for the initial training of young people between 16 and 20 are not adequate to meet the needs of industry for continual updating of skills. It will be necessary from now on for people to have further training almost continuously to keep up with both the changes to technology and to work situations and requirements. In fact the concept of new technologies may itself be challenged, as it seems to imply a once and for all change which achieves a new status quo. In fact, the only constant in this status quo is continuous change itself, and the pace will increase. During the third quarter of the 20th century the rate of major change in manufacturing shifted from once every 20 years to once every five to seven years. This rate is still visibly increasing, and in the most advanced countries, major new manufacturing and product technologies are now being adopted every two to four years. There is no longer time for changes in technology to proceed through leisurely development and implementation stages which are mirrored, after a decent interval of several years, by changes to education and training curricula. Training has to begin immediately the market implementation of new basic technologies (such as microprocessors) starts and has to be applied quickly to the current workforce as well as to the next generation coming through initial education.

Under these conditions of change — which it is tempting, but foolish, to call extraordinary — the relationship between new technology and training needs to be completely rethought and the adaptation of old mechanisms will no longer suffice. A difficulty in the UK traditionalist culture is that even radically new solutions tend to be put in the hands of, or to be controlled by, institutions which have previously not responded effectively to change. Nonetheless, changes that have taken place are worth reviewing briefly as they show the patterns likely to be increasingly employed in the future.

Education sector provision

Looking first at the UK formal education sector, there has been a considerable effort on the part of a number of FE colleges, polytechnics and universities to build up a repertoire of short courses of interest to local industry. Some have been very successful in this, but they are relatively few, and there is no coherent country-wide pattern for employers to rely upon. The difficulties for the institutions attempting this are twofold. Both the incentives to do it and the resources for these developments are inadequate.

In the case of incentives, the pressures to maximize external revenue by going to the trouble of investigating local and regional priority training needs (market research) and then to provide matching training opportunities (product development) are relatively small, so long as the vast bulk of institutional funding is provided through recurrent grants from government. Also, in many institutions, the arrangements to benefit by the retention of any income generated are still lacking, and any earnings are likely to be clawed back by the funding authority.

The resources for what is, in effect, a commercial operation (market research, product development, marketing and selling) are usually not strong within institutions. Few existing staff have been recruited with commercial, marketing and management skills, and the structures and procedures of the institutions are not geared to this type of work. There is also the serious problem that specialist staff in institutions find it very difficult to keep up with the current pace of industrial and techno-logical change, and most institutions are not funded to acquire the rapidly changing and often expensive equipment for new technology. Nonetheless, these activities are growing slowly in the formal educa-tion sector although sums earned and services provided are still very limited. It may be that the incentive will be increased and that govern-ment policy will be to make institutions earn more of their revenue requirement through the meeting of important local training needs and, if so, ways will have to be found around the resource problems. But it is clear that, in this formal education sector, the initial training courses for 16–20 year olds which are the current 'bread and butter', paid for by government recurrent funding, are not appropriate or available to people in employment. They occur mostly during the day, and they are lengthy and inflexible, and tend to emphasize theoretical and mathe-matical principles rather than current industrial practice.

Suppliers'/manufacturers' courses

A new phenomenon, which has always existed but was of little sig-nificance when replacement or upgrading of capital equipment was infrequent, is the supplier's training course. Most equipment suppliers provide some kind of training for end users who have installed their equipment in manufacturing or process plants. Now that equipment installation and upgrading is relatively frequent and leading to increas-ingly sophisticated operational and maintenance skills to get full value, these courses are crucial. Often they may be the only source of techni-cal updating available to those in employment. However, there are drawbacks and limitations:

☐ Manufacturers' courses often assume a prior level of background knowledge (eg in digital electronics or microprocessors) which trainees do not have — leading to confusion and inability to 'stay with' the course.

☐ They only occur when new equipment is first installed — people coming along later do not get the benefit.

☐ The lack of a suitable background of fundamental knowledge leaves trainees feeling 'uncomfortable' that they do not really understand what the equipment is doing or how it is doing it.

☐ Such courses are of variable quality — many suppliers treat them as a necessary evil which reduces the margins from selling the equipment, rather than as an important activity which, when well done, can add to margins and competitiveness.

It goes without saying that these courses do not form a coherent and consistent pattern of updating and, as noted earlier, neither are they supported by such a pattern from the formal education sector.

Government training intervention

Official government policy for the past few years has been that British industry must take responsibility for the retraining and updating of people already employed, in the same way and to the same extent that industry in competitor countries does. Despite this, however, four government initiatives have affected the training and updating of employees in a positive way.

1. Training grants for employers have been introduced. These are paid to employers (preferably in medium and smaller sized firms) to meet, typically, half the costs of a new training venture for employees to improve their skills and productivity. These grants are seen by government as 'pump-priming' to developing the training habit more widely in British industry and can amount to up to £30,000 per company per annum.

2. The development of MSC Open Tech Programme 1983–87 to encourage the use of innovative learning methods for vocational training of people already employed. Approximately 120 pilot projects were funded in companies, training boards, colleges and local education authorities (to a total of £45 million) to develop and deliver packaged training materials using open learning techniques. Most of these projects were based on existing national curricula or internal training requirements of a specific company or industry. However, several focused specifically on new technologies and produced generic training for a broad market. In general, the projects were not planned or resourced to make an effective entry into the competitive training market and most have had limited impact to date. However, the concept of open learning has been much more widely understood and applied as a result.

3. A parallel was the Department of Education and Science's PICKUP programme (started in 1983), designed to inject relatively small sums of money (typically £15–50,000) into local and regional schemes from the education sector. The schemes were

intended to increase the amount of training which institutions were making available to local industry and business. The success of this programme is difficult to estimate, since reports tend to focus on the number of contacts made and enquiries received rather than the increase in the number of trainee hours delivered. This points up one of the main difficulties which the formal education sector has in coming to terms with the needs of those in employment. The education industry is not 'consumer led' and its structure and responses tend to be dominated by the formal and academic concerns of the providers. It is not therefore the ideal vehicle to respond rapidly to highly defined and specific skill needs coming from industry. Educationalists tend to believe strongly in their own pre-eminence in being best able to define (or redefine) their 'customers' needs, and are usually loath to take a prescription from their consumers.

4. The government training centres mentioned earlier have been made over into a national network of Skillcentres under the Manpower Services Commission's Skills Training Agency (STA). Many have been re-equipped to a high standard in new technology but their primary focus has remained the relatively low level reskilling of the unemployed. However, they are under increasing pressure to generate income from selling sponsored training to local employers and whilst most hover between 5 and 10 per cent of turnover from this source, one or two are approaching 30 per cent. But the bulk of their income still comes from selling their courses back to the other arm of MSC responsible for retraining unemployed adults (Vocational Education and Training Group, or the VET Group). It is believed that government policy will increasingly be to modernize both the instructor skills and new technology resources of these Skillcentres and to make them earn more of their income in fully costed courses for local employers.

Innovation for training during employment

Despite the problems encountered in the recent Open Tech programme, there is no doubt that this MSC innovation has already had a considerable impact on industrial training provision and may have more in the near future. Open Tech not only created a number of projects which produced effective training materials, but it also managed to create industrial interest in the techniques and benefits of open learning. Briefly, these may be stated as:

☐ Training can be delivered at a time and place suitable to the trainee and his or her employer.

☐ Generic training can be devised to suit the greatest number of employees and their job needs and tailored locally to a specific situation.

☐ Training can be modular and designed in short packages (typically 8 to 30 hours) to be highly flexible.

☐ Because training packages are designed for independent study by individuals, with support from a tutor or adviser, the individual proceeds at his or her own pace, depending on aptitude, previous skills and experience.

Many companies are now coming to see that these benefits can reduce the cost and increase the availability and effectiveness of their training. Until recently, one of the outcomes of the British manager's attitude to the workforce was to let go of employees who proved not to have skills relevant to future needs, and to hire new employees who did. The increasing pace of technical change and the inadequacy of national training systems now make this impossible, because there is a great scarcity of people with new technology skills. Employers are beginning to recognize that people are potentially flexible, and with the right motivation and assistance can often retrain and upgrade themselves to meet new needs.

This scarcity of skills may also go a long way to change another attitude which has in the past impeded training in UK industry. One of the most frequent reasons given, in private, by managers for not training the workforce has been that people are likely to leave their current employer to better themselves if given training that makes them attractive to other employers. Of course, this whole proposition assumes that the employee would have no loyalty or commitment to the present employer. The evidence from industry in countries other than the UK is that motivating and rewarding employees, and not treating them as disposable, does lead to commitment and an environment in which training is regarded as a benefit and enhances loyalty as well as skills. It seems that skill shortages will more and more force employers to regard their individual workers as valuable assets and to develop ways of retaining their loyalty and commitment in order to retain the investment benefit of training. The human side of this is that people clearly have no respect for or commitment to employers who do not demonstrate by their actions the high value they place on employees.

Open learning in employment training

In this changing situation, where training in new technology for those employed is seen not only as essential to maintain competitive production ability but also to build and retain loyalty and commitment, open learning has a considerable role to play. While more and more employers are recognizing the need for such training, the options open to them are relatively few, so that open learning or packaged flexible training provides an attractive answer. Some of the characteristics of good open learning materials for people in employment can be seen as:

□ Short attractively designed packages that focus on essential work-related skills and use many practical work-based examples.

□ The opportunity built into the package to practise the essential skills in as near to a work situation as possible.

□ Content broken down into short one to two hour sections, each having its own clearly stated skill and performance objectives.

□ Diagnostic pre-tests for each module to allow individuals to determine whether they have the necessary entry skills for that package.

□ Frequent test-yourself items to build confidence and check that essential skills are being learnt.

□ Periodic progress checks every four to eight hours, externally monitored by tutor or supervisor to ensure that difficulties are soon detected.

□ Use of more than one medium, to provide variety, motivation and alternative learning modes (eg print, practical work/projects, group work, audio, video, computer-based simulation).

□ Achievement tests at the end of each package based exactly on specified objectives and skills of each section of the training package and, wherever possible, on practical activities to demonstrate competence.

Training packages with features such as these are now being developed or are available in a growing number of fields. While many employers are able to make use of generic packages, supplied by colleges or industry training bodies, larger firms are beginning to commission purpose-designed training packages from suppliers.

A key point which requires considerable planning and attention is the setting up of support for this open learning mode of training. In-company trainers and work supervisors need to learn in the most effective way of organizing and supporting open learning and in their new roles as facilitators and managers of learning rather than teachers and trainers. Even when well supported and briefed, the process of adoption of such an innovative training system is lengthy and 12 to 18 months is often taken in a company for initial exploration, evaluation of materials, small-scale trials and fuller implementation. Together with the scale of input required from the training supplier during this phase, the time factor can form a powerful disincentive to the marketing and selling of this innovative type of training. It may also restrict its usage initially to larger companies and organizations where ultimate levels of uptake produce a return on the significant set-up costs.

However, major open learning industrial users in the UK with several years' experience have calculated the full costs per trainee hour as between £7 and £10 depending on the number of individual users following parallel programmes. This is considerably better than the costs of conventional training and includes time off the job and the costs of transport and subsistence.

A recent development which seems likely to extend the vocational effectiveness of open learning in the UK and to bring to full flower the seeds sown by the Open Tech programme is the Open College. Announced in Spring 1986, it will use national television broadcasts to highlight training opportunities, many produced as open learning training packages under its own auspices.

The future

While the pattern described in this chapter has used examples drawn from the United Kingdom, the problems are very similar in all post-industrial societies. The recent and rapidly accelerating switch over to electrical and electronic equipment for control and communication will give companies, industries and countries chronic skill shortages. Two requirements are central. Firstly, to bring up to date the remains of the workforce still in employment with skills in a range of new technologies, electrical, electronic and mechanical. Secondly, to create systems of training and education which from now on will be able to update and maintain the skills of working people to match the continuous changes in technology, the organization of industry, and the varying roles of the flexible worker.

These needs will have to be met in a variety of ways, all of which call for much greater flexibility and speed of response by trainers and educators to changing circumstances. To stay in the game, those working in the education and training sector will need to become much more entrepreneurial and client-centred. They will need to focus less on syllabus and curriculum content and formal standards and more on needs analysis, skill and performance specification and the design and marketing of an effective training product.

Part 4:Some questions

14. No flowers, no fences: is NIT paving the road for our children's future?

Roland Lauterbach

Summary: With the introduction of microcomputers into education an exceptional situation is declared and a fundamental change is proposed. The educational community finds itself confronted by claims and demands, promises and hopes, apprehensions and admonitions. At present, there is no theory on computers for elementary education, just a number of practical approaches. In the Federal Republic of Germany these are not readily accepted. In this chapter it is argued that any pedagogically sound perspective for dealing with the new technologies has to be developed out of one's own educational culture.

The metaphor

Gefunden

Ich ging im Walde
so für mich hin,
und nichts zu suchen,
das war mein Sinn.

Im Schatten sah ich
ein Blümlein steh'n,
wie Sterne leuchtend,
wie Äuglein schön.

Ich wollt' es brechen,
da sagt' es fein:
Soll ich zum Welken
gebrochen sein?

Ich grub's mit allen
den Würzlein aus,
zum Garten trug ich's
am hübschen Haus.

Und pflanzt' es wieder
am stillen Ort;
nun zweigt es immer
und blüht so fort.

Found

I roamed through the forest
just by myself,
searching for nothing,
aimless my mind.

In the shade of the trees
a flower I found,
like sparkling stars,
like beautiful eyes.

I wanted to break it,
but it asked me fair:
Why should I be broken,
then wither and die?

So I dug with care,
took roots and all,
carried it home
to my garden place.

I planted it safely
on a spot in the shade,
now it grows and blossoms
for ever more.

(Johann Wolfgang von Goethe, freely translated into English by RGL)

Goethe's poetic episode has metaphorical intentions. Using it freely, one can imagine a child exploring the world, having nothing special on its mind. What would it do, when discovering a phenomenon of singular beauty? Pick the flower? Put the salamander in its pocket? Carry home the bubbling clear spring water? Whatever the child might want to do, it will discover that nature's beauty and productivity needs care and understanding of its fundamental laws, if we want to have it grow and develop for our pleasure or subsistence.

We are not over-interpreting Goethe by assuming that his poem is an epistemological metaphor, valuing the unique and holistic quality of phenomena for the growth and development of knowledge and humane existence. He is not only considered the greatest German poet (John Steinbeck appreciates his drama *Faust* as the most profound piece of literature). Goethe was also an excellent scientist, who in his time fundamentally questioned Newton's analytic and abstract approach towards nature on philosophical and empirical grounds. Today, his ideas on nature and science, mainly his research on colours, are reconsidered and valued as highlights of the (nearly) lost empathetic phenomenological approaches to natural history.

The issue

There may be 99 ways of experiencing a flower. With the computer we are offering the child perhaps only one — the geometric abstraction of its form. And yet, by doing so, we are opening up mind space free of the material bondage to reality; we are presenting a tool at service to the child's imagination. As, for instance, Seymour Papert's *Mindstorms* (1980) illustrates: with Logo children can make flowers of any shape and size, arrange them in a garden, a field, just anything that comes to a child's mind — a world commanded by its fingers. What will happen to the child who has been put on this path of its own mind and learned to like its smooth progress without noticeable restrictions? Will it ever want to stop and attend to the flower in its totality, leave the world of its own creation and return to the world of material laws which does not conform to the child's wishes but forces obedience instead?

We have no answers yet. Up to now, children have spent relatively little time at computers. Our knowledge about so-called computer freaks and about the effects video games have on many players offers little encouragement for positive speculation. The competence to take decisions for real-life situations is not increased and the readiness to take responsibility for one's own decisions is decreased. Contrary effects are identified with experts in their field. They improve the quality of judgement on the basis of computer-assisted problem analysis and trend anticipation. We are thus faced with the question of moral development: where and how are we preparing our children to take responsibility for the reality of their (and our) existence, be it with respect to themselves, to other people, or to nature? It may turn out that what we can offer our young children at the computer is the least important experience to develop this responsibility. I want to pose my core questions in relation to the introductory methaphor.

How intimately do children have to experience flowers, nature, life's totality, so they themselves will optimally grow and develop?

Is richness of holistic sensual perception a developmental prerequisite before imagery and abstraction can extend experience and transform it into anticipation and consciousness?

And subsequently, how is the child's relationship to nature (the material world), to people (the social world) and to him- or herself affected by the use of computers?

It might be too early to give clear answers to these questions. But it certainly would be too late asking them, after the empirical answers have turned out negatively for our children. If we want to avoid the hit and miss approaches of goodwill and wishful thinking often experienced in the past, we will have to invite and acknowledge pessimistic analysis, then engage in integrative planning and come up with an optimistic strategy.

The German situation

Who would be taken seriously today by American or English politicians or, for that matter, educators, announcing that computer use by children of elementary school age is pedagogically irresponsible and, therefore, must be banned? Indeed, whoever has watched children work and play at computers in American or British elementary schools could not but classify this idea as an absurdity, hardly different from asking for a ban on candy bars for children.

In the Federal Republic of Germany the situation is different. More or less all of the 11 Ministries of Education who are independent in cultural matters have made the elementary school off-limits for computers. The programmatic declaration at the political level does not mean that there are no elementary schools with computers, that teacher trainers are ignoring the new technologies completely, or that all educational ministries are unaware of developments in other countries. But all in all, the response from most teachers has been in agreement with the official policy, the reaction of parents so far at least acceptant. (But then, 90 per cent of German school children have carious teeth and about 70 per cent require dental fillings due to excessive consumption of sweets.)

Three considerations seem to justify the political decision that, at present, new information and communication technologies are not introduced into German elementary schools.

The first one is fiscal. Nearly all resources in the educational sector, be it financial, personnel, administrative or training, have been activated to introduce computers and computer education into all secondary schools. This task is developing, leaving no room for any additional fiscal efforts within the education system. The situation may change when the equipment of secondary education becomes obsolete and thus available to the elementary schools. Or parents may start to offer direct support to their schools following some of the well-known macroeconomic arguments that for the purpose of individual qualification and international competition computer literacy should be introduced as early as possible.

The second one is educational. In the Federal Republic of Germany elementary education is considered a well-to-do level of schooling: small classes, well-trained teachers, sufficient equipment and materials, good facilities, excellent pedagogical tradition. After four years of elementary school our children continue into one of the secondary school types. While secondary education often finds itself confronted with internal and external problems, eg comprehensive schooling or girls' disinterest in science and technology, German elementary education has experienced a steady course of incremental development after a short period of destabilization about two decades ago. Some of the states have re-introduced conservative ideals and tightened organizational controls, others have steadily delegated curricular and organizational decision-making to the school level. The present state of affairs should not imply that improvements are not desirable or changes possible. But there are simply neither pressing requirements imposed upon primary schools nor internal difficulties forcing attention.

The third reason is pedagogical. There is fundamental scepticism among many educators, be they teachers, teacher trainers, pedagogical and developmental psychologists, or educational philosophers, about having young children work at computers. Although lack of experience and familiarity with computers may well be involved in some cases when aversion is expressed, the strong arguments are derived from the educational culture of German elementary schools. While practical demands such as learning the cultural techniques of reading, writing and arithmetic often dictate the daily routines, the idealistic position emphasizes the developmental relationship between child and nature, child and society, child and educator. It is this relationship which is seen to be endangered by a programmatic introduction of computers as teaching and learning machines for the first level of schooling. But as there is no royal road of safe conduct for educators in this matter, teachers will find themselves caught between claims and demands, promises and hopes. Especially for elementary education the pros and cons are formulated emphatically. Without thorough examination, affirmative response seems educationally as irresponsible as brusque rejection.

The task

We are historically at the beginning of a new educational age. And most of the pedagogically relevant questions have not yet been researched. This is my assumption. As teachers and educators we, therefore, will find ourselves stripped down to the fundamentals of our profession: being the child's advocate. I want to elaborate this point in the light of the proposed issue because it touches the core of educational theory and practice and thus contains the chance for long range educational perspectives in dealing with the new information and communication technologies. How well are we prepared for this task and what are our chances?

The professional stamina of educators is rooted in the educational culture they are part of. Research into teacher effectiveness clearly indicates that teachers need to be certain that what they teach is valuable and how they teach is successful (Lauterbach, 1984). A sound educational culture with explicit pedagogical principles to follow makes it easier for teachers to experience that certainty.

In the German case the reformulation of pedagogical principles for elementary education was completed during the first half of this decade and it can be interpreted as a fairly successful synthesis of traditional values and developmental opportunities. These principles are in line with German educational philosophy. It has oriented its pedagogical efforts towards the ideal of the mature and morally responsible individual who takes an active part in developing the natural and man-made environment, improving individual and social welfare, and enhancing cultural tradition and differentiation. This, at least, is the idea mounted on a rather more earthy reality. In most European countries the emphasis will be similar, differing only slightly. Indeed, we have a fair chance, if we self-confidently design the future of elementary education from our cultural roots.

The perspectives — principles of elementary education

Principles are best described as regulating ideas (Hübner, 1979) indicating the direction of action and efforts a society intends to take from a definite historical situation. As they are historical derivatives of a theoretical and practical synthesis, often not explicitly available but nevertheless underlying theory and practice, they are best understood in the light of historical analysis. As I am going to extrapolate five principles of German elementary education, translation of the terminology is necessary. I hope it is not altogether misleading. The principles are influenced by educational theories dialectically mediating between the developing subject (child) and the object in education (content) (eg Weniger, 1952; Klafki, 1965; Walgenbach, 1979).

From child-centredness (Kindgemässheit) *to subjective generality*

Education starts with the child and ends with the person while enhanc-

ing the developmental identity of the growing individual. For the child
each thing has a subjective reality. Even those things a child meets for
the first time may induce associations, fear or delight, attention, motivation to act. This educational principle would need to begin with this
subjective reality (*vom Kinde aus*). The child is then confronted with
the intersubjective validity of things: names, usages, relationships,
characteristics, semantics in different contexts, etc. Education leads the
child to recognize, learn about and critically accept as his own what
is generally accepted as valid in society. During this socially determined
process of assimilating and accommodating, subjective reality is transformed into categories of intersubjective generality, be it in terms of
knowledge, attitudes, values or behaviour. Ideally, education withdraws
its guidance step by step in accordance with the individual's ability to
regulate his own dvelopment, and it terminates when the person reaches
consciousness of him- or herself as a legitimate participant in the making
of the world.

How much do we know about the subjective reality a computer has
for children? Is it of a kind that justifies educational intervention or
demands educational efforts? Are computers becoming indispensable
for child development?

The production and sale of personal computers is increasing rapidly.
Eventually, they may be found in most homes like TV sets, home worker
tools, or electronic toys of today. This is one vision used to construct
the rationale for computer use in schools. Indeed, as computers become
part of the human environment they will also become reality for children and, thereby, demand educational decisions. From this point of
view the above stated questions are of a historical nature and cannot
be answered *a priori*.

Nevertheless, anticipation of the probable seems imperative for educators. A glance at the American scene is highly instructive. Sherry
Turkle (1984) gives us first impressions of what the subjective reality
of computers may be for children.

She describes, for instance, how children explore life and death,
killing and resurrection, by causing the computer to crash at will. She
follows up how feelings of power and control grow, how children shape
their 'second self', how the idea of the human being as an intellectual
animal is substituted by that of the emotional machine. Can we but
speculate what this would mean for the educational goal of fostering
the child's development to a responsible individual?

These first examples indicate that computers will influence child
development very fundamentally. Educators need to respond when the
time comes; but their preparation for adequate response has to begin
as early as possible. In my country the time to start was yesterday.

I would like to illustrate this point. In elementary education nature
study intended to have the child experience and appreciate beauty,
creativity and the order of our world, things in the sky and on earth;
eg sun, stars, rivers, plants, another way around. But already today

apples come in containers with a hygienic plastic film. They are called Golden Delicious or Granny Smith. Each of a kind is guaranteed to look and taste more or less like the other. They are available all year round, just around the corner at the supermarket. And if they are out just ask for more from the storage room or wait until tomorrow. The reality of apples is that of any merchandise: attractive, buyable, disposable — man-made! Many educators do not tell the whole story of trees, the birds and the bees — of monocultures, fertilization, pesticides and insecticides, cadmium content, surplus destruction, price control, South Africa and the American Fruit Company. Even if they do, they most often forget to make sure that the children really know what they are talking about.

Commanding the computer may foster the belief that the world is controlled by one's fingertips — and if its edges and corners show one either has to dull them or withdraw from them.

Another problem may be magnified as computers are used to substitute human functions in education. Children already learn less and less from real people how to live, ie experience the material world, each other, themselves, how to use senses, language, or tools, how to communicate, interact, or create. They learn most often from idealized pictures. As meaning is not just verbal or pictorial information, but concern, intention, context, biography, history, what effects must we consider on children who — by age — have had only a few experiences enabling them to learn about meaning?

As we are just at the beginning of computer experience, the truly promising visions for elementary education are rare. One is offered by Papert (1980). He wants children to learn the rules of dealing with the computer in order to foster their independence from the computer by turning it into an instrument to extend human thinking whenever there are good reasons for it.

'I have described myself as an educational utopian — not because I have projected a future of education in which children are surrounded by high technology, but because I believe that certain uses of very powerful computation technology and computational ideas can provide children with new possibilities for learning, thinking, and growing emotionally as well as cognitively.'

In agreement with this first principle he designed Turtle geometry. It had 'to be something children *could* make sense of, to be something that would resonate with their sense of what is important' (p 63). It had to be firmly related to the children's sense and knowledge about their own bodies and be coherent with children's sense of themselves as people with intentions, goals, desires, likes, and dislikes. This sounds promising. We are expectant, but the first empirical studies are not yet keeping the promise.

From nearness (Lebensnähe) *to vernacular universality*

Education starts at home and ends in the world. The individual child lives in a community with other people, with animals and with objects. They are close to him; they belong. This geographical, social, ideological, aesthetic, emotional, and personal environment constitutes his home. It includes the personal experiences of the distant made possible by modern transport and communication. Other people have other homes. Being at home is different in different cultures. Education begins at home and conceptualizes the things at home in its vernacular structure. It then confronts the child with 'foreign' cultures and things. Getting to know them, to accept them in their uniqueness, and dealing with them on their terms will expand as well as deepen the child's perception of home.

Wherever the vision of personal computers in every home turns into reality, education will have to deal with it under this principle. The use of computers and their home-shaping influence would then, most probably, make them physically, emotionally and intellectually near to the children. Yet we do not know if the status of computers in homes will be that of common tools or that of cars and television. Television, for example, has had striking home-shaping effects. Research evidence shows how television can increase the degeneration of personal nearness, living experiences, and creative home-making wherever its use is uncontrolled. Antagonistically, it can also expand human experience when self-control is exercised. Alienation from home and family is not uncommon as is an increase of brutality and cynicism when films of this kind are accessible to children. It seems that the social context and the social controls which are in effect determine how children are influenced.

In accordance with similar developments in other areas of life, cultural traditions are less valued and creatively developed. We need not argue for those that constructively and effectively retaliate. Children do not belong to the socially powerful. Today there is little difference between children living in different cities of industrialized societies: food at MacDonalds or Kentucky Fried Chicken, TV series with American stars, cars and Shell Oil, aspirin and Alka-Seltzer, learning new maths and science, Pepsodent and Lux soap, and even music and language adapt to one another.

This trend toward cultural uniformity would not be topical, if it were not for the loss of traditional individuality. The personal computers from Apple or Texas Instruments with the same language just focus this issue. If the children's experiences outside of school tend toward uniformity obliterating traditions, should education reinforce this development or does it become necessary to promote the regeneration of culturally deprived areas?

At the moment, the overwhelming use of computers by children is for games. We have no indication that computer games improve home-making through social, physical, emotional or intellectual contributions or that computers in the home prove to be more useful for daily chores than hand-made activities. Therefore, we hardly find good reasons to deal with computers in elementary school under this principle except for preventive or compensatory activities. This, surely, is not a desirable educative perspective.

Pertaining to games, elementary education may have to offer compensatory play — with dolls, face-to-face with other children, sporting activities, etc. Thereby, computer games most probably would not receive any reinforcement.

Another compensatory effort may be a greater challenge: communication with people. Already, teachers are fighting the communicative deficiencies of children, be it in social relationships, language use, speaking as well as reading and writing or non-verbal communication. The deficiencies which have been identified are related to the growth of comic strip, television and video storytelling with its mere passive perception of over-detailed settings, leaving little room for individual conceptualization and creativity. These pictorial stories are void of descriptive and dynamic terminology for context and process, space-time orientation and interactive experience. Computers may extend this development or they may redirect it into a new formalized type of communication behaviour.

Ivan Illich pointed out an interesting historical paradigm. He considers Columbus' discovery of America the lesser historical event of 1492 compared to the introduction of an artificial Spanish language for all official communication and documentation. This new language reduced the autonomy of the provinces and started a cultural deprivation which continues to the present time. Wilhelm von Hulboldt, a German historian and later an architect of Prussia's school system, noted about 1800 how the richness and independence of Basque culture, which had not complied with this monoculturalization, had fascinated him. He describes its intellectual and aesthetic harmony with everyday life, and its lively uniqueness uniting all people regardless of their social status. This led him to develop his concept of education which still is alive in German educational culture and mainly responsible for what has been illustrated in the first of my five principles.

The conclusions to be drawn here are similar to those of the first principle: the introduction of computers as topic will be an educational task, whenever the need arises. The decision would be with the teachers. They have to be prepared to respond and be able to identify what needs to be done and they need to know how to do it when the time for response arrives.

From wholeness (Ganzheitlichkeit) to analytic integration

Education starts with unique things and ends with meaningful systems. A thing is an entity. It is perceived in its wholeness. As entities, things have their own value. They seem simple by just being there and well defined by their names. Education begins with this simple thing and guides the child to explore its existence. Thereby, the boundaries of meaning are extended. A thing can appear as bearing a mixture of properties, it can be taken as an example for a class of things, it can be seen as a system of interrelated parts, or it can be looked at as part of another system. These analytic views are developed functionally to integrate things into higher order systems, ie into new entities. Thereby, things turn into determinants of the new entities as those in turn redefine the original things. In all of this, meaning and value are not lost but extended and enriched.

Computers are perceived as concrete objects. To the children they are not yet the concrete abstractions of human activities. As with many other technical objects of this kind they eventually will become part of the children's environment appearing as normal or fascinating as cars, telephones or television. This would make them, at first glance, neither more nor less attractive for an educational topic than any of these. Their meaning would be sufficiently defined by the way they are used: at first at home, later on at school or at other places children will visit. Differentiation as well as integration of meaning will inevitably occur even without the assistance of formalized teaching.

A closer look reveals a few remarkable characteristics of computers concerning holistic dimensions. Computers split up into hardware and software of remarkable independence not unlike the body and mind dichotomy known in philosophy. Sherry Turkle offers some evidence that children become aware of this after dealing with a computer over a longer period of time. At first, the computer is perceived as a quasi-living thing that even 'cheats' in order to win a game. Or children may identify a specific computer as their partner with an identity of 'his' own, like that girl who signed the letters she wrote on the computer with 'Tanya and Peter', Peter being 'her' computer and 'friend'. Later on, children become aware of the software aspect as that part of the computer they put into it making it a bit like people. The experiences children go through and the conceptualizations they attempt have not been explored yet. But there seems to be a new developmental question arising as the possibility of forming the mind of a thing and handling it like an object becomes a reality.

Even though the intensively experienced quasi-living thing is eventually argumentatively differentiated in its hardware and software components, an unconscious perceptional singularity of computers often remains. The attribution of this individualistic quality, its personality feature, is not just a child's projection but is common to adults working with computers. For a programmer it may be the second, maybe even the better half; for the user it is another being.

Let us have a look at the analytic and constructive potential of the computer for the elementary school level. Because there seems little didactical sense in having children discover the man-made rules a certain program works on, except for the fun of solving puzzles, the constructive power of computers is of prime interest. Papert's turtle on the screen, for example, is neither a composition of sub-units nor does it constitute new entities of which it is a maintained part. The reasons are obvious: for one, the constructions in turtle geometry are not material systems; for another, the symbolic turtle is a tool (a pointer) in the generation of symbolic systems. Tools may leave their marks on products but they are not part of them. And yet, the mental activity required in Logo needs attention under this principle. The construction of each new entity (eg flower, house, windmill) by trial and error experiences, which are transformed into analytical steps, is the prototype procedure in constructing artificial systems. The similarity to construction procedures in technology are striking. The difference is that for today's technology the physical, chemical, or biological basic units as well as the natural laws regulating their interaction have to be discovered first, before they are synthesized.

In view of this analogy one may well follow Papert's statement: 'Children are builders (Piaget), therefore, give them materials to build with' (p 7). We do not know if toy blocks and bricks, sticks and wheels, cars and houses, etc, will suffice. Although one may well argue that building with material objects is of greater developmental value than building activities with abstractions and, therefore, artefacts of representations, one cannot lightly put aside the notion that reflective processes for material experiences may be enhanced by using the computer as an assisting tool after the material experience has been made.

From vividness (Anschaulichkeit) to conceptual concreteness

Education starts with offers to the senses and ends with thinking of the world. Perceiving things is a sensory as well as a cognitive, affective, and motor development. Education begins to offer a multi-sensory perception of things, it conceptualizes the experience in concrete operations, places them in meaningful contexts, and abstracts from symbolic operators as well as interpretations of the world. The conscious use of the senses and the available concepts, interpretation schemes and operative powers increase the quality and quantity of perception and conceptualization as well as that of concrete actions.

There is little controversy among educationalists and developmental psychologists that a fundamental basis for child development is, among other things, the complete sensual perception of things. The more of the senses used in getting to know the world, the better for the child. Papert is aware of that. He introduces a movable robot turtle. The children are asked to identify with the turtle in moving back and forth, right and left, speeding up and slowing down. This permits the children to conceptualize their own movements and improves their physical awareness of themselves. Only after that, the turtle is symbolized on the screen. And by identifying with it geometric forms are produced of geometric representations of real objects.

While this attempt towards perceptual enrichment is to be highly appreciated when comparing it with bookish approaches in mathematics teaching it still remains a complementary approach, for instance, to Montessori.

Computers are used to represent reality and to reconstruct concrete things in terms of conceptual reductions. These simulations can be powerful instruments to explore certain aspects of real as well as of imagined systems.

No doubt, on the developmental pathway from complete sensual perception to conceptual concreteness the simulative capacity of computers can be a stimulating and enlightening tool to understand better and deal with the represented parts of reality. The decisive question is when is the proper time to start with simulating. The notion that we ourselves need to simulate reality in order to act adequately in it puts the question to the point. If our simulative abilities need the reality in its totality in order to develop optimally, how do reductions which intervene too early influence child development?

As we know too little about computer effects on child development, a simple analogy will have to do. Children communicate before they learn how to write. It is common practice to let them sing and make sounds before they are introduced into a system of notation. And this is done in relation to the children's ability to produce sounds in accordance with the symbolic representations. Some children even become proficient in playing an instrument without learning the notation system. Similar experiences exist with children learning to 'play' the computer. But in language as well as in music the perceptual basis lies before its representation. One would concede a similar sequence of development for pictorial representation in drawing and painting.

While there is no definite developmental criterion for the optimal age level, we again need to maintain that prior to pictorial representation and computer simulation the children need to have had extensive experiences with the things of their world as totally as possible. Thereafter, piece by piece, representations will be attempted in the direction of conceptual clarity. Here, indeed, the computer may turn out to be the tool that extends the children's simulative powers beyond our present capabilities. We must take care that they are not replaced by it. The final and most important step to be taken will be the conceptual comprehension of concrete reality. Conceptual abstractions and operative powers are needed in different contexts of living and learning. We have sufficient research evidence that the ability to operate successfully and in a morally responsible way in a certain context usually requires context experience and not just conceptual schemes.

From active learning (Selbsttätigkeit) *to self-reliance*

When child and object meet, two entities interact. The interaction changes both, child and object, however small the change may be. The child experiences how the object determines his actions, the object undergoes change depending on the child's inventiveness. Education starts with offers of interaction. It enhances the child's change as learning and growth. Growing awareness of the limitations objects set as well as the chances they offer for actions increases the child's competence and confidence to participate in shaping objects and self. Advice Jean-Jacques Rousseau is said to have given a young mother may illustrate the point: 'If your child cries for an apple, don't bring the apple to the child, but take the child to the apple. This will teach him from the beginning that nature is not man's servant.' One may add: it will also make him confident that taking action enhances self-development.

The greatest attraction computers have for parents and non-educationalists is their apparent superiority over textbook learning. In the US, for instance, national surveys on science and mathematics teaching during the 1970s revealed about 80 per cent of book learning. This was a discouraging result for a country whose educational philosophy was brilliantly developed by John Dewey, who coined the slogan 'learning by doing', and whose outstanding efforts for active learning in science and mathematics during the 1970s are second to none. Learning with the computer can be more active than learning with the book — but it need not be, as too many examples of computer-assisted instruction show.

If active learning is intended the computer will become part of it. But it would be educational short-sightedness to claim its advantages against the book school or mediocre lectures. Empirical evidence comes to a non-encouraging tie-up on effectiveness terms (Lehmann and Lauterbach, 1985).

The central theme of this principle envisions the child as the originator and controller of action. The child is the interactive constructionist, the 'builder' as Piaget suggests. Keeping Rousseau's advice in mind, children need the resistance of reality to develop the abilities required to cope with it in a self-reliant and responsible way: eg fire that burns, food that deteriorates, flowers that die — once and for all, people who get hurt. With them children learn actively nature's laws and the rules of human interaction. Experiences of this kind are of primary importance as they eventually determine the true potential to act.

But there is also the aesthetic dimension of action, the creation of quality, the making and shaping of the world from imagination — the domain of art and, perhaps, creative technology.

Already, computers are occasionally used to bridge what CP Snow termed the two cultures of human existence: science and art. At present, commuting between these two cultures seems to require proficiency in the sciences as well as in the arts. The principle of active learning demands discovery and creation to build proficiency in both. In Papert's scene children experience how their intention (eg to create flowers) has to adapt to the computer's structure. But after accepting these determinants they learn to construct their own creation. And when they would like a garden, the appropriate command forces the computer to make one.

The limitations of these experiences are obvious: neither biological laws are discovered nor aesthetic expressions are developed. But there is a perspective beyond the present. Children who actively learn to operate and to shape their environment may well find in the computer a tool for extending their capability to act, eg when solving problems, designing or planning a project. At present, these applications are functionally available mainly to the world of adults. The computer tool needs further didactization.

Conclusion

The conclusion arrived at in this chapter declares the coming of computers as a historical reality which elementary education will have to deal with. It is argued that from the educational culture of this school level long-range perspectives on what and how to teach with computers can be generated to satisfy the developmental needs of children. How to establish favourable frame conditions at the policy level, for teacher training and for the schools, has been described elsewhere (Lauterbach 1985; 1986). Now it is necessary that those responsible for elementary education, ie teachers, parents, administrators, need to take on the challenge of

☐ making and keeping themselves competent in their knowledge of computers, their development and their usages;

☐ observing changes in children and in their environment due to the increasing availability and use of computers;

☐ becoming and remaining sensitive to the basic or prerequisite needs of children;

☐ insisting that child development comes first regardless of economic or modernistic arguments;

☐ daring to approach the uncertain if it promises improvement and development of one's own educational culture.

References

Hübner, K (1979) *Kritik der wissenschaftlichen Vernunft* Freiburg

Klafki, W (1965) *Studien zur Bildungstheorie und Didaktik* Weinheim

Lauterbach, R (1984) Staff development with regard to science education in primary schools *Council of Europe: Education Research Workshop on Science and Computers in Primary Education. Edinburgh, Scotland 3-6, September 1984* Council of Europe: Strasbourg

Lauterbach, R (1985) Towards a generative strategy for computers in education: the research base *Conference on Children in an Information Age: Tomorrow's Problems Today, May 6-9, 1985*, Proceedings, Volume II, 545-564 Varna: Bulgaria

Lauterbach, R (1986) Preparing for change - anticipating new information technology in German primary education *Programmed Learning and Educational Technology* 23, 4, 337-345

Lehmann, J and Lauterbach, R (1985) Die Wirkungen des Computers in der Schule auf Wissen und Einstellungen (Effects of computers in school on knowledge and attitudes) *LOG IN 5*, 1, 24-27

Papert, S (1980) *Mindstorms* New York
Turkle, S (1984) *Die Wunschmaschine. Vom Entstehen der Computerkultur* Rowohlt: Reinbek bei Hamburg
Walgenbach, W (1979) *Ansätze zu einer Didaktik ästhetisch-wissenschaftlicher Praxis* Weinheim
Weniger, E (1952) *Didaktik als Bildungslehre* Beltz: Weinheim

15. The myth of vocationalism

George Chryssides

Summary: It is indefensible to train students exclusively for vocation when only a small proportion of life is spent in paid employment. 'Vocationalism' has its roots in the Protestant work ethic, and is reinforced by arguments that the financial sponsors of education (industry, the government and society) have the right to determine students' curricula. Such arguments are questioned, and the implications are explored for education which is not exclusively vocationalist. In particular, it is claimed that higher education needs a more flexible structure, particularly with regard to entry requirements and to part-time modes of study, if it is to become a continuing process rather than a once-and-for-all 'initiation'.

The problems of vocationalism

The belief that we should educate students for paid employment is a strange one. In a typical working day, only one third of one's time is spent on work. Bearing in mind that those who work, work on average a 40 hour week, the proportion of working time is reduced even further. And, of course, one does not work for the whole of one's life. Making the somewhat generous assumption that a person works from the age of 16 until the age of 60, on my reckoning we arrive at the statistic that only some 15 per cent of one's life is actually spent in paid employment, and this figure reduces even further when we take into account holidays, time spent off sick, early retirement, shorter working hours, and, of course, the spectre of redundancy and unemployment.

In a situation in which there are approximately three million unemployed, and in which the figures for long-term unemployment are the highest since the depression of the 1930s, the problems which are posed for the educational system are obvious. First, is there any point in training students for a degree or even a vocational qualification when these are no longer passports to employment? Second, how are we to respond to the situation in which a student actually has to choose between receiving an education or getting a job? I recall very clearly an occasion when an extremely able student sought my advice on whether he should abandon the prospect of a first class honours degree in order to accept a post as a chef. Understandably, when jobs are scarce, a significant number of students yield to the temptation to abandon their education

if they are offered a job, for there is no guarantee that at the end of
a course of study the student will be able to find suitable employment.
Equally, there is a growing number of applicants for further and higher
education who have already taken up the opportunity of employment,
but now want to undertake further study, either for educational purposes or to enhance future career prospects.

Such candidates, through accepting early employment, have failed
to secure the normal prerequisites for higher education and can find
difficulty in securing re-entry into an educational environment.

It is understandable that, in the face of mass unemployment, an
educational establishment should take the view that its curriculum
should be geared to greater employability by its students. From the student's point of view this may make sense: if I cannot get a job, I will
want to improve my qualifications for employability so that I can
increase my chances. In response to this kind of demand, we therefore
not only ensure as far as possible that students acquire appropriate vocational skills, but we know that they also develop basic employment-
seeking skills such as writing a job application, compiling a curriculum vitae, and learning interview techniques.

Such training may well assist those individuals who are fortunate
enough to obtain employment. But they are really of little value to those
who fail to secure paid employment, and it is questionable whether they
help to improve the overall unemployment situation. If I am well trained
in how to perform at an interview, I may be offered the job, but inevitably this will be at the expense of someone else who was not so well versed
in interview strategies. The more techniques of this kind that we teach,
the higher the requirements for attaining employment will become, and
in the long run the unemployment problem is simply redistributed. Those
who have learned the relevant additional skills will perhaps secure
employment, whereas those who have not, but formerly might have had
a serious chance, will not. To advise an individual to stand on tip-toe
in order to see a spectacle makes sense; but to invite the whole crowd
to do so makes the activity of seeing universally more difficult. In fact,
it may with some justification be contended that to go on training people
for jobs when the available jobs are diminishing is absurd.

The underlying rationale of emphasizing vocational training, I
suspect, is a political one. If it is possible to persuade people that one
fundamental reason for unemployment is that the unemployed are
insufficiently trained, then one may hope to persuade the unemployed,
and indeed the public at large, that those who have failed to secure paid
employment are in their present situation through their own negligence:
if only they had taken the trouble to better themselves they would not
be in their present predicament. Thus it is possible for a government
to exonerate itself from blame in the face of mass unemployment.

The roots of vocationalism: the work ethic

It seems likely that the diminution of time spent in paid employment
will continue, partly on account of the unemployment situation, and

partly because of increased automation and computerization. If this is so, then it behoves the educational system to respond to such a change in society. I want to suggest a number of ways in which it might do this.

Firstly, and most obviously, there is a need to recognize the value of 'education for life'. The other 85 per cent of one's life still needs to be taken into account by the educational system. It is a fallacy to suppose that what is done outside working hours is less demanding and more mindless than the work for which one is paid. The tendency to exalt paid employment and to downgrade leisure is largely the result of the Protestant work ethic which stems from the Puritans. The whole philosophy on which the work ethic is based is questionable. The notion stemmed from the Protestant doctrine of predestination: that God had pre-ordained that certain individuals should form the 'elect' who would, through divine grace, and not through their own efforts, inherit God's kingdom, whereas the damned, equally through no choice of their own (but rather through sin, which they inherited genetically in any case), are destined to eternal torment. As a confirmation of this doctrine, the Puritans looked to the earthly realm to discover whether they could find this doctrine reflected in human affairs, and they detected a reflection in the respective economic prosperity of the rich and poor. Although material prosperity was not a means of attaining God's favour (for one's eternal fate was decreed from the moment of creation), nevertheless it was a sign of God's blessing and a reasonable indication that one was on the way to the right eternal destiny.

The theological doctrines on which such contemporary materialism is based are now, to say the least, somewhat suspect. Nevertheless the conclusions which the Puritans drew about the value of work and the desirability of financial reward continue to prevail. Yet it is not the case that work is necessarily absorbing, ego-involving and significant, while leisure, by contrast, is not. Much of one's paid employment can be trivial, even unskilled. Equally, one's unpaid activities can be highly significant.

Reading a newspaper, voting in an election, identifying with a particular movement or cause, even pursuing a hobby or engaging in a stimulating conversation, can demand as much skill and intelligence, if not more, than paid employment does. It was John Dewey who, of all educationalists the most celebrated for his insistence that there is more to the self than one's paid employment, said:

'There is doubtless — in general accord with the principle of habit — a tendency for every distinctive vocation to become too dominant, too exclusive and absorbing in its specialized aspect. This means emphasis upon skill or technical method at the expense of meaning. Hence it is not the business of education to foster this tendency, but rather to safeguard against it, so that the scientific enquirer shall not be merely the scientist, the teacher merely the pedagogue, the clergyman merely one who wears the cloth and so on' (Dewey, 1944, p 308).

Dewey is here propounding a philosophy of education which contrasts sharply with three currently prevalent views on the function of education. It is often suggested that education should be directed towards 'the demands of industry', 'the needs of the economy', and 'the needs of society'. Each of these views entails the autonomy and self-development of the student being subservient to some assumed wider need.

Vocationalism and financial sponsorship

The controversy amongst these competing positions on the function of education is sometimes based on considerations about who is providing the finance for students to pursue their courses of study. Some students are sponsored by business organizations, who may take the view that their financial backing and their vested interests in the quality of the finished product — the graduate or diplomate — entitle them to play a substantial part in determining the educational path which the student follows. Equally, some academic posts and a substantial number of research projects are funded by industry, and inevitably teaching and research staff can be expected to develop their professional expertise along lines which are consistent with the aims of their sponsors.

A government or local authority may also take the view that it is the sponsor of the bulk of educational provision. Ultimately, in the UK the funds which are available to the University Grants Committee (UGC) and to the five research councils are derived from central government, and the financing of the non-university sector, with only a few exceptions, comes indirectly from central government and from local authorities. It is not surprising, therefore, that one often hears the view expressed that polytechnics should provide a strong emphasis on catering for 'local needs', and that the universities should look towards the 'needs of the nation' in their curricular planning.

This philosophy of higher education has been expressed forcibly since the time of the expansion of higher education in the UK in the mid-1960s. For example, the University Grants Committee made the following statement in its Memorandum for Guidance for the 1967-72 quinquennium:

'The Committee fully recognize that a university has other objectives besides providing industry with ready-made recruits and that much has already been done to promote closer collaboration with industry. But there is no doubt that it would be valuable if the universities collectively made a further deliberate and determined effort to gear a larger part of their 'output' to the economic and industrial needs of the nation, for few things could be more vital to the national economy at the present time than the proper deployment of highly qualified scientific manpower and the application of research to the solution of current technological and economic problems... There are a good many comments from industry which reveal a gap between what postgraduate studies have traditionally provided and what industry would like to receive... it follows, in the Committee's view, that in present circumstances special attention should be given... to: (a) a shift of postgraduate effort from the more traditional types of course to something which is avowedly more 'vocational' and often shorter in duration; (b) training method designed to ease the transition from the academic to the industrial world...; (c) a greater emphasis on applied research than has hitherto been customary' (Quoted in Arblaster, 1974).

Of course, the government in turn derives its monies from society, and it is therefore also understandable that a body of opinion is expressed that education should be directed towards 'social needs' and that one principal aim of the educational system is to produce 'good citizens' who are capable of taking their place within our liberal-democratic community.

Recent proposals to abolish the student grant system and to replace it with 'student loans', if implemented, may have the interesting effect of providing a salutary counter to the claims which are exerted by those who are currently putting up the money to finance further and higher education. This is not to contend that such proposals are desirable, but if the provision of finance were accepted as entitlement to decide on the appropriateness of educational provisions at least the student — who is, after all, the immediate client — could claim the right to demand that the 'needs of the student' should be given as serious consideration as national, industrial and societal 'needs'. Yet, although a student loan system might enable students to determine what kind of education they wished to buy on credit, there would undoubtedly be a strong incentive for students to opt for vocational courses which secured a good financial return, thus enabling them to pay back their loans with minimum discomfort. Courses which might prove to be of greater inherent interest might be discounted in favour of those which offered the prospect of more immediate and more lucrative careers.

However, it is questionable whether ability to pay should serve as an entitlement to determine the availability of educational curricula. There is no logical connection between ability to pay for education and competence to decide what is desirable. Even an industrial sponsor can often have only a vague, or even an erroneous, notion of what will improve the operation of the company. Politicians, and even a Secretary of State for Education, can be accused, often with justification, of having little more than naive impressions of the content and aims of a curricular area. One teacher of computing recently criticized the Minister of State for Education for enthusing that the use of computers in primary schools would help children with sums, when in reality, she insisted, computers are used much more widely in teaching skills such as visual and manual co-ordination. Since teaching staff are the ones who are most fully conversant with their subject areas, there is a strong

case for contending that the control of educational curricula should not
rest with those who are making financial provision, but rather the academic communities who are the competent authorities on education.
This does not mean, of course, that curriculum planning should take
place within the confines of an academic ivory tower, and indeed this
rarely happens: validating bodies in the UK such as the Business and
Technician Education Council (BTEC) and the Council for National
Academic Awards (CNAA) normally require institutions seeking
approval to provide information demonstrating that there is potential
student demand, that industrialists and relevant professional bodies have
been consulted, and that the course is likely to have a good record in
securing the employability of students. Allowing academics to decide
need not involve subjecting students to some esoteric ivory-towerish
research in which members of staff have been engaging.

The 'needs of society'

Apart from the question of who has the right to decide what students
should study, there remains an equally important question of precisely
how one should understand expressions like 'the demands of industry',
'the needs of the economy', and 'the needs of society'. As Anthony
Arblaster noted in his provocative book *Academic Freedom* (1974), published over a decade ago, the 'demands of industry' have tended to be
equated with the demands of the controllers of industry. Institutes of
higher education typically teach management studies to a much larger
extent than trade union studies. Within faculties of business studies,
the presuppositions of capitalism manifest themselves in courses which
are run on self-employment, personnel management, company law and
the like. It would be foolish to deny, of course, that these have a place;
but the truly educated student is not the one who is processed on an
educational conveyor belt to take his or her place in business industry
like a cog in a machine. Education is not equivalent to the ability to
perform a set of vocational tasks, and if we are concerned to educate
our students, it is equally important to expose them to the problems
and criticisms related to contemporary capitalism. As Arblaster writes:

> 'It needs to be said, as dogmatically as may be necessary, that
> the needs of capitalism are not the needs of the 'nation', and may
> even be in direct conflict with those needs. It is significant that
> it is of 'the nation' and not 'the people' that they always speak.
> No doubt the term 'the people' has uncomfortably radical associ-
> ations. But it also has human ones; and here lies the rub. For time
> and again it becomes clear that the policies implied in responding
> to what are called the 'national' needs are policies which involve
> the sacrifice of people, of their rights, of their freedom, of their
> chance of obtaining a humane and personally valuable education.
> Policies of making research more 'useful' have involved a loss of

freedom and variety in this area. Policies of encouraging, and even of only permitting, vocational studies have cramped and distorted education, especially in the non-university sector. The habit of thinking of education solely in economic terms, as an 'investment', as a matter of producing trained manpower, has led to a situation in which it seems quite acceptable to propose a reduction of the quality of post-school education, deprive students of the opportunities to which they are entitled and even deter them from seeking any higher education at all.

'This may be what 'industry' needs. This may even be what some dismal abstraction called 'the nation' needs. But this is not what an open and vital society needs. It is not what the real living people who receive education need, or, very often even what they want either. In endorsing the rhetoric and the requirements of 'national needs', the academic elite, so far from behaving with the 'responsibility' which they would undoubtedly claim for themselves, have been betraying the very principles of a humane and open education which it is their professional duty to defend.'

Similar criticism can be directed with justification at the view that it is 'the needs of society' which can serve as the criterion which should determine what is put on a curriculum. There are no objective 'needs' which society has, apart from the basic necessities of food, clothing and shelter. Any so-called needs which extend beyond these basic biological needs can only reflect the political ideologies of the society which defines them. Thus, to say that society *needs* more production engineers is to express a political view that our society should increase its gross national product, and that it is more important to achieve certain economic goals than to produce educated men and women who will be sufficiently critical to assess whether such goals are worth pursuing in the first place.

To attempt to provide students with an education which reflects only one model of 'what society needs', without enabling students to become aware of alternative models and without enabling them to entertain criticisms of the prevailing model, is to transform education into a form of social control. To aim to produce 'good citizens' may sound a laudable enough aim, until one realizes that what is a good citizen is a contentious question. What should we say about a group who engages in civil disobedience by physically obstructing the setting up of a nuclear base? If our criterion is obedience to the law, then perhaps not. Yet, on the other hand, the group has arguably taken a responsible and reflective stance on a highly important issue. Whether or not one supports causes like the Campaign for Nuclear Disarmament in the UK or similar organizations elsewhere, it seems vital that the educational system should enable individual students to support or even initiate *changes* in society, rather than to conform mindlessly.

A 'good citizen' is certainly not identical with a conforming citizen, and in particular a good citizen is not necessarily one who accepts the

Protestant work ethic and regards gainful employment as a virtue and unemployment as a stigma. The value of paid employment is in fact grossly overrated. It is highly questionable whether someone who works, let us say, in the advertising industry is doing society a service by persuading people to adopt standards of living which they cannot afford, or to buy commodities which they do not need or necessarily even want. Conversely, if one is unemployed, it is not the case that one is on the scrap-heap or incapable of doing anything useful. Much unpaid work in our society is grossly undervalued, for example, the Citizens Advice Bureau worker who accepts no payment for his or her services, the prison or hospital visitor, and so on. I recently met one of my former students who, as yet, has not secured a full-time paid position. He was undertaking some full-time unpaid work to travel round the city ascertaining what facilities various stores offered for the disabled, and what provisions they would be willing to implement. The work was unpaid, but yet surely much more valuable than many a paid job.

The alternative to vocationalism

Subject matter

If, as I have argued, life is more than paid employment, we should expect to see this reflected in the patterns of our education system. It does not follow from what I have said that this is a plea for the old-fashioned 'liberal studies' approach, where it used to be fashionable in the UK to inject students of plumbing, mechanical engineering or electronics, with a timetabled slot of 'high culture' to which the unfortunate students were dragged along unwilling — often on a Friday afternoon between four and six o'clock — to receive doses of modern poetry, drama, ballet or whatever. Such an approach was patronizing in the extreme, implying that those who were studying science or engineering subjects, or those who were learning a trade, lacked culture, which we, the high priests and custodians of this esoteric knowledge, could dispense as a great privilege. It was always assumed that the scientific and technical subject students lacked 'culture', and it was only rarely suggested that there might be a reciprocal ignorance on the part of the humanities student: indeed, many teachers of humanities lack the basic skills of car mechanics, electrical engineering or computer programming, all of which are now as much part of our culture as Shakespeare, Beethoven and Picasso.

To acknowledge the fact that life is wider than paid employment, rather more radical changes are needed to education than the occasional injections of liberal studies for engineers or 'scientific culture' courses for humanities students. First, the requirement that educational courses should have to justify themselves in terms of available job opportunities for graduands is one which should be radically reconsidered. True, if one is to be in a position to afford to go to the theatre or take up a leisure pursuit, one needs a certain earning capacity, which can generally only be achieved through paid employment. However, with the rapid changes in technology and the corresponding and often unpredictable changes in job opportunites, it becomes increasingly difficult to predict what occupational skills a student will require. A very high proportion of students, in fact, end up in paid employment which bears little, if any, relationship to their formal qualifications. If it makes sense to train students vocationally, then arguably the best vocational commodity which one can teach is the ability to be versatile and adaptable. Where one's graduands or diplomates fail to secure employment, that is not necessarily a failure for the institution (and certainly not for the individual concerned). Indeed, if one's course of study has been devised with regard to the current situation, what one has acquired during one's course of study may be precisely what enables the graduand to lead a fulfilled life *without* paid employment. When a polytechnic is briefed to meet the 'needs of the community', this need not be construed as vocational skills, but the individual psychological and human needs of those applying to undertake courses of study.

The structure of the educational system

But it is not just the subject matter which requires reappraisal in the light of dwindling employment opportunities. What is needed is a reappraisal of the entire structuring of the system of higher and further education. The conventional stereotype of the undergraduate is that of one who is preparing for employment and who is using a course of study as a kind of apprenticeship for a paid vocation. Many graduates will testify that one's education, if not wholly geared to the employment which one attains (if one is successful), provides one with many indispensable skills and much necessary experience for coping with the 'outside world': one is able to be more confident and assertive, to argue one's case well, to appear well-informed on the matters one has studied, and so on. Yet, while education provides valuable experience for work and for life, it is also true that a background of employment and experience in the 'outside world' can stand one in better stead for receiving an education. The mature student is often much more able to see the value of the subject matter with which he is presented, to be more articulate in discussion, and to bring to bear on the taught material a profitable background of skills and experiences. There therefore does not seem to be any good reason why the accepted norm should be that full-time education should precede vocation, rather than *vice versa*. Indeed the prevalent convention that full-time education is the precursor of full-time vocation is precisely what gave rise to my student's conflict about whether to continue his course of study or to accept the chef's job. If one is to cope with such dilemmas effectively, and if one is to recognize that it is just as desirable for employment to precede education as for the reverse, then much more flexible patterns in our educational system ought to be emerging.

If we are to make higher education possible for those who are already in paid employment, we need to look afresh at some of our admissions procedures. Apart from the Open University, British higher education courses demand qualifications which are not normally held by those who have accepted offers of employment before obtaining the requisite number of English advanced level points (or their Irish and Scottish equivalents). It is generally agreed that such entry requirements are not reliable indicators of a student's final achievement, and many educators will confirm that 'mature' students who have gained experience of the world of work after leaving school can bring to bear on their studies a much greater wealth of insight and motivation. Indeed school leavers who have recently completed A levels are often required to 'unlearn' techniques encouraged within the school system. In the absence of solid research, there is no obvious alternative to A levels as prerequisites for higher education, but it behoves educators to discover some form of prognosis which will facilitate the optimum selection of suitable students for higher education and simultaneously ensure that those who intend pursuing a degree or diploma course undergo preliminary study which provides adequate preparation for higher education.

Another strategy which requires much greater exploration is the possibility of providing more educational courses which are pursued in a part-time mode. The existence of more part-time courses of study would enable those who had secured employment to undergo further education without sacrificing a career on which they had embarked after considerable difficulty. A pattern which enabled more transference from full-time to part-time modes of study would assist the student who, midway through a course of study, secured employment.

When one looks at the conventionally accepted norms for undergoing education, they really seem on reflection to be illogical in the extreme. To take a degree one must normally be fairly immature, in one's teens (preferably 18). One normally qualifies for the privilege of higher education by having passed two examinations (A levels), which need not have any bearing whatsoever on the subject to be studied, and at which one's success bears no correlation to the quality of the degree which one finally earns. During one's course of study, one may not earn, with the possible exception of holiday jobs, and one is condemned to a period of poverty, in which one is deprived of the opportunity to earn a proper wage or salary, but rather must survive on a very low 'grant'. One may not normally interrupt one's course of study, and if one wishes to do so, a convincing case has to be made and accepted by the institution. After three years, one's education is deemed to be complete: one is not normally permitted to return, and few normally do so. Those who wish to do so find that the chief barrier is that no awarding body will sponsor them: after all, have they not *'been* educated'?

When stated in this way such attitudes, of course, seem absurd, as indeed they are. What requires recognition is that education is not something which one 'completes'. To complete an educational qualification is often to abandon it entirely, and to annul many of the benefits which one's formal education has endowed. As someone who has actually secured employment in what is basically a not very marketable subject — namely, philosophy — I can recall my former philosophy professor taking aside his intending specialist philosophy students and counselling them that philosophy was not a subject by which one could normally expect to earn a living. Predictably, most of my fellow-students ended up in professions which demanded different skills — the legal profession, the civil service, the church. Having lost the ability to pursue their specialist subject, on their own admission, they have now forgotten most of what they ever learned. This points to a case for enabling a subject which is studied to become part of a continuing process of education, with facilities for erstwhile students to return, if they so desire, to keep abreast with what has developed in that subject since their undergraduate days.

'Initiation' versus continuation

The institutional barriers to enabling erstwhile students to return to continuing education are not merely administrative and financial. They reflect, I believe, a prevalent philosophy of education which is most notably expressed in contemporary writers such as R S Peters, who has pioneered the field in endowing this area of philosophy with a clear methodology which emphasizes the importance of subjecting key educational concepts to linguistic analysis rather than attempting explicit recommendations for curricular innovation. Peters is therefore ostensibly less prescriptive than Dewey, and this has lulled readers into supposing that his writings on the philosophy of education are ideologically neutral and non-judgemental on questions of educational practice. Such an interpretation of Peters, however, overlooks the fact that the terminology which he uses to unravel the meaning of concepts such as 'education' reveals on closer inspection some important hidden assumptions about attitudes to educational practice to which he and many other educators subscribe.

One revealing piece of terminology which Peters uses when analysing the concept of education is the word 'initiation' (see Peters, 1966). For Peters, education is, amongst other things, the initiation of a student into 'worthwhile activities'. (In fairness to Peters, his insistence that education entails initiation into 'intrinsically' worthwhile activities means that he attaches greater importance to general education than to narrower vocational training.) The problem with a word like 'initiation' is not so much that it marks finality: strictly speaking, an initiate is one who has only just started in (usually) some spiritual path. The problem lies in the fact that, in Gilbert Ryle's terminology, it is an 'achievement word' (see Ryle, 1949): that is to say, initiation is 'episodic' — it marks a moment in time which creates a sharp break between the non-achievement and the achievement, just as, for instance, the footballer who scores the goal (an achievement) creates a sharp break between, say, a nil-nil draw and a state of one-nil superiority.

'Initiation' may be an appropriate term to characterize education to the extent that it implies that there lies a further and more complex path for the initiate to pursue subsequently. But it is singularly inappropriate in its implication that there is a sharp break between being uneducated and being educated. People do not divide neatly into the educated and the uneducated, but rather form a continuum of degrees of educatedness. 'Initiation' connotes the kind of sharp break which we find in religious contexts such as baptism and confirmation. These are all-or-nothing matters: either one is baptized or confirmed or one is not, and neither rite is repeatable. Further, although a newly confirmed convert to Christianity may still have much to learn about the Christian faith, paradoxically formal instruction often terminates once confirmation has been granted.

This initiation — confirmation model — when applied to education, leads to the kinds of fallacies about completed education which I have been attempting to expose. Although education itself is not episodic, the educational system devises certain rites of passage which are themselves episodic in nature. Passing GCE (or equivalent) examinations, matriculation at college or university, and graduation are all events which can be pinned down to a single episodic moment. The episodic nature of such moments can therefore cause educationalists and philosophers of education to view education as a once-and-for-all event which finds its completion when a particular educational rite has been celebrated. But to view education in this manner ignores the obvious point that events like obtaining diplomas, first degrees or even doctorates are only like milestones in a potentially endless journey. Education does not cease with the completion of a traditional period in further or higher education, but can continue indefinitely, and, obvious though this point may seem, much work remains to be done to ensure the provision of continuing education for adults throughout life, even when it is not instrumental in securing employment or enhancing career prospects.

For those who are unemployed, or for those who have time which they wish to use outside their main employment, education can actually form *part* of life, as well as preparation *for* life. Classes in university extra-mural departments or in organizations such as the Workers' Educational Association perform a highly important task here. The Open University also fulfils a role in continuing education, with its much more flexible patterns of study than those of conventional universities and polytechnics. It is unfortunate that increasing financial demands on its students have meant that for many it is no longer a live option: if the concept of 'openness' is to mean availability to all, then financial barriers should not be permitted to close off such educational opportunities from a significant proportion of the country's population.

I have put the case for placing education more in the context of life than of paid vocation, and argued that much greater emphasis should be placed on the former. Of course, any system which is more flexible than our present one will involve enormous logical problems in order to make it successful. It is not my task as a philosopher to suggest how my proposals might be tackled logistically, although it cannot be denied that what is educationally desirable has often to be subordinated to what is practically possible. What I hope I have done, however, is to suggest by my analysis of the function of education that such a reappraisal of our educational system would be worth working on, and that it would place the respective roles of paid employment and life in general in a much more balanced perspective.

References

Arblaster, A (1974) *Academic Freedom* Penguin: Harmondsworth
Dewey, J (1944) *Democracy and Education* The Free Press: New York
Peters, R S (1966) *Ethics and Education* Allen and Unwin: London
Ryle, G (1949) *The Concept of Mind* Penguin: Harmondsworth

16. How should new technologies be used in education?

Steen Larsen

Summary: Based on relevant research, some important questions concerning the use of information technology in education are discussed. First, the common argument that extrinsic reinforcement systems facilitate learning is examined, and it is shown that extrinsic reward can even undermine the students' own intrinsic interest. Second, the difference between information and knowledge is considered. It is shown that these are not identical concepts, and that a distinction between them is necessary if one's theory of teaching and learning is not to be reduced to a simple theory of transferring information to the students. In accordance with these considerations, some principles for the use of information technology in education are proposed, based on the fundamental view that our schools should be changed from auditoriums of isolated listeners into laboratories of active co-operation.

Introduction

'Every day we read of the many serious problems plaguing our educational system. In Des Moines, a teacher is stabbed by a student. In Boston, parents stone a school bus carrying black children into their white neighborhood. In Detroit, teachers stay home on strike while kids roam the streets looking for fun and trouble. Homeowners in Oregon protest that soaring property taxes are squandered on increasingly ineffective schools. Despite the billions of public dollars poured into our educational system, Johnny still can't read and Johnny's teacher can't teach. American education seems to be a hydra-headed monster — **the more we hack at it, the more ugly problems it sprouts.**'

This is a short description of the current educational situation as Linnehan (1984) sees it. Even if it concerns the American school system, similar descriptions of the educational situation in other countries can be found as well. Generally such descriptions are made in a state of frustration because no concrete solutions to the problems can be offered. But not this one:

'The solution to all these difficulties is so simple and obvious that I am amazed that no one, to my knowledge, has even mentioned it', Linnehan continues. 'I happened upon this happy solution to

our country's educational crisis not by any stroke of genius but
by simple observation of recent technological developments.'

And what is then the solution?:

'My proposal is this: every American child be educated at home
by a computer.'

Indeed, it is a very concrete proposal which is based on the following
arguments:

'Parents will again assume responsibility for educating their children. Individuals, no longer slaves to the group, will learn at their
own pace and will reap immediate satisfaction from their newly
acquired knowledge when their computers beep that their
responses are correct. No more delaying of positive reinforcement
for days or weeks while the teacher gets around to making up a
test or grading a paper.'

Furthermore, there are no reasons for hesitation, no argument against
this solution of the current educational problems:

'If I have overlooked any valid objection to my proposal, I will
be most grateful to have them pointed out, but I am confident
there are none.'

Certainly, there are. Let us point them out by examining the four arguments, not out of regard for Linnehan, but because these arguments
raise some questions about education and the new technologies which
are of general importance.

The first argument, that parents will again assume responsibility for
educating their children, if they are educated at home by a computer,
is based on the assumption that parents are home too. But are they?
At least in Western Europe the pattern has changed during the last
decades from families with a home-working mother to families where
most frequently both parents are out-working. Furthermore, we see an
increasing number of families with only one parent who works outside
the home. If general education by computers in the home was established in this situation, the child would in most families be the only
home-working person, and the parents would not have much better conditions than they have today for assuming responsibility for educating
their children.

However, even if this is indeed an important question, it is not directly
related to questions on education and educational methods in a strict
sense. Therefore, and because I have dealt with computers in the home
elsewhere (Larsen, 1986a), the present chapter will concentrate on the
other three arguments and examine the following questions:

1. Does positive reinforcement in educational software facilitate
   learning?
2. Can computers transmit knowledge?
3. Is education an individual process?

Does positive reinforcement in educational software facilitate learning?

Linnehan's argument, which is frequently found in discussions concerning computer-assisted education, is that one of the advantages of this kind of instruction is the possibility of giving the student immediate feedback and reward. Due to this, different kinds of motivational reward systems are very often found in educational software.

However, even if it is commonly accepted that verbal or graphic reinforcers increase the student's motivation for the program, a number of studies (Atkinson and Suppes, 1968; Suppes and Morningstar, 1972; Brebner et al, 1981) have found that studerts are not always interested in or motivated by positive reinforcers or even verbal feedback on the screen (Roblyer, 1981).

Concerning such reinforcement features, it should be realized that they can be a more or less integrated part of the learning process. Thus in most traditional drill-and-practice software we frequently find a kind of extrinsic reward which is without relation to the academic content of the program. A smiling face, for instance, appearing on the screen, when the student has solved a number of arithmetical problems correctly, does not relate to the calculations just carried out. This kind of reward can be called extrinsic because it does not contain instructional cues. It does not belong to this specific learning situation, and can therefore just as well be used in programs on geography, biology or language.

However, programs of another type have recently been designed which are more game-like, where the reinforcing features are integrated with the academic content. In these programs, we do not see a number of calculations carried out on the screen followed by the reward of a smiling face, but now a graphical scenario is established on the screen. For instance, in the program 'Fractions Basketball' (Dugdale and Kibbey, 1980), a program designed to teach children about the addition and subtraction of fractions, a scenario from a basketball match is used. A ball is placed on the line between the two baskets, indicating a certain fraction of the line, and the student has to type the right answer on the keyboard. If the answer is correct he has scored two points which are displayed on the screen.

In such game-like scenarios the reinforcing features are an integrated part of the program, and Lepper (1985) argues that such kinds of instructional computer games stimulate the child's intrinsic motivation. Lepper's view is based on an important distinction between what he calls 'intrinsic interest' and 'extrinsic reward'. Thus when the child on a certain task is motivated by its own immediate intrinsic interest, no artificial extrinsic reward is necessary. In a previous study (Lepper, Greene and Nisbett, 1973) Lepper has shown that the use of extrinsic reward can even undermine the child's intrinsic interest in a task. Corresponding results have been obtained by Deci (1971), who found that college students who had been paid for solving a number of puzzles, which they initially found immediately interesting, tended to show a greater decrease in their intrinsic interest compared to subjects who had not been paid. Deci hypothesized that during the work, the rewarded subjects had changed the character of their engagement from an intrinsic interest in the task itself to an interest in obtaining some extrinsic goal.

In the study by Lepper, Greene and Nisbett (1973), which included 69 pre-school children, the same phenomenon was found, and this led to the following conclusion:

> 'Many of the activities we ask children to attempt in school, in fact, are of intrinsic interest to at least some of the children; one effect of presenting these activities within a system of extrinsic incentives, the present study suggests, is to undermine the intrinsic interest in these activities of at least those children who had some interest to begin with.'

However, let us return to the game-like scenarios which according to Lepper (1985) stimulate the child's intrinsic interest. Is this true? Does the fact that the reinforcing features in these scenarios are integrated aspects of the learning activity change the extrinsic reward systems into intrinsic motivation? Yes and no. It can be assumed that many children will be motivated to use these game-like scenarios through an immediate interest in the programs. They simply find them amusing to play with. However, the question is whether this intrinsic interest in such cases is directed towards learning about the arithmetical problems, or whether it is directed towards the basketball scenario in which the arithmetical problems are inherent? Even if the children are motivated by intrinsic interest in playing basketball on the screen, these same reinforcing features must be regarded as extrinsic in relation to the actual learning subject, namely learning about the addition and subtraction of fractions.

In the implementation of educational software we must thus distinguish between three kinds of motivational interests:

1. an interest based on unintegrated extrinsic rewards as found in many traditional drill-and-practice programs;
2. an interest based on integrated extrinsic reward systems as found in the game-like scenarios; and
3. the child's immediate intrinsic interest found in situations where the child is engaged in the task itself, and is not working in order to obtain some extrinsic goals.

Thus, it must be realized that the use of extrinsic reinforcement can be even counterproductive in learning settings, due to its undermining of the child's own intrinsic interest.

Can computers transmit knowledge?

At present a number of experiments with computer-assisted instruction have been carried out. Most frequently the educational software in these projects involves learning activities such as drill-and-practice, simulations and presenting information to the student.

A survey covering 33 investigations of the effect of computer-assisted instruction reveals that this kind of instruction in general seems to have a positive effect, particularly as regards drill-and-practice and interactive use of the computer. However, retention of what had been learned through computer-assisted instruction was lower compared with normal instruction (Splitberger, 1979).

Similarly, in another overview of 20 investigations (Edwards, Norton, Taylor, Weiss and Dusseldorp, 1975), it was also found that computer-assisted instruction took less time, but again most investigations showed retention to be lower in students who had learned through computer-assisted instruction compared with students who learned through normal instruction.

Finally, Kulik, Bangert and Williams (1983) reviewed 51 evaluations of computer-based teaching in Grades 6 through 12 and found that the computer reduced substantially the amount of time that students needed for learning. However, only five of these studies included follow-up examinations, investigating retention over periods from two to six months. In four of these, no significant difference between computerized and normal instruction was found, and in the remaining study, retention was significantly higher in the control group of students who had attented normal instruction.

Apparently, children thus learn faster by computer-assisted instruction, but are obviously unable to retain as much compared to traditional methods. How can this phenomenon be explained?

Information is not identical to knowledge

One of the words most frequently used in current educational discussions is 'information'. That precisely this concept is dominating in a period where the use of new information technology in education is debated, is certainly not surprising. However, the strong emphasis on information involves a tendency to disregard the concept of 'knowledge'. Often these concepts are even regarded as just different words referring to identical matters, and are used as synonyms. This is perhaps one of the most serious and widespread mistakes in the current use of information technology, and it leads to the attitude that giving the students information is identical to giving them knowledge.

Certainly, there are fundamental differences between information and knowledge (Larsen, 1986b). To understand the nature of these differences, we must realize the difference between what can be termed personal and public. The individual person can bring his inner thoughts, feelings and opinions into the public domain by the process of communication. The name of this process is derived from the root 'common', which means 'pertaining or belonging to the whole community' (Hamlyn, 1972). Thus, to communicate means to turn one's thoughts and feelings into common formulas, ie formulas belonging to the whole community. This means that our personal thoughts and feelings must be transformed. Like Cinderella's two sisters, we must cut a mental 'toe and heel' to put our personal experiences into the common formulas which can bring them publicity. Thus to communicate involves the process of formation and in an almost literal sense its product is 'in-formation'.

Now the fundamental difference between 'knowledge' and 'information' can be defined: the difference between knowledge and information belongs to the process of communication, which means that when personal knowledge is communicated it is transformed into public information.

Thus through the transition from personal knowledge into public information, something disappears. How can we describe this 'something'? In the psychology of perception we speak of *gestalts* and define them as integrated wholes that contain more than the mere summation of their units or parts. According to this definition we can say that knowledge is organized like *gestalts*, always containing something more than the mere summation of the information that can be communicated.

In education it is important to understand this difference between *gestalts* of knowledge and informational facts, because they each represent indispensable necessary dimensions of the educational process. Education is not solely a matter of absorbing as much information as possible on a certain subject, but also a question of establishing a coherent *gestalt* of knowledge concerning this subject. To simplify this a little, we could say that knowledge of a certain subject is what you have left if all information has been forgotten. And due to your *gestalt* of knowledge, the necessary information can easily be searched for when it is needed in a certain situation. Thus, solely to concentrate on transmitting information to children in an information age is really no wise educational strategy.

Semantic and episodic memory

If we analyse the process of concept formation in the child, we will recognize that concepts can be established in different ways. Take for instance the concept 'dog'. Through its daily life activities the child frequently encounters a phenomenon which adults call 'dog'. However, these dogs can be highly different but are still named by the same word. The child's problem is to overcome these authentic differences, to abstract the common characteristics and to establish it as a general linguistic category.

The cardinal point is, however, to which degree this process of concept formation is based on authentic experiences or on semantic and lexical derivations from already established concepts. If, for example, the child has established the concept 'dog', it is possible through purely linguistic explanations to derive the concept 'cow' by modifying the old concept: 'A cow is an animal like a dog. It is bigger, has two horns and you get milk from it.'

It is important to realize that the differences between authentic and derived concepts are not at the manifest level. Both types of concept can work efficiently on the surface level of the child's language. In the linguistic development of the child, attention is generally directed towards pronunciation, syntax and other manifest features, but the question, nevertheless, if not one of the most important linguistic aspects, is how deeply the concepts are rooted in authentic life experiences derived from concrete episodes.

Episodes, yes. Just the importance of concrete episodes has occupied memory research in the past decade. Already in 1972 the Canadian psychologist Tulving proposed a distinction between what he called episodic and semantic memory (Tulving and Donaldson, 1972), concepts which in many respects are parallel to the distinction made here between personal knowledge and public information. Thus episodic memory is derived from 'temporally dated episodes and events, and temporal-spatial relations among these events...always stored in terms of its autobiographical reference'.

On the other hand, semantic memory refers to organized structures of facts and concepts, information about 'verbal symbols, their meaning and referents, about relations among them, and about rules, formulas and algorithms for the manipulation of these symbols, concepts, and relations'.

Let us illustrate the difference between episodic and semantic memory by an example: one day I meet a friend on the street. He tells me about a certain meeting he had attended recently. While listening, I simultaneously experience the situation on two different levels: the semantic content of his description of the meeting he had attended, which I am now publicly informed about, and the immediate circumstances in which his description is made, which constitute an episode of my life. Looking back later I can remember his description of that certain meeting he had attended, stored as semantic information, and I can recollect it as a certain episode where I met a friend at a certain place at a certain time. If I were not able to recollect the episodic knowledge, I would still be able to refer to the meeting he had told me about, but would no longer be able to ascertain whether I had attended it myself or if somebody had just informed me about it.

Lexicon and biography

If education is regarded as a process by which I become capable of handling my own life and taking part in the further development of the society, thinking must be my way of thinking and semantic information must be turned into my own *gestalts* of knowledge. From such a view, semantic memory and information established through computer-based instruction is no longer sufficient, because of its lack of autobiographical reference.

This does not mean, however, that semantic information in any way should be avoided. This would be impossible. But it implies that computers, due to the lack of autobiographical references, should not be used as the children's main source of information or as a sparring partner in general thinking. The programmed micro-worlds have been described by Minsky and Papert (1970) as 'fairyland(s) in which things are so simplified that almost every statement about them would be literally false if asserted about the real world'.

If education is considered to be a process by which one becomes capable of handling everyday situations, this is a crucial point. Because the semantic micro-worlds are built up of separated information, they are ill-adapted to the elusive, shifting world of everyday episodes. Our everyday expertise does not consist in terms of explicit facts and rules, but in our episodic memories of past situations already successfully confronted. If what the learner was acquiring were still more sophisticated rules and principles, then episodic aspects could be neglected and the semantic micro-worlds could just gradually be complicated as the child developed. But if the child was able to see the general principles as aspects of concrete episodes of everyday life, then keeping the learner in a micro-world could actually be counterproductive.

This problem can be illustrated by the terms 'lexicon' and 'biography'. The semantic memory can be compared to the lexicon and the episodic memory to the biography. The question now is how far these faculties of mind are dissociated. Do they constitute different libraries into which the student places new memory records, or is the lexical information due to the presence of autobiographical references turned into coherent personal knowledge?

The interaction with the computer is cyclical. Even if the semantic content of this interaction changes from situation to situation, the educational circumstances remain unchanged: the screen is the same, the starting procedures, the commands of the programs and the actual surroundings are the same. The educational situations cannot be separated and recollected as different episodes of life, even if their lexical content can be reproduced. In fact, this means that the autobiographical reference is suspended in such educational settings.

Now we can answer the question: information can be presented to the children faster through computer-assisted instruction compared to traditional methods. However, the children are apparently unable to retain as much because this information is not automatically turned into coherent personal knowledge.

Information can be transmitted but knowledge must be induced

The consequence of this understanding leads to an almost provocative statement, namely that knowledge cannot be transmitted. It cannot be directly transmitted from a knowing person, a teacher, to a learning person, a student, in a simple and direct way — not even through the process of communication. The process of teaching and learning is not simply a matter of transmission, but involves the much more fundamental and complicated processes of transformation.

Let us use a metaphor to clarify this. Electricity can be transmitted from one place to another through a wire. However, where very long distances are involved, the voltage is often changed to avoid a huge transmission loss. This process is carried out in a transformer, an electrical device, without continuously moving parts, which by electromagnetic induction transforms electric energy from a primary circuit to a secondary. Contrary to transmission, there is no direct wire connection between the two circuits in the transformer. It is the very existence of electric energy in the primary circuit that raises electric energy in the secondary, not by direct transmission but by indirect induction.

Similarly, in the teaching process, knowledge cannot be transmitted directly; it must be induced due to its informal character. Like the electrical system, two transforming processes can therefore be found in an effective teaching process: the transformation of personal knowledge into public information, by which the teacher so to speak breaks down his *gestalts* of personal knowledge into systems of information that can be transmitted to the students, and the opposite process where *gestalts* of personal knowledge are developed in the student, based on the obtained information.

Simple and developed theories of teaching and learning

Fox (1983) investigated teachers' personal theories of the process of teaching and learning. On this background he distinguishes between what he calls 'simple' and 'developed' theories. Most inexperienced teachers used analogies which fell mainly into the category of what Fox calls 'the transfer theory of teaching, because the subject material is viewed as a commodity to be transferred to the students' minds'. This conception belongs to the category of simple theories because it views the student as a container or vessel to be filled. Teachers who more or less explicitly base their educational philosophy on the transfer theory do not distinguish between information and knowledge, the result being that they regard knowledge as a commodity which can be directly transferred to the student by the act of teaching, from one container to another. Such teachers tend to describe their view of the teaching process as 'imparting knowledge' or 'conveying information', and they are described by Fox in this way:

'Conscientious transferrers spend a great deal of time preparing their material and making sure that it is accurate and up to date. Some of them also go to great lengths to develop and refine their methods of transfer and they often devise elaborate teaching aids to inject the essence of their subjects accurately into the heart of the container...The simple theories of teaching express a very simple relationship between teaching and learning. If a topic has been taught it must have been learned. If the tea has been poured, the cup must be full.'

This means that because the teacher's attention is first concentrated on the commodity before it is transferred, and then on the very act of transfer, he often tends to overlook what happens to the commodity after the transfer. Thus, in this perspective, efficient teaching and learning is seen to be the result of well-prepared material, effectively organized and imparted.

This simple transfer theory is the one on which most of today's computer-assisted education is based. In the same way, no distinction is made between information and knowledge, simply because it is taken for granted that transferring information to the children is identical to giving them knowledge.

Is education an individual process?

'No longer slaves to the group', Linnehan put it in his argument for individual education at home by the computer. But how efficient is learning as an individual process? And what is the impact on the children's development of social functions?

According to Piaget, thinking and social function are closely related to engagement in actions and operations which are both individually and socially organized. He states that 'it is precisely by a constant interchange of thought with others that we are able to decentralize ourselves... to co-ordinate internal relations deriving from different viewpoints' (Piaget, 1950).

The development of social function is nothing isolated, but a part of the child's general cognitive development. According to Piaget, 'co-operation is the first of a series of forms of behaviour which are important for the constitution and development of logic' (Piaget, 1950).

Such arguments stress the importance of social interchange in learning situations. However, how do the cognitive operations controlling the interaction between the individual and his environment develop? This is not just a question of how the individual manipulates and interacts with the physical objects in his environment, but includes interaction with other individuals.

Social learning theorists such as Murray (1974) and Bandura (1977) explain the child's acquisition of social behaviour by processes of imitation, in particular imitation of superior models. However, both Mugny and Doise (1978) and Weinstein and Bearison (1985) have shown that subjects who interacted with less advanced partners showed as much progress as subjects who interacted with more advanced partners. Therefore, the conception that imitation is the fundamental mechanism in social learning must be modified.

Thus Marion, Desjardins and Breante (1974) observed that 'interaction among participants increases when a cognitive conflict is felt by all'. According to this, Doise, Mugny and Perret-Clermont (1975) established a socio-cognitive conflict model of development in children, based on the hypothesis of 'cognitive conflict experienced and resolved socially'. In a number of experiments they have shown that when children are working together in dyads and thus have the opportunity to generate so-called socio-cognitive conflicts, they are able to solve problems at a more advanced level compared to children working individually on the same problems. Furthermore, it has been shown by Mugny and Doise (1978), that in dyadic combinations where subjects who functioned at different levels of mastery worked together, both the less and the more advanced partners progressed.

Apparently, cognitive structuring is stronger in groups than in individuals because the social interaction opposes different views which leads to cognitive conflicts between the subjects. And as stated by Piaget (1975) 'the most productive factors in acquisition (are) the disturbances brought about by conflict'.

Such conflicts oblige the subjects to co-ordinate their actions, which brings about a disequilibrium in the encounter with other points of view which can only be assimilated if cognitive restructuring takes place. According to Perret-Clermont (1980), cognitive conflicts of this kind

'bring about the disequilibrium which make cognitive elaboration necessary, and in this way cognitive conflict confers a special role on the social factor as one among other factors leading to mental growth.

'Social-cognitive conflict may be figuratively likened to the catalyst in a chemical reaction: it is not present at all in the final product, but it is nevertheless indispensable if the reaction is to take place.'

Very few of the investigations concerning the effect of computer-assisted instruction have related to such questions and distinguished between changes in academic and social behaviours. One of them was carried out by Feldman and Sears (1970) at Stanford University's Center for Research and Development in Teaching. Their results revealed that children who had received computer-assisted instruction exhibited less social behaviour compared to children who were given normal instruction. According to the authors, this result might be due to the more individualized character of computer-based instruction compared to conventional classroom techniques, and they conclude:

'The decrease in social behaviour for children receiving CAI instruction does suggest that critics may have some justification for suggesting that CAI leads to more sedentary, constricted behaviour' (Feldman and Sears, 1970).

Such criticism has, for instance, been raised by Hilgard (1964). His main objection against programmed learning is just that it is sedentary and passive:

> 'But if we wish to encourage a spirit of inquiry, we have to encourage students to move about in the library or the laboratory: social participation acquires a certain amount of motility, if only to be able to sit in a circle and talk; there is creative work to be done that requires a shop or studio.'

Research on the difference between individual and collective work with computers

Until now there has been only a little systematic investigation of the character of social interaction between students working with the microcomputers. Some more or less anecdotal descriptions have been published concerning students sharing ideas when using text editing programs (Rubin, 1980; Collins, Bruce and Rubin, 1982; Zacchei, 1982) and of computer programming in group settings (Jabs, 1981).

However, a few systematic studies have been carried out which enlighten us about the difference between individual and collective work with computers. Thus Reid, Palmer, Whitlock and Joner (1973) observed that some children solved problems more effectively in a group than they did when working alone. Furthermore, Cheney (1977) found that students who worked in pairs on learning computer programming did much better in an exam compared to those who had worked individually. In accordance with this, Klaus and Grau (1976) found in a study where 48 seventh graders, below the performance median in arithmetic, worked both individually and in groups with computer-controlled tasks of increasing difficulty, that on the average 60 per cent less time was required in group work as compared to individual work.

It could be suggested that students of high mastery will dominate and even render passive their lower achieving peers when working together in small groups. Apparently, this is not necessarily the case. Thus Webb (1984) found in a study of learning to program microcomputers in small groups, that the number of turns and the amount of time at the keyboard had almost no relationship with computing outcomes. The students not at the keyboard seemed to be at least as involved with the material as the students at the keyboard. Furthermore, the cooperation in the groups seemed to be less based on verbalization as compared to normal classroom settings:

> 'In group work in the typical classroom setting, students can verbally explain how to do the work or can show another student the solution, for example, by writing the solution to a mathematics problem on paper or on the blackboard. Even while "showing" the work, students often rely on verbal cues when the written solution is not complete. With a computer, however, the strategies

or approaches to solving a problem (the program) and the results are clearly seen by everyone because they appear on the screen in standardized fashion. In this way, students can learn from what other group members do as well as from what they say.'

Concerning the importance of social interaction in learning, it can thus be concluded that a child, when working alone on a certain task, might more easily remain enclosed in an egocentric approach compared to children working together. The socio-cognitive conflicts, due to different points of view, make cognitive restructuring necessary in the subjects and make the children able to solve problems at a more advanced level compared to children who work individually on the same problems.

An alternative proposal for the use of computers in education

After the discussion of Linnehan's three arguments for the use of computers in education, we can now state an alternative proposal, based on the following views:

1. Education should be based on the student's intrinsic motivation.
2. Teaching should be based on developed theories, realizing the difference between transmission of information and induction of knowledge.
3. Learning situations should be based on co-operation and social interaction.

That education should be based on intrinsic interest implies that it is heavily based on the student's own learning-by-doing. Brown (1983) suggests that computer technology will give learning-by-doing a renaissance in the schools:

'I believe that technology will fundamentally change both the use and content of learning-by-doing. In particular, it will make possible a wider range of learning-by-doing scenarios as well as extending the kinds of knowledge that can be taught. Namely, it will facilitate the learning and improvement of metacognitive skills — skills for thinking about thinking, learning, remembering, and diagnosing.'

However, this vision does not relate to the original educational philosophy behind learning-by-doing. Due to the lack of authentic, practical work in the schools, reality is replaced by scenarios. And working with these is much closer to learning-by-thinking than to learning-by-doing.

Learning is closely connected to problem-solving, and the computer is a powerful tool for this purpose. But what kind of problems does the learner actually solve when the computer is used in education?

'The student, working on several strands simultaneously, begins at the bottom of a strand and moves upward on each strand as a function of his ability to perform correctly on the strand. Since

movement along a strand depends on the student, the level of performance on one strand relative to the level of performance on other strands
creates a problem set for one student different from the problem set
for another student. Thus, unlike in the traditional classroom, each
student is solving a different set of problems, and each set of problems
contains problem types from each strand appropriate to the ability level
of the student involved' (Suppes, 1971).

This description represents much of the current use of computers in
education, where it is seldom used as a tool for solving authentic problems, but rather as a generator of artificial problems.

In fact it all seems to end in a paradox: in the schools we now have
a powerful tool for problem-solving, but what are the problems to be
solved with it? Due to the isolation of the schools from the rest of societal life, most problems the children are dealing with in the school are
still of an artificial and abstract character. This creates the need for
external reward systems.

The attitude that extrinsic reward is necessary for efficient learning
overlooks the power of the student's own intrinsic interest. Instead of
just working out extrinsic and artificial reward systems in a certain educational software, the relevance and authenticity of the subject matter in
question should be considered. Thus, there is a close connection between
abstract, boring and irrelevant subject matters on the one hand, and
the need for extrinsic reward on the other. Therefore, we should ask
ourselves why it is necessary to motivate the students for a certain task
or subject matter. Why are they not simply intrinsically interested in
it? Thus, the use of new information technology also implies a critical
attitude towards the content of the existing curricula, a critical attitude
towards partly antiquated curricula, which are frequently more in line
with the needs of an industrial or even a pre-industrial society than a
society based on modern information technology. The more the existing curricula grow out of date, the more will extrinsic reward systems
be needed. But, as has been shown, such extrinsic reward can undermine the student's own intrinsic interest. Therefore, new information
technology should not be introduced to compensate for partly antiquated
school systems; it should be used for changing them.

Furthermore, if the view is accepted that information can be transmitted but knowledge must be induced, the transfer theory is no longer
a sufficient educational philosophy. As already described, the induction of knowledge is not just a matter of simple direct transfer of
information to the student, because the two processes of transformation are involved. According to this, the teaching process can be
described in three stages:

1. the knowing person's transformation of personal knowledge into
    public information,
2. transmission and distribution of information, and

3. the learner's transformation of the obtained public information into personal knowledge.

Stage 1: Transformation	Stage 2: Transmission	Stage 3: Induction
The expert's transformation of personal knowledge into public information	Transmission of information to the learner	The learner's transformation of public information into personal knowledge
ANALYSIS	SPEECH	PERCEPTION
DEFINITION	SCRIPT	UNDERSTANDING
EXPLANATION	PICTURES	INTEGRATION
DISPOSITION	RADIO	RECOLLECTION
SEPARATION	TV	DIALOGUE
FORMULATION	VIDEO	DISCUSSION
SCHEMATIZING	COMPUTERS	CO-OPERATION
VISUALIZATION	EXPERT SYSTEMS	EXPERIMENTATION
ETC	ETC	ETC

Figure 16.1 *Public knowledge into personal knowledge*

Since most of today's computer-based education is based on the transfer theory, it generally concentrates the attention on stage 1, the teacher's transformation of his personal knowledge into public information, and stage 2, the transmission and distribution of information to the child.

In the implementation of educational software, these two stages are well known, and much time and effort is used on developing programs and databases which can present all the relevant information to the students. However, the third stage, where the obtained information is so to speak digested by the student, is often overlooked. This is a serious mistake which simplifies the educational situation according to the principle of a mere transfer of information. Thus, to transform the obtained information into personal knowledge demands two important functions, namely that the objective and public information gets subjective and personal references, and that it is integrated into already existing coherent patterns of knowledge in the student's mind. However, due to their subjective character, these functions cannot be built into the software, but must be stimulated from other parts of the situation in which the learning takes place. This is the reason why knowledge cannot simply be transmitted but must be induced.

What are then the activities which establish autobiographical references and turn information into personal knowledge? They are activities such as co-operation, social interaction, restructuring of knowledge due to socio-cognitive conflicts, discussion, explanation, recollection of

previous experiences, and solving of real-life problems. Such activities
can never be part of educational software, but educational software can
be part of them. Therefore, education must be based on both communication, transmission and personalization, and the use of information
technology should never be seen in isolation but as part of a much
broader educational situation. It is a tool, not an end in itself.

When we work with this new technology in education, we should
have this three-stage model in mind and be especially aware of the activities in stage 3. Thus when we, for example, introduce new educational
software we must ask ourselves: what are the necessary pedagogical
activities which are needed to complement my software to be sure that
the presented information is digested into knowledge in my pupils?

As Daniel Boorstin (1980), chief librarian in the American Congress,
has put it:

> 'It is a cliché of our time that what this nation needs is an
> "informed citizenry"... I suggest, rather that what we need — what
> any free country needs — is a knowledgeable citizenry. Informa-
> tion, like entertainment, is something someone else provides. It
> really is a service! We expect to be entertained, and also to be
> informed. But we cannot be knowledged! Each of us must acquire
> knowledge for ourself.'

A new educational sociology

The further integration of new information technology in education
therefore implies the understanding that education is not merely a matter
of instruction. The new technology will then no longer be regarded as
teaching machines, for which qualified software must be developed, but
as devices which, controlled by the learner, can be a powerful tool for
the development of personal knowledge. However, in this perspective
information technology is just an aspect of the social setting in which
education is taking place. Thus what is needed now is not more sophisticated technology or stronger interest and attention toward its
characteristics and use, but a revised 'educational sociology'. The principles on which the present educational systems are based are more in
accordance with thoughts belonging to the former century than with
the possibilities inherent in the new technology. The buildings, classrooms, curricula and textbooks do not simply electrify these old systems.

It must be realized that education is not identical with instruction
and therefore the schools are not solely occupied with teaching and
instruction, but have also important social purposes. If education is
changed into a private act, for instance carried out by the computer
in the home, some very important social dimensions in education could
possibly be lost.

Thus, the interaction between the child and the computer forms an
artificial dyad which immediately seems to be parallel to that between
teacher and pupil. However, effective learning is not solely a matter

of establishing teacher-pupil relationships. Such relationships can be effective in the initial stages of a new learning process where much instruction and new information is necessary. But according to the child's progress this instructional relationship becomes less important as the child begins to use its skills and knowledge in a larger social perspective in co-operation with others.

However, in obtaining this social extension of the learning processes, the private computerized instruction in the home could be counterproductive due to its individual character. Thus, the relationship between the computer and the pupil in this artificial dyad can in certain cases be so intense that it almost replaces other social relations, and almost leads into a situation which might be called social deprivation.

Social function demands the ability of anticipatory imaginations which are part of the very basis of human relationships. Through the imagination of how it must be to be another human being, and how it must be to be exposed to what I do now, I can simulate the consequences of my actions mentally and think them over before I carry them out into the real world.

However, such abilities can only be developed in social settings where co-operation with other individuals is necessary, not through a co-operative solving of artificial and abstract problems constructed solely for instructional purposes, but through the solution of real-life problems. The important question is what consequences the new information technology will have on this development of social function.

The immediate answer would appear to be that the new technology will expand the educational possibilities, partly because an overwhelming amount of information will be at hand for the students, and partly because the computers apparently open a more practical kind of learning activity than the mental operations which dominate most traditional learning in the classroom.

Indeed, a possible change in our schools from auditoriums to laboratories should be welcomed. However, the advantages of the new information technology can in the educational perspective be turned into disadvantages if it is not used according to explicit and well-defined educational philosophy. Thus, the new information technology can be used as a powerful tool to bring almost any kind of information into the classroom. But is this a reasonable educational strategy when we speak of the development of social function? Thus, to bring the world to the child does not contribute to the diminishing of the isolation of the schools from the surrounding parts of society.

A more reasonable educational strategy will be to do the opposite: to bring the child to the world. In accordance with the fact that social function must be developed through participation in social life, our schools must be changed from auditoriums of isolated listeners into laboratories of active co-operation. The present challenge is to investigate how the new information technology can be used in the realization of this necessary development.

References

Atkinson, R C and Suppes, P (1968) *An Automated Primary Grade Reading and Arithmetic Curriculum for Culturally-Deprived Children. Final Project Report* Stanford University: California

Bandura, A (1977) *Social Learning Theory* Prentice-Hall: Englewood Cliffs, New Jersey

Boorstin, D (1980) Remarks by Daniel Boorstin, the Librarian of Congress, at White House Conference on Library and Information Science *Journal of Information Science*, 111-113

Brown, J S (1983) Learning by doing revisited for electronic learning environments in White, M A (ed) *The Future of Electronic Learning* Hilldale: New Jersey

Cheney, P H (1977) Teaching computer programming in an environment where collaboration is required *AEDS Journal*, 11, 1-5

Collins, A, Bruce, B C and Rubin, A (1982) Microcomputer based activities for the upper elementary grades *Proceedings of the Fourth International Learning Technology Congress and Exposition* Society for Applied Learning Technology: Warrenton, VA

Deci, E L (1971) Effects of externally mediated rewards on intrinsic motivation *Journal of Personality and Social Psychology* 18, 105-115

Doise, W, Mugny, G and Perret-Clermont, A-N (1975) Social interaction and the development of cognitive operations *European Journal of Social Psychology* 5, 367-383

Dugdale, S and Kibbey, D (1980) *Fractions Curriculum of the PLATO Elementary School Mathematical Project* Computer-Based Education Research Laboratory: Urbana-Champaign: Illinois

Edwards, J, Norton, S, Taylor, S, Weiss, M and Dusseldorp, R (1975) How effective is CAI? A review of the research *Educational Leadership* November, 147-153

Feldman, D H and Sears, P S (1970) Effects of computer assisted instruction on children's behavior *Educational Technology* 10, 11-14

Fox, D (1983) Personal theories of teaching *Studies in Higher Education* 8, 151-163

Hamlyn Encyclopedic World Dictionary (1972) Hamlyn: London

Hilgard, E R (1964) Issues within learning theory and programmed learning *Psychology in the Schools* 1, 129-139

Jabs, C (1981) Game playing allowed *Electronic Learning* 1, 5-6

Klaus, F and Grau, U (1976) Soziale Anregungsbedingungen als Motivationsfaktor in einen Ubungsprogramm *Zeitschrift für Entwicklungspsychologie und Pedagogische Psychologie* 8, 37-43

Kulik, J A, Bangert, R L and Williams, G W (1983) Effects of computer-based teaching on secondary school students *Journal of Educational Psychology* 75, 19-26

Larsen, S (1986a) Computerized instruction in the home and the child's development of knowledge *Education and Computing* 2, 47-52

Larsen, S (1986b) Information can be transmitted but knowledge must be induced *Programmed Learning and Educational Technology* 23, 331-336

Lepper, M R (1985) Microcomputers in education. Motivational and social issues *American Psychologist* 40, 1-18

Lepper, M R, Greene, D and Nisbett R E (1973) Undermining children's intrinsic interest with extrinsic reward: a test of the 'overjustification' hypothesis *Journal of Personality and Social Psychology* 28, 129-137

Linnehan, P J (1984) A modest proposal for the improvement of American education *English Journal* 73, 44-45

Marion, A, Desjardins, C and Breante, M (1974) Conditions experimentales et développement intellectuel de l'enfant de 5-6 ans dans le domaine numérique in *Pourquoi les échecs dans les premiéres années de la scolarité? Recherches Pédagogiques* (CRESAS, Ed) No 68 INRDF: Paris

Minsky, M and Papert, S (1970) *Draft of a proposal to ARPA for Research on Artificial Intelligence at MIT*

Mugny, G and Doise, W (1978) Socio-cognitive conflict and structure of individual and collective performances *European Journal of Social Psychology* 8, 181-192

Murray, J P (1974) Social learning and cognitive development: modelling effects on children's understanding of conservation *British Journal of Psychology* **65**, 151-160

Perret-Clermont, A-N (1980) *Social Interaction and Cognitive Development in Children* Academic Press: London

Piaget, J (1950) *The Psychology of Intelligence* Routledge and Kegan Paul: London

Piaget, J (1975) L'equilibration des structures cognitives. Probléme central du développement. *Etudes d'Epistemologie génétique* Vol XXXIII PUF: Paris

Reid, J, Palmer, R, Whitlock, J and Joner, J (1973) Computer-assisted instruction performance of student pairs as related to individual differences *Journal of Educational Psychology* **65**, 65-73

Roblyer, M D (1981) When is it 'good courseware'? Problems in developing standards for microcomputer courseware *Educational Technology* Oct 47-54

Rubin, A (1980) Making stories, making sense *Language Arts* **57**, 285-298

Splitberger, F L (1979) Computer-based instruction: a revolution in the making *Educational Technology* **19**, 20-25

Suppes, P (1971) *Computer-assisted Instruction at Stanford Technical Report No. 174* Stanford University: Stanford

Supples P and Morningstar, M (1972) *Computer-Assisted Instruction at Stanford, 1966-68: Data Models and Evaluation of the Arithmetic Programs* Academic Press: New York

Tulving, E and Donaldson, W (1972) *Organization of Memory* Academic Press: New York

Webb, N M (1984) Microcomputer learning in small groups: cognitive requirements and group processes *Journal of Educational Psychology* **76**, 1076-1088

Weinstein, B D and Bearison, D J (1985) Social interaction, social observation, and cognitive development in young children *European Journal of Social Psychology* **15**, 333-343

Zacchei, D (1982) The adventures and exploits of the dynamic storymaker and textman *Classroom Computer News* **2**, 28-30

Part 5: Bibliography and biographical notes

Bibliography

Elizabeth Wilce

Books and pamphlets

Adams, A and Jones, E (1983) *Teaching Humanities in the Microelectronic Age* Open University Press: Milton Keynes

Alloway, B S and Mills, G M eds (1985) *Aspects of Educational Technology XVIII: New Directions in Education and Training Technology* Kogan Page: London

Anderson, J ed (1985) *Computers in the Language Classroom* Australian Reading Association: Perth

Anderson, R C, Osborn, J and Tierney, R J eds (1984) *Learning to Read in American Schools* Erlbaum: Hillsdale, New Jersey

Anderson, R C, Spiro, R J and Montague, W E eds (1977) *Schooling and the Acquisition of Knowledge* Erlbaum: Hillsdale, New Jersey

Anwyl, J E and Harman, G S eds (1984) *Setting the Agenda for Australian Tertiary Education* Centre for the Study of Higher Education, University of Melbourne: Parkville Victoria

Arblaster, A (1974) *Academic Freedom* Penguin: Harmondsworth

Ashton, D N and Maguire, M J (1986) *Young Adults in the Labour Market* Research Paper No 55, Department of Employment: London

Atkinson, R C and Suppes, P (1968) *An Automated Primary Grade Reading and Arithmetic Curriculum for Culturally-Deprived Children* Final Project Report, Stanford University: California

Baker, K (1982) *Teaching for Tomorrow's Technologies*. The 28th Fawley Foundation Lecture, University of Southampton: Southampton

Baldridge, J V, Roberts, J W and Weiner, T A (1984) *The Campus and the Microcomputer Revolution: Practical Advice for Nontechnical Decision Makers* American Council on Education/Macmillan: New York

Bandura, A (1977) *Social Learning Theory* Prentice-Hall: Englewood Cliffs, New Jersey

Bannon, L, Barry, U and Holst, O eds (1982) *Information Technology: Impact on the Way of Life* A selection of papers from the EEC Conference on the Information Society held in Dublin, Ireland, 18–20 November 1981, Tycooly: Dublin

Barker, P G (1987) *Author Languages for CAL* Macmillan: Basingstoke

Barron, I and Curnow, R (1979) *The Future with Microelectronics: Forecasting the Effects of Information Technology* Open University Press: Milton Keynes

Bates, A W ed (1984) *The Role of Technology in Distance Education* Croom Helm: London

Baumgart, N, Low, B and Riley, S (1982) *Student Assessment Project* (A set of seven modules developed for inservice use by teachers) Macquarie University, School of Education: Sydney

Beech, G (1983) *Computer Based Learning: Practical Methods for Microcomputers* Sigma Technical Press: Wilmslow

Bennis, W G, Benne, K D and Chin, R eds (1970) *The Planning of Change* Holt, Rinehart and Winston: New York

Benson, I and Lloyd, J (1983) *New Technology and Industrial Change: the Impact of the Scientific-Technical Revolution on Labour and Industry* Kogan Page: London

Bernbaum, G ed (1979) *Schooling in Decline* Macmillan: London

Bessant, J et al (1985) *IT Futures: What Current Forecasting Literature Says about the Social Impact of Information Technology* National Economic Development Office: London

Bessant, J et al (1986) *IT Futures Surveyed: A Study of Informed Opinion Concerning the Long-Term Implications of Information Technology for Society* National Economic Development Office: London

Block, J H ed (1971) *Mastery Learning: Theory and Practice* Holt, Rinehart and Winston: New York

Bolter, J D (1984) *Turing's Man: Western Culture in the Computer Age* Duckworth: London (reprinted 1986, Pelican Books, Harmondsworth)

Bond, D, Landbeck, R and Trigwell, K (1986) *Computer Literacy: The Intake Characteristics of First Year GU Students* Centre for the Advancement of Learning and Teaching, Griffith University: Brisbane

Bork, A (1985) *Personal Computers for Education* Harper & Row: New York

Braverman, H (1974) *Labor and Monopoly Capital* Monthly Review Press: New York

Brochet, M (1985) *Computer Conferencing as a Seminar Tool: a Case Study* Workshop on Computer Conferencing and Electronic Mail, University of Guelph: Guelph, Canada

Campbell, D and Connor, S (1986) *On the Record: Surveillance, Computers and Privacy: the Inside Story* Michael Joseph: London

Cerych, L (1982) *Computer Education in Six Countries: Policy Problems and Issues* Institute of Education: Paris

Chartrand, R L and Morentz, J W eds (1979) *Information Technology Serving Society* Pergamon: Oxford

Cherry, C (1971) *World Communication: Threat or Promise* Wiley Interscience: London

Christensen, G ed (1987) *Datalaere i 5.klasse 1985/86* Horsens Kommune: Horsens, Danmark

Conabere, T and Anderson, J (1985) *Towards a Rationale for the Educational Use of Computer Technology* Occasional Paper No 8, Australian College of Education: Melbourne

Costello, N and Richardson, M eds (1982) *Continuing Education for the Post-Industrial Society* Open University Press: Milton Keynes

Coutts-Stern, A (1985) *The Education and Support of Non-Specialist Computer Users at Macquarie University* Macquarie University (internal report): Brisbane

Critchlow, J (1985) *The Use of Computers in Schools: Constraints to Further Development* Department of Education Management, Sheffield City Polytechnic: Sheffield

Curnow, R and Curran, S (1980) *The Silicon Factor: Living with the Microprocessor* National Extension College: Cambridge

Daiute, C (1985) *Writing and Computers* Addison-Wesley: Reading, Massachusetts

Dale, R ed (1986) *Education Training and Employment: Towards a New Vocationalism?* Pergamon Press: Oxford

Dancsuly, A, Ionescu, M, Radu, I and Salade, D (1979) *Pedagogie* Editura Didactică şi Pedagogică: Bucureşti

Dean, C and Whitlock, Q (1983) *A Handbook of Computer-based Training* Kogan Page: London

Dewey, J (1944) *Democracy and Education* Free Press: New York

Dick, W and Gagné, R (1982) *Instructional Psychology, 1976–81* N66001-81C-0456 US Navy Personnel Research and Development Center: San Diego

Donovan, K (1986) *Management of Information Technology in Further Education* Council for Educational Technology: London

Drăgănescu, M (1987) *Informatica şi societatea* Editura Politică: Bucureşti

Dugdale, S and Kibbey, D (1980) *Fractions Curriculum of the PLATO Elementary School Mathematical Project* Computer-based Education Research Laboratory: Urbana-Champaign, Illinois

Duke, J (1983) *Interactive Video: Implications for Education and Training* Council for Educational Technology: London

Duncan, K and Harris, D eds (1986) *Computers in Education* Proceedings of the IFP TC-3 4th World Conference on Computers in Education, Norfolk, Vancouver, 29 July-2 August. 1985, North Holland: Amsterdam

Dylander, B et al (1987) *Education, Skills and Informatics — a Danish Contribution to the EEC FAST-Programme, TWE 3, Network 2* CPI (Danish Centre for Education and Information Technology): København, Danmark

Elkjaer, B (1987) *Are the Girls the Problem? Gender and Computer Science in the Danish Secondary School System* Institute of Information, Royal Danish School of Educational Studies: Copenhagen

Ellington, H and Harris, N D C (1986) *Dictionary of Instructional Technology* Kogan Page: London

Ellis, M L and McCreary, E K (1985) *The Structure of Message Sequences in Computer Conferences: a Comparative Case Study* Computer Conferencing and Electronic Messaging, University of Guelph: Guelph, Ontario

Ennals, R and Cotterell, A (1985) *Fifth Generation Computers: Their Implications for Further Education* Further Education Unit: London

Entwistle, N and Hounsell, D eds (1975) *How Students Learn* Institute for Research and Development in Post-Compulsory Education, University of Lancaster: Lancaster

Eraut, M (1972) *Inservice Education for Innovation* Occasional Paper No 4, National Council for Educational Technology: London

Evans, C (1979) *The Mighty Micro* Victor Gollancz: London

Evans, H (1931) *Cwm Eithin* Gwasg y Brython: Liverpool

Evans, N (1986) *The Future of the Microcomputer in Schools* Macmillan: Basingstoke

Feigenbaum, E A and McCorduck, P (1983) *The Fifth Generation: Artificial Intelligence and Japan's Computer Challenge to the World* Addison-Wesley: Reading, Massachusetts

Forester, T ed (1985) *The Information Technology Revolution* Basil Blackwell: Oxford

Gagné, R (1977) *The Conditions of Learning* (3rd Edn) Holt, Rinehart and Winston: New York

Gagné, R and Briggs, L (1979) *Principles of Instructional Design* (2nd Edn) Holt, Rinehart and Winston: New York

Gershuny, J and Miles, I (1983) *The New Service Economy: The Transformation of Employment in Industrial Societies* Frances Pinter: London

Gerver, E (1986) *Humanizing Technology: Computers in Community Use and Adult Education* Plenum Press: New York

Gibson, D G and Gray, P D (1986) *Pedagogic Skills in IT: an Analytical Framework* St Andrews College: Bearsden

Glaser, R ed (1978) *Advances in Instructional Psychology* (Vol 1) Erlbaum: Hillsdale, New Jersey

Godfrey, D and Parkhill, D eds (1985) *Gutenberg Two* (4th Edn) Press Porcepic: Toronto

Goldsworthy, A W ed (1983) *Technological Change: Impact of Information Technology 1983* AGPS: Canberra

Gosling, W (1981) *The Kingdom of Sand: Essays to Salute a World in the Process of Being Born* Occasional Paper No 9, Council for Educational Technology: London

Goulet, L R and Bates, P B eds (1970) *Life-Span Developmental Psychology: Theories and Research* Academic Press: New York

Gross, N, Giacquinta, J B and Bernstein, M (1971) *Implementing Organizational Innovations* Harper & Row: New York

Gwyn, R (1987) *Visions and Scenarios for Education and Teacher Training* FAST Occasional Paper No 138, Commission of the European Community: Brussels

Hamlyn Encyclopedic World Dictionary (1972) Hamlyn: London

Hansen, K F and Jacobsen, J (1987) *Datamaterne i skolerne* Skolen NU: Gyldendal, Danmark

Hansen, K F and Jensen, P E (1986) *Informationsteknologi og skole. Status og udviklingslinier* Danmarks Paedagogiske Institut: Munksgaard, Denmark

Hargreaves, D (1982) *The Challenge for the Comprehensive School* Routledge and Kegan Paul: London

Havelock, R G (1968) *Planning for Innovation Through the Dissemination and Utilization of Knowledge* University of Michigan: Ann Arbor

Hawkridge, D (1983) *New Information Technology in Education* Croom Helm: London

Hawkridge, D, Vincent, T and Hales, G (1985) *New Information Technology in the Education of Disabled Children and Adults* Croom Helm: London

Heinich, R, Molenda, M and Russell, J D (1985) *Instructional Media and the New Technologies of Instruction* (2nd Edn) Wiley and Sons: New York

Hills, P J (1987) *Educating for a Computer Age* Croom Helm: London

Hiltz, S R (1984) *Online Communities: a Case Study of the Office of the Future* Ablex: Norwood, New Jersey

Hiltz, S R and Turoff, M (1978) *The Network Nation: Human Communication via computer* Addison-Wesley: Reading, Massachusetts

Hofmeister, A (1984) *Microcomputer Applications in the Classroom* Holt, Rinehart and Winston: New York

Howe, J A M and Ross, P M eds (1981) *Microcomputers in Secondary Education: Issues and Techniques* Kogan Page: London

Hubner, K (1979) *Kritik der Wissenschaftlichen Vernunft* Verlag Karl Alber: Freiburg, München

Hubner, K (1983) *Critique of Scientific Reason* (Translated by P R Dixon and H M Dixon) University of Chicago Press: Chicago

Hurley, P, Hlynka, D, Hurley, J and Thompson, J (1982) *Videotext — an Interactive Tool for Education and Training, Teleconferencing and Interactive Media* University of Wisconsin Extension: Madison, Wisconsin

Jamieson, I M and Lightfoot, M (1982) *Schools and Industry: Derivations from the Schools Council Industry Project* Methuen: London

Jenkins, C and Sherman, B (1979) *The Collapse of Work* Eyre Methuen: London

Jenkins, C and Sherman, B (1981) *The Leisure Shock* Eyre Methuen: London

Jennings, H (1985) *Pandaemonium, 1660-1886: The Coming of the Machine as seen by Contemporary Observers* André Deutsch: London

Jensen, P E and Klewe, L (1987) *Undersøgelse af Datalaere 1* Danmarks Paedagogiske Institut: Munksgaard, Danmark

Johansen, R, Vallee, J and Spangler, K (1979) *Electronic Meetings: Technical Alternatives and Social Choices* Addison-Wesley: Reading, Massachusetts

Johnston, A and Sasson, A eds (1986) *New Technologies and Development* Unesco: Paris

Jonassen, D H ed (1984) *The Technology of Text: Principles for Structuring, Designing and Displaying Text* (Vol 2) Educational Technology Publications: Englewood Ciffs, New Jersey

Jonassen, D ed (1987) *Instructional Design for Microcomputer Software* Erlbaum: Hillsdale, New Jersey

Jones, A, Scanlon, E and O'Shea, T eds (1987) *The Computer Revolution in Education: New Technologies for Distance Teaching* Harvester Press: Brighton

Jones, B (1982) *Sleepers Wake!: Technology and the Future of Work* Wheatsheaf Books: Brighton

Kail, R V and Hagen, J W eds (1977) *Perspectives on the Development of Memory and Cognition* Erlbaum: Hillsdale, New Jersey

Kaye, T (1985) *Computer Mediated Communication Systems for Distance Education: Report of a Study Visit to North America* (Project Report CCET/2) Institute of Educational Technology, Open University: Milton Keynes

Klafki, W (1979) *Studien zur Bildungstheorie und Didaktik* Beltz: Weinheim

Klatzky, R (1980) *Human Memory* (2nd Edn) W H Freeman and Co: San Francisco

Kleiman, G M (1984) *Brave New Schools: How Computers can Change Education* Reston Publishing Company: Virginia

Knowles, C (1984) *Distribution of Educational Software Through PRESTEL: Report of the CET Telesoftware Project* Council for Educational Technology: London

Kuhn, T S (1970) *The Structure of Scientific Revolutions* (2nd Edn) University of Chicago Press: Chicago

Large, P (1984) *The Micro Revolution Revisited* Pinter: London
Le Roy Ladurie, E (1978) *Montaillou: Village Occitan de 1294-1324* Editions Gallimard: Paris
Le Roy Ladurie, E (1978) *Montaillou: Cathars and Catholics in a French Village, 1294-1324* (Translated by B Bray) Scolar Press: London
Lewis, R and Pates, A (1987) *Learning Workshops: a Manual of Guidance on Setting Up and Running Flexible Learning Workshops* Longman/Further Education Unit: York
Lewis, R and Tagg, E D eds (1981) *Computers in Education* Proceedings of the IFIP TC-3 3rd World Conference on Computers in Education, Lausanne, Switzerland, July 27-31, 1981, North Holland: Amsterdam
Lewis, R and Tagg, E D eds (1982) *Involving Micros in Education* North Holland: Amsterdam
Lewis, R and Tagg, E D eds (1987) *Trends in Computer Assisted Education* Proceedings of the 1986 conference on computers in higher education, held at Lancaster University, Blackwell Scientific: Oxford
Lloyd, J, Taylor, J and West, C (1984) *Computer Literacy* (2nd Edn) (4 vols) Further Education Unit: London
Locatis, C N and Atkinson, F D (1984) *Media and Technology for Education and Training* C E Merrill Publishing Company: Columbus, Ohio
Lockhead, J and Clements, J eds (1979) *Cognitive Process Instruction: Research on Teaching Thinking Skills* Franklin Institute Press: Philadelphia

McCombs, B and Dobrovny, J (1982) *Student Motivational Skill Training Package: Evaluation for Air Force Technical Training* Logistics and Training Division, Lowry Air Force Base: Colorado
McConnell, D (1987) *A User Guide to the Open University CoSy Computer Conferencing System* (Prepared for students taking the educational technology 2 course in the School of Education, University of Bath) School of Education, University of Bath: Bath
Mackintosh, I (1986) *Sunrise Europe: the Dynamics of Information Technology* Basil Blackwell: Oxford
Maddison, J (1983) *Education in the Microelectronics Era: a Comprehensive Approach* Open University Press: Milton Keynes
Mallet, S (1975) *The New Working Class* Spokesman Books: Nottingham
Mandrou, R (1973) *Des Humanistes aux Hommes de Science: XVIe-XVIIe Siécles* Editions du Seuil: Paris
Marland, M ed (1981) Information skills in the secondary curriculum *Schools Council Curriculum Bulletin* No 9 Methuen: London
Martin, J (1981) *Telematic Society: a Challenge for Tomorrow* (Originally published as 'The Wired Society') Prentice Hall: Englewood Cliffs, New Jersey
Masuda, Y (1981) The information society as post-industrial society *World Future Society* Washington, D C
Meadows, A J, Gordon, M and Singleton, A (1982) *Dictionary of New Information Technology* Kogan Page: London
Megarry, J, Walker, D R F, Nisbet, S and Hoyle, E eds (1983) *World Yearbook of Education 1982/83: Computers and Education* Kogan Page: London
Michie, D (1979) *Expert Systems in the Microelectronics Age* Edinburgh University Press: Edinburgh
Minsky, M and Papert, S (1970) Draft of a proposal to ARPA for research on artificial intelligence at MIT

Nora, S and Minc, A (1978) *L'Informatisation de la Société Rapport de la Republique* la Documentation Française: Paris
Norman, D, Rumelhart, D and LNR Research Group eds (1975) *Explorations in Cognition* W H Freeman: San Francisco
Northcott, J and Rogers P (1985) *Microelectronics in Industry. An International Comparison: Britain, Germany and France* PSI: London

O'Neil, H F ed (1978) *Learning Strategies* Academic Press: New York
O'Neil, H F and Speilberger, C D eds (1979) *Cognitive and Affective Learning Strategies* Academic Press: New York
O'Shea, T and Self, J (1983) *Learning and Teaching with Computers* Harvester Press: Brighton

Papert, S (1980) *Mindstorms: Children, Computers and Powerful Ideas* Harvester Press: Brighton
Pask, G (1982) *Micro Man: Living and Growing with Computers* Century Publishing: London
Pearson, D P ed (1982) *Handbook of Reading Research* Longman: New York
Percival, F, Craig, D and Buglass, D eds (1987) *Aspects XX: Flexible Learning Systems* Kogan Page: London
Perret-Clermont, A-N (1980) *Social Interaction and Cognitive Development in Children* Academic Press: London
Peters, R S (1966) *Ethics and Education* Allen & Unwin: London
Piaget, J (1950) *The Psychology of Intelligence* Routledge and Kegan Paul: London
Pitariu, H (1979) *Dictionar de Pedagogie* Editura Didactică şi Pedagogică: Bucureşti
Pogrow, S (1983) *Education in the Computer Age: Issues of Policy, Practice and Reform* Sage Publications: London
Pressley, M and Levin, J R eds (1983) *Cognitive Strategy Research: Educational Applications* Springer-Verlag: New York

Radu, I T (1974) *Sisteme de Învăţămînt General-Obligatoriu* Editura Didactică, şi Pedagogică: Bucureşti
Rajan, A (1985) *Recruitment and Training Effects of Technical Change* Gower: Aldershot
Rajan, A and Pearson, R (1986) *UK Occupation and Employment Trends to 1990* Butterworths: Guildford
Ramsden, E ed (1984) *Microcomputers in Education 2* Ellis Horwood: Chichester
Reinecke, I (1984) *Electronic Illusions* Penguin: Harmondsworth
Robinson, F P (1946) *Effective Study* Harper & Row: New York
Rogers, C R (1983) *Freedom to Learn for the 80's* (2nd Edn) Merrill: Columbia, Ohio
Rumberger, R W and Levin, H M (1984) *Forecasting the Impact of New Technologies on the Future Job Market* Project Report No 84-A4, Institute for Research on Educational Finance and Government, School of Education, Stanford University: Stanford
Rushby, N J (1979) *An Introduction to Educational Computing* Croom Helm: London
Rushby, N J ed (1981) *Selected Readings in Computer-Based Learning* Kogan Page: London
Rushby, N J (1983) *Computer-Based Learning: State of the Art Report* Pergamon Infotech: Maidenhead
Rushby, N J ed (1987) *Technology Based Learning: Selected Readings* Kogan Page: London
Rushby, N J and Howe, J A M eds (1986) *Aspects of Educational Technology XIX: Educational, Training and Information Technologies — Economics and Other Realities* Kogan Page: London
Ryle, G (1949) *The Concept of Mind* Penguin: Harmondsworth

Saettler, P (1968) *A History of Instructional Technology* McGraw-Hill, New York
Salomon, G (1979) *Interaction of Media, Cognition and Learning* Jossey-Bass: San Francisco
Segal, J W, Chipman, S F and Glaser, R eds (1985) *Thinking and Learning Skills* (Vol 1) Erlbaum: Hillsdale, New Jersey
Sendov, B and Stanchev, I eds (1986) *Children in an Information Age: Tomorrow's Problems Today* Pergamon Press: New York
Sewart, D, Keegan, D and Holmberg, B eds (1985) *Distance Education: International Perspectives* Croom Helm: London
Shallis, M (1985) *The Silicon Idol: the Micro Revolution and its Social Implications* Oxford University Press: Oxford
Sharples, M (1985) *Cognition, Computers and Creative Writing* Ellis Horwood: Chichester
Short, J, Williams, E and Christie, B (1976) *The Social Psychology of Telecommunications* Wiley and Sons: London
Sleeman, D and Brown, J S eds (1982) *Intelligent Tutoring Systems* Academic Press: London

Smith, D J ed (1985) *Information Technology and Education: Signposts and Research Directions* Economic and Social Research Council: London

Smith, I C H ed (1982) *Microcomputers in Education* Ellis Horwood: Chichester

Smith, P R ed (1984) *CAL 83: Selected Proceedings from the Computer Assisted Learning 83 Symposium* Pergamon Press: Oxford

Sorge, A, Hartmann, G, Warner, M and Nichols, I (1983) *Microelectronics and Manpower in Manufacturing* Gower: Aldershot

Stonier, T (1983) *The Wealth of Information: a Profile of the Post-Industrial Economy* Thames Methuen: London

Stonier, T and Conlin, C (1985) *The Three Cs: Children, Computers and Communication* Wiley and Sons: Chichester

Strachan, R M ed (1983) *Guide to Evaluating Methods: a Manual for Microtechnology Innovation* National Extension College: Cambridge

Suppes, P (1971) *Computer-assisted Instruction at Stanford* Technical Report No 174, Stanford University: Stanford

Supples P and Morningstar M (1972) *Computer Assistld Instruction at Stanford, 1966-68: Data Models and Evaluation of the Arithmetic Programs* Academic Press: New York

Taylor, R ed (1980) *The Computer in School: Tutor, Tool, Tutee,* Teachers' College Press: New York

Terry, C ed (1984) *Using Microcomputers in Schools* Croom Helm: London

Toffler, A (1970) *Future Shock* Pan Books: London

Toffler, A (1980) *The Third Wave* Morrow: New York

Tourain, A (1974) *The Post-Industrial Society* Wildwood House: London

Townsend, C et al (1982) *London Into Work Development Project* Institute of Manpower Studies, University of Sussex: Brighton

Travers, R ed (1973) *Second Handbook of Research on Teaching* Rand Mcnally: Chicago, USA

Tucker, J ed (1984) *Education, Training and the New Technologies* A report of the Scottish Council for Educational Technology Conference 'Look out for Learners', held 16-17 March 1983, Kogan Page: London

Tulving, E and Donaldson, W (1972) *Organization of Memory* Academic Press: New York

Turkle, S (1984) *Die Wunschmaschine. Vom Entstehen der Computerkultur* Rowohlt: Reinbek bei Hamburg

Twining, J, Nisbet, S and Megarry, J eds (1987) *World Yearbook of Education 1987: Vocational Education* Kogan Page: London

Vand der Veer, G C, Tauber, M J, Green, T R G and Gorny, P eds (1984) *Readings on Cognitive Ergonomics — Mind and Computers* Springer-Verlag: Berlin

Van Weert, T J (1984) *A Model Syllabus for Literacy in Information Technology for all Teachers* ATEE: Brussels

Vian, J (1977) *L'Ecole CAP 2001 Editions* ESF: Paris

Vincent, B and Vincent, T (1985) *Information Technology and Further Education* Kogan Page: London

Vockell, E L and Rivers, R H (1984) *Instructional Computing for Today's Teachers* Macmillan: New York

Walgenbach, W (1979) *Ansätze zu einer Didaktik ästhetischwissenschaftlicher Praxis* Beltz: Weinheim

Watts, A G (1983) *Education, Unemployment and the Future of Work* Open University Press: Milton Keynes

Weiner, M (1981) *English Culture and the Decline of the Industrial Spirit: 1850-1980* Cambridge University Press: Cambridge

Weizenbaum, J (1984) *Computer Power and Human Reasoning* (2nd Edn) Penguin: Harmondsworth

Wellington, J J (1985) *Children, Computers and the Curriculum: an Introduction to Information Technology and Education* Harper & Row: London

Wellington, J J et al (1987) *Skills for the Future* HMSO: London

Weniger, E (1952) *Didaktik als Bildungslehre* Beltz: Weinheim

White, M A ed (1983) *The Future of Electronic Learning* Erlbaum: Hillsdale, New Jersey

Whiting, J and Bell, D A eds (1987) *Tutoring and Monitoring Facilities for European Open Learning* Elsevier/North Holland: Amsterdam

Wicklein, J (1981) *Electronic Nightmare − the New Communication and Freedom* Viking Press: New York

Wilkinson, A C ed (1983) *Classroom Computers and Cognitive Science* Academic Press: New York

Winterburn, R and Evans, L (1980) *Aspects of Educational Technology XIV: Educational Technology to the Year 2000* Kogan Page: London

Wood, S ed (1982) *The Degradation of Work* Hutchinson: London

Woodhouse, D and McDougall, A (1986) *Computers: Promise and Challenge in Education* Blackwell: Oxford

Yazdani, M ed (1984) *New Horizons in Educational Computing* Ellis Horwood: Chichester

Zinsser, W (1983) *Writing with a Word Processor* Harper & Row: New York

Official and corporate publications

Alvey Committee (1982) *A Programme for Advanced Information Technology: the Report of the Alvey Committee* HMSO: London

Assessment of Performance Unit (APU) (1981) *Understanding Design and Technology* APU; London

Association for Educational Communications and Technology (AECT) (1977) *Educational Technology: Definition and Glossary of Terms* AECT: Washington, DC

Central Policy Review Staff (1980) *Education, Training and Industrial Performance* HMSO: London

Central Statistical Office (1986) *Social Trends* No 16 HMSO: London

Commission of the European Communities (1986) *Draft Final Report to the DELTA Proposals* Directorate General XIII 'Telecommunications, Information Industry and Innovation', Commission of the European Communities: Brussels, Belgium

Computer Teaching Working Party (1985) *Report of the Computer Teaching Working Party* University of New South Wales: Sydney

Coopers and Lybrand Associates (1985) *A Challenge to Complacency: Changing Attitudes to Training* A report to the Manpower Services Commission and the National Economic Development Office, Manpower Services Commission: Sheffield

Council for Educational Technology (CET) (1979) *The Contribution of Educational Technology to Higher Education in the 1990s − a Statement* CET: London

Council for Educational Technology (CET) (1978) *Microelectronics: Their Implications for Education and Training: a Statement* CET: London

Council for Educational Technology (CET), Further Education Unit (FEU) and Further Education Staff College (FESC) (1984) *Information Technology and Educational Development* Report of a conference organized by CET, FEU and FESC, 13 March, Blagdon, Further Education Staff College: Blagdon, Bristol

Council for National Academic Awards (CNAA) (1979) *Implications of the Development of Information Technology for CNAA Undergraduate Courses* CNAA 2a/27: London

Dansk Center for Paedagogik og Informatick (CPI) (1987) *Forslag vedrorende informatik og edb i folkeskolens og gymnasiets undervisning i trearsperioden 1987-90* CPI: København, Danmark

Department of Education and Science (DES) (1981) *Microelectronics Education* DES: London

Department of Education and Science (DES) (1984) *Survey of Examining Boards in England* HMSO: London

Department of Education and Science (DES) (1985a) *Education and Training for Young People* Cmnd 9482 HMSO: London

Department of Education and Science (DES) (1985b) *Better Schools* Cmnd 9469, HMSO: London

Department of Education and Science (DES) (1987) *Aspects of the Work of the Microelectronics Education Programme* DES: London

Economic and Social Research Council (ESRC) (1987) *Document on Teachers' Use of Electronic Mail* ESRC funded seminar on the role of electronic mail in education: Southampton

Further Education Staff College (FESC) (1985) *Training for Jobs: Comments and Views on the White Paper* FESC: Blagdon, Bristol

Further Education Unit (FEU) (1984a) *Information Technology in FE: a Survey of IT Policy and of Current Practice in a Sample of Colleges* FEU: London

Further Education Unit (FEU) (1984b) *A Framework for Action in IT* FEU: Stanmore

Further Education Unit (FEU) (1985) *Computer Based Learning in FE: a Staff Development Model* FEU: London

Her Majesty's Inspectors of Schools (1985) *The Curriculum from 5–16* HMSO: London

House of Lords Select Committee on Science and Technology (1984) *Education and Training for New Technologies: Volume 1 Report,* HMSO: London

Information Technology Advisory Panel (1986) *Learning to Live with IT: an Overview of the Potential of Information Technology for Education and Training* HMSO: London

Manpower Services Commission (MSC) (1982a) *The Aims of TVEI* MSC: Sheffield

Manpower Services Commission (MSC) (1982b) *The Criteria of TVEI* MSC: Sheffield

Manpower Services Commission (MSC) (1983) *Towards an Adult Training Strategy: a Discussion Paper* MSC: Sheffield

Manpower Services Commission (MSC) (1984) *The Open Tech Programme Explained* MSC: Sheffield

Manpower Services Commission (MSC) (1985a) *Open Learning: It Gets Results* MSC: Sheffield

Manpower Services Commission (MSC) (1985b) *TVEI Review* MSC: Sheffield

Manpower Services Commission (MSC) (1987) *TVEI Students and Studies-Three Years On* MSC: Sheffield

Manpower Services Commission (MSC) Training Services Division (1981) *An 'Open Tech' Programme, to Help Meet Adult Training and Retraining Needs at Technician and Related Levels: a Consultative Document, May 1981* Open Tech Programme, MSC: Sheffield

Manpower Services Commission (MSC) Training Services Division (1982) *An 'Open Tech' Programme: Response to a Consultation* Open Tech Programme, MSC: Sheffield

South Australian Council on Technological Change (1982) *Communications Technologies: An Introductory Summary* Technological Change Office: Adelaide

University Grants Committee (UGC) (1983) *Report of a Working Party on Computing Facilities for Teaching in Universities* UGC: London

University of Western Australia (1984) *University Use of Microcomputers Project* Interim Report, University of Western Australia: Nedlands

World Confederation of Organizations of the Teaching Profession (WCOTP) (1981) *Implications of New Technology for Society and the Impact on Educational Policy and Provision* WCOTP: Morges, Switzerland

Yorkshire and Humberside Association for Further and Higher Education (1982) *FE Staff Development in the Use of Microcomputers* PAVIC Publications: Sheffield

Articles, periodicals and working papers

A'Herran, A (1986) The extent and nature of primary school children's access to computers in homes *ACE News*

Ahl, D H (1984) Progress on the project: an interview with Dr Kazuhiro Fuchi *Creative Computing* **10** 8: 113-114

Anderson, J (1985) Communication and the information age *in* Anderson (1985)

Anderson, R, Spiro, R and Anderson, M (1978) Schemata as scaffolding for the representation of information in connected discourse *American Educational Research Journal* **15**: 433-450

Andre, M and Anderson, T (1979) The development and evaluation of a self-questioning study technique *Reading Research Quarterly* **14**: 605-623

Armbruster, B and Brown, A (1984) Learning from reading: the role of metacognition *in* Anderson *et al* (1984)

Ausburn, F B and Ausburn, L J (1986) Directions for educational computing and implications for professional skilling requirements *Australian Journal of Educational Technology* **2** 1: 33-42

Ausubel, D (1960) The use of advance organizers in the learning and retention of meaningful verbal material *Journal of Educational Psychology* **51**: 267-272

Baker, L and Brown, A (1982) Metacognitive skills in reading *in* Pearson (1982)

Barclay, C (1979) The executive control of mnemonic ability *Journal of Experimental Child Psychology* **27**: 262-276

Barker, P (1985) Information technology, education and training *British Journal of Educational Technology* **16** 2: 102-115

Beattie, C (1985) Computers: an assessment of their educational potential *New Education* **7** 1-2: 63-77

Belanger, J and Sapp, R (1983) Project U-Train/CAL: NATAL as an authoring language *Programmed Learning and Educational Technology* **20** 3: 174-186

Bell, M (1985) The Coventry computer-based learning project *Programmed Learning and Educational Technology* **22** 3: 218-223

Bentley, T and Wrightson, S (1986) New technology solutions to training problems *Interactive Learning International* **3** 2: 21-22

Bernard, R (1985) Strategy cueing for activating students' use of illustrations in text: a report of two studies *in* Alloway and Mills (1985)

Bertrand, O (1985) The NIT revolution and educational strategies *European Journal of Education* **20** 2-3: 193-201

Black, P J and Ogborn, J (1977) Inter-university collaboration in methods of teaching science *Studies in Higher Education* **2** 2: 149-159

Bloom, B S (1968) Learning for mastery *Evaluation Comment* **1** 2: 1-13

Boorstin, D (1980) Remarks by Daniel Boorstin, the Librarian of Congress, at White House conference on Library and Information Science *Journal of Information Science*: 111-113

Bowden, J (1984) Applying new technology to tertiary teaching: possibilities and problems in the large-scale introduction of computers *in* Anwyl and Harman (1984)

Brezin, M J (1980) Cognitive monitoring: from learning theory to instructional applications *Educational Communications Technology Journal* **28**: 227-242

Britell, J K (1982) The social consequences beyond school *New York Times Spring Survey of Education* 25 April

Brooke, P (1984) New eras in education *Journal of Educational Television* **10** 3: 157-160

Brown, A (1978) Knowing when, where, and how to remember: a problem of metacognition *in* Glaser (1978)

Brown, A, Campione, J and Day, J (1981) Learning to learn: on training students to learn from text *Educational Researcher* **10** 2: 14-21

Brown, J S (1983) Learning by doing revisited for electronic learning environments *in* White (1983)

Canadian Journal of Educational Communication **16** 2 (spring 1987) A special issue on computer mediated communication in education

Cane, A (1983) More expected to work from home. *Financial Times* 1 September

Carl, D R (1983) Creating a duet: using video and video teleconferencing to meet the needs of the community *Programmed Learning and Educational Technology* **20** 3: 187-189

Cerych, L (1985) Problems arising from the use of new technologies in education *European Journal of Education* **20** 2-3: 223-232

Chalk, P (1987) PROLOG-based computer-aided learning environments *Programmed Learning and Educational Technology* **24** 2: 102-107

Cheney, P H (1977) Teaching computer programming in an environment where collaboration is required *Association for Educational Data Systems Journal* **11**: 1-5

Child, J (1984) New technology and developments in management organisation *Omega* **12** 3

Chin, R (1970) General strategies for effecting change in human systems *in* Bennis *et al* (1970)

Clark, R and Vogel, A (1986) Transfer of training principles for instructional design *Educational Communication and Technology* **33** 2: 113-123

Coffey, J (1986) Individualised training, OL, and modular training systems in the EEC *Training and Development* **5** 5: 16-19

Colbourne, M (1984) Computer-guided diagnosis of reading difficulties *Australian Journal of Reading* **6** 4: 199-212

Collins, A, Bruce, B C and Rubin, A (1982) *Microcomputer Based Activities for the Upper Elementary Grades* Proceedings of the Fourth International Learning Technology Congress and Exposition, Society for Applied Learning Technology: Warrenton, VA

Collins, L (1985) Cultural attitudes to the implementation of telephony: the significance for the development of training materials for UK users of audioconferencing *Teleconferencing and Electronic Communications* **IV**: 93-100

Cowan, J (1987) Learner centred learning: the key issues (or seven deadly sins which frustrate facilitation) *in* Percival *et al* (1987)

Daniel, A E, Encel, S and Barnes, J (1986) Education in the computer industry *Australian Universities Review* **29** 1: 13-16

Dansereau, D (1978) The development of a learning strategies curriculum *in* O'Neil (1978)

Dansereau, D (1985) Learning strategy research *in* Segal *et al* (1985)

Dansereau, D, Collins, K, McDonald, B, Holley, C, Garland, J, Diekhoff, G and Evans, S (1979) Development and evaluation of a learning strategy training program *Journal of Educational Psychology* **71**: 64-73

Dansereau, D *et al* (1979) Evaluation of a learning strategy system *in* O'Neil and Speilberger (1979)

Davies, P N (1985) The electronic office: responding to the challenge *BACIE Journal* **40** 3: 67-77

Davies, R L and Howard, E B (1985) Whither tele-shopping? *Economic & Social Research Council Newsletter* **55** June

Deci, E L (1971) Effects of externally mediated rewards on intrinsic motivation *Journal of Personality and Social Psychology* **18**: 105-115

Dede, C (1985) Educational and social implications *in* Forester (1985)

Delai, N (1985) A new culture for the computerized society: the implications for vocational training *Vocational Training* **19**: 9-13

Denholm, R (1983) Computer managed learning as a pilot project in TAFE Victoria *Proceedings of the Conference on Computer-Aided Learning in Tertiary Education* University of Queensland: Brisbane

Derry, S and Murphy, D (1986) Systems that train learning ability *Review of Educational Research* **56** 1: 1-40

Dickinson, W (1986) Industry shakes hands with vocational education: results positive *Florida Vocational Journal* **11** 4: 3-5

Diekhoff, G (1982) Cognitive maps as a way of presenting the dimensions of comparison within the history of psychology *Teaching of Psychology* **9** 2: 115-116

Doise, W, Mugny, G and Perret-Clermont, A-N (1975) Social interaction and the development of cognitive operations *European Journal of Social Psychology* **5**: 367-383
Doulton, A (1984) Interactive video in training *Media in Education and Development* **17**
4: 205-206
Dunnett, C W (1985) The technologies of education, communication and distance education *Programmed Learning and Educational Technology* **22** 4: 368-373

Edwards, J, Norton, S, Taylor, S, Weiss, M and Dusseldorp, R (1975) How effective
is CAI? A review of the research *Educational Leadership* November: 147-153
Emms, S J (1984) The MSC's skill centre CBT project *Programmed Learning and Educational Technology* **21** 3: 211-217
Emms, S J and McConnell, D (1987) *An Evaluation of Tutorial Support Provided by Electronic Mail and Computer Conferencing* Paper presented at the 22nd Annual Conference
of the Association for Education and Training Technology, University of Southampton, April 1987 (To be published in *Aspects of Educational Technology XXI* (forthcoming)
Kogan Page: London)
Ennals, R (1985) New technologies in training *Training and Development* **3** 9: 23-24
Ennals, R (1986) The fifth generation and training strategies *Interactive Learning International* **3** 1: 4-7

Feldman, D H and Sears, P S (1970) Effects of computer assisted instruction on chil-
dren's behaviour *Educational Technology* **10**: 11-14
Ferguson, M (1985) The family and new technologies *Economic and Social Research Council
Newsletter* **55** June
Flavell, J and Wellman, H (1977) Metamemory *in* Kail and Hagen (1977)
Ford, L (1986) A new intelligent tutoring system *Interactive Learning International* **3** 4: 23-26
Foster, D (1984) Computer simulation in tomorrow's schools *Computers in the Schools* **1**
3: 81-89
Fox, D (1983) Personal theories of teaching *Studies in Higher Education* **8**: 151-163
Friedman, R B (1984/85) The impact of technology on medical education *Journal of Educa-
tional Technology Systems* **13** 2: 137-141

Gershuny, J (1986) Time use, technology and the future of work *Journal of the Market
Research Society* **28**: 4
Gershuny, J (1987a) The leisure principle *New Society* **79**: 1259
Gershuny, J (1987b) Lifestyles, innovation and the future of work *Journal of the Royal
Society of Arts* **CXXXV**: 492-502
Glaser, R and Colley, W (1973) Instrumentation for teaching and instructional manage-
ment *in* Travers (1973)
Goodman, L (1984) New training technology: the MSC's view *Programmed Learning and
Educational Technology* **21** 3: 202-204
Gordon, A (1986) Education and training for information technology *Studies in Higher
Education* **11** 2: 189-198
Greeno, J (1985) Some examples of cognitive task analysis with instructional implica-
tions *in* Segal *et al* (1985)
Greer, W R (1982) In New York, a zest for learning is ignited *The New York Times Spring
Survey of Education* 25 April
Guellette, D (1987) *Psychotechnology as Instructional Technology: Systems for a Deliberate Change
in Consciousness* Paper presented at the annual meeting of the Association for Educa-
tion Communications Technology: Atlanta, Georgia
Gwyn, R (1982) Information technology and education: the approach to policy in England,
Wales and Northern Ireland *European Journal of Education* **17** 4: 355-368

Haeckel, S (1985) Some view! *Information Processing (IBM)* **4** 2: 12-13
Hall, K (1986) Developing learning in the workplace: the travel industry's experience
Programmed Learning and Educational Technology **23** 3: 228-235
Handy, C (1987) The future of work — the new agenda *Journal of the Royal Society of
Arts* **CXXXV**: 515-525

Harris, N D C and Tarrant, R D (1983) Teleconferencing and distance learning *British Journal of Educational Technology* 14 2: 103-108

Hartley, J and Davies, I (1976) Preinstructional strategies: the role of pretests, behavioural objectives, overviews, and advance organizers *Review of Educational Research* 46 2: 239-265

Hayes, J (1985) Three problems in teaching general skills *in* Segal *et al* (1985)

Heafner, K (1985) The challenge of information technology to education *Education and Computing* 1 3: 173-178

Hewitt, C and Cairns, J (1984) Catching up with technology: distance training for industry *Media in Education and Development* 17 3: 146-149

Hilgard, E R (1964) Issues within learning theory and programmed learning *Psychology in the Schools* 1: 129-139

Hlynka, D and Hurley, P (1982) Correspondence education and mass media: some issues and concerns *Programmed Learning and Educational Technology* 19 2: 158-165

Hodgson, V E (1986) The interrelationship between support and learning materials *Programmed Learning and Educational Technology* 23 1: 56-61

Holley, C, Dansereau, P, McDonald, B, Garland, J and Collings, K (1979) Evaluation of a hierarchical mapping technique as an aid to improve processing *Contemporary Educational Psychology* 4: 227-237

Holligan, P (1986) Patchwork academe *The Times Higher Education Supplement* 27 June: 20-21

Hopkin, D (1986) Back to the future *The Times Higher Education Supplement* 27 June: 24

Howe, A F and McConnell, D (1984) Teaching electronics at a distance by CYCLOPS: an assessment of the telewriting system *International Journal of Electrical Engineering Education* 21 3: 237-249

Howe, J A M (1982) The microelectronic revolution: a challenge to education *Scottish Educational Review* 2: 3-13

Ibbotson, C (1985) Embedding technology in the educational process *ACT Papers in Technical and Further Education* 86-91

Jabs, C (1981) Game playing allowed *Electronic Learning* 1: 5-6

Jamieson, I M (1986) Corporate hegemony or pedagogic liberation?: the schools industry movement in England and Wales *in* Dale (1986)

Johanssen, R and Bullen, C (1984) What to expect from teleconferencing *Harvard Business Review* 62 2: 164-173

Jonassen, D (1984) Developing a learning strategy using pattern notes: a new technology *Programmed Learning and Educational Technology* 21 3: 163-175

Jonassen, D (1985a) Learning strategies: a new educational technology *Programmed Learning and Educational Technology* 22 1: 26-34

Jonassen, D (1985b) The electronic notebook: integrating learning strategies in courseware to raise the level of processing *in* Alloway and Mills (1985)

Jonassen, D (1986) Improving recall using database management systems: a learning strategy *Association for Educational Data Systems Journal* 19: 109-123

Jonassen, D (1987) Integrating learning strategies into courseware to facilitate deeper processing *in* Jonassen (1987)

Jones, B (1982) Destruction or redistribution of engineering skills? The case of numerical control *in* Wood (1982)

Jones, B (1984) Schools mesmerised by hardware *Pivot* 11 1: 5-6

Jones, B and Scott, P (1987) FMS in Britain and the USA *New Technology and Work Environment* 2 1 Spring

Kang, Z (1987) PROLOG with interactive graphics for CAL *Programmed Learning and Educational Technology* 24 2: 122-127

Kerr, E B (1986) Electronic leadership: a guide to moderating online conferences *IEEE Transactions on Professional Communications* 29 1

Kestner, J and Borkowski, J (1979) Children's maintenance and generalization of an interrogative learning strategy *Child Development* **50**: 485-494

Klaus, F and Grau, U (1976) Soziale Anregungsbedingungen als Motivationsfaktor in
einen Ubungsprogram *Zeitschrift fur Entwicklungspsychologie und Pedagogische Psychologie*
8: 37-43

Knutton, H (1987) Information technology: its impact on work, education and training
in Twining *et al* (1987)

Kulik, J A, Bangert, R L and Williams, G W (1983) Effects of computer-based teaching
on secondary school students *Journal of Educational Psychology* **75**: 19-26

Laaser, W (1987) Effective methods for meeting student needs in telecommunications-
supported distance education *in* Whiting and Bell (1987)

Lange, J C (1986) New technology and distance education: the case of Australia *Distance
Education* **7** 1: 49-67

Larsen, S (1986a) Computerized instruction in the home and the child's development of
knowledge *Education and Computing* **2**: 47-52

Larsen, S (1986b) Information can be transmitted but knowledge must be induced
Programmed Learning and Educational Technology **23**: 331-336

Lăscus, V (1986) The principle of permanent orientation *Studia Universitatis Babes-Bolyai,
Philosophia* **31** 2: 66-69

Laurillard, D M (1984) Interactive video and the control of learning *Educational Technology* **14** 6: 7-15

Lauterbach, R (1984) *Staff Development with Regard to Science Education in Primary Schools*
Council of Europe: Education Research Workshop on Science and Computers in
Primary Education, Edinburgh, Scotland, 3-6 September 1984, Council of Europe:
Strasbourg

Lauterbach, R (1985) *Towards a Generative Strategy for Computers in Education: the Research
Base* Proceedings of conference on children in an information age: tomorrow's problems
today, May 6-9, 1985, volume 2, Varna, Bulgaria, 545-564

Lauterbach, R (1986) Preparing for change — anticipating new information technology
in German primary education *Programmed Learning and Educational Technology* **23** 4:
337-345

Lehmann, J and Lauterbach, R (1985) Die Wirkungen des Computers in der Schule auf
Wissen und Einstellungen (Effects of computers in school on knowledge and attitudes) *LOG IN* **5** 1: 24-27

Lepper, M R (1985) Microcomputers in education: motivational and social issues *American Psychologist* **40**: 1-18

Lepper, M R, Greene, D and Nisbett, R E (1973) Undermining children's intrinsic interest
with extrinsic reward: a test of the 'over justification' hypothesis *Journal of Personality
and Social Psychology* **28**: 129-137

Linnehan, P J (1984) A modest proposal for the improvement of American education
English Journal **73**: 44-45

Long, J P and Zahniser, G (1984) Microcomputers in vocational education: current and
future uses *Journal of Studies in Technical Careers* **6** 2: 132-141

Lougher, J (1985) Computer-based training project in the British Steel Corporation: basic
mathematics in industry *Programmed Learning and Educational Technology* **22** 3: 230-236

McAleese, R (1985) Some problems of knowledge representation in an authoring environment: exteriorization, anomalous state meta-cognition and self-confrontation
Programmed Learning and Educational Technology **22** 4: 299-306

McCombs, B (1982) *Enhancing Student Motivation Through Positive Self-Control Strategies*
Paper presented at the annual meeting of the American Psychology Association,
Washington, DC

McConnell, D (1986) The impact of CYCLOPS shared-screen teleconferencing in distance tutoring *British Journal of Educational Technology* **17** 1: 41-74

McConnell, D (1987) *Student-Tutor Co-operation in the Design of an Educational Technology and Development Course* Paper presented at the ETIC conference, University of Southampton, April 1987 (To be published in *Aspects of Educational Technology XXI* (forthcoming) Kogan Page: London)

McConnell, D and Sharples, M (1983) Distance teaching by CYCLOPS *British Journal of Educational Technology* 14 2: 109–126

McKenzie, G (1984) Using microcomputers to increase productivity in academia *Journal of Geological Education* 32: 171–175

McQuade, E and Petty, E (1984) Computers in engineering education *European Journal of Engineering Education* 9 2: 123–133

Marion, A, Desjardins, C and Breante, M (1974) Conditions experimentales et développement intellectuel de l'enfant de 5–6 ans dans le domaine numérique *in* Pourquoi les échecs dans les premières années de la scolarité? *Recherches Pédagogiques* (CRESAS, Ed) No 68 INRDP: Paris

Marton, F (1975) What does it take to learn? *in* Entwistle and Hounsell (1975)

Mayer, R (1980) Elaboration techniques that increase the meaningfulness of technical text: an experimental test of the learning strategy hypothesis *Journal of Educational Psychology* 72 6: 770–784

Meadow, C T (1979) Information science and scientists in 2001 *Journal of Information Science* 1 4: 217–222

Michie, D (1979) Expert systems: the cost effective consultants of computing *University of Edinburgh Bulletin* 15 11: 24

Mihkelson, A and Carswell, D (1985) The microcomputer as a teaching aid in tertiary chemistry *IUPAC International Newsletter on Chemistry Education* 23: 7–9

Miller, C A (1956) The magical number seven, plus or minus two: some limits on our capacity to process information *Psychological Review* 63: 81–97

Milne, J A and Anderson, J S A (1984) The Microelectronics Education Programme — dissemination and diffusion of microelectronics technology in education *Programmed Learning and Educational Technology* 21 2: 82–87

Mortimer, R J (1984) Using a viewdata system for training *Programmed Learning and Educational Technology* 21 3: 192–195

Mugny, G and Doise, W (1978) Socio-cognitive conflict and structure of individual and collective performances *European Journal of Social Psychology* 8: 181–192

Mugridge, I (1985) Distance education: a major role to play in the third world *Canadian Universities International Development Journal* Winter 1985/1986

Murray, J P (1974) Social learning and cognitive development: modelling effects on children's understanding of conservation *British Journal of Psychology* 65: 151–160

Nichol, J, Briggs, J, Nichol, R, O'Connell, K and Raffan, J (1987) PROLOG in the classroom *Programmed Learning and Educational Technology* 24 2: 108–116

Nightingale, P (1987a) *Microcomputers and Academic Work: Survey of Academic Staff at the University of New South Wales* Research and Development Paper No 66, Tertiary Education Research Centre, University of New South Wales: Sydney

Nightingale, P (1987b) Multiple and conflicting expectations of 'units' in higher education *Programmed Learning and Educational Technology* 24 1: 55–61

Noble, D (1984) Jumping off the computer bandwagon *Education Week* 3 24 October

Norman, D and Rumelhart, D (1975) Memory and knowledge *in* Norman *et al* (1975)

Oettinger, A and Zepol, N (1972) Will technology help learning? *Teachers' College Record* 74 1: 5–52

O'Farrell, J (1984) The European strategic programme for research and development in information technology *Journal of Information Science* 8 3: 31–35

Ogborn, J (1987) New technologies and the classroom *Programmed Learning and Educational Technology* 24 2: 94–101

O'Neill, G (1987) Interactive video as an aid to learning *Programmed Learning and Educational Technology* 24 2: 137–144

O'Shea, T (1978) Artificial intelligence and computer based education *Computer Education* 30: 25–28

Paine, N (1985) Open learning: the wider context *Media in Education and Development* **18** 1: 6–9

Paivio, A (1980) Imagery as a private audio-visual aid *Instructional Science* **9** 4: 295–309

Palmarozza, P H (1984) Trends in training: a historical perspective *Interactive Learning International* **1** 1: 9–11, 14

Papert, S (1982) Tomorrow's classrooms? *Times Educational Supplement* 5 March: 31–41

Peterson, P and Swing, S (1983) Problems in classroom implementation of cognitive strategy instruction *in* Pressley and Levin (1983)

Piaget, J (1975) L'equilibration des structures cognitives. Problème central du developpement *Etudes d'Epistemologie genetique* **33**, PUF: Paris

Pitariu, H (1984) Psychological selection of personnel for data processing professions *in* Vand der Veer *et al* (1984)

Plomp, T and Van de Wolde, J (1985) New information technologies in education: lessons learned and trends observed *European Journal of Education* **20** 2–3: 243–256

Plummer, H G (1985) Teacher training and interactive videodisc technology *Programmed Learning and Educational Technology* **22** 3: 245–249

Polanyi, M (1966) The logic of tacit inference *Philosophy* **41**: 1–18

Pollock, W J B (1983) Developing a national telecommunications infrastructure for the information era *in* Goldsworthy (1983)

Ragsdale, R G (1985) Educating teachers for the information age *McGill Journal of Education* **20** 1: 5–18

Rajan, A (1987) Technology in the workplace: assessing the impact *Manpower Policy and Practice* **2** 4, Summer

Reeder, D (1979) A recurring debate: education and industry *in* Bernbaum (1979)

Reese, H and Overton, W (1970) Models of development and theories of development *in* Goulet and Bates (1970)

Reid, J, Palmer, R, Whitlock, J and Jones, J (1973) Computer-assisted instruction performance of student pairs as related to individual differences *Journal of Educational Psychology* **65**: 65–73

Richardson, F (1978) Behaviour modifications and learning strategies *in* O'Neil (1978)

Rigney, J (1978) Learning Strategies: a theoretical prespective *in* O'Neil *ed* (1978)

Ringel, B and Springer, C (1980) On knowing how well one is remembering: the persistence of strategy use during transfer *Journal of Experimental Child Psychology* **29** 2: 322–333

Roblyer, M D (1981) When is it 'good courseware'? Problems in developing standards for microcomputer courseware *Educational Technology* **21**: 47–54

Roger, J (1979) Theories of the transfer of learning *Educational Psychologist* **14** 53: 53–69

Rubin, A (1980) Making stories, making sense *Language Arts* **57**: 285–298

Rumelhart, D E and Ortony, A (1977) The representation of knowledge in memory *in* Anderson *et al* (1977)

Rumelt, R P (1981) *The Electronic Reorganisation of Industry* Paper presented at the Global Strategic Management in the 1980's Conference, London (Quoted in Child, (1984)

Runquist, R W (1985) From paper flow to electronic flow *Educational Media International* **2**: 15–19

Sasscer, M F and Moore, D (1984) A study of the relationship between learner control patterns and course completion in computer assisted instruction *Programmed Learning and Educational Technology* **21** 1: 28–33

Schonfeld, A (1979) Can heuristics be taught? *in* Lockhead and Clements (1979)

Self, J (1987) User modelling in open learning systems *in* Whiting and Bell (1987)

Sheppard, M (1986) Communications technologies: challenges and solutions for isolated school learners *Media in Education and Development* **19** 3: 130–133

Shirley, S (1987) The distributed office *Journal of the Royal Society of Arts* **CXXXV**: 503–514

Simon, B (1984) Breaking school rules *Marxism Today* September

Singer, R (1978) Motor skills and learning strategies *in* O'Neil (1978)

Smith, D J and Sage, M W (1983) Computer literacy and the education/training interface *Computers and Education* **7** 4: 227–234

Snowman, J and McCown (1984) *Cognitive Processes in Learning: a Model for Investigating Strategies and Tactics* Paper presented at the annual meeting of the American Educational Research Association, New Orleans

Splitberger, F L (1979) Computer-based instruction: a revolution in the making *Educational Technology* **19**: 20–25

Stein, B, Bransford, J, Franks, J, Owings, R, Vye, N and McGraw, W (1982) Differences in the precision of self-generated elaborations *Journal of Experimental Psychology* (General) **111** 4: 399–405

Sternberg, R (1983) Criteria for intellectual skills training *Educational Researcher* **12** 2: 6–12

Sturdivant, P (1985) Technology in the classroom — students preparing for the world of tomorrow *Association for Educational Data Systems Monitor* **24** 3–4: 8–10

Thomas, G (1986) Writing and thinking: some effects of a new technology *Teaching News* **28** 2

Thompson, V (1984) Information technology in education and training: the CET view *Programmed Learning and Educational Technology* **21** 3: 196–201

Thompson, W (1985) A practitioner's perspective on the Chicago Mastery Learning Reading Program with Learning Strategies *in* Segal *et al* (1985)

Tremlett, L R (1985) The continuing education of professionals with special reference to engineers and scientists *International Journal of Innovative Higher Education* **9** 2: 23–28

Warner, M (1984) New technology, work organisation and industrial relations *Omega* **12** 3

Washburne, C W (1922) Educational measurements as a key to individualizing instruction and promotion *Journal of Educational Research* **5**: 195–206

Webb, N M (1984) Microcomputer learning in small groups: cognitive requirements and group processes *Journal of Educational Psychology* **76**: 1076–1088

Weinstein, B D and Bearison, D J (1985) Social interaction, social observation, and cognitive development in young children *European Journal of Social Psychology* **15**: 333–343

Weinstein, C and Underwood, V (1985) Learning strategies: the how of learning *in* Segal *et al* (1985)

Wellington, J J (1987) Employment patterns and the goals of education *British Journal of Education and Work* **1** 3

White, M and Snowman, J (1985) *Learning to Remember: a Memory-Directed Strategy that Transfers* Paper presented at the annual meeting of the American Educational Research Association: Chicago

Whiting, J (1984) Cognitive and student assessments of a CAL package designed for mastery learning *Computers and Education* **8** 1: 58–67

Whiting, J (1985) The use of a computer tutorial as a replacement for human tuition in a mastery learning strategy *Computers and Education* **9** 2: 101–112

Whiting, J (1986) Student opinion of tutorial CAL *Computers and Education* **10** 2: 281–292

Wildman, T M (1981) Cognitive theory and the design of instruction *Educational Technology* **21** 7: 14–20

Wildman, T M and Burton, J K (1981) Integrating learning theory with instructional design *Journal of Instructional Development* **4** 3: 5–14

Williams, B (1987) Necessity disguised as luxury *The Times Educational Supplement* 23 January

Williams, V (1984) Employment implications of new technology *Employment Gazette* May

Wilson, R (1979) Looking towards the 1990's *British Journal of Educational Technology* **10** 1: 45–91

Winders, R (1985) Teleconferencing: student interaction by telephone — the PACNET experience *Programmed Learning and Educational Technology* **22** 4: 327–333

Wittrock, M C (1974) Learning as a generative activity *Educational Psychologist* **11**: 87–95

Yeates, D (1986) How expert systems can make education more effective *Computer Weekly* **1037**: 38–39

Zacchei, D (1982) The adventures and exploits of the dynamic storymaker and textman *Classroom Computer News* **2**: 28–30

Biographical notes on contributors

Jonathan Anderson (Chapter 3) is Professor of Education at Flinders University of South Australia where he was appointed in 1973. His academic qualifications include BA, Master of Education, Diploma in Computing Science, and PhD. His teaching and research interests are in the fields of reading, communication, and the instructional uses of computers. This work has taken him to the Regional Language Centre in Singapore as Research Fellow, to the University of Stockholm under a Spencer Fellowship, to the Open University as research collaborator, and to Seattle Pacific University as adjunct professor. His published books include *Computing in Schools*, *Psycholinguistic Experiments in Foreign Language Testing*, and *Developing Computer Use in Education*. As well, he has authored reading tests, educational computer software and many journal articles. Professor Anderson is Australia's representative on Unesco's Intergovernmental Committee on Informatics. He was foundation editor of the *Australian Journal of Reading*, is editorial consultant for several international journals including *Reading Research Quarterly*, and writes regular columns on computing. He is a past president of the Australian Reading Association.

Chris Bell (Chapter 10) taught physics at secondary school prior to studying for a master's degree in educational technology in 1980. He subsequently worked on research and development into evaluation and distance learning. Currently he is a senior lecturer within the Learning Resources Centre at Plymouth Polytechnic, UK, where he is involved with a wide range of professional staff development activities, including course design, evaluation, assessment, open learning and new information technologies. With Duncan Harris he is the author of *Assessing and Evaluating for Learning*, also published by Kogan Page.

George Chryssides (Chapter 15) is senior lecturer in philosophy at Plymouth Polytechnic. He teaches professional ethics to students of business studies and philosophy of education for in-service courses aimed at FE and HE staff. A graduate of the universities of Glasgow and Oxford, he has presented papers at numerous international conferences and contributed articles to journals including *Religious Studies*, *Sophia*, *The Scottish Journal of Theology* and *Religion Today*.

Mikhail Draganov (Chapter 6) is a graduate in computer science of the Lenin Higher Institute of Mechanical and Electrical Engineering, Sofia. He has been teaching programming ever since and has conducted research on the various aspects of computer uses, including those in education. He was a lecturer at the department of computer science at the Higher Institute of Mechanical and Electrical Engineering, Sofia, then was deputy manager and manager of the Educational Computer Centre at the Higher Institute of Chemical Engineering. In 1983 he rejoined the staff of the Lenin Higher Institute.

At present he is a lecturer at the department of programming and application of computers and head manager of the computerization of secondary education board with Bulgaria's Ministry of Education. His PhD thesis is on computer vision and the understanding of 3D line drawings. His chief interests lie in the application of computers in education and computer vision.

Richard Ewen (Chapter 12) began work as TVEI Project Director in Hillingdon in January 1986 after 18 months as TVEI consortium co-ordinator in the Northamptonshire TVEI project.

He began teaching in 1972 in a Leicestershire comprehensive upper school after graduating from London University. In 1974 he took up a teaching post with the Ministry of Education in Jamaica in a rural comprehensive school for three years. Upon returning to England he completed an MA degree in educational research at Lancaster University and then took up a post as head of department in a Northampton upper school which subsequently became directly involved with TVEI developments.

Lise Fogh (Chapter 8) graduated from Copenhagen University in 1984 with a degree in literature, and is currently working as an information officer at the Danish Centre for Education and Information Technology.

Rhys Gwyn (Chapter 5) is joint head of the Centre for Information Technology and Education, Manchester Polytechnic. He has been a teacher trainer since 1967. Formerly a teacher of English literature, he made the transition to information technology in the early 1980s. He has extensive experience at the European level, having acted as consultant variously to the Commission of the European Community, the Centre for Research and Innovation (OECD), Unesco, the Council of Europe and the European Cultural Foundation. He chairs the IT Study Group of the Association for Teacher Education in Europe, of which he is a past president, and is also Chairman of the International Planning Committee for the Plovdiv Seminars on IT and Education (Unesco and Ministry of Education, Bulgaria). He edits the *European Journal of Teacher Education* and is the author of numerous articles and reports. Recent research (for the FAST Programme of the EEC) entailed an examination of the implications for education of the socio-economic consequences of IT, and he is currently researching the educational take-up of interactive video. He speaks (in order of preference) Welsh, French and English.

Duncan Harris (Introduction) graduated in physics at bachelor level and by research at master's level at Nottingham University. His doctorate was in education from the University of Bath.

After being an instructor officer in the Royal Navy, and a teacher in schools, he became lecturer in education and then senior lecturer in education at the University of Bath. He is currently Professor and Head of Education at Brunel, the University of West London. His current interests include educational technology, assessment and evaluation. He has written and edited several books including a *Dictionary of Instructional Technology* (with H Ellington) and *Evaluating and Assessing for Learning* (with C Bell).

Clive Hewitt (Chapter 13) managing director of Macmillan Intek, which produces and distributes training materials for industry and business, was the originator of Southek, the first and largest of the Open Tech projects which became part of the Macmillan Publishing Group in 1985. He was previously head of learning resources at Brighton Polytechnic and qualified in economics at LSE and in film, TV and communications at the University of North Carolina, USA. After four years producing vocational training television broadcasts in the US, he returned as a founder member of the University of Leeds Media and AV Service before going to Brighton in 1973.

Ian Jamieson (Chapter 1) is lecturer in education and industry at the University of Bath. He was formerly head of sociology and later reader in business and management studies at Ealing College of Higher Education; between these two appointments he was evaluator and research director of the Schools Council Industry Project (SCIP). His main publications include *Capitalism and Culture* (Gower, 1980) and *Schools and Industry* (with Martin Lightfoot) (Methuen, 1982); he has also edited *We Make Kettles: Studying Industry in the Primary School* (Longman, 1984) and *Industry in Education: Perspectives and Developments* (Longman, 1985). He is editor of the *British Journal of Education and Work*.

David Jonassen (Chapter 2) is Professor of Instructional Technology at the University of Colorado at Denver, where he is chair of the department of instructional technology. Dr Jonassen has a number of articles and books in the field of instructional design, including the two-volume series *The Technology of Text*. His publications and research interests are in the areas of learning strategies, computer-assisted instruction, and text design.

Steen Larsen (Chapter 16) is lecturer in psychology at the department of education and psychology, Royal Danish School of Educational Studies.

He has published a number of books in Denmark, Sweden and Finland concerning the following issues: neuro-psychological and cognitive function in children, cerebral laterality and dyslexia, and the possible impact of new technology on children's cognitive development and education.

Roland Lauterbach (Chapter 14) is working in research, development and teacher training of science and computer education at the national Institute for Science Education at the University of Kiel, Federal Republic of Germany.

After having been a teacher of science and mathematics he continued studies in psychology, sociology and educational anthropology. Diverse research and development projects in science education followed. Since 1982 he has been especially concerned with effects of computers on child development, learning science and educational culture.

David McConnell (Chapter 11) took a BA in biology and education at the University of Stirling, and a PhD in educational technology at the University of Surrey.

He has worked at Murdoch University, Western Australia and the UK Open University. He is currently lecturer in educational technology and development in the School of Education, University of Bath.

His current interests include adult education, open and distance education, especially the educational applications of new information technologies, student learning, values in education and qualitative research methods.

Peggy Nightingale (Chapter 9) is a lecturer in the Tertiary Education Research Centre of the University of New South Wales. She holds a PhD from Macquarie University and has published in the area of new literatures in English as well as in higher education research and development. Main areas of interest have been the improvement of student writing and supervision of research students. She is editor of *HERDA News*, a publication of the Higher Education Research and Development Society of Australasia.

Raina Pavlova (Chapter 6) graduated from the Leningrad Higher Institute of Electrical Engineering, USSR in computer science in 1969. She has been teaching programming at the Lenin Higher Institute of Electrical and Mechanical Engineering since 1970. Her PhD thesis is on evaluation of the performance of multiprocessor systems. She has been working on using new information technologies in education — higher, secondary and primary.

Horia D Pitariu (Chapter 7) is currently an assistant professor at Cluj-Napoca University, Department of Pedagogy-Psychology. He received his PhD in industrial psychology (1976), which is the field of his research interest. He has published papers on topics concerning personnel selection, appraisal and training of data processing personnel and other categories of industrial personnel. He was written the following books: *Industrial Psychology*, *The Psychology of Professional Selection and Training* and *Dimensions of Professional Success (in press)*. He has also adapted and translated several personality tests and questionnaires for use in Romania.

Mary Tasker (Chapter 1) is a lecturer in education at the University of Bath. She is a member of the Values in Education Research Group which is exploring the relationship between values, industry and education. Her publications include *Teaching the History of Technology* (Historical Association, 1980) and articles in the journal *Resurgence*.

Martin Tessmer (Chapter 2) is assistant professor of instructional design at the University of Colorado at Denver, where he serves as a teacher and consultant to faculty on instructional design. He has a PhD in instructional design from Florida State University, and an MS in instructional technology from Southern Illinois University at Edwardsville. His publications and research interests are in the areas of cognitive strategies, intellectual skills learning, and subject-matter expert consultation.

John Whiting (Chapter 4), after a short and abortive career in forestry and a variety of other jobs, trained as a medical laboratory technician, and later became a lecturer in medical microbiology at the Ulster Polytechnic. An increasing fascination with computers and education led to his appointment as a lecturer in information systems at the University of Ulster in 1985 where he has been engaged upon research and development in the areas of computer assisted learning, user modelling and authoring systems. In 1986 he held a contract with the European Commission under the DG XIII DELTA project, dealing with tutoring and monitoring facilities for European open and distance learning systems. He has recently edited a book for Elsevier-North Holland on tutoring and monitoring facilities which contains contributions from a wide variety of European experts in fields which relate to open and distance learning. He has contributed to several international conferences on education and training since 1982 and is currently establishing an interdisciplinary research centre within his university to promote research into the educational application of intelligent knowledge based systems and user modelling.

Elizabeth Wilce (Bibliography) graduated in botany from the University College of Wales, Aberystwyth and gained a postgraduate diploma in librarianship from the College of Librarianship, Wales. She is currently senior library assistant in the library for the Faculty of Education and Design, Brunel University.

Index